TRAVAUX
D'HUMANISME ET RENAISSANCE

N° CLXXIX

BY THE SAME AUTHOR

The Italian Renaissance of Mathematics. Studies on Humanists and
Mathematicians from Petrarch to Galileo (Droz).

Selected Writings of Jean Bodin on Philosophy, Religion and Politics
(James Cook University).

PAUL LAWRENCE ROSE

Reader in European History
James Cook University of North Queensland, Australia

BODIN

AND THE

GREAT GOD OF NATURE

The Moral and Religious Universe
of a Judaiser

GENÈVE

LIBRAIRIE DROZ

11, rue Massot

1980

TO MY PARENTS

PREFACE

Much of this book was written while I was working on a study of Wagner's anti-semitism and I may say that after the chaotic vileness of Wagner's mind it was often a relief to turn to the humanity and (comparative) sanity of Bodin. Yet both thinkers have this in common: each of their mental worlds revolves around a vision of Judaism, in the case of Wagner a disgusted vision, in Bodin an admiring one.

For those readers who are accustomed to think in Greek, Christian or modern terms of moral philosophy this book may present an unfamiliar point of view. Much of what I have to say lacks grace but readers may be glad to know that many of the Judaising ideas described may be found expressed in a more elegant and lucid form in the novels of Isaac Bashevis Singer. The reader who is aroused to learn more of a culture which is fundamental for Western thought but has lain unheard and discredited for two thousand years in the West could have no better introduction than Mr. Singer's books. It was my wife Susan who introduced me to these novels and that is the least of the ways in which this book is indebted to her.

Working in an isolated university a thousand miles from its nearest sister institution makes one particularly grateful for facilities offered by our University Library and its heavily used Inter-Library Loans Office. I have also been most fortunate in being awarded travel and research grants by the James Cook University Research Committee and by the Australian Research Grants Committee which allowed me to undertake further research in European libraries. I should like to express my thanks to these bodies for their generosity.

I am in the debt of two foreign institutions for their hospitality while working abroad: through Marshall Clagett's good offices the Institute for Advanced Study, Princeton granted me the privilege of membership in 1978 while the previous year Dermot Fenlon arranged for me to be taken under the roof of Gonville and Caius College, Cambridge. I appreciate their kindness very much indeed.

For their support in a number of professional capacities my warmest thanks go to John Hale, Geoffrey Elton, Roy Porter, William Bouwsma and Robert Kingdon. To John Maguire I am very grateful for his discussion and reading of the book; his suggestions have diminished its defects. For typing a difficult text I thank Helen Stokes as well as my wife Susan who also compiled the index.

Finally, I should like to acknowledge the energy of Professor Brian Dalton in building a department which is a natural home for research and scholarship.

P.L.R.

1979

ABBREVIATIONS

I. WORKS BY BODIN

Oppian
: *Oppiani de venatione libri IIII, Joanne Bodino interprete* (Paris, 1555).

Oratio
: *Oratio de instituenda in Republica iuventute ad Senatum Populumque Tolosatem* (Toulouse, 1559). All references are to the modern edition in Jean Bodin, *Œuvres philosophiques*, ed. P. Mesnard (Paris, 1951), I.

Methodus
: *Methodus ad facilem historiarum cognitionem* (Paris, 1566). References are to the edition in Bodin, *Œuvres philosophiques*, ed. Mesnard, I; they are followed in parentheses by the relevant page number in the English translation, *Method for the Easy Comprehension of History* (trs. B. Reynolds, New York, 1945; repr. 1969). I amend some of the quoted translations.

République
: *Six livres de la République* (edition of Paris, 1583).

Republica
: *De Republica libri sex. Latine ab autore reddita* (Paris, 1586).

Démonomanie
: *De la Démonomanie des sorciers* (Paris, 1580).

Sapientia
: *Sapientiae moralis epitome* (Paris, 1588; under alleged authorship of "Elie Bodin").

Consilium
: *Consilia Johannis Bodini et Fausti Longiani de principe recte instituendo*, ed. J. Bornitius (Weimar, 1602).

Paradoxon
: *Paradoxon, quod nec virtus ulla in mediocritate, nec summum hominis bonum in virtutis actione consistere possit* (Paris, 1596).

Paradoxe
: *Le Paradoxe ... qu'il n'y a pas une seule vertu en médiocrité, ny au milieu de deux vices*, transl. by Bodin, according to the colophon in January 1596 (Paris, 1598).

Theatrum
: *Universae naturae theatrum* (Lyons, 1596).

Heptaplomeres
: *Colloquium Heptaplomeres de rerum sublimium arcanis abditis*, ed. L. Noack. (Schwerin, 1857). References are followed within parentheses by the relevant page numbers in the translation, *Colloquium of the Seven about Secrets of the Sublime*, trs. M.L.D. Kuntz (Princeton, 1975). I have amended some of the translations quoted.

II. SCRIPTURE AND PHILO

Biblical references are generally to the King James Authorised Version. In some cases I have translated Bodin's French versions quite literally since the Authorised Version reads differently. When translating Bodin into English I have, however, changed Bodin's references to books and chapters in the French Bible so as to correspond to the Authorised Version's arrangement.

Philo   References are to the paragraphs in the Loeb edition: *Philo in Ten Volumes with an English Translation,* ed. F.H. Colson *et al.* (Cambridge, Mass., 1929-62).

CHRONOLOGICAL TABLE

JEAN BODIN 1529/30 - 1596

1529-30	Born at Angers.
1544-48?	Spends two years as a Carmelite student in Paris.
1548	Tried for heresy.
ca. 1548	Leaves Carmelites.
ca. 1549-60	Studies law at Toulouse.
1555	Publishes commentary on Oppian.
1559	Publishes *Oratio*.
ca. 1560-	Practises law at Paris.
1562	Swears Catholic oath at Paris.
1566	Publishes *Methodus*.
1568	Publishes *Response à M. de Malestroit*.
1567-69	Prophetic transfiguration.
1568-69	Letter to Bautru.
1569-70	Imprisoned for refusing religious oath.
1571	Joins household of the duc d'Alençon.
1576	Marries widow of Laon.
1576	First edition of *République*.
1576	Leads opposition to Henri III at the Estates of Blois.
1580	Publishes *Démonomanie*.
1581-82	Accompanies Alençon to England and to Antwerp.
1584	Death of Alençon.
1584-96	Bodin retires to Laon as lawyer and later *procureur du roi*.
ca. 1576-88	Later educational writings.
1586	Latin *Republica* published.
1587	Questioned for Huguenot sympathies and acquitted.
1589	Declares for the League.
1590	Arrested on suspicion and released.

BIBLIOGRAPHICAL NOTE

The following sources have been reprinted in *Selected Writings of Jean Bodin on Philosophy, Religion and Politics,* ed. Paul Lawrence Rose (James Cook University Publications, Queensland, Australia, 1980):

1. *Epître à son Neveu* (1586).
2. *Consilium de institutione principis* (Weimar, 1602).
3. *Sapientiae moralis epitome* (Paris, 1588).
4. *Paradoxon* (Paris, 1596), dedication.
5. *Paradoxe* (Paris, 1598).
6. *Letter to Jean Bautru des Matras* (1568-69).
7. *Lettre de M. Bodin* (Paris, 1590).

TABLE OF CONTENTS

PART C.

"It's a war (of the demons)."
"Why did God create them?"
"In order that there be free choice."

I.B. Singer, "Stories from Behind the Stove",
in *A Friend of Kafka*.

INTRODUCTION

THE ENIGMA OF BODIN'S RELIGION

a) Remarks on Methodology

The traditional ways of dealing with the writings of major figures in the history of thought, particularly political thought, have their weaknesses. Recently Quentin Skinner has voiced dissatisfaction with the "textualist" practice of simply reading the relevant works of an author in a close fashion without any reference to the context in which they were originally written.[1] Professor Skinner proposes a more genuinely "historical" approach to the history of political thought which would rather be a history of ideologies embracing the major works themselves, those less distinguished writings by contemporaries which form part of the same discussion, and the social and political context of the period in which those major works were composed.

While recognising the weakness of traditional accounts and the force of Prof. Skinner's methodology, I must confess that I do not think that his suggestions are sufficient to obtain a full understanding of a number of major thinkers. It seems to me that Prof. Skinner's proposals for reforming the historiography of ideas go only half way in that they help us to grasp better how Bodin's contemporaries understood the *République,* but do not really tell us how Bodin himself understood his writings or for what purpose he intended them to serve. In the *République* Bodin may have used the same words and examples as many of his contemporaries; but it seems to me that his intentions and meaning were very remote from what the other writers of his time could have accepted or even comprehended.

In order to mount an exploration of Bodin's mind I should like to propose a somewhat different methodology based on two principles: (1) the completeness or integrality of Bodin's thought and writings and (2) the integration of Bodin's ideas and personality.

Some readers may think that any attempt to understand what goes on inside anyone else's head — particularly one dead these 400 years — is a

---

[1] Q. Skinner, *Foundations of Modern Political Thought* (Cambridge, 1978), I, introduction.

chimerical undertaking. I should not myself wish in the least to deny the power and reality of individualism and idiosyncrasy which is so much in evidence in each of us and our acquaintances, not to say our dogs. Yet most writers are publicists and write, not only out of vanity or for profit, but to enlighten and convince their readers. Such persuasion may not always be manifest and blatant; sometimes indeed plain speaking may be impossible for reasons of censorship. Yet the writings of a major thinker like Bodin are sufficient in variety and bulk to allow us to grasp his thought in the round and as a whole.

I am not advocating here any Straussian thesis which sees all great authors as having hidden messages which they are obliged to conceal for fear of persecution (although it happens that Bodin was compelled to be devious because his ideas were wildly heretical and destructive of Christianity). My main suggestion is simply that, rather than divide the thought of someone like Bodin into separate compartments, one should endeavour to understand his total vision and then his individual writings on politics, history, law and so forth in the light of that vision. If this is done then what appear to scholars who read no further than the *République* to be contradictions, confusions and paradoxes, very often will disappear.

No amount of reading in the everyday political literature of the later sixteenth century is really going to tell us how Bodin understood or intended his own work. What may guide us into Bodin's mind is a knowledge of *all* his writings and of the vision which they represent. Many sentences in the *République* may appear pretty straightforward but if one tries to analyse a single one of them without first understanding Bodin's general purpose, only distortion of greater or lesser degree can result.

How then are we to grasp Bodin's vision? If there is one area of belief that embodies human thinking about the most fundamental aspects of life it is religion. Religion conveys the most general perceptions of reality, for example, in its particular doctrines of divinity, creation, transcendence and immanence; it formulates ideas of man through such doctrines as free will and sin; it expresses the sensibility of the individual man in his predilection for harsh religious attributes such as judgement, retribution, and suffering, or softer ones such as mercy, repentance and compassion. *La religion, c'est l'homme.* [2]

It should be clear by now that I believe that intellectual history cannot be written simply as the history of abstracted ideas. Ideas must first be set in the general context of a writer's religious vision; but I would go further and state that the religious vision itself cannot be understood as a purely intellectual system. The emotional charge is vital to an individual's religion and this takes us into the realm of personality.

There is a long-standing orthodoxy that in writing intellectual history, whether it be the history of political thought or the history of science, one must

---

[2] For an appreciation of the theological premises of Locke's political thought see J. Dunn, *The Political Thought of John Locke. An Historical Account of the Argument of the Two Treatises of Government* (Cambridge, 1969), pp. xi, 87ff.

at all costs keep separate the *thought* and *personality* of a thinker. Nothing seems to me to be such a dead hand on the study of thinkers of the past or present than this prescription. Of course it is difficult to integrate thought and personality without slipping into banalities yet this is hardly a reason for not trying. Let me cite two examples from the biography and thought of Bodin. In 1569 Bodin was arrested for heresy and spent the next year unrepentant in prison even though a simple recantation and oath of Catholicism such as he had sworn in 1562 (and swore again in 1589) would have sufficed to gain his release. Surprising conduct, one would agree, for a reputed *politique*. My second example adds to the confusion for it apparently contradicts the former one; it is Bodin's apparently zealous subscription to the Catholic League and support of the League's claimant to the throne in 1589-90. This episode has proved a major thorn in the side of conventional interpretations of Bodin, yet I believe that it, like the paradoxical imprisonment of 1569, can be understood if one has first grasped the nature of Bodin's religion. Hidden in the pages of Bodin's writings are details of a conversion to prophetic religion, indeed of the author's own transfiguration as a prophet. It was this transfiguration that provoked Bodin's stubbornness in 1569 and twenty years later convinced him that the Catholic League was the instrument of God's retribution on France. In this conversion and its resultant effects on Bodin's thought and behaviour we may see clearly illustrated the interplay of religion, politics and personality.

My account of Bodin's conversion (or rather conversions, for the phenomenon was enacted in three stages) will be found in Chapter VIII. I wish it could have been less conjectural but Bodin is an elusive thinker and the sources are not as full as one would like. Nevertheless, I have tried to construct an account which might shed some light on some of the central riddles of conversion: what are the constants in thought and personality which are present in the convert before and after conversion?; what are the particular sources of psychic unrest before conversion?; how is the convert restored to inner peace? Any study of a conversion-experience must take us to the heart of the convert's religion and raises in an acute form the problem of the relationship between thought and personality.

The methodology I propose does not seek to "prove" anything. Historical proof is not the same as legal proof, and belongs to a different category of demonstration altogether; intellectual history is a different animal again from political and social history and the most that can be hoped for is a certain plausibility and persuasiveness of argument. In the case of figures like Bodin that plausibility must, it seems to me, depend on whether the general picture of his thought holds together. If one has got Bodin's "religion" right then one should be able to pick virtually any page of his works and understand and clarify it in the light of his religion; equally one should be able to interpret any biographical fact by reference to his religion. It seems to me that there is no point in taking isolated phrases about sovereignty out of the *République* and seeking to understand their meaning unless one already has a clear idea of where those sentences belong in the general structure of Bodin's thought. This kind of purely logical dissection leads inevitably to our misconceiving the meaning of Bodin's political ideas no matter how publicly and directly they may seem to be expressed.

b) Categories

This study began as an attempt to solve the problem of reconciling Bodin's religious vision with his reputedly naturalistic and secular thinking on politics and history. It soon emerged that it was a misconception to contrast, or even to separate, his religious and secular thought for even in Bodin's most apparently secular writings such as those on politics and economics there is a religious aura permeating the whole work. Bodin certainly uses such categories as "natural" and "divine" but it would be wrong to suppose that these reflect a basic dichotomy in his mind between what we would call religious and secular thought. "Natural" and "divine" refer more to the modes in which Bodin's religious sense organises itself; history, politics, law and economics are natural disciplines, whereas theology is a divine discipline. There is no opposition in Bodin between nature and religion for nature is part of religion. Thus it is that Bodin is able to speak of the Decalogue as "the revealed law of nature"; the Ten Commandments are *divine* law in that they are promulgated by God but they also represent *natural* law. Bodin in this way distinguishes formally between natural and divine law, but in essence both kinds of law really are different manifestations of what one may call a fundamentally *religious* understanding of law. For these reasons it is ill-conceived to think of Bodin's political theory as falling into our modern categories of secular or religious thought. Such categories are not even separate ones in Bodin but rather interpenetrating.

At several points in his political career Bodin actually put into practice this religious perception of politics, most notoriously in his decision to join the Catholic League in 1589. As our last chapter will explain, Bodin's writings on the League not only reveal how unhistorical it is to apply such artificial categories to Bodin as "religious" and "secular", but also discredit the seemingly concrete labels of *politique* and *ligueur*. Bodin himself was simultaneously *politique* and *ligueur* and his understanding of the entire political problem was dictated by a profusion of political, legal, natural and above all, moral and religious ideas. Politics, ethics and religion, far from forming separate categories, were fused by Bodin into unaccustomed and dynamic modes of thought.

As one reads Bodin in this light then a great deal of what appears to be confused and obscure in his writings begins to make sense. It seems indeed that many of the charges of muddled thinking laid by modern critics against Bodin have arisen out of applying traditional Greek and Christian categories or those of jurisprudential thinkers of the seventeenth and later centuries to this uniquely original philosopher. Bodin was not a Hobbesian, nor a Lockean, nor a "predecessor of Montesquieu". And if Bodin was neither an absolutist nor a liberal theorist, neither can he be said to fall into the mainstream of Christian theocratic thought. Bodin's categories were not those of Calvin, nor of Aquinas, nor even those of the Gospels. Bodin's categories and religious vision stemmed, it will be argued, from the Jewish tradition represented by the works of Philo and Maimonides. In the case of his political philosophy Bodin built upon these foundations but constructed his edifice to take account of the shifts in terrain which a thousand years of political and legal development had produced. It is Bodin's shrewdness in grafting the realities of

4

French history on to a Jewish theocratic vision that explains both the genius of his works as well as their enduring capacity to be interpreted in misconceived categories.

c) Judaising

The term Judaiser has a long history in Christianity. The original Judaisers were those Christian adherents of St. Peter who against St. Paul urged conformity to Jewish ritual law. Later the term came to be applied to Christian heretics like the fourth century Byzantine Photinus or the Russian "Judaisers" of the fifteenth century who denied the Trinitarian divinity of Christ though admitting Him as the Redeemer and as such as a part or mode of the Father.

The European Reformation saw an extension of Judaising activity in such forms as an increasing knowledge of Hebrew and a reawakened interest in the Old Testament. [3] In general the Protestant Reformation's simplifying attack on traditional doctrines and ecclesiastical organisation had the effect of an unconscious Judaising campaign. It was, however, the more radical reformers who found themselves denounced by the Lutherans and Calvinists as "Judaisers"; the radicals were taxed with advocating a modern Pharisaic legalism based upon the New Testament and denounced for trying to reproduce in Christian form various aspects of Hebraic conduct and belief, or merely for refusing to consider the Old Testament superseded by the New.

The phenomenon of Judaising in the sixteenth century still awaits a full investigation but from existing studies we can see already how Judaisers of the period seized upon new categories of thought which had been purposely excluded from Christian tradition, or indeed (as in the case of Bodin) had simply been unthinkable to the minds of Christians. Such new modes of thought were exploited to the full for their ability to open up new dimensions of religious and moral philosophy. [4] Pico della Mirandola and Guillaume Postel availed themselves of the Jewish mystical Kabbala in order to achieve a reform of Christianity which would transform the Christian religion into a universal creed. Michael Servetus and Lelio and Fausto Sozini, on the other hand, applied their Judaising so as to destroy the creedal doctrines of the Trinity and the divinity of Christ. These radical Judaising tactics scarcely met with magisterial approval. Calvin shuddered that "it is indeed an abomination to see how this miserable man Servetus excuses the Jew's blasphemies

---

[3] In general see S.W. Baron, *A Social and Religious History of the Jews* (2nd ed., New York, 1952-   ), XIII, chs. 47 and 48. L.I. Newman, *Jewish Influence on Christian Reform Movements* (New York, 1925). G.H. Williams, *The Radical Reformation* (Philadelphia, 1967), pp. 834-39. J. Friedman, *Michael Servetus. A Case Study in Total Heresy* (Trav. d'Hum. et Rena., 163, Geneva, 1978), ch. 12.

[4] J.L. Blau, *The Christian Interpretation of the Cabala in the Renaissance* (New York, 1944). W.J. Bouwsma, *Concordia Mundi. The Career and Thought of Guillaume Postel (1510-81)* (Cambridge, Mass., 1957). F. Secret, 'Un cheval de Trois dans l'église du Christ: La Kabbale chrétienne', in *Aspects du libertinisme au seizième siècle*, éd. J. de Boisset and A. Stegmann (Paris, 1974), pp. 153-166. Friedman, *Servetus*.

against the Christian religion". Yet Servetus' Judaising strategy was directed towards the restoring of Christianity to its original purity of doctrine; no wonder he countered Calvin's accusations by charging the theologian with "Jewish legalism" in *his* preference for the "irrational, impossible, Mosaic law" over that of the New Covenant of Christ. "You have shocked me with your true Jewish zeal", Servetus sadly remarked. [5]

Some Socinians went further than Servetus in their Judaising and argued that Christ's death had restored freedom of the will to man and so expurgated original sin. [6] They admitted, however, that original sin had been incurred by Adam whereas Jewish belief held that there never had been a transmissible original sin but only the Fall of Adam. Yet for all the wildness of their heresies the Socinians and other Christian Judaisers remained Christians. Christ may not have been accepted by them as part of the divine godhead itself but He was still more than a mere man and was superhuman in nature. Moreover, their thought is almost always characterised by the presence of such concepts as "justification" (by faith or belief in Christ if not by His death itself) or "redemption" (in which Christ has greater or lesser functions). All these Judaisers who sought to use Jewish concepts to revolutionise Christianity were actually heretics *within* Christianity.

Not so Bodin who Judaised, not to reform Christianity, but to refute its claim to be the true religion. It was a largely discredited Christianity that was to be absorbed into Bodin's vision of a universal *vera religio,* a true religion closer to Judaism than to any other positive religion.

*
* *

Bodin's Judaising took various forms. In his published writings he made no secret of his extensive knowledge of Jewish sources (though he occasionally concealed some of his most radical Judaising in such printed works as the *Paradoxe* by citing a Christian source rather than a Jewish one). [7] Nor did Bodin seek to hide a generally sympathetic attitude towards the Jews. He was ready to tolerate them as a minority on account of their antiquity, their unconcern about gaining converts and their abstention from politics. [8] These were political reasons for a Judaeophile policy but there were much deeper

[5] 'Accusation et procès de Michel Servet (1553)', in *Registres de la compagnie des pasteurs à Genève au temps de Calvin,* eds. R.M. Kingdon, J.-F. Bergier, A. Dufour (Tr. Hum. Ren., 55, Geneva, 1962), II. Cf. Baron, *History,* XIII, 283f. Friedman, *Servetus,* for bibliography.

[6] E.M. Wilbur, *A History of Unitarianism* (Boston, 1945). Williams, *Radical Reformation,* pp. 742f, 839.

[7] For Bodin's knowledge of Jewish sources see F. Bezold, 'Jean Bodin als Okkultist und seine *Démonomanie*', *Historische Zeitschrift,* CV (1910), 1-64 (pp. 50ff). J. Guttmann, 'Jean Bodin in seinen Beziehungen des Judentums', *Monatschrift für Geschichte und Wissenschaft des Judentums,* XLIX (1905), 315-348; 459-489. M. Isnardi-Parente, 'Le volontarisme de Jean Bodin: Maimonide ou Duns Scot?', in *Verhandlungen der internationalen Bodin Tagung in München,* ed. H. Denzer (Munich, 1973), pp. 39-51, takes Bodin's public reliance on Duns too literally, to my mind. See below, Chapters IV and V.

[8] Baron, *History,* XV, pp. 94ff.

reasons of a religious nature governing Bodin's attitude. Judaism was for him the source of all religions :

> Such is the religion of the Jews from which all others save demonolatry seem to derive their origin. Whence Judaism is called by Chrysostom the mother of the gentiles. 9

(Note the typical use of a Christian source to validate what is in fact a Judaising statement). And in the *Heptaplomeres* :

> But the purest and simplest religion of the Hebrews has no impurity mingled within it and no heresies attached; it knows the worship of the one true God. 10

This archetypal quality of Judaism was to prove irresistible to a religious thinker engaged in the discovery of a universal *vera religio* who held no special brief for Christianity.

Yet in dealing with Bodin's religious ideas one immediately runs up against the problem caused by sixteenth century censorship. In a major religious work like the *Paradoxe* Bodin had to step very cautiously indeed in advancing a theory of religious virtue which effectively repudiated Christian doctrines of theological virtue and grace in favour of a Judaised approach portraying faith, hope and charity as natural virtues. Such opinions, if made explicit, would have quickly brought Bodin to the stake. Bodin, therefore, was forced to express his radical ideas in ambiguous terminology and in a form which appears full of logical errors and confusion. Each sentence may read simply but paragraphs rarely make sense unless the reader has first fully appreciated the whole Judaising tendency of Bodin's thought. My treatment of the *Paradoxe* in Chapter V may appear to make Bodin's writing more straightforward than it is but it seemed essential to attempt to unravel some of the involutions of this cryptic text.

If Bodin's printed works do not easily yield up information about his religion, nor can we go direct to the clandestine and startlingly original *Heptaplomeres* in search of straightforward indications. It is true that the speeches of the Jew Salomon in the *Heptaplomeres* put forward some forthright Judaising opinions, but any work written in dialogue form presents numerous difficulties of interpretation. Above all the form of the *Heptaplomeres* precludes us from easily assuming that the remarks of Salomon or any other participant unequivocally express Bodin's own ideas. In order to be able to use the *Heptaplomeres* as evidence of Bodin's authentic religious views we must first carry out a methodological sieving of the work. Two kinds of filters suggest themselves. In the first place we may ascertain his religious beliefs from

---

9 *Republica* (1586), p. 344: "Qualis est Iudaeorum religio, a qua caeterae praeter demonolatria origines duxisse videntur; quam propterea Chrysostomus gentium matrem appellat."

10 *Heptaplomeres*, ed. Noack, p. 197 (trs. p. 258): "Sed Hebraeorum purissima ac simplicissima religio nihil impuri admistum habet, nullas haereses adjunctas, nullum praeterquam unius Dei cultum agnoscit." For Bodin's use of Jewish ideas see G. Roellenbleck, *Offenbarung, Natur und jüdische Überlieferung bei Jean Bodin* (Gütersloh, 1964), pp. 97-113. C.R. Baxter, 'Jean Bodin's Daemon and his Conversion to Judaism', in *Verhandlungen*, ed. Denzer, pp. 1-21.

other sources such as the *Paradoxe* and the *Démonomanie* and use this knowledge as a control upon the ambiguities of the *Heptaplomeres*. In the second place we may use an internal filter, examining his statements in the *Heptaplomeres* on some key themes such as prophecy, ethics and happiness, ascertaining the extent of agreement among speakers on these themes, and using the resulting knowledge to control the disputation by the participants upon other themes. One of the main objectives of this book has been to design a fruitful method for the decoding of that enigmatic work — perhaps the first masterpiece of comparative religion — the *Heptaplomeres*. (I hope to apply the method more extensively in a future work).

From this method it results that Bodin *largely* agreed with the sentiments he put into the mouth of Salomon, but not *completely* so; Bodin did not become a Jew but remained a Judaiser. This circumscription did not, however, save Bodin from being condemned as a secret Jew by some contemporaries, or from being derogatorily accused of being of Jewish ancestry in later centuries,[11] or from having his religion described as "Judaism" by modern writers.[12] (In fact Bodin seems to have been descended from a French provincial family although it would be unwise to rule out entirely the remote possibility of some Marrano ancestry).[13] For Bodin the real attraction of Judaism was that it supplied him with new ways of thinking about universal religion which broke out of the old constricting arena of Christian theology; for Bodin to have adhered to Judaism proper and to have observed Jewish rites would have meant renouncing that very universalism towards which his whole Judaising strategy was directed.[14]

Bodin originally Judaised in order to achieve a universal *vera religio* but by the time of the *Paradoxe* and *Heptaplomeres* his religious vision had become so thoroughly Judaised that it entailed the destruction of the fundamentals of Christian doctrine. Only this purged Christianity could be admitted as a constituent of *vera religio*. Bodin's Judaising eventually accomplished a critique of Christianity which repudiated Christian doctrines of grace, original sin, theological virtue, justification and redemption. All these themes came to seem to Bodin to be fallacious categories of Christian thought which obstructed the path to true religion. Man, for example, cannot in any sense ever be *justified,* concluded Bodin; this was a Christian category and any discussion of justification is futile. But, said Bodin adopting Jewish categories, man can be made *happy* or *blessed* by the gift of divine prophetic illumination. Man's natural powers enabled him to prepare himself for this divine illumi-

---

[11] Baron, *History,* XV, 94ff, 420f, for bibliography on these charges. P. Mesnard, 'La conjuration contre la renommée de Jean Bodin: Antoine Tessier (1684)', *Bulletin de l'Association Guillaume Budé,* XVIII (1959), 535-559. R. Chauviré, *Jean Bodin, auteur de la République* (Paris, 1914), pp. 158ff.

[12] E.g., by Roellenbleck, *Offenbarung.* Baxter, 'Bodin's Daemon'. D.P. Walker, *Spiritual and Demonic Magic from Ficino to Campanella* (London, 1958), p. 171. See below, Chapters VIII, note 141.

[13] J. Levron, *Jean Bodin et sa famille. Textes et commentaires* (Angers, 1950). Cf. P. Mesnard, 'État présent des études Bodiniennes', *Filosofia,* XI (1960), 687-696.

[14] P. Mesnard, 'Jean Bodin et la critique de la morale d'Aristote', *Revue Thomiste,* LVII (1949), 542-562, comes close to grasping the nature of Bodin's Judaising. But see Chapter V. (In his later articles Mesnard lost sight of this Judaising theme).

nation through cultivating the virtues of righteousness, faith, hope and charity; precisely this natural self-preparation or purification constituted the subject of moral philosophy and ethics. It was thanks to the new categories of understanding made available to him by Jewish thought that Bodin was able to formulate this unusual conception of religion and ethics.

The anti-Christian thrust of Bodin's Judaising sets him apart from the Christian Judaisers of the sixteenth century and the uniqueness of his position becomes apparent if the attitudes of Bodin and Servetus towards their Jewish mentors are compared. One of Servetus' motives for Judaising Christianity was to attract Jewish converts by abolishing the obstacle of the Trinity which prevented Jewish acceptance of Christ as the messiah. Bodin, on the contrary, never sought to convert the Jews and indeed saw no reason why they should forsake their pure monotheism for the rather unsatisfactory doctrines of Christianity which he regarded as tainted with superstition. Again Servetus generally corrupted Jewish ideas to make them fit his idiosyncratic conception of Christianity, while Bodin left the concepts of Jewish theologians intact and remained faithful to their spirit and content. This applies particularly to the cardinal Judaising themes which Bodin expounded in his writings as the foundations of *vera religio*, namely the Decalogue, the Deuteronomic choice of good and evil, and purification and prophecy.

d) Bodin's Judaised Religion. Purification, Prophecy and the Great God of Nature

Bodin's vision of *vera religio* was Judaised in its very structure — its two poles of purification and prophecy were also the pillars of Philo's Judaism. For Bodin purification and prophecy are more than a mere formula; they are ideas embodied in the actuality of his religious biography. As a youth Bodin had been trained in a Carmelite spirituality which also revolved around purification and prophecy but his quest for a universal religion isolated him from these religious feelings on account of their Christian setting. It was only after Bodin had subsequently encountered purification and prophecy in a quite alien Jewish context that he was able to resume them so as to fill a troubling vacuum in his religious sensibility. Thanks to this Judaising of purification and prophecy Bodin was eventually able to reconcile his earlier Carmelite spirituality with his leanings towards a universal religion devoid of Christian specificity. These developments comprise the first two stages of Bodin's conversion to true religion. The first of these — the shift away from Christianity to universal religion — I would date to before 1559; the second, in which Bodin embraced a Judaised religion based upon purification and prophecy, had occurred, it seems, by 1566. The third and final stage was to be marked by Bodin's own transfiguration as a prophet, an illumination that took place probably in 1567-68. The analysis of the third stage (Chapter VIII) reveals just how Bodin's religious ideas of purification and prophecy were fulfilled biographically in the sequence of his conversions; having first purified himself by the cultivation of religious virtue, Bodin was prepared to receive a prophetic illumination which was indeed not denied to him.

For Bodin, all the virtues are religious, not just the theological virtues of faith, hope and charity. [15] This is because all the virtues contribute to the purification of the soul which is the first part of *vera religio* and the prelude to prophecy. Ethics is, therefore, one of the two great sectors of Bodin's religion. It is vitally important here to recognise that Bodin has adopted a Judaised understanding of ethics. Greek and Christian ideas of ethics tend to be abstract and systematic in contrast with the concrete and practical nature of Jewish ethics. The difference is to be seen in the appeal of Greek and Christian moral philosophy to a systematic psychology; in Jewish tradition all virtue was the manifestation of a general "righteousness" which in a unitary soul depended entirely on free will. This concrete view of virtue as "righteousness" is quite foreign to the Christian tradition of seeing virtue as an abstract concept rooted in ideas of "the good" and depending, furthermore, on the operation of divine grace. Grace itself in Christian thought is an abstract metaphysical concept whereas in Judaism grace refers rather to particular acts of God's will and love.

The concreteness of Jewish ideas of virtue, free will and grace is likely to create confusion in the mind of a reader accustomed to the categories of Greek or Christian thought. In Christian thought free will is a religious concept but in Judaism it is both religious and "naturalistic" since it is intrinsic to man and not limited by the constant Christian control of grace. For this reason Jewish ethics seems to be a confused mixture of naturalistic and religious thinking, yet it is really a religious theory which incorporates naturalistic elements.

According to Bodin's Judaised theory of ethics, virtue is achieved by the natural powers of man. This is not the naturalistic theory it appears to be for it is set within a religious framework. To Greek, Christian and modern secular ways of thinking Bodin's ethics may seem even contradictory, a mixture of the religious and the natural. But viewed in the context of Jewish religious and ethical thought, Bodin's moral philosophy shapes itself into a lucid and coherent theory of ethics.

Ethics in fact occupies a pivotal position in Bodin's thought, uniting politics with religion. "Righteousness" for example is not merely an ethical or a religious notion but incorporates moral virtue, the pursuit of justice and the worship of God. Righteousness in its role as justice lies at the heart of Bodin's political thought just as it animates that of Philo and Maimonides. In the Jewish tradition taken up by Bodin politics are neither autonomous nor secular but rather are conducted within a moral and religious universe. It is within this Judaised context that Bodin's political thought, whether as expressed soberly in the *République* (Chapter II below) or more luridly in the writings on the Catholic League (Chapter IX), must be understood. For all their naturalistic appearances Bodin's political writings are ultimately moral and religious.

The integration of Bodin's ethical and religious thought means that our knowledge of one of these spheres is essential for an understanding of the other. In particular the ideas of virtue outlined in the *Paradoxe* have great significance for Bodin's religion. Bodin's belief that man has a natural capacity

---

[15] I have not used the term "moral theology" to describe Bodin's religious ethics since that term connotes a particular Christian theory.

for virtue carries the implication that man's will is not flawed by original sin and this in turn means that man has no need of a redeeming saviour. We therefore find embedded in Bodin's moral philosophy the roots of his non-Christian religious beliefs in free-willed Deuteronomic choice and the redundancy of any sort of Christian redeemer. Although Bodin for purposes of formal convenience dealt with moral philosophy in the *Paradoxe* and religious doctrine in the *Heptaplomeres* the two works are intimately linked and cannot really be read in isolation from another.

Bodin's ethics also throws a great deal of light on his religious conversions. For it is the *free-willed* purification of the soul and the achievement of virtue that paved the way for his final prophetic conversion. The virtuous purification of the soul, according to both Philo and Bodin, is not an end in itself but rather prepares the soul to receive that rarest gift of prophetic illumination which God bestows only upon His elect.

*
**

Bodin's religion hinges on prophecy for it is prophecy which unifies the crucial theophanies of *illumination* and *revelation*. Following Philo and Maimonides, Bodin argued that prophecy was the result of the influx of divine light or spirit into the soul, a light communicated by means of the active-intellect of the universe and the various angelic intelligences. Prophecy was conferred by God's will alone on selected men whose purification had prepared them to receive the gift which their free will, however, could not secure. For Philo, Maimonides and Bodin perfect happiness consisted in the ecstatic vision, knowledge, love and enjoyment of God which the prophetic light produced in the soul. It is clear from the manner in which Bodin expunged the terminology of grace in his later writings that he understood prophecy as based not on a Christian idea of divine grace but rather upon Judaised notions of "extraordinary divine help" (Chapters V and VI).

In its other function prophecy is the vehicle of divine revelation. The first purpose of revelation is to communicate God's will to men but revelation also serves an ethical purpose in recalling men to virtue. Here again we may see how misconceived it is to impose on Bodin the conflicting categories of nature and revelation. For Bodin revelation is the natural law; it is required only because men stray from nature. In the *Heptaplomeres* Bodin cites Philo to the effect that "the Ten Commandments depart not at all from nature... the tables of Moses contain nothing but the law of nature and the life of our ancestors".[16] Bodin's notion of a "revealed law of nature" may seem paradoxical but it was no paradox in the Jewish tradition which he adopted.

Bodin's theory of prophetic revelation has a yet more pregnant role to play in Bodin's religion in that it provides the key to his solution of the fundamental problem of how the transcendent and immanent aspects of God are to be reconciled: The active intellect and angels who transmit to human prophets the commands of a transcendent God are immanent spirits inhabiting the universe of nature.

*
**

[16] *Heptaplomeres*, pp. 190f (249).

If God is extrinsic to nature how does He manifest Himself in the natural universe? Philo's solution was that "God is everywhere in His powers, nowhere in His essence". According to Philo the chief of these immanent powers or spirits is the *logos* which he sees as the directing immanent executive of God's commands. The *logos* is emphatically not God Himself as it is in Christianity (though Philo may have been responsible for influencing the early Christian adoption of the term). Below Philo's *logos* are ranged the angels (who transmit prophecy and other forms of good to men) and the demons (who inflict evil as punishment for the sins committed by human free will). These immanent spirits are "natural" in that they are part of the natural universe rather than divinity but they are "supernatural" in being spirits.

Philo's general approach to the problem of immanence was followed by later Jewish thinkers although for obvious reasons his Christian term *logos* was replaced by such terms as *shekina* in rabbinical writers, by *active-intellect* in Maimonides, and by *sefirot* or emanations in the Kabbala. This was also to be Bodin's line. Rather than accept the Trinitarian solution of Christianity which saw the Holy Ghost as the bridge between transcendence and immanence and envisioned Christ as the reconciler of the rift between God and nature, Bodin turned to Philo and a Judaised vision of God and nature. God and nature are different in quality but God acts in nature through the immanent powers and spirits which are always under His control. This attempt to explain divine immanence led Philo and Bodin to understand God's law as the law of nature. For both thinkers God Himself is not part of nature but His law *is*.

God's revealed law comprehends the law of nature:

> God wished to renew (*for Moses*) that same law of nature by His own word and comprehend it in the Decalogue... When men grew deaf to the law of nature the divine voice was required so that those who contemned nature might hear the Father of nature proclaiming His words. [17]

Divine and natural law are thus different sides of the same coin. The Hebrews, says Bodin in the *Démonomanie,*

> were not ignorant of the difference between the works of God and of nature. For Solomon remarked in his allegories that the wise son obeys the commands of his father and does not forget the law of his mother. That is, he heeds the commands of God and the law of nature. [18]

Thanks to this essentially religious vision of law Bodin's natural universe becomes a moral universe. The moral and the natural are held together by two major bonds — one is free will, which is a fact of nature making moral choices; the other is the immanent powers of the angels and demons which by rewarding good and punishing evil operate the whole system of divine

---

[17] *Ibidem.* Latin quotation given below in Chapter VII.

[18] *Dèmonomanie,* I, fol. 37: "Ce n'est pas que les Hébrieux ayent ignoré la différence des œuvres de Dieu et de nature: car Salomon l'a souvent remarqué, quand il dict aux allégories, 'L'enfant est sage, qui obeist aux mandements du père, et n'oublie pas la loy de la mère.' Il entend les commandements de Dieu, et la loy de nature". See Chapter VIII.

cosmic justice. It is impossible to divorce Bodin's idea of the moral from his notion of the natural: both are facets of his religious understanding of God and nature. [19]

That understanding is summed up in the formulae connecting God and nature which recur in Bodin's writings — "the Father of nature", "this great prince of nature", "this great legislator of nature", "the sovereign of nature", "the Great Great God of Nature". [20] This God is not part of nature but nature cannot be considered, cannot exist, without constant providence. It is this God who maintains the peace and justice of nature, preservative functions dimly and imperfectly reflected in the actions of His earthly counterparts, the sovereign kings. According to Bodin, the universe and all its parts including political states are inherently unstable; there is in all things which are part of universal nature an intrinsic tendency to degenerate, and it is only the preserving power of God which averts the collapse of all orderly structure and a return to chaos. [21]

For Bodin the triumph of God's preserving power over a degenerative universe is attested by the astonishing harmony of the natural universe:

> For one sees how this great God of Nature has bound all things by means which reconcile the extremes and compose the harmony of the intelligible, celestial and elemental universe through indissoluble powers and links. Just as harmony perishes if the opposite voices are not joined by the middle voices, so too it is with the world and its parts. [22]

This universal harmony is the cosmic justice of the Great God of Nature.

Bodin's idea of the Great God of Nature suggests that it is wrong to enquire whether he was a follower of theistic or of natural religion. In Bodin the two forms of religion are not exclusive of one another but rather are mixed together. Most of the modern inclination to keep these categories separate stems from those Enlightenment thinkers who had opposed *natural* theology to *revealed* theology and opted for the former to the exclusion of the latter. Aquinas had distinguished between natural and revealed theology but, accepting natural theology as dependent on a revealing God, he had taken both theologies as complementary modes of perceiving God. In this perspective natural religion does not appear as necessarily deistic although it has often been taken as

---

[19] See Chapter V.

[20] E.g., *Methodus*, ed. Mesnard, p. 114 (trs. p. 15); *République*, I, i, p. 5; *Démonomanie*, fol. 7 (see below); *Paradoxe*, p. 33; *Heptoplomeres*, p. 190 (249). See Chapters II, V and VII.

[21] This comes through most clearly in the *Theatrum Naturae* which I hope to treat in detail in a future work.

[22] *Démonomanie*, fol. 7: "Car on void que ce grand Dieu de nature a lié toutes choses par moyens, qui s'accordent aux extremitez, et composé l'harmonie du monde intelligible, celeste et élémentaire par moyens et liaisons indissolubles. Et tout ainsi que l'harmonie périroit, si les voix contraires n'estoyent liées par voix moyennes, ainsi est il du monde, et de ses parties".

such since the eighteenth century. Aquinas and Bodin were able to conceive of such a thing as theistic natural religion without regarding it as a glaring contradiction in terms such as it has subsequently become. Yet they apprehended this mixture of theism and natural religion in ways that differed profoundly. Bodin refused to allow Aquinas' ideas of grace and redemption; instead he embraced a *vera religio* whose combination of nature and revelation was founded not on Christ but on a Judaised theory of prophecy. The revelation of a revealing God is communicated by means of prophecy which reinforces and explains nature.

In prophecy then lies the heart of Bodin's *vera religio* for it is prophecy that transmutes natural religion into *vera religio*. [23] Bodin's true religion was neither Christianity, nor deistic natural religion, nor even Judaism; it was in fact a Judaised religion whose fusion of elements of nature and revelation was achieved by recourse to an exalted idea of prophecy.

e) Synopsis

This book attempts to examine Bodin's ideas on religion, ethics and politics at various levels. The difficulty of the material and complexity of the argument has led me to adopt what may be a confusing and possibly a tedious method of exposition which will involve the patient reader in going over some texts as many as three times. In extenuation the author would like to think that each circuit is made on a deeper level of understanding. Nevertheless readers who find themselves bored by the first tour (Chapters I - III) might find themselves revived if they proceed to the second section where the proper deciphering of Bodin's enigmatic religion begins. I wish I could have dispensed with these dry opening chapters yet they seem essential if the reader is to gain an impression of the significance of Bodin's concept of virtue for all aspects of his thought.

Part A (Chapters I - III) offers a straightforward, summary account of the role of virtue in Bodin's political and educational thought. For the most part I have not tried to indicate here the Judaised character of his ethics and moral philosophy. That virtue is a major concern of Bodin's from 1559 until his last writings suggests that his reputed shift from political thought to religion and ethics in his later life is not as real as it appears. Ethical and religious preoccupations inform all Bodin's works including the *Methodus* and the *République;* this is the point which the rather cursory treatment of these two works in Chapter II is intended to make.

The discussion of a little-known group of Bodin's educational writings in Chapter III (the *Epître à son neveu,* the *Consilium* and the *Sapientia*) brings to the surface further aspects of Bodin's sense of the connections between society, ethics and religion. In the social sphere Bodin saw education as

---

[23] An important article by P. Mesnard, 'La pensée religieuse de Bodin', *Revue du Seizième Siècle,* XVI (1929), 77-121, drew attention to the prophetic theme in Bodin's religion but I hope to have explored more deeply the nature of Bodin's idea of prophecy by interpreting it as a salient feature of his Judaising.

inculcating moral and intellectual virtue which served to promote amity and peace. At the same time education was seen to have a vital religious function which consists in showing men the relation between father and son, or teacher and pupil, so prescribing the proper relation between God and man. Before God the adult always remains a minor and the relationship between man and God is seen by Bodin as based on an unequal love which is further mixed on the side of man with fear and reverence. Adult wisdom consists of this recognition of human pupillage.

Part B (Chapters IV-VII) is an exposition of the systematically Judaised character of Bodin's moral and religious philosophy. Adopting the Philonic idea of religion as purification and prophecy Bodin perceived ethics in its guise of purification as essentially religious and indeed as the prelude to prophecy. If Bodin's religion can be used to elucidate his ethics the reverse process is also feasible. Our investigation of the religious basis of Bodin's ethics has presented an opportunity to penetrate the ambiguities of the *Hepta-plomeres* by using the *Paradoxe* as a control on certain key passages in the clandestine work.

Part C (Chapters VII-VIII) adds a biographical dimension to the religion of Bodin and examines the evolution of his religious thought. The main framework for this religious biography is a study of Bodin's successive conversions. Chapter VIII seeks to understand the psychological motives of these experiences and perhaps to shed some light on the general phenomenon of conversion. The study of conversions is one of the most fertile fields of biographical interpretation for these transfigurations are accompanied by intense dynamic interaction between the ideas and personality of the convert. The impulse for conversion seems to come from a psychic disturbance in the personality, but the disturbance is expressed and formulated in theological terms. With Chapter VIII I hope to have clarified the fascinating and difficult problem of Bodin's conversions and also to have demonstrated how vital for an understanding of Bodin's religious biography is an awareness of his Judaising strategy.

The last chapter illustrates the impact of Bodin's religion on other aspects of his biography. In this account of Bodin's political conduct at Laon after 1589, one may see again how ideas and biography interact and at the same time how Bodin's Judaised prophetic religion directed his political behaviour.

The present book is intended merely as *prolegomena* to a more rounded intellectual biography of Bodin. But I hope it is sufficient to vindicate the effectiveness of the two methodological principles announced at the beginning of this introduction: (1) That Bodin's thought must be comprehended in its completeness if any one compartment of his thought is to be understood without distortion, and (2) That a true understanding of Bodin can only be achieved through the integration of his thought with his personality and biography. If these principles are to be observed, we have need of a full understanding of Bodin's religion. The Judaising programme which Bodin pursued so unflinchingly is the key to that enigmatic religion.

PART A.

VIRTUE, WISDOM AND THE STATE

Chapter I

BODIN'S EARLY MORAL AND RELIGIOUS THOUGHT: THE "ORATIO" OF 1559

Bodin's *Oration to the Senate and People of Toulouse concerning the Education of Youth in the Republic* was published at Toulouse in 1559 in an effort to promote the founding of an academy which might instruct the youth of the city in the humanities and philosophy. [1] In its own right it is an important educational treatise and has even been described as "le monument le plus important de l'histoire de l'école française au seizième siècle". [2] But for our study of Bodin's thought the *Oratio* has a significance that goes beyond the merely pedagogic, for it is a superb account of the diverse intellectual strands which formed Bodin's outlook in 1559. Bodin intended the *Oratio* to be a vividly creative synthesis of his thoughts on virtue, learning, reason, society and religion, showing how each of these elements affect and determine one another. Already by 1559 Bodin had evidenced that taste for encyclopaedism which was to dominate his mature works. But the *Oratio* went further than this in setting the stage for Bodin's later thought, for in this early rhetorical work Bodin revealed a tendency to think in mixed terms of the religious and the natural which was to achieve its full power and development only in his last works written three decades after.

---

[1] *Oratio de instituenda in republica juventute ad senatum populumque Tolosatem,* reprinted in Jean Bodin, *Œuvres philosophiques,* ed. P. Mesnard, 1 vol., (Paris, 1951), I, 5-30.

[2] P. Mesnard, 'L'importance de la cité dans l'education nationale au temps de la Renaissance française', in *Pierre Mesnard: Images de l'homme et de l'œuvre* (Paris, 1970), pp. 238-243. The *Oratio* is discussed briefly by R. Chauviré, *Jean Bodin, auteur de la République* (Paris, 1914), p. 27; J.L. Brown, *The Methodus ad Facilem Historiarum Cognitionem of Jean Bodin. A Critical Study* (Washington D.C., 1939), pp. 20ff; P. Mesnard, 'Jean Bodin devant le problème de l'education', *Revue des Travaux de l'Académie des Sciences Morales et Politiques,* (1959), 217-228, at pp. 218ff; Idem, 'Jean Bodin à Toulouse', *Bibliothèque d'Humanisme et Renaissance,* XII (1950), 31-59, at pp. 51ff; 'Jean Bodin et Toulouse' (exhibition catalogue Toulouse, 1961, with essay by P. Mesnard), *Annales de la Faculté de Droit de Toulouse VIII,* fasc. 2 (1960), 151-208. M. Duby, *Jean Bodin et Toulouse* (thèse en droit, Toulouse, 1944). A fuller analysis is in V. De Caprariis, *Propaganda e pensiero politico in Francia durante le guerre di religione. I, 1559-1572* (Naples, 1959), pp. 327-340. For recent bibliography on Bodin see *Jean Bodin. Verhandlungen der internationalen Bodin Tagung in München,* ed. H. Denzer (Munich, 1973).

Three main aspects of this tendency appear, as we shall see, in the *Oratio*. There is first the conviction that natural knowledge of God (though not of His essence) is possible through the universe of nature and that nature's workings direct men to God. Secondly, Bodin praises as the bounty of God the diversity of nature and its miraculous harmony which he symbolises as the "choir of nature". And lastly the soul, although immortal, is seen as constituting part of this universe of nature.

Does the religious orientation of the *Oratio* betray leanings towards Judaising? Muted and inconclusive as they may be, there are hints that Bodin was indeed already a Judaiser, and that he had adopted the religious philosophy of Philo which attempted to reconcile Jewish monotheism with natural truths. (Philo's works were available in Greek from 1552 and in Latin from 1554). The idea of God as the unifier of the diversity of nature, the concept of the soul as a natural spirit that is immortal, the belief in the harmony of all the virtues and sciences, the view of virtue as a religious phenomenon as well as a natural one, the religious character of wisdom and education — these notions are all to be found in Philo as well as Bodin's *Oratio* (as also indeed in Christian thought!). [3]

But whatever use of Philo was made here by Bodin quarried mostly the naturalistic side of Philo's religion, that side which drew a large portion of its stock of ideas from the Platonic tradition. It was only in the following decade that Bodin turned once more to Philo, this time with recourse to the philosopher's Jewish strains of religion, above all those of Mosaic revelation and prophecy. In 1559 Bodin's attachment to Philo was only partial, a situation reflected in the only faintly Judaised attitudes of the *Oratio*. For that work is very much a transitional one representative of an early stage in the evolution of Bodin's mind, though nevertheless indicative of future directions to be taken. The second last chapter of this book will return to this problem and attempt to describe where this sketch of Bodin's religion as it was in 1559 stands in his religious biography as a whole; it will at the same time examine the progress of Bodin's Judaising from 1559 until his death. [4] The present chapter seeks only to describe this early work of synthesis so as to reveal the connections which Bodin believed existed between virtue, learning, society and above all religion.

Bodin spent the decade of the 1550's at Toulouse and it is tempting to see the *Oratio* as a product of a Toulousain university culture that was permeated with fervent Protestant religiosity as well as legal humanism. One should beware of thinking, however, that Bodin assimilated Protestant beliefs at Toulouse, although it seems inevitable that he must have been affected by

[3] See below for the appearance of these topics in the *Oratio*. For details of Philo's moral philosophy see Chapter IV, and for his religion Chapter VIII.

[4] For the different successive forms in which Philo and Jewish tradition influenced Bodin see Chapters IV and VIII.

the feverish religious climate in which he found himself. [5] There is certainly evidence in the *Oratio* of deep reflection on religion but Bodin was perhaps unique in Toulouse in being neither a *croyant* Protestant nor Catholic but rather a believer in an idiosyncratic form of natural religion.

This is not to say that Bodin kept himself apart from the Protestant legists of Toulouse. A close friend and patron of Bodin's in these days — to whom he later dedicated the *République* — was Guy du Faur de Pibrac (1529-84), a member of the family on whose support Bodin depended for his educational project of 1559. [6] Pibrac himself was no Protestant and he held Gallican reformist opinions which were politically congenial to Bodin with whom he shared a serious interest in moral philosophy. [7] But Pibrac's brother involved the family in heretical scandal in 1559, thus putting paid to Bodin's hopes of becoming principal of the proposed academy and perhaps hastening his departure for Paris. Several Protestant professors of law also had close ties to the du Faur family including the humanist poet Jean de Boissoné (1505-59) and the Huguenot extremist Jean de Coras (1513-72), sometime city councillor and rector of the university. [8] Although Coras' religious dogmatism may not have appealed to Bodin his French translation and paraphrase of the *Altercacion de l'empereur Adrian et du philosophe Epictète* (Toulouse, 1558) may have influenced some of Bodin's early moral thought as it did that of such later neo-Stoics as Guillaume Du Vair. [9]

Perhaps the most fruitful Toulousain influence on Bodin was Etienne Forcadel (1520-76) who was suspected of Protestantism but whose true religious

[5] For the Protestant jurists see *La Réforme à Toulouse*. In 1560 400 scholars, many of them no doubt from the law school, demanded a Calvinist church. Religious tensions erupted into the riots and massacre of 1562. See R. Gadave, *Les documents sur l'histoire de l'Université de Toulouse et spécialement de sa faculté de droit civil et canonique (1229-1789)* (Toulouse, 1910), pp. 164ff.

Bodin was accused of heresy at Paris in 1548 but the main reason for assuming his susceptibility to Toulousain Protestantism has been the dating of his allegedly Huguenot letter to Jean Bautru des Matras to 1561-63. I shall argue in Chapter VIII that this letter dates from 1568-69. (See P.L. Rose, 'Two Problems of Bodin's Religious Biography: The Letter to Jean Bautru des Matras and the Imprisonment of 1569', *Bibliothèque d'Humanisme et Renaissance*, XXXVIII (1976), 459-465).

Mesnard, 'Bodin à Toulouse', p. 57, thinks that Bodin remained Catholic and was driven from Toulouse by the religious unrest there. This view rests in part on interpreting the *Oratio*'s call for a single state religion as being a Catholic attitude. I doubt whether it was necessarily Catholic. See below, notes 56ff.

[6] *Oratio*, p. 30 for the family. Bodin, *Methodus (Œuvres*, ed. Mesnard, I, p. 108) also mentions Pibrac. Cf. A. Cabos, *Guy du Faur de Pibrac. Un Magistrat poète au XVIe siècle (1529-84)* (Paris, 1922).

[7] Although Pibrac was probably not a Huguenot in 1559 he seems to have followed Bodin into heresy at Paris in 1568 where he was listed among suspects and fined 1,000 *livres*. See *La Réforme à Toulouse de 1562 à 1762. Exposition* (Toulouse, 1962), p. 31. For his moral philosophy see below Chapters III and IV.

Bodin, *Oratio*, p. 30, praises another Gallican reformer, Odet de Coligny, cardinal de Châtillon, who was at Toulouse from 1534-50 and 1559-62. Other non-Protestant legists perhaps known to Bodin at Toulouse were Barnabé Brisson and Jacques Cujas.

[8] *La Réforme à Toulouse*, pp. 31, 79ff. Coras was hanged in his robes in the aftermath of St. Bartholomew in 1572.

[9] See Chapter IV.

feelings are somewhat hazy. [10] Forcadel's writings suggest a fluid religious imagination far more plastic than that of a doctrinaire Huguenot and there are several parallels to be found between his ideas and those of Bodin who seems to have known him personally. Like Bodin, Forcadel allowed religious and naturalistic habits of thought to overflow into his legal philosophy; this is to be found in what is a rather bizarre series of legal treatises. The *Necyomantia jurisperiti sive de occulta philosophia dialogi* (Lyons, 1544, 2nd ed., 1549) recreated the psychic and religious life of the ancients and incorporated a rich fund of material on paganism and cultic religions, including those of the druids, the Egyptians and the Persians. With its universal invocation on "Serva me, o Deus, o Alla, o Theos, o Theut", this curious work may have fostered Bodin's own syncretistic inclination which was to culminate in the *Heptaplomeres*.

In the *Sphaera legalis* of 1549 Forcadel dilated on the mythological and astrological origins of law and pointed out the connection between law and the religious imagination. Saturn was seen as the patron god of the Twelve Tables, Jupiter as the god of imperial Roman law; the sterile moon was aptly associated with the medieval commentataries on Roman law.

A quaint but perhaps significant parallel between Forcadel's thought and the interests of Bodin in these early years consists in their mutual interest in what might be called the domestic aspects of natural history. Forcadel's *Penus juris civilis* (Lyons, 1542), dedicated to Arnaud Du Ferrier (born 1506) who had taught both him and Bodin, contained a section on the identification of ancient foods mentioned in Roman law treatises; and when Forcadel came to reprint it in 1550 he added an *Aviarium juris civilis* investigating the birds known to the ancient lawyers. Around this time Bodin was working on an edition of Oppian's treatise on hunting (*Cynegetica*) and he may have been the editor of the Greek text published at Paris in 1549. Certainly Bodin did bring out his own Latin translation and ample commentary on Oppian a few years later in 1555. [11] Many lawyers in this period were of course pursuing the application of humanistic philological techniques but what is striking in this case is that legal interests were expanding into the study of natural history and the natural universe. In both Forcadel and Bodin we find that law was being fertilised not only by religious modes but also by naturalistic categories.

With Forcadel this two-fold tendency reached its high point in his *Cupido jurisperitus* (Lyons, 1553). Here Forcadel founded his conception of human society and peace on the harmony of the created universe. Love and justice lead men to the restoration of concord, says Forcadel, and the same notion reappears in Bodin's discussion of *amicitia* and concord in the closing pages of the *Oratio*. [12]

---

[10] Forcadel defeated Cujas in competition for a chair in law in 1555. Much of the following information on his works comes from Etienne Forcadel, *Œuvres poétiques*, ed. F. Joukovsky (Geneva, 1977), introduction. P. Mesnard, 'Un rival heureux de Cujas et de Bodin: Etienne Forcadel', *Zeitschrift der Savigny-Stiftung für Rechtsgeschichte*, LXVII (1950), 440-458.

[11] The Greek text of Oppian published by an anonymous editor (Vascosanus, Paris, 1549) seems to have been Bodin's work. Oppian, *De Venatione*, ed. and comm. by J. Bodinus (Paris, 1555), exacerbated Bodin's rivalry with A. Turnebus who also published his own edition in the same year in which he accused Bodin of plagiary. See Chapter VIII.

[12] See below, notes 59ff.

This odd Toulousain legist may also have reinforced Bodin's anti-feminism for both writers were obsessed with female guile and the moral nihilism of women. Forcadel's *Cupido* had single-mindedly insisted that the ability of women to arouse men's desire represented the enchantment of man's will and Bodin had personified this phenomenon in the form of Circe, the enchantress who de-natured men by robbing them of virtue. [13]

*
**

The grand theme of the *Oratio* is the indissolubly moral nature of education and its fundamental role in the life of man and the state.

> The arts and sciences are the companions and ministers of virtue. Without them there is no way that life may be lived happily, or lived at all. You may have a fortunate and flourishing state if its youth are educated in the best virtues and learning. [14]

The alliance of virtue and learning (*virtus ac doctrina*), its significance for human happiness, the notion that a state flourishes when it is best satisfying its moral purpose of furthering human happiness — these form the central cluster of ideas around which the *Oratio* is constructed. Bodin approaches these ideas from various angles and directions — historical, moral, social, political, religious and anthropological — for only through such a diversity of illustration can he show that education is the very summation of man.

Bodin's first avenue of approach is historical and consists of his famous panegyric of the French Renaissance. The point here is to illustrate the universal truth that education and learning are inextricably bound up with the political fortunes of nations. The collapse of Rome had been accompanied by the near extinction of European learning and only in the last hundred years had the final act of the tragedy been played out when the Byzantine remnant of ancient civilisation had finally succumbed to the scourge of war.

> Greece itself, which had so excellently created and developed the arts, first began to burn with civil wars, then sought foreign wars, and finally was laid waste by the barbarians. Its cities were plundered, its academies burnt, its libraries, books and memorials all set aflame. [15]

The Renaissance had then been launched by the Italians but it achieved its full flower in France under François I who had been "born to repair the fall and

[13] See below, note 46.

[14] *Oratio*, p. 8: "aguntur artes ac scientiae, quae cum sint virtutis comites & administrae, tum sine iis beate vivi, aut etiam vivi, nullo modo potest: agitur denique summa Reipub. cuius seminaria si optimis virtutibus ac disciplinis exculta fuerint, Rempub. fortunatam ac florentem estis habituri." For the rich classical tradition of thought — especially that of Plato — on education, man and the state which helped shape Bodin's views see W. Jaeger, *Paideia. The Ideals of Greek Culture*, 3 vols. (Oxford, 1939-45), II, 235ff and passim.

[15] *Oratio*, p. 8: "Graecia ipsa, quae humanissimas artes tanta cum laude pepererat & educarat, primo bellis civilibus flagrare, tum externis appeti, postremo a barbaris vastari, civitates diripi, gymnasia incendi, bibliothecae, libri, monimenta denique Graecorum omnia ardere visa sunt."

ruin of Greece." The *dignitas scientiarum,* the torch of learning, had passed from Byzantium and French culture, in decline since Tiberius' suppression of the ancient druids, had now entered its triumphant phase. [16] For Bodin the Renaissance was therefore at once a European and a particularly French phenomenon.

Underneath this ebb and flow of learning Bodin recognised the operation of a universal principle of change:

> There is a vicissitude of letters, as of all things. In certain countries the arts are first born through the efforts of wise men and thereafter increase. They flourish, then they languish and grow old with ancience. At the end they die and are buried in oblivion.... Among the Greeks the disciplines matured gradually until they reached what might be thought their apogee for they could progress no further nor could they rest longer in the same place. Surely then they had to retreat. [17]

Neither superficial nor accidental, this intellectual cycle was embedded in the natural order of things.

> This then is the vicissitude of learning, this is the process of change in human affairs so certain that none may doubt that with human minds there occurs by the marvellous ordering of nature the same (process) as happens on the land, which, after lying fallow, renders its thanks for rest by bringing forth in greater abundance. Thus, nature, after giving forth a wealth of genius, always seems to rest and after resting for a long time at last arouses herself again. [18]

Bodin's naturalistic interpretation of the French Renaissance granted a certain autonomy to the cycle of intellectual growth and decay. But he also saw that this cultural process coincided with that political cycle whereby states matured and perished. In fact culture and society shared a common agent of destruction — war. If the political collapse of Greece and the ancient world was marked by the eruption of civil and foreign wars, so too war signalled the eclipse of classical civilisation.

> The daily calamity of wars carried men away from humanity to bestiality, from letters to arms. [19]

[16] *Oratio,* p. 10.

[17] *Oratio,* p. 10: "vel quod rerum omnium, sic literarum quoque sua quaedam est vicissitudo; ut primum quibusdam locis, ingeniosorum hominum experientia & labore, artes oriantur, deinde incrementa suscipiant, post aliquantum in statu vigeant, tandem sua vetustate langueant ac senescant, ad extremum emoriantur, & oblivione diuturna sepeliantur .... nonne apud Graecos disciplinae cum sensim adolevissent, ut ad summum pervenisse crederentur, quia longius progredi non poterant, nec eodem loco stare diutius, regredi necesse habuerunt."

[18] *Oratio,* p. 11: "haec illa est disciplinarum vicissitudo, haec illa rerum humanarum ingeniis, mirabili quodam naturae ordine, quod in agris, eveniat, qui intermisso cultu, majori ubertate gratiam referre quietis solent: sic natura, postea quam magnam vim ingeniorum simul effudisset, visa semper est conquiescere, & cum aliquandiu conquiesset, denuo seipsam excitare."

[19] *Oratio,* p. 10: "vel quod bellorum diuturna calamitas, ad feritatem homines, ab humanitate; a literis, ad arma efferarit."

War de-natured man, stripping him not only of his intellectual dignity but also of his social being, reducing him to the status of an animal.[20] (Animality supplies one of the central recurring metaphors of the *Oratio*.)[21]

Yet was war really the cause, as opposed to the agent, of these disasters? Bodin's attitude to war was ambivalent. While it might prove fatal to a state war might also be the making of an empire. Its effect was fatal only to those states which had already grown weak and where war took the form of civil conflict or foreign invasion. In such states the bonds of society and the morality of the state had long since decayed. The question, therefore, was really what caused this decay of civic virtue laying a state open to the depredations of war. The answer, according to the *Oratio*, lay in the failure of education. It was the task of education to ensure the cultivation of virtue and learning in the state. A state which neglected education was doomed to lose its civic virtue and culture and was destined within a short time to enter the fateful cycle of political decline. The vicissitude of virtue and learning not only paralleled the political cycle but actually triggered the process.[22]

After this historical perspective on the role of education Bodin turns to a mixture of moral and political considerations. For Bodin education is a fundamental response to the nature of both man and the state. Education is basic to the state and takes precedence even over filial duty to fathers.

> I believe the public interest (*causa publica*) to be affected in the first instance by those things which are useful to all, harm none, and whose neglect bring ruin to the state.... What is more useful to all than that the citizens' children be well educated? What is more beneficial to your city than that those to whom you entrust the preservation of the state be provided with virtue and learning (*virtus ac doctrina*)? For indeed those who founded the first states and shaped men from bestiality to this society (*societas*) which we practise thought it so necessary that they believed that no laws of the state would be valid without education.... Thus Solon was inspired to the most severe sanctions aginst those who infringed the requirements for the education of youth.... Fathers who failed to educate their children lost all rights over them, forfeiting that duty which sons owed them by the law of nature and out of humanity.... Such a (negligent) father was to be disowned by his son.... Who will therefore deny that learning and piety and the education of children pertain to public law?[23]

---

[20] For similar views in contemporary literature see A. Roubichou-Stretz, *La vision de l'histoire dans l'œuvre de la Pléiade* (Paris, 1973).

[21] See analysis below of passages from *Oratio*, pp. 14, 24, 26. See also, note 69.

[22] *Oratio*, pp. 14-16, quotations given below.

[23] *Oratio*, pp. 11f: "Ea primis ad caussam publicam pertinere duco, quae cum prosunt omnibus, detrimentum afferunt nemini, tum vero si negligas ac deseras, magnam Reipub. ruinam as allaturus.... quid est autem omnibus tam utile, quam civium liberos optime institui? quid tam salutare vestrae civitati, quam virtute ac doctrina praeditos esse eos quibus Rempub. traditis sustinendam? enimvero ii qui primi civitates fundarunt, & a feritate homines ad hanc, quam colimus, societatem impulerunt, non modo juventutis institutionem summe utilem, sed ita necessariam putarunt, ut sine qua nullas in Repub. leges quicquam valituras arbitrarentur.... Solon ... quod leges de instituenda in Repub. juventute, severius quam caeteri sanxit... primum parentes, qui liberos ex lege non instituerent, ... tum ne a liberis colerentur, neve in egestate constituti sublevarentur; postremo ne legitimam bonorum partem, quam filius parenti jure quodammodo naturae atque humanitatis debet, consequerentur, prohibuit .... omnia pietatis, & grati erga parentem animi officia, in pravae educationis poenam, denegari a filio jubet ... qui literas, quis disciplinas, quis mores, quis pietatem, quis doctrinam, quis educationem liberorum ad jus publicum negabit pertinere?"

Bodin next argues that learning and virtue, the two components of education, are natural to human character.

> Certainly nature has bred into each and everyone such a loving attraction to the increase of knowledge (*scientia*) that even the most abject and menial of men are moved by a natural or divine instinct to admire and respect a deeply learned man. [24]

Since man's mind is a part of universal nature it follows that he should seek to understand nature. In an eloquent passage which anticipates the encyclopaedic naturalism of the *Theatrum Naturae* Bodin expounds the relation between mind and universe.

> What is more admirable in the universe than excellence in the sciences? We wonder at the vastness of the earth, the depth of the sea, the immensity of the heavens, the splendour of the sun, the courses of the planets, the influences of the stars, the eclipse of the heavenly bodies; we marvel at lightning and thunder, storms and earthquakes, the forms of animals, the qualities of plants, the properties of metals, the variety of gems, the birth and death of all things; we are astounded by the virtue and power of immortal souls, the incredible divinity and nature of man. Yet none of these things is more admirable than that which is able to measure and comprehend these things. For this truly is the astounding miracle of the universe. And what pleasure can surpass the discovering of the hidden causes of these grand phenomena? What spectacle can be more beautiful than nature shedding profusely such a diversity of forms? [25]

There is too a moral dimension to learning for it restrains those evil passions which drive men to madness. Learning is indeed the natural ally of virtue. [26]

> True wisdom (*sapientia*) is a conflation of firm morality (*virtus*) and the knowledge of important things (*scientia*). Those who separate virtue and knowledge think they can combine virtue with ignorance. Nothing is more absurd than this. You may say that virtue without learning keeps its own value, nor do I deny that

[24] *Oratio*, p. 13: "& certe tantam amoris ad scientias amplexandas illecebram ingeneravit unicuique natura, ut etiam abjectissimi homines, & qui sordissimas artes profitentur, illud sentiant, si quem modo iis literis, quibus homo homini praestat, excultum vident, hunc nescio quo naturae vel numinis impetu, quamvis ipsi nullam humanitatis partem attigerint, colunt & admirantur."

[25] *Oratio*, p. 13: "ac mehercule jure id faciunt. quid. n. scientiarum praestantia in rerum universitate admirabilius? miramur terrae vastitatem, maris altitudinem, coeli profunditatem, solis splendorem, siderum cursus, stellarum vim, defectus luminum; miramur fulgura, tonitrua, ventorum impetus, terrae tremorem: miramur animantium formas, plantarum vires, caussas metallorum, lapidum varietatem, rerum omnium ortus ac interitus: miramur animorum immortalium virtutem ac potestatem, miramur huius mundi excellentiam & amplitudinem, miramur incredibilem hominis divinitatem ac naturam: nihil tamen ex omnib. quae dixi, quicquam potest esse admirabilius eo, qui haec omnia dimetiri, & mente complecti potuit. hoc illud est mundi miraculum magnopere visendum ac stupendum. at quae voluptas major est, si quidem voluptates quaerimus, quam abstrusas rerum illarum caussas tenere? quid pulchrius quam naturam, in tanta rerum varietate, ludentem intueri?"

[26] *Oratio*, p. 13. For relevant Platonic views of wisdom and virtue see Jaeger, *Paideia*, II, 91ff. E.F. Rice, Jr., *The Renaissance Idea of Wisdom* (Cambridge, Mass., 1958). Bodin's views are certainly closer to Plato than to Aristotle, but for what seems to me to be the crucial influence of Philo's idea of wisdom on Bodin see Chapters IV and V. See also footnotes 66f below.

some men have been endowed either by nature of God with the ability to develop the greatest virtues without learnings. But how much more superior to themselves they would be if they possessed also knowledge of the human and divine sciences? For he who combines these sciences with perfect virtue is as much above his fellows as they are above the beasts. Indeed this man comes close to the divinity of immortal God. [27]

Bodin's attitude to learning and knowledge is thus rooted in his concept of the moral nature of man. His *virtus ac doctrina is* reminiscent of the Erasmian formula *pietas et humanitas* but what clearly distinguishes Bodin's view of man and knowledge is his pervasive sense of the natural and of man's place in nature. That man could come near to divinity through the cultivation of his own natural instincts for virtue and learning hints at a belief in natural religion in sharp contrast with the firmly Christian context of Erasmus' views on education. There is, it should be noted, no mention here of an intermediary Christ.

That Bodin by 1559 had arrived at a partial belief in natural religion appears likely from his consideration of barbarian religion in the *Oratio*.

> Whence arose the impiety and false religion of the barbarians? Certainly out of ignorance. On the other hand, how was it that wise men recognised that the soul was an immortal principle, personal to them and flowing from the eternal mind? Whence did they extract the most certain knowledge (*certissima scientia*) of the one God? Assuredly out of the first principles and hidden causes of nature. They saw that these causes were all interrelated and led eventually as though by some necessity of nature, to a single one. Thus, even if nothing were published in our literature and books concerning God, the creator of the universe and of nature, if no voice from heaven had ever taught that souls live immortally, nevertheless that knowledge (*scientia*) which reveals the causes of things would educate us completely and give us faith of a kind that enraged Epicureans could not dissipate. Is it not enough to contemplate that admirable might and nature of the most powerful God which is inscribed and comprehended in the causes of nature? [28]

This religious combination of naturalistic ideas and belief in a transcendental creator of nature is very similar to the picture which emerges from Philo's

---

[27] *Oratio*, p. 14: "vera sapientia, quae ex solida virtute, ac rerum magnarum scientia conflatur. qui autem virtuti adimunt rerum scientiam, cum ignorantia, quo nihil est absurdius, virtutem conjungi posse putant. at virtus, inquies, sine doctrina suam per se dignitatem tuetur: haud equidem nego, quosdam tantum naturae vel numinis bonitate valuisse, ut sine magna eruditione egregias sint virtutes consequuti: sed quanto intervallo seipsis superiores fuissent, si divinarum atque humanarum rerum scientias tenerent? has enim si quis cum virtute perfecta conjungat, tanto reliquis hominibus praestiterit, quanto illi belluis; immo vero hunc hominem proxime ad Dei immortalis numen accedere oportet."

[28] *Oratio*, p. 15: "nam unde profecta barbarorum impietas est, & falsa religio? certe ab ignorantia: unde vero sapientes homines, immortalem & in se collectam animi vim, ex aeterna mente derivari ac fluere intellexerunt? unde certissimam unius Dei scientiam hauserunt? profecto ex naturae initiis, & abditis caussis, quas cum inter se contulissent omnes, quadam necessitate naturae, ad unam, in qua consistendum erat, viderunt referri. quapropter si de Deo, mundi ac naturae totius opifice, nihil esset literis nostris atque libris proditum; si nunquam coelo delapsa vox illa, docuisset animos immortaliter vigere; haec nos scientia, quae rerum caussas in lucem eruit, penitus erudiret, ex qua fidem ejusmodi haberemus, quam Epicurei abrogare, si vel disrumpantur, non possint. parumne est igitur admirabilem praepotentis Dei vim ac naturam, quae in rerum caussis insculpta & comprehensa est, intueri?"

writings. In both Bodin and Philo the unitary God of nature presides over the diversity of creation and instills both religion and morality into men's souls, endowing man with a rational capacity for knowledge. [29] There is here even a hint of revelation — the critical third element in Philo — in the phrase "if no voice from heaven had ever taught that souls live immortally...". Nevertheless the religion here is far more rationalistic than Philo's which emphasises rather the free-will of Deuteronomic choice. In the *Oratio* divinely instilled reason alone seems to suffice to direct man towards God; there is but a weak suggestion of the power of man's instinct for good and for love of God, or of the supreme importance of the will in choosing to seek virtue, or of the role of prophecy as the medium of divine revelation — yet these were the elements which were dominate to Bodin's later religion. [30] Instead of the will, it is reason which, in the form of learning and letters, shapes men's virtue. So virtue becomes almost an adjunct of learning and Bodin even remarks that without learning, virtue will disappear.

> Is it not enough that these things are known in themselves? This is why letters teach us not merely those arts necessary for living, but instruct us fully as to which things are to be sought after and which avoided, as to what is shameful and what proper, what is true and what is false, what is wholesome, what pernicious. It tells us of the virtues, the best laws, the best state (*respublica*), of the happy life. If learning were to disappear, then of necessity the divine oracles, faith, piety, religion would all be carried off in the general decay of things (*decursu temporum*). Ignorance must yield to learning, foolishness to wisdom, error to certain knowledge (*scientia*), falsehood to truth, shadow to splendour, bestiality to humanity, profit to merit. [31]

Not surprisingly the state (*respublica*) in which man's life is lived becomes a necessarily moral institution.

> Do you think that the worth of a state is to be measured by utility rather than by morality (*honestas*)? Or do you believe that state happy in which your citizens seek only the useful and avoid the good (*honesta*)? [32]

Imagine a rich city ruled only by *utilitas* where *honestas* and *virtus* are forgotten and all learning and knowledge   shunned.

> Its citizens, like animals destitue of reason (*ratio*) are driven by instinct alone to those things which are at hand. Although they are plunged in the worst darkness of error, they refuse the light (*lux*) so divinely sent down to them. Compare

---

[29] The seeding of virtue is made more explicit at *Oratio*, p. 25, quoted below. See also Chapter VI. For Philo's religion see Chapter VIII.

[30] See Chapters V-VIII.

[31] *Oratio*, p. 15: "parumne est seipsum nosse? quamobrem cum literis doceamur, non solum artes ad vitam degendam necessarias, sed etiam omnino quae sint homini expetenda, quae fugienda; quid turpe, quid honestum; quid verum, quid falsum; quid salutare, quid perniciosum; quae virtutes, quae optimae leges, quae optima Respub. quae beata vita: cum sublatis literis divina oracula, fidem, pietatem, religionem, decursu temporum, convelli sit necesse; cedat, opinor, ignoratio disciplinis, stultitia sapientiae, error scientiae, caligo luci, mendacium veritati, umbra splendori, feritas humanitati, lucrum dignitati."

[32] *Oratio*, p. 14: "an tu Reipub. dignitatem, utilitate potius quam honestate metiendam putabis? aut beatam Rempub. arbitrabere, in qua tui cives non nisi utilia consectentur, ab honestis abhorreant?"

28

... those citizens of a less wealthy state which educates its citizens in virtue and learning until they no longer seem to have been moulded but rather born for the good and prudent governing states. Which state is the better, which citizens the happier? Those who greedily pursue the useful, forgetting all uprightness (*honestas*) and virtue, or those who rejoice in the good? ... Is the former life (if you can call it life) to be compared with the latter? [33]

A state without morality and learning is indeed not a human state but an association of animals.

> For not only are we composed of a soul and body, but men would be nothing better than the beasts if societies (*societates*) were joined merely for the care of bodies and the amassing of wealth and not for the education (*erudiendorum*) of souls (I shall show in another place that the material end cannot be satisfied if you neglect the spiritual).

> If it might be possible that any state (*respublica*) based only on its material resources and devoid of learning might stand for long then that state would be a wholly miserable one, nor would its inhabitants differ from the beasts which also have their associations (*coetus*) and protect and maintain, as it were, their states (*respublicae*) by a fair — and because of that inviolable — law of nature (*aequabili quodam, eoque inviolabili, jure naturae*). [34]

Bodin here seems to accept a basic law of nature, common to both man and animal, which instigates the formation of societies for the satisfaction of bodily needs. Such an instinctive law of nature had some precedent in Roman law, having been sanctioned by Ulpian. To judge from the phrasing of the passage Bodin perceived the essence of this instinctive law of nature to be its fairness or equability. But it seems impossible that he could have regarded the equability or equity of animal societies as comparable to that justice which is the bond of the human state. For the point of his argument is that virtue is the essence of human society and that virtue itself — like justice — consists in the domination of the passions by natural reason. This places Bodin more in the tradition of Gaius which interpreted natural law as uniquely human and held it to be justified by its inherent rationality and virtue. For Bodin, therefore, any human state which was to be more than an animal association had to be based upon a law of nature quite different from that which applied

---

[33] *Oratio*, p. 14: "ut animalia rationis expertia, solo sensu, ad ea quae praesto sunt, moveantur; & cum maximis errorum tenebris offusi sint, lucem tamen divinitus ad se delatam refugiant: ... illos ... his qui tenues admodum facultates habent, prudentissimè tamen Rempub. gerunt, suum omne otium in reb. honestis collocant, ... ad omne virtutum ac scientiarum genus tantisper instituunt, dum ad Respublicas bene ac prudenter gerendas non facti, sed nati videantur: utra tandem Respub. melior, utri ciues beatiores? an illi qui utilitatem nescio quam nimis avare consectantes, omnis honestatis ac virtutis obliviscuntur; an vero hi qui tenue utcunq. aerarium exhauriunt, ut eo, quod pulchrum ac honestum est, summa cum gloria fruantur? ... tu vitam illam (si hoc vivere est) cum hac comparandam arbitrere?"

[34] *Oratio*, p. 14: "nos non solum ex animo esse & corpore conflatos, sed etiam nihilo praestantiores homines bellius ipsis futuros, si corporum curandorum, & cogendarum opum, non etiam animorum erudiendorum causa, societates inter se coeant (ostendam alio loco, ne illud quidem effici posse, si hoc negligas) attamen si posset ulla Respub. suis opibus, sine literarum cognitione, stare diutius, misera omnino videretur, nec illi homines quicquam a bestiis discreparent, quae suos caetus habent, ac suas veluti Respub. aequabili quodam, eoque inviolabili jure naturae tuentur & conservant."

29

to both man and the animals. The natural law of the human state had to be rooted in the moral nature of man. The state had to be moral, or it was no state. [35]

In these passages one may sense a connection between Bodin's vision of the natural and moral state and his theory of historical cycles: "If it might be possible that a miserable state (i.e. *an animal-like state which had lost its moral nature*) might stand for long..." reflects Bodin hypothetically, and he goes on to develop the link between the vicissitudes of virtue and of politics. [36] Among the foremost intellectual pursuits of the citizens of a happy state, says Bodin, should be a study of the history of all peoples which contemplates "as in a mirror the origin, consolidation, alteration and ruin of towns, realms, cities and states (*respublicae*)". [37] Through an understanding of the causes of the rise and fall of empires, he implies, an educated citizenry may be able to avoid the fate of other nations.

> I shall show that those states in which learning flourished, also prospered in population, in empire and in power, and in wealth and abundance.... The Athenians would never have achieved so much had they not abounded in resources, nor would they have set firm (*stabilissent*) the fortunes of their state had they not zealously cultivated the liberal arts which they spread over the globe. [38]

The political ascendancy of Athens, Alexandria, Rome and France was accompanied by the rise of learning in those states. Nor was the parallel merely coincidental, for the two developments were causally and necessarily linked. Just as virtue is inextricably joined with learning to form *honestas*, so *honestas* is intimately associated with *utilitas* — the material wealth and power, the resources of the state.

> (True) *utilitas* is so much a part of *honestas* that if you take away one from the other, neither may exist.... And do you not see that what some imagine to be utility not only differs from *honestas* but may exist entirely separately? When you separate the pursuit of the good (*honesta*) and the useful you err and are guilty of imprudence. Therefore if you do love the public interest (*utilitas*) remove from the state the conflict between the useful and the good. [39]

[35] The *Distributio juris universi* written at Toulouse but published only in 1578 separates the *jus naturale* of men from that of animals. So too in the *Methodus*, p. 123 (trs. p. 39) Bodin is reluctant to grant animal societies the same status as human societies which are "associations of law and justice". Animals have a sort of prudential equity, men have justice. See below Chapter II (note 10). Cf. *Paradoxe*, (1598), pp. 70, 79 (and Chapter VII) for prudence and its relationship to justice in Bodin's later thought.

[36] *Oratio*, p. 14, quoted above.

[37] *Oratio*, p. 14: "denique urbium, regnorum, civitatum, Rerumpublicarum initia, status, conversiones, ruinas in libris, quasi in speculo, contuentur ac prospiciunt."

[38] *Oratio*, p. 15: "ostendo igitur civitates eas, in quibus literarum studia florent, civium frequentia florere, imperio & potentia florere, rerum omnium ubertate & copia florere .... quas res nunquam Athenienses gessissent, nisi magnos opibus abundarent, nec tantas Reipublicae fortunas stabiliissent, nisi artes ingenuas, quibus ipsi terrarum orbem implerunt, studiosissime colerent."

[39] *Oratio*, p. 16: "utilitas enim ita cum honestate confusa est, ut si alteram ab altera divellas, neutra consistere possit ... non vides illam, quam tute fingis, utilitatem, non solum ab honestate discrepare, verumetiam penitus ab ea distrahi? quoties autem honestorum ac utilium studia dividis, toties peccas, toties imprudentia laberis. quamobrem tolle mihi de Republica discrimen illud utilis ac honesti, si utilitatem publicam amas."

Thus, the utilitarian purpose of the state is bound up with its moral and natural life, the political cycle of the state with the cycle of the rise and decay of learning.

It was in this context that Bodin understood the history of France. The *Oratio's* optimistic descriptions of the French Renaissance are rooted in Bodin's experience of contemporary French culture and in a sense distort a specific instance into a general theory of history. Surrounded by the fresh vitality of French culture and inspired by the magnificence of François I Bodin might feel equally confident about the political fortunes of the French state, for politics and culture were bonded together in the natural cycle of history. As long as culture flourished the French nation would be prosperous and powerful. So for Bodin the *Oratio* was more than a mere plea for educational patronage; its insistence on the necessity of learning and education had a political significance — the survival of France. The particular portrait of the French Renaissance with which the *Oratio* begins, far from being a separate theme, is rather an integral part of the general theme of the fundamental role of education in the moral and natural republic.

A constant interaction between the unique and the universal is one of the most striking characteristics of Bodin's thought. On the one hand there are his specific perceptions of French culture and of "France", on the other his abstract and general theories of cyclical history which apply to all nations. Again one might cite his interpretation of the relation between concrete Roman law and philosophical concepts of law and justice. Both these examples are to be seen in juxtaposition in the *Oratio* where Bodin sets out his discussion of Roman law in the context of the French Renaissance.

Of all the achievements of the French Renaissance Bodin selects the recovery of a true understanding of Roman law as the most momentous. The French universities and particularly Toulouse were in the forefront of this revival of Roman Law, which, for Bodin, is fundamentally civil law, that is "law for the governing of states and the ordering of nations". [40] Thanks to Budé, Alciat, Connan and the rest of the humanist jurists, civil law (says Bodin) has been purged of the filth and ignorance which surrounded it. Now the path to a true science of law has been cleared of the brambles, hedges and ditches which beset it. Instead of the rocky wilderness overrun by the thickets and thorns of the Bartolist commentators, humanist jurisprudence presents a well-cultivated garden, planted with the flowers of letters, eloquence and philosophy. In this inclusion of philosophy in the lawyer's intellectual equipment we may see the convergence of Bodin's knowledge of the particulars of civil law with his philosophical vision of justice.

> At last there have appeared jurists worthy of the name who have understood clerly that the nature of justice (*justitiae naturam*) is not changeable at the will of men, but permanent and defined by eternal law (*lege*). They have inquired deeply into the power and majesty of the laws (*legum*). They have discussed with skill what equity should be (*normam aequitatis*). They have assiduously traced

---

[40] *Oratio*, p. 16: "jus civile ... id est, ut ad gubernandas civitates, ad populos instituendos erudiantur." Cf. De Caprariis, *Propaganda*, pp. 336ff.

back the origins and roots of law, even from its first principle. They have passed on to a complete history of legislators and jurists, and a true knowledge (*cognitio*) of antiquity. They have understood wholly the jurisdictions and powers of the emperor, senate, people and magistrates of Rome. They have brought to the interpretation of law (*jus*) the writings of the Philosophers on the laws (*legibus*), on the state and on virtue. They have been learned in the Greek and Latin languages in which the laws are written. They have combined famously legal and political duties with teaching. Finally they have mapped out the boundaries of the whole science (*ars universa*), noted its genera, set out its parts, assigned its terminology and elucidated it with precedents. With such zeal have our youth now begun to embrace this science (*scientia*) which before lay spurned and squalid that we may think no other science more divine or useful for the state or more salutary for the human race. [41]

This passage is a remarkable attempt at reducing law to a true science, resting on the most certain principles. To penetrate to the inner and real nature of law — *vis ac majestas legum,* the *norma aequitatis,* the *ultimum principium juris,* as he variously calls it — Bodin has conscripted the historical and philological armament of humanist jurisprudence and placed it under the command of his philosophical and moral imperatives. Only after this campaign has been successful may law be construed as a certain science with a comprehensible and rational structure (*ars universa*).

We know that Bodin was engaged in the composition of the *Distributio Juris Universi* — his systematisation of the science of law — during his years at Toulouse. But the passage quoted above hints that Bodin had also embarked by 1559 on the enterprise of a universal history which would illuminate the nature of law. The *Oratio*'s emphasis on natural law, its insistence on the historical interpretation of civil law and its repeated recommendation to study the history of all legislators and peoples, suggest that by 1559 Bodin had already formed in his mind the nexus of ideas which was to emerge fully elaborated in the *Methodus* seven years later. [42]

[41] *Oratio*, pp. 17f: "at postea quam inventi sunt jurisconsulti, hoc tam gravi nomine digni, qui justitiae naturam non instabilem illam, & ad hominum voluntates mutabilem, sed aeterna lege definitam clare intuerentur; qui legum vim ac majestatem penitus perspicerent; qui normam aequitatis perite tractarent; qui juris ortum ac stirpem diligenter, & ab ultimo principio repeterent; qui legumlatorum ac juris-consultorum omnem historiam, & antiquitatis cognitionem accurate traderent; qui principis, senatus, populi, magistratuumq. Romanorum jurisdictionem, potestatem, officia plane tenerent; qui philosophorum libros de legib. & Repub. deq. virtutibus ad jus interpretandum afferrent; qui Graecam & Latinam linguam, quib. latae ac descriptae leges sunt, minime ignorarent; qui literas forenses ac senatorias, cum praeceptis haud obscure conjungerent; qui denique artem universam suis finibus circunscriberent, generibus notarent, partibus distribuerent, verbis designarent, exempli illustrarent; tanto studie juventus scientiam illam, quae antea spreta ac sordidata, contra quam decuit, jacebat, amplexari coepit, ut nullam vel diviniorem, vel Rebuspub. utiliorem, vel hominum generi magis salutarem putet."

[42] Compare also the echoes in the *Methodus* of Bodin's remarks in the *Oratio* on the flowers of eloquence and philosophy which are humanistic jurisprudence contrasted with the rocky crags and thorns of Roman law (*Methodus,* p. 108 (trs. p. 4)); on the skill of those legal theorists who are establishing the science or *ars* of law (p. 108 (p. 6)); and on the manner in which the investigation of nature's workings draws man on to knowledge of God (pp. 15f (p. 114)). See also for Bodin's ideas of 1566 J.H. Franklin, *Jean Bodin and the Sixteenth Century Revolution in the Methodology of Law and History* (New York, 1963).

Reflecting on his theory of education in the final section of the *Oratio,*
Bodin turns to some of the central problems of moral philosophy and presents
a rationalistic theory of ethics which he was to abandon in his later writings.
The core of morality is the dominion of reason (*recta ratio, mentis lumen*)
over the passions. [43]   Only by this dominion may man attain the virtue for
which he is born (*virtus...pro qua fruenda nascimur*).   But this victory has to
be fought for just as Cyrus "learnt to govern himself and to subdue his
appetite to reason which is the summation of all justice and natural law
(*rationi... quae totius justitiae ac legis naturae summa est*)". [44]   The need for
such a moral education is the cue for one of Bodin's bitterest attacks on
women, the class to whom the private education of children is usually entrusted.
Such education is as devoid of true moral content as the women who give it.
The archetype of women is the enchantress Circe.

> Circe changed men into beasts ... making them forget their children and
> country until they lost their dignity and honour and even their divinity.... Ulysses'
> men refused to heed him, preferring a life of misery to hapiness, madness to reason,
> to be animals rather than men....   Thus too it happens with those boys who are
> nourished, taught, reared and pass their adolescence under the tutelage and in
> the company of women.   Such feminine education must be suppressed. [45]

These seductive mistresses who teach letters without morality prevent men
being truly rational human beings. [46]   The great vice of the age is truly effemi-
nacy.

Seen in this context Bodin's notorious misogyny arises out of the conviction
that women symbolise the divorce of the moral and intellectual powers of man,
a divorce fatal to both man and the state.   That learning without virtue is
simply perversion is one of the chief lessons of the *Oratio.* [47]

> What is more pernicious than intelligence without integrity?   What more
> hateful to immortal God than knowledge (*scientia*) allied with crime?   Indeed I
> am wrong in using the word "knowledge" here.   But whatever one calls it, nothing
> is more monstruous than that which lacking all goodness (*probitas*) usurps the sacred

[43] *Oratio*, p. 23.   Compare Plato's theory of psychic conflict.   But Bodin's later
usage distinguishes between two forms of the will — the rational will (*voluntas*) and
desire or passion (*appetitus*).   This is dealt with, for instance, in the *Universae naturae
theatrum* (Lyons, 1596), pp. 468f.   For the difference between the rationalistic theory of
ethics of the *Oratio* and Bodin's later voluntaristic ethics see below, Chapter VI.

[44] *Oratio*, p. 23.   Cf. *République* (Paris, 1583), pp. 19-20, where a similar remark
prefaces a discourse on the subjection of wives to husbands.   There is a clear implication
that wives represent the passions, men reason.

[45] *Oratio*, p. 24: "homines in bestias a Circe mutatos tradunt ... ut capti atq. impliciti
quasi laqueis miserrimi homines, non modo liberorum ac patriae, sed etiam nomines &
famae, suaeq. divinitatis penitus obliviscerentur ... vellent ad se [Ulissem] redire; licere
per Circem: illi contra renitentes, vitam miseram quam beatam ducere, furere quam
sapere, pecudes quam homines esse maluerunt ... quales futuri sunt, qui in contubernio ac
coetu foeminarum aluntur, instituuntur. educantur, adolescunt? tollenda igitur disciplina
illa muliebris."

[46] Bodin admits that women may be learned, if not virtuous.   See his praise of
Clémence Isaure, founder of the Jeux Floraux at Toulouse (27-28).   Compare Forcadel's
warnings against women and "venal love" (above).

[47] The dark ages were in part the result of men turning salutary learning to evil
ends and so bringing down on themselves the just punishment of the gods (10).

name of *scientia*. To know nothing is certainly unhappy. But by far the greatest of miseries is to pervert to evil that which ought to be beneficial. [48]

Equally damnable are the theory and practice of politics when conducted without reference to virtue.

> Some explain the books of the philosophers on gods and demons, on destiny, on nature, on the greatest good, yet do so without any mention of *pietas*, as though it were unremarkable that so many men have taken up the teachings of the Stoics and Epicureans, not for the purpose of intellectual debates but that they might learn a way of living. What greater treachery can there by, what more deadly for states, for law, for good morals [than sophistry?].... Cato the Elder, we are told, could not bear the discourse of the Athenian ambassador Carneades who delivered a eulogy of injustice for the sake of a rhetorical exercise.... [49]

How then will one curb the un-virtuous education practised by women and those licentious poets, their allies? Only through a system of public education may this immorality be censored effectively. [50] One may be amused at Bodin's preoccupation with women and dubious books but his prejudices arise out of his fundamental views on the nature of man and the state. The earnest proposal in the *République* to revive the Roman office of censor is not a paradoxical slip by the libertarian Jean Bodin. It is a logical expression of his moral and political beliefs. [51]

One of the perennial topics of sixteenth century French thought was the translation of the psychic conflict between reason and passion into the social language of war and peace. [52] By 1559 Toulouse had been disturbed by bitter religious hostilities and in the *Oratio* there is already a sense of the impending

---

[48] *Oratio*, p. 24: "nam quid est tam pestiferum quam intelligentia sine integritate? quid immortali Deo tam invisum quam scientia cum scelere conjuncta? quanquam non sum eo verbo usus quo debui: neq. enim scientia dici meretur, quod abest ab ea, distatque plurimum: sed tamen quid tam nefarium istuc quicquid est, quod detracta probitate scientiae sanctum nomen arripit? miserum est omnino nihil scire, miserius eo quod scias uti non posse, sed longe miserrimum, id, quod salutare esse debuerat, ad malitiam convertere."

[49] *Oratio*, p. 24: "alii philosophorum libros de diis ac daemonibus, de fato, de natura, de summo bono ita explicant, ita nihil ad pietatem referunt, ut minime mirum videri debeat, si multi jam in Epicureorum ac Stoicorum placitis, non disputandi animo, sed ita vivendi acquiescent. at quae fraus ulla capitalior? quid Rebuspublicis, quid legibus, quid bonis morib. exitiosius?...dicitur Cato major Carneadem legatum Atheniensium, de injustitiae laudib. exercendi animi caussa dicentem."

It seems to me that the vexed question of Bodin's early Machiavellism is largely misconceived. Bodin never divorced politics from morality and law, even as an analytical or literary exercise.

[50] *Oratio*, p. 24f.

[51] M. Reulos, "Une institution Romaine vue par un auteur du XVIe siècle: La censure dans Jean Bodin', *Etudes offertes à Jean Macqueron* (Aix-en-Provence, 1970), pp. 585-590. The *Oratio's* treatment is cited at p. 847 of the 1583 edition of the *République*. Bodin links the decline of Rome with the abandoning of the censorship.

[52] See the letter to Bautru for the relation of psychic peace to religious war. Rose, 'Two Problems'. And Chapter VIII below.

catastrophe of the Wars of Religion. Peace, claims Bodin, is the true and highest end of the state as universal history shows.

> One thing in the state (*civitas*) is to be sought above all from immortal God. It is that the will of the citizens in both spiritual and temporal matters (*divinae ac humanae res*) always be the same and in harmony (*consentiens*). This is the end of human society and of all public life. The laws of all nations, the religions and cults of all peoples, all the duties of judges and magistrates, indeed all institutions, rites and customs relate and are directed to one instance — that men may live happily in affection and trust. [53]

How may such peace be achieved? Education is the best pacifier for it encourages the innate tendency of man towards virtue and religion.

> Of those laws which reconcile society in the state (*in rebuspublicis societatem conciliare*) none is so sacred or divine as the common and identical education of children. Indeed in religious matters it is necessary that the citizens agree among themselves in the greatest harmony (*conspiratio*). For God has placed in the souls of all of us the seeds of piety and religion, and these are so deeply rooted that they cannot be torn out without destroying also honour, trust, integrity and that justice without which not even God would reign. [54]

Bodin sees two main social aspects to religion. Firstly he treats it as virtue and as such inseparable from those virtues which make for social harmony. Secondly and more politically he regards religion as a formal expression of political duty. Outward uniformity in matters of religion contributes to the peace and unity of the state.

> As adults we are full of errors. Nor may one realise religious unanimity among all the citizens except that people receive a common education from infancy, learn the same texts, acquire the same customs, honour the same God and finally be initiated in to the same rites and imbued with the same learning. [55]

But Bodin then goes on to make a further distinction between the spiritually true religion of the pontiffs and the formal state-religion of the magistrates.

> If it is the duty of pontiffs to ensure that true religion (*religio vera*) is not polluted by the filth of any superstition or impiety, so it is the duty of the magis-

[53] *Oratio*, p. 25: "Una res est in civitate a Deo immortali summe optanda, ut divinarum ace humanarum rerum eadem sit inter cives, & semper sibi consentiens voluntas. hic societatis humanae, ac rerum omnium publicarum finis est. omnes. n. omnium gentium leges, omnes populorum religiones ac ceremoniae, omnia judicum, omnia magistratuum munera, omnia denique instituta, ritus, mores, in hunc exitum spectant ac diriguntur, ut scilicet communi hominum charitate ac fide beate vivi possit."

[54] *Oratio*, p. 25: "nullas esse leges tam sanctas ac divinas, quae firmiorem in Rebuspub. societatem conciliare valeant, quam communis & eadem liberorum educatio. ac de reb. quidem divinis, necesse est in iis ut summa conspiratione civium sensus inter se congruant. etenim jacta sunt a Deo uniuscujusque nostrûm animos, pietatis quaedam ac religionis semina, quae cum altissimis defixa radicib. haerent, tum erui nullo modo possunt, nisi pudorem, fidem, integritatem, & eam, fine qua ne Deus quidem regnarit, justitiam una convellas."

[55] *Oratio*, p. 25: "sed quoniam adulti variis saepe replemur erroribus, qui porterit omnium civium de reb. diuinis eadem esse scientia, nisi ab ineunte aetate disciplinam eandem hauserint, easdem literas didicerint, eosdem mores imbiberint, idem numen coluerint, denique iisdem sacris initiati, eadem doctrina imbuti fuerint?"

trates who hold the helm of state to prevent the distraction of its youth from the one and the same religion to a multiplicity of religions, that is if we hope to have a state (*rempublicam*) at all. But with private education some learn pure religion (*pura religio*), some another religion, others none at all. [56]

This distinction between *vera religio* and state-religion remained central to Bodin's religious thought and outward behaviour. As we shall see in Chapter VIII Bodin's inner religion changed little of its main lineaments between the *Oratio* and the *Heptaplomeres,* although some remarkable shifts of emphasis occurred. On the other hand his formal religious behaviour fluctuated wildly between extremes of apparently stubborn Protestantism in 1569 and fanatical Catholicism in 1590. This confessional indifference aptly illustrates Bodin's conviction that formal religion — which largely performed a social function — had little or no bearing on inner *vera religio*. In consequence the actual church and dogma which constituted the religion of a particular state mattered little to Bodin. In this regard a definite reticence in the passage just quoted is highly revealing, for Bodin declines to name either the Catholic or Reformed churches as the representatives of *pura religio*, nor does he specify which church is to be regarded as the religion of the state. The only criterion Bodin has in mind seems to be pragmatic — whichever religion commands the allegiance of the majority and of the powerful is the religion of the state. [57]

Without religious unity, religion becomes a double-edged sword. Just as it may consolidate peace so too it may sow war.

> Whence have so many varied errors invaded the minds of men? Whence the multiplication of sects? Why do so many groups not only oppose their rivals but also differ internally among themselves if it is not because they think it well to follow their own sect and founder? From here begins that limitless evil which creeps slowly over all states. Here originate those calamitous storms, those hatreds, brawls, rivalries, enmities, complaints, accusations, factions; and after them come the plots, the civil wars, the pillaging of cities, the overthrow of states, the slaughter of illustrious men. It is not long since we have had neighbouring realms and nations tossed about in the waves of civil wars. Nor have they yet achieved true peace, nor will they unless they educate in one and the same way all their children under a public provision. [58]

[56] *Oratio*, p. 275: "sed si quidem pontificum munus est, uti est, conniti ne religio vera superstitionis ullius aut impietatis fuco polluatur, magistratuum itidem est, qui clavum Reipub. tenent, dare operam, ne juventus ab una & eadem religione in varias distrahatur, si nos ullam Rempub. habituros speramus. at in privata educatione, alii quidem puram religionem, alii aliam, alii nullam didicerunt."

[57] Cf. De Caprariis, *Propaganda,* pp. 329ff. In the *Methodus* (ed. Mesnard), p. 135, Bodin is also careful not to specify just which church is the *vera religio*.

[58] *Oratio*, p. 25: "unde tot ac tam varii errores in hominum animos irrepserunt? unde tot sectae? unde tanta raritas eorum qui unum sentiunt atque idem? aut cur tam multi non modo ab aliis, sed etiam ipsi a se discrepant, nisi quod suam quisq. sectam sequi suum quisq. magistrum, a quo est institutus, tueri pulchrum putat? hinc igitur serpit in omnes Respub. infinitum malum: hinc calamitosae tempestates oriuntur: hinc odia, rixae, contentiones, inimicitiae, querelae, accusationes, sectiones; postremo conjurationes, intestina bella, direptiones urbium, Rerumpublicarum eversiones, & clarorum, virorum interitus. atque iis quidem bellorum civilium fluctib. jactari finitima regna, finitimas nationes non ita pridem vidimus, quae nondum plane conquierunt, nec conquieturae videntur, nisi publica lege suorum civium liberos uno & eodem modo instituant."

Bodin's vision of peace here is fundamentally religious in that it depends on both divinely instilled virtue and formal religious unity. But even if the religious elements were removed social harmony would still require the uniform education of children. [59]

> Some have disengaged themselves from religious matters (*res divinae*) and attended only to human affairs even though the temporal sphere cannot endure (*stare*) without the religious, and the religious sphere does not decline without involving the temporal in its ruin. But suppose there were a people [60] so primitive and barbarous as to lack all piety towards God, to think human affairs governed by chance and the accident of fortune rather than by divine kindness and prudence — then those men would have to live like animals (even though the beasts themselves do not live like this) unless they gave their children the common education necessary for the good of the state (*civitas*), and education that will bind the citizens both to one another and to the state (*respublica*) by some kind of relationship. [61]

Bodin's concept of public education, like his notion of public religion, has an anthropological sense of the relativism of social rituals and of the function of these rituals in reconciling social conflict.

> This need has been wisely foreseen by all legislators who have not stopped at a common system of education, but also instituted for all the citizens a common feasting, ceremonial meals, distribution of meat, public games and finally sacred banquets. By this common engagement of life are the citizens led to live in peace (*se conciliare*), to initiate friendships, to dispel hatred, to forget anger. [62]

The rites of education, the companionship of youth and the shared joys of learning — all these combine to produce the fundamental social virtue — amity.

> The whole of nature proclaims amity as the firmest bond (*vinculum*) for the protection and preservation of states, empires and cities, of communities (*societates*), houses, families and of all human life. [63]

---

[59] For the power of social friendship even where religious agreement is lacking see Bodin's letter to Bautru (ed. Chauviré, *Bodin*, pp. 521ff): "In the absence of religion or any fear of divine majesty even justice, one of the most beautiful virtues, together with the social trust which comes of it, could scarcely stand fast. Nevertheless sometimes the force and bounty of nature is so great as to pull together hostile and competing men in mutual love." But although amity is a powerful social bond it can be strengthened still further by agreement in matters of religion.

[60] Compare Bodin's hypothesis of a people who lived without regard for virtue and learning (*Oratio*, p. 14). Their state could endure only in hypothesis also.

[61] *Oratio*, p. 26: "quod si qui sunt qui res divinas omittant, humanas tantum curent, quanquam sine divinis humana stare nullo modo possunt, nec illa corruere, ut haec non eodem quassata & labefactata motu concidant: sed si qua gens esset tam immanis ac barbara, quae, sublata adversus Deum pietate, casu quodam ac fortunae temeritate res humanas ferri, non bonitate numinis ac prudentia geri arbitraretur, omnino tamen aut unicuiq. vivendum esset soli ferarum in modum, quamvis ne sic quidem ferae vivant; aut liberorum educatio illa communis, ad optimum civitatis statum necessaria fuerit, ut cives necessitate quadam, & inter se, & cum Repub. conjungantur."

[62] *Oratio*, p. 26: "quod persapienter est ab omnibus legumlatorib. provisum, qui non solum eandem liberorum educationem, verumetiam communem omnium saepe civium convictum, festas epulas, viscerationes, ludos, postremo sacra convivia instituerunt; ut cives seipsos sibi communi vitae fructu conciliarent, amicitias inirent, odia depillerent, irarum obliviscerentur."

[63] *Oratio*, p. 26: "amicitiam vero non solum ad Respub. imperia, civitates; verumetiam ad societates, domos, familias ,deniq. ad hominum vitam tuendam & conservandam, vinculum, firmissimum esse tota rerum natura clamat."

So Bodin has arrived at the two basic principles which underlie society and its peace. Amity (*amicitia*), that benevolence which is the essence of reconciliation between men ; and religion (*religio*), which acts both as a spirit of peace and as the formal cement which unifies society.

> All states and all social relations (*illam societatem, quae est hominum inter homines*) between men are secured solely by those two guardians of divine and human affairs, religion and amity. [64]

In the encouragement of these two cardinal social virtues — "connected with learning by the tightest of knots" — lies the objective of Bodin's theory of education.

What has been said so far should indicate the impossibility of drawing a simple division between virtue and learning in Bodin's theory of education. For Bodin the central purpose of education was that it should make man a good citizen *and* a good man at the same time, a double object faithfully reflected in each of the components of his educational theory. As we have seen *doctrina* might lead men to a sense of civic virtue and amity and make them in consequence good citizens; yet *doctrina* also inculcates moral virtue by its perfection of man's reason which curbs the passions. In promoting both civic and moral virtue, therefore, learning contributed to the formation both of the good man and the good citizen. In fact, the good man and the good citizen were inseparable from one another, for in Bodin's eyes the state was above all an association of virtuous men, men whose rational soul gave them an idea of justice which was *denied* to the animals.

Plato and Aristotle had also associated virtue with education but Bodin's theory of education is distinguished from Greek views by its religious colouring. In this we may see another reflection of Bodin's early Judaising which was taking him not only beyond Christian religious ideas into the realm of natural religion, but also enabling him to transcend Greek concepts of ethics. [65]

---

[64] *Oratio*, p. 26: "quapropter cum duo rerum divinarum & humanarum praesidia, res omnes publicas, atque illam, quae est hominum inter homines, societatem sola tueantur, religio nimirum & amicitia, quae literarum communione quasi arctissimo inter se nodo conjugantur."

Amity is more than sociability. Bodin (p. 26) believes that a young man brought up in solitude may acquire an instinct for *societas* but not *amicitia*. On amity, cf. the letter to Bautru cited in note 59. Compare also Forcadel's view that *amor et jus* lead men to *concordia* (see above).

Although there are some resemblances Aristotle's *philia* (*Ethics*, book VIII) is scarcely a fundamental virtue of the same kind as Bodin's *amicitia*. But Plato sees a link between amity and concord (*Laws*, VI, 759b).

In the *Paradoxe* (1598), p. 87f, Bodin identifies amity with justice itself. There is also a shift in Bodin's later works from *amicitia* as a rational to a willed virtue. See Chapter V, note 42.

[65] It should be stressed that Bodin's thought for all its Platonic aspects is very much his own. In any case most of the Platonic flavour comes from Philo. Curiously P. Mesnard, 'Le Platonisme de Jean Bodin', in *Actes du Vᵉ Congrès de l'Association Guillaume Budé* (Paris, 1954), pp. 352-361, did not cite the "Platonic" themes in the *Oratio* as evidence for his case that Bodin was a Platonist.

Bodin's main Judaising resource (if there is indeed one at this stage) seems to have been the writings of the Alexandrian Jewish philosopher Philo which, while embodying several Platonic elements, fused these with an essentially religious attitude. For Philo's theory differed from Greek ethics in that he adapted the moral virtues to the religious soul rather than merely to the natural man as in Platonic or Aristotelian ethics. [66] This ethical attitude permeates Philo's theory of education. Philo's main educational work (*De Congresu eruditionis*) had emphasized the necessity of a religious dimension of the soul; in this allegorical account Abraham symbolising the soul consorted with Hagar representing learning, but his true wife Sarah stands for religious virtue and wisdom. The lesson is that the soul should love learning but be bound even more closely to religious experience. The same orientation is to be found in the *Oratio*. "True wisdom is a conflation of virtue and science", says Bodin in a naturalistic way, but when he follows this with the remark that "the wise man approaches more closely the divinity of immortal God" he adds a religious element which owes nothing to Plato but perhaps a great deal to Philo. [67]

In constructing his theory of man and the state Bodin argued that virtue, intellect, justice, religion and peace or amity were natural to both man and his artefact the state. How then was one to explain the existence of vicious men and unjust states? Bodin's answer was that these represented de-natured men and societies. Nature was the norm of all things and nothing might deviate from its nature without destroying itself. Such de-natured things might exist for a time but they were doomed in the long run. A state without justice was destined to collapse, just as a man without virtue would bring unhappiness on himself. [68] To illustrate these truths Bodin conceived two series of metaphors, one derived from the animals, the other from women. When a man fails to follow his natural reason and abide by natural law, then he reduces himself to the condition of an instinctive animal; when a plurality of men form a society which violates natural justice then they are on the same level as the flocks and herds of beasts. Women too are inferior to man in that they are deficient in

[66] See E. Bréhier, *Les Idées philosophiques et religieuses de Philon d'Alexandrie* (3rd ed., Paris, 1950), pp. 272-296, 307-310, etc. Education is part of a scheme of moral progress which also includes the religious ideas of hope, joy, repentance and justice as well as nature. For Philo the idea of a transcendent God inspiring love and fear of Himself in men produced the notion of a moral conscience.

This religious idea of moral conscience does not appear in the *Oratio* although it may be implied in Bodin's simultaneously held conceptions of natural virtue and learning, religious wisdom and a transcendent God.

[67] *Oratio*, p. 14, quoted more fully above. For Philo's impact on Bodin's ethics and religion see Chapters IV and VIII respectively. The combination of naturalism and a transcendent God in the *Oratio* seems to come in part from Philo's *De Opificio mundi*. (See Chapter VIII, section C). Apart from the notion of the choir of creation Bodin also seems to have drawn the musical metaphor of the harmony of all the virtues from Philo. (*Oratio*, p. 17, see below Chapter VIII). See Bréhier, *Les Idées*, p. 291. Cf. *Paradoxe* (1598), p. 76 and below Chapter V, Note 41.

[68] *Oratio*, pp. 14, 24.

virtue and endeavour to de-nature man by appealing to men's passions and seducing their natural reason and virtue just as Circe did with Ulysses' men. In Bodin's mind women represent the bestialising passions which must be tamed by the male reason in the war of the soul. When man's reason finally prevails then he attains a state of justice and peace.[69] "In rendering the appetite subject to reason — there lies the sum of all justice and natural law (*legis naturae*)".[70]

Unjust states hasten their decline by voluntarily betraying their moral nature. But there was also a tragic and inevitable character to the decline of states which reflected Bodin's pessimistic sense of the omnipresence of degeneration in the universe of nature, a general idea which appears in all of his writings in different guises. Even in the glowingly optimistic canvas of the French Renaissance painted in the *Oratio* Bodin recognised that decay was part of the natural process of all states, good or evil.[71] While seeing the French Renaissance as the natural corollary of the nation's devotion to justice and natural law, Bodin sensed that the flourishing French State, by reason of its participation in the natural cycle of states, was bound to decay eventually. In the *Methodus* some years later this tension was incorporated in Bodin's framework of a universal history which both exalted France's national history and yet viewed French eminence as but a transient phase in an endless historical flux.[72]

Since the natural was the key to the understanding of all things, true knowledge (*vera scientia*) meant comprehension of the individual natures of things. Bodin's intellectual ambition was to obtain certain and true understanding, whether the subject was man, the state, history, religion, the natural universe or law. Such knowledge was achieved by reducing all the various aspects of the subjects to their inner elements of truth, "penetrating the essence and sovereign power of law (*vis et majestas legum*)".[73] Bodin's principle of sovereignty was one of the fruits of this process for it demonstrated the inner reality of the state which lay beneath the diversity of forms of government.

[69] References in the *Oratio* to Circe (24) and to animality and bestiality (10, 11, 14 passim, 15, 24, 26). Cf. *Démonomanie* (Paris, 1580), fols. 8v-9, for "men living like pigs". See above, note 45. For the tyrant as a beast who has lost his reason see Plato's *Republic* and Aristotle's *Ethics*, Book VII. Etienne de la Boétie in his *Discours de la servitude volontaire* (*circa* 1552) insisted that virtue redeems men from the vice of tyranny which leads them to "abandon their natural right and become animals again". The correlation of women, animality and the reign of the passions is a recurrent motif in Agrippa d'Aubigné's *Misères*. For Italian examples see G. Paparelli, *Feritas, humanitas, dvinitas. L'essenza umanistica del Rinascimento* (Naples, 1973).

[70] *Oratio*, p. 23: "appetitum rationi obsequentem reddere consuesset, quae totius justitiae ac legis naturae summa est." See note 44 above.

[71] For the undercurrent of pessimism see *Oratio*, p. 15 (quoted in the text above). Cf. *Methodus*, proemium (in *Œuvres philosophiques*, ed. Mesnard), p. 114A.

[72] For the cycles see *Oratio*, pp. 10-11, 15. P. Mesnard, 'Le nationalisme de Jean Bodin', *La Table Ronde*, CXLVII (1960), 66-72, does not see the ambiguity of Bodin's sense of nation. For a more subtle view see M. Yardeni, *La conscience nationale en France pendant les guerres de religion (1559-1598)* (Paris-Louvain, 1971).

[73] *Oratio*, p. 17: "aeterna lege definitam clare intuerentur; qui legum vim ac majestatem penitus perspicerent; qui normam aequitatis perite tractarent."

Once one understood the true nature of a subject then all else followed easily and logically. The science of law had to be based on the true nature of law. [74]

Yet Bodin did not believe in a pure naturalism. Ultimately he was concerned with understanding not just the principle behind the details of individual sciences but rather with the single principle which gave unity to the diversity of forms in the created universe. Such an encyclopaedic vision of nature demanded a universal and unifying principle and it was in the omnipotent and all powerful God of nature that Bodin found the key. [75] In the *Oratio* God is not an absconding deity hidden from men's eyes but a providential and intervening presence governing human history. God has given man an instinctive knowledge of the divine and instilled a moral sense, which, cultivated, shapes him in the divine image. [76] So too man is able to construe the order, structure and harmony with which God the creator has infused all nature. [77] It was in nature that God revealed himself so that man could penetrate to a true recognition (*vera scientia*) of the deity which would merge with true religion (*vera religio*) to produce the true knowledge that was wisdom.

> Whence did the wise men extract the most certain knowledge of the one God? Assuredly out of the first principles and hidden causes of nature. They saw that these causes were all inter-related and led eventually as though by some necessity of nature to a single one. [78]

Already in 1559 Bodin had glimpsed the Great God of Nature. [79]

---

[74] For Bodin's interest in the *ars universa* and *vera scientia of law* see *Oratio*, pp. 17ff. Cf. K.D. McRae, 'Ramist Tendencies in the Thought of Jean Bodin', *Journal of the History of Ideas*, XVI (1955), 306-323. Franklin, *Jean Bodin*, pp. 28f. For *vera religio* see *Oratio*, p. 25.

[75] See L. Febvre, 'L'universalisme de Jean Bodin', *Revue de Synthèse* LIV (1934), 165-168. A current tendency to regard order as the dominant theme of Bodin's philosophy seems questionable to me. For Bodin the fundamental thing was that the universe be *moral*. Order served to mediate and reveal this divine morality.

[76] *Oratio*, p. 14.

[77] *Oratio*, pp. 13, 25.

[78] *Oratio*, p. 15, quoted above.

[79] See Chapter VIII.

CHAPTER II

THE MORAL STATE IN THE "METHODUS"
AND THE "RÉPUBLIQUE"

The *Methodus* of 1566 attempted a full scale application to human society of the naturalistic ideas of history and law adumbrated in the *Oratio*. At the same time the *Methodus* elucidated and expanded many of the moral and religious notions which had been expressed nebulously, if fulsomely, in the earlier work. In some cases Bodin offers in the *Methodus* merely superior technical definitions (for example of wisdom) but more often connections left loose or simply asserted rather than demonstrated in the *Oratio* are now argued more cogently. And in one crucial innovation — its sudden insistence on the power of the will — this work of 1566 marks a great step forward in the development of Bodin's ethics and religion and clearly reflects the progress of Bodin's Judaising.

The religious character of wisdom was suggested in the *Oratio* but in the *Methodus* Bodin incorporated it into his very definition of wisdom which is a new tripartite one instead of the *Oratio*'s "virtue and learning".

> From the three virtues together (*prudentia, scientia, religio*) is created true wisdom (*sapientia*), man's true and final good. [1]

Where the *Oratio* had vaguely commented that the wise man approaches divinity, the *Methodus* sees wisdom as a definite stage in what has become the mystic ascent of the soul towards God. Happiness now achieves a religious definition.

> Men turn to survey the exact causes of nature and hence come those sciences (*scientiae*) and virtues which, because they rest solely on the recognition of truth. we call speculative.... By these steps man is carried on to things grasped only by the mind — that is to the strength and power of immortal souls (*ad animorum immortalium vim ac potestatem*) [2] — until ... he is closely united (*conjungatur*) to God. In this consists the goal of human action, the final peace and the highest

---

[1] *Methodus*, p. 114B (trs. p. 15): "ex his tribus virtutibus inter se conjunctis, conflatur vera sapientia, summum hominis extremumque bonum." For prudence see below. For further remarks on Bodin's concept of virtue in the *Methodus* and *République* see Chapter VI. For the religious content of the *Methodus* see Chapter VIII.

[2] Note the echoed phrasing of *Oratio*, pp. 13B, 15A.

felicity. Towards this all plans, words, deeds, all striving, all learning (*disciplinae*) and virtues are directed. [3]

The highest happiness is therefore mystical but a lesser happiness consists in moral virtue which may be pursued in the setting of man's own individual being, or in the family, or in the state. The state actually becomes in Bodin's scheme an exemplar of moral virtue.

> Men's interests are divided between civil, domestic and moral training (*morali disciplina*). The one teaches him to control himself, the second his family, the third the state. It is fitting to impose upon oneself the rule of reason — in which resides the culmination of all justice and all laws — before it is possible to rule a family, and then the state. [4]

Indeed Bodin outrightly declares that virtue, not liberty or prosperity, is the end and purpose of the state.

> States are formed not for the sake of liberty (*libertas*) but for living well; for if we measure human happiness by wealth, honours, empire, pleasure and the greatest liberty, then that state would be happy which abounded in these things (as Venice does). But if we consider virtue more important then I do not see why Venice should be regarded as the most excellent of states. [5]

But since Bodin's idea of virtue is coloured here as in the *Oratio* by religious conception, the state is not only moral but in a sense religious, as is to be seen in the manner in which Bodin makes justice and other virtues the concomitants of the fear of God.

> Where fear of the divine will exists, there piety, justice and all the virtues must flourish. I say nothing of that loftiest knowledge of heaven and natural things... I discuss only the state. [6]

---

[3] *Methodus*, p. 120A (p. 30): "hinc illae scientiae ac virtutes, quae quod in veri sola cognitione acquiescunt, theoricae vocantur ... sed his veluti gradibus ad ea fertur quae sola mente percipiuntur, id est ad animorum immortalium vim ac potestatem ... cum Deo penitus conjungatur: in quo finis humanarum actionum & quies extrema, summaque foelicitas consistit. huc omnia consilia, dicta, facta: huc humanae actiones, huc disciplinae ac virtutes referuntur." For the mystical ascent see Chapters V and VI.

[4] *Methodus*, p. 120B (p. 31): "praecipuae hominum actiones conspirant, sunt autem in civili, domestica, & morali disciplina positae: una sibi ipse imperare docet: altera familiae: tertia Reipublicae: prius enim apud se rationis imperium stabilire consentaneum est, in quo quidem justitiae totius ac legum omnium summa consistit, quam uxori, liberis, ac servis imperari possit: & familiae prius imperium habere quam Reipublicae." Compare *Oratio*, p. 23: "rationi ... quae totius justitiae ac legis naturae summa est."

[5] *Methodus*, pp. 217B-218A (p. 276): "at libertatis causa non sunt Respublicae constitutae, sed bene vivendi. vix est autem ut ullus virtuti sit in ea civitate locus, in qua suis quisque moribus ac libidini tam effuse blanditur, nam si hominis foelicitatem opibus, honoribus, imperiis, voluptate, summaque libertate metimur, beata sit Respublica quae his omnibus abundat : sin virtutem potiorem ducimus, non video cur Venetia Rerumpublicarum praestantissima sit."

[6] *Ibidem*, p. 207A (250): "at ubi numinis metus est, illic pietatem, justitiam, virtutes omnes florere oportet. omitto summam rerum coelestium ac naturalium cognitionem ... de Republica duntaxat disputo."

One obvious role of religion in the state lies in the ability of religions to promote social stability by "impelling (men) towards honour and virtue". [7] But as in the *Oratio* Bodin is careful to distinguish two different but complementary kinds of religion, the religion of the pontiffs and that of the magistrates, state-religion as opposed to *vera religio*.

> We should not consider religion a part of civil training even if we see priests and pontiffs controlled by the power of the magistrates. This happens because the sacrifices and approved rites in the state must be zealously defended. But religion itself, that is, the direct turning of a cleansed mind towards God, can exist in the solitary man without civil training or association. [8]

Nevertheless *vera religio,* though independent of society, contributes much to the political and social life of men. True religion depends on the belief that man has a soul different from that of the animals. Just so too are human societies distinct from those of animals for the very reason that man has a higher soul which is the source of the exclusively human idea of justice.

> Because man has been endowed by God with the gift of an immortal soul and is associated with Him in a certain likeness, it is inconsistent with men's superiority to unite him with the beasts in a society of the highest good (*boni societate summi*). This would indeed be the case if in political associations man should live happily but not (morally) well (*beate, tantum non etiam bene viverentur*). [9]

Bodin's religious belief in the soul is therefore the basis of his argument that human states, unlike animal groups, are dedicated to the promotion of virtue. One may observe here how far Bodin has clarified the rhetorically lax reasoning of the *Oratio*.

This intensely moral view of the state leads Bodin to criticise severely Plato's theory of justice and in the course of doing so to suggest that although prudence is in a sense a virtue it is one shared by the animals and so not a virtue derived, as justice is, from religion. The critique of Plato is somewhat opaque but is worth quoting and elucidating at length, not least because it shows a strengthening impulse towards Judaising in its open preference for Philo's ethics over Plato's.

> Let the division of virtues and vices embrace four classes — prudence, temperance, bravery and integrity. Philo (*Post. Cain.* 85) avoiding ambiguity of words

---

[7] *Ibidem*, p. 121A (p. 32).

[8] *Ibidem*, p. 121A (p. 33): "neque tamen existimare debemus religionem disciplinae civilis partem esse, si pontifices & sacerdotes imperio magistratuum contineri videmus: quod eo pertinet, ut sacrificia ritusque in Republica probatos acerrime tueantur. religio vero ipsa. id est purgatae mentis in Deum recta conversio, sine civili scientia, sine coetu, in unius hominis solitudine esse potest."

[9] *Ibidem*, p. 120AB (p. 31): "homo vero cum sit immortali animorum munere a Deo subornatus, eique similitudine quadam conjunctus, alienum est ejus praestantia cum beluis summi boni societate copulari: quod quidem fieret si in civitatibus beate tantum non etiam bene viveretur." Bodin's meaning here is that it is impossible for men to live "happily" if they do not live "morally well". For *bene vivere* as the virtuous life see *Methodus*, pp. 217B-218A (p. 276) quoted above. Bodin's description of animal society as *bona coetus animantium, quae gregatim coeunt* parallels that of the *Oratio*, p. 14, where he had used *societas* to denote human society and *coetus* that of the animals. See Chapter I (note 35).

preferred to call the supreme good that justice which is nothing else than a certain righteousness and integrity in all plans, words and deeds. When Plato taught that each man develops justice in himself first (as the Hebrews would have it, that each man initiates charity in himself) he placed prudence in the higher soul as a guide to the desirable and a warning of danger, bravery in the heart (*fortitudo*), temperance in the liver; but he made common to all that justice which assigns command to reason, compliance to the rest. That is, he gave to each its own (*Rep.* IV. 443). But either this means nothing at all, or justice has been utterly confused with prudence. That virtue by which one can judge what everybody should give to everyone else jurisconsults do not call moral virtue, but prudence. The man who restores their own to others, or orders it to be restored, is not good, since he would be wicked who did otherwise, unless we are to say that there is virtue in rogues who boast that they have given life to those from whom they did not take it. If we grant this type of justice to the lower soul, the difficulty will arise that we shall join brute beasts, *which have that lower power,* in an association of law and justice with men. But if any virtue is common to both souls certainly prudence is the bond, as well as between all virtues and bodies of knowledge (*virtutum ac scientiarum commune vinculum*). If indeed we grant this we shall eliminate from philosophy that obscure argument as to whether prudence is a virtue or not. We shall have as authority Plato himself who in the last book of the *Laws* (XII, 963) measured all activities of everyone by virtue alone, and virtues by prudence. [10]

Bodin seems to agree with Philo's view that justice means a general sort of integrity or righteousness. [11] Nor does he dissent from Plato's opinion that justice consists in the command of reason, justice being seen as a moral virtue dominating the whole soul; indeed Bodin had concurred already with this notion (*Methodus,* p. 120 B, quoted above). What Bodin takes issue with is the Platonic

[10] *Methodus,* p. 123AB (pp. 38f): "quod si quem minus delectat ea vitiorum ac virtutum partitio, quatuor generibus complectatur, scilicet, prudentia, temperantia, fortitudine & integritate. sic enim Philo maluit verborum ambiguitate sublata justitia illam, quae aliud nihil est quam in omnibus consiliis, dictis, & factis, rectitudo quaedam & integritas, αγαθοτητα vocare. cum enim Plato justitiam in se quenque prius stabilire doceret (sic enim Hebraei charitatis a se quenque initium ducere volunt) prudentiam in anima superiore, veluti normam expetendorum ac fugiendorum collocavit, fortitudinem in corde, temperantiam in hepate: justitiam vero quae rationi quidem imperium, aliis obsequium, id est, suum cuique tribueret, omnium communem fecit. sed ea aut nulla est, aut omnino cum prudentia confusa. sic enim virtutem illam, quae judicare potest quid quenque cuique praestare oporteat, jurisconsulti non virtutem moralem, sed prudentiam vocarunt. neque vero bonus est qui aliis suum restituit, aut restitui jubet, cum sceleratus sit qui aliter faciat: nisi dicamus virtutem esse latronum, qui jactant se iis vitam dedisse quibus non ademerunt. illud etiam incommodum sequetur, si quis illam justitiam inferiori animae tribuat, quod animantia bruta, quae vim illam inferiorem habent, juris ac justitiae societate cum hominibus conjungemus. quod si qua virtus est utriusque animae communis, profecto prudentia est utriusque animae, tum etiam virtutum ac scientiarum commune vinculum, quod quidem si demus, obscuram illam disputationem, utrum prudentia virtus sit necne, de philosophia sustulerimus, ejusque opinionis authorem habebimus Platonem ipsum, qui extremo libro de legibus, omnes omnium actiones sola virtute; virtutes omnes sola prudentia metitur." Compare the similar passage in *République,* pp. 19f, quoted beow, note 26. For the divided soul see below notes 14 and 18. Although Bodin here believes that prudence links the rational and animal souls (*utriusque animae*) of man his later writings explicitly rejected the conventional Platonic theory of the multiple souls of man in favour of his own idea of a unitary soul with differentiated functions. (Chapter V below). For more on this difficult passage see Chapter VI.

[11] For the appearance of Philo's ethics — particularly his four natural virtues — in the *Paradoxe* see Chapter V.

45

interpretation of the command of reason as being an instance of the ultimate principle of justice which is that of giving each his own (*suum cuique*). For Bodin, "giving each his own" is not a principle rooted in moral virtue as justice properly should be, but rather describes the operation of prudence. To construe this sort of prudence as justice and allow it to govern the soul would mean conceding that even the animals which exercise prudence (or as the *Oratio*, p. 14, has it, equity) in their assemblies are in fact practising justice. Yet justice as we have seen is a purely human concept with which man alone is endowed by reason of his possession of a rational soul. Prudence, therefore, is, unlike justice, not a moral virtue in itself, indispensable though it may be as a guide to justice and the moral life. [12]

By elucidating the nature of prudence in the *Methodus* Bodin was able to argue more cogently the relationship between justice and virtue which he had posited in the *Oratio*. At the same time he was able to cement the *Oratio*'s connection between the virtues and learning by identifying prudence as the chain which linked them all. In 1559 Bodin had defined wisdom as the conflation of virtue and learning but in 1566 he added prudence to the compound. [13] This massive enlargement of the role of prudence to the extent that it emerges as a powerful and distinct faculty in its own right constitutes a critical development in Bodin's theory of virtue and wisdom between 1559 and 1566, but it stems from a more fundamental shift in Bodin's ethics involving recognition of the dominating power of the will. Philo's theory of prudence had emerged out of his acknowledgement of the supremacy of free will in ethics and Bodin's adoption of the same theory signified an important advance in his exploitation of Philo amounting to a real extension of his Judaising technique. There had been little room in the rationalistic *Oratio* for the notion of free will. "Will" appeared there in the unedifying guise of irrational animal *appetitus*. But now in the *Methodus* Bodin grasped that free will or *voluntas* is distinct from both appetite *and* reason.

> Those activities are human which spring from the plans, sayings and deeds of men when will (*voluntas*) leads the way. For the will is the mistress of human actions whether it turns to reason or the lower quality (*vis*) of the soul in seeking and avoiding things. [14]

Bodin seems here to have arrived at the mainspring of his mature psychology, for he now sees the will as the director of activity and able to choose whether it will follow the counsels of animal feeling or those of reason. (He still, however, adheres to a divided rather than a unitary soul). In the *Theatrum* and especially in the *Paradoxe* Bodin was to elaborate these insights at length, describing the precise relationship between the will, reason and prudence;

---

[12] For prudence in Bodin see Chapters V and VI.

[13] *Oratio*, p. 14. *Methodus*, p. 114B (p. 15). *Religio* also replaces *virtus*.

[14] *Methodus*, p. 119B (p. 29): "actiones igitur humanae sunt, quae ab hominum consiliis, dictis, & factis praeeunte voluntate oriuntur. est enim voluntas, humanarum actionum magistra, sive ad rationem, suae ad vim animae inferiorem sese converterit in rebus expetendis ac fugiendis." Cf. notes 10 above and 18 below; in contrast to his mature concept of the unitary soul, Bodin still divides the soul into rational and animal entities. See Chapter VI.

prudence becomes intellectual virtue which mediates the will's commands and translates its choices into action. [15]

***

In the *République* we find stated in an explicit form Bodin's views on the place of virtue in political and social life. Here he attacks the problem from two perspectives; the first chapter of Book I examines the relationship between virtue and the state, while in the third chapter of the same book the connections between virtue and justice are explained.

In the first chapter Bodin pursues his earlier disagreement (voiced in chapter six of the *Methodus*) with the conventional definition of a well-ordered and happy state. Just as he had doubted in the *Methodus* whether Venice for all its liberty and wealth was truly the happiest state in the world, so Bodin here takes pains to reject the common use of the term "happy" to mean material prosperity and power; the happy state may be neither powerful nor wealthy, may even be racked with calamity, and yet may still be a happy republic, well-governed and well-ordered because it is founded on virtue. [16] In the *Oratio* (p. 14), Bodin had contended that that state is the happiest which has honest virtuous citizens and he now tries to prove this.

Bodin's idea of happiness is ultimately religious and it is this religious underpinning which permits him to insist that the true happinesses of both man and the state are identical; the happiness of both resides in the pursuit of virtue, virtue directed towards the enjoyment of the sovereign good, God himself, "ce grand Prince de nature".

> Or si la vraye felicité d'vne Republique, & d'vn homme seul est tout vn, & que le souuerain bien de la republique en general, aussi bien que d'vn chacun en particulier, gist és vertus intellectuelles, & contemplatiues, comme les mieux entendus ont resolu: il faut aussi accorder, que ce peuple-là iouït du souuerain bien, quand il a ce but deuant les yeux, de s'exercer en la contemplation des choses naturelles, humaines & diuines, en rapportant la louange du tout au grand Prince de nature. Si donc nous confessons, que cela est le but principal de la vie bien heureuse d'vn chacun en particulier, nous concluons aussi que c'est la fin & felicité d'vne Republique sans faire difference entre l'homme de bien & le bon citoyen. [17]

What exactly is this "virtue"?

As in the *Methodus* Bodin puts forward a theory of virtue which while adopting some Platonic themes modifies them by a sapiential concept of his own. He defines the moral virtues in terms of Plato's notion of the command

---

[15] *Paradoxe*, pp. 66-77. See Chapter V.

[16] *République* (Paris, 1583), pp. 4-5. Cf. *Oratio*, pp. 14-15. (Unfortunately I have had access only to the 1583 edition of the *République* which may represent a later stage in the evolution of Bodin's ethics than the original edition of 1576).

[17] *République*, p. 5.

of reason but treats the intellectual virtues, constituting wisdom, as being superior; the moral virtues are the bond between the body and lower soul, while the intellectual virtues have as their domain the upper soul.

> ... & la felicité de l'ame inferieur, qui est la vraye liaison du corps & de l'intellect, gist en l'obeissance que les appetits doyuent à la raison: c'est à dire, en l'action des vertus morales: tout ainsi que le souuerain bien de la partie intellectuelle gist aux vertus intellectuelles: c'est à sçauoir, en prudence, science, & vraye religion: l'vne touchant les choses humaines, l'autre les choses naturelles, la troisieme les choses diuines: la premiere monstre la difference du bien & du mal: la seconde, du vray & du faux: la troisieme, de la pieté & impieté, & ce qu'il faut choisir & fuir: car de ces trois se compose la vraye sagesse, où est le plus haut poinct de felicité en ce monde. [18]

Bodin explains with great care how his system of moral and intellectual virtue arises out of his religious thought. After rehearsing the great chain of being (la suite des causes enchaînées), which he first described in the Oratio as leading the contemplative mind to the intellectual love of God, he remarks that

> Par ce moyen de contemplation, les hommes sages & entendus, ont resolu vne tres-belle demonstration, c'est à sçavoir, qu'il n'y a qu'vn Dieu eternel & infini : & de là ont quasi tiré vne conclusion de la felicité humaine. [19]

Such a religious form of contemplative virtue which leads to God is further-more at the same time the measure of individual human happiness and of the happy state.

> Si donc vn tel homme est iugé sage, & bien heureux, aussi sera la Republique tres-heureuse, ayant beaucoup de tels citoyens, encore qu'elle ne soit pas de grande estendue, ny opulence en biens, mesprisant les pompes & delices des cités superbes, plongees en plaisirs: & ne faut pas pourtant conclure, que la felicité de l'homme soit confuse & mestee: car combien que l'homme soit composé d'vn corps mortel, & d'vne ame immortelle, si faut il confesser, que son bien principal depend de la partie la plus noble: car puis que le corps doit seruir à l'ame, & l'appetit bestial à la raison diuine, son bien souuerain depend aussi des vertus intellectuelles. [20]

For Bodin, in sum, "la république bien ordonnée" and "l'homme bien reiglé" are mutual reflections of one another. [21]

---

[18] *Ibidem*, p. 6. Cf. *Methodus*, p. 114B (p. 16). See Chapter VI. For the still divided soul see notes 10 and 14 above.

[19] *République*, p. 7. Cf. *Oratio*, p. 15. (Although Bodin acknowledges his debt here to Aristotle's doctrine of the first cause his religion of course is nothing like the Philosopher's; Bodin, as we have seen in the previous chapter, believed at the same time in a transcendent revealing God quite inconceivable to Aristotle's Greek way of thinking. See chapters VII and VIII for discussion).

[20] *République*, pp. 7-8. Bodin goes on to criticise Aristotle's "action of the intellect" as a confused contradiction in terms which had nevertheless been framed to allow for the primacy of intellectual virtue. Cf. *République*, p. 586, for an extreme statement of the supremacy of contemplation over action.

[21] *République*, p. 9.

But Bodin is realistic enough to see that a state devoted to the pursuit of contemplation would not last long in the real world. Hence he goes on to advocate a combination of moral and intellectual virtue as the best form of conduct in social and political life.

> Et neantmoins il est bien certain, que la Republique ne peut estre bien ordonnee, si on laisse du tout, ou pour long temps les actions ordinaires, la voye de iustice, la garde & defense des subiects, les viures & prouisions necessaires à l'entretenement d'iceux, non plus que l'homme ne peut viure longuement, si l'ame est si fort rauie en contemplation, qu'on en perde le boire & le manger. [22]

In any event there is a good religious reason, as well as a practical one, for the practise of moral virtue.

> ... aussi l'action des vertus morales est bien fort louable: par ce qu'il est impossible, que l'ame puisse recueillir le doux fruict de contemplation, qu'elle ne soit esclarcie & purifiee par les vertus morales, ou par la lumiere diuine: de forte, que les vertus morales se rapportent aux intellectuelles. [23]

But there is no doubt that it is in the development of intellectual contemplative virtue — that virtue which leads the soul to knowledge of God in the end — that the main purpose of the state lies.

> Nous ferons mesme iugement de la Republique bien ordonnee, la fin principale de laquelle gist aux vertus contemplatiues, iaçoit que les actions politiques soyent preallables, & les moins illustres soyent les premieres: comme faire prouisions necessaires, pour entretenir & defendre la vie des subiects: & neantmoins telles actions se rapportent aux morales, & celles-cy aux intellectuelles, la fin desquelles est la contemplation du plus beau subiect qui soit, & qu'on puisse imaginer. Aussi voyons nous, que Dieu a laissé six iours pour toutes actions, estant la vie de l'homme subiecte pour la plu part à icelles: mais il a ordonné, que le septieme, qu'il auoit beni sur tous les autres, seroit chommé, comme le sainct iour du repos, à fin de l'employer en la contemplation de ses œuures, de la foy, & de ses louanges. Voila quant à la fin principale des Republiques bien ordonees, qui sont d'autant plus heureuses, que plus pres elles approchent de ce but: car tout ainsi qu'il y a plusieurs degrés de felicité és hommes, aussi ont les Republiques leurs degrés de felicité. [24]

For Bodin the happy state is the virtuous state; and the virtuous state, in that it is not an end in itself but rather a path to God, is a religious state. Bodin's theory of virtue emerges therefore, as the foundation of a unique vision of theocracy. [25]

---

[22] *Ibidem,* p. 9. Cf. M. Isnardi-Parente, 'A proposito di un'interpretazione cinquecentesca del rapporto teoria-prassi in Aristotele e Platone', *Parola del Passato,* LXXXVII (1962), 436-447.

[23] *République,* p. 8. Cf. Chapter VI, note 28. For Bodin's opinion that virtue prepared man for the infusion of the divine spirit of prophecy see Chapters V and VIII.

[24] *République,* pp. 9-10.

[25] For the theocratic ideas of a later thinker see J. Dunn, *The Political Thought of John Locke* (Cambridge, 1969).

The second main juncture at which the moral and virtuous foundations of Bodin's political thought break surface is the third chapter of Book I. Here the Platonic notion that justice consists in the rule of reason over the passions — already acknowledged in the *Oratio* and *Methodus* — is developed in a long passage combining moral and religious allegory of a Philonic kind with political argument. Bodin's idea of justice, his theory of law as command and indeed his whole concept of sovereignty are revealed here as resting ultimately on the moral and religious principle that man's reason has been instituted by God to command the appetite and passions. The entire passage intensifies the Judaised character already present in the parallel paragraph in the *Methodus* already quoted.

> Nous appellons liberté naturelle de n'estre subiect, apres Dieu, à homme viuant, & ne souffrir autre commandement que de soy-mesme: c'est à dire, de la raison, qui est touiours conforme a la volonté de Dieu. Voila le premier & le plus ancien commandement qui soit, c'est à sçauoir, de la raison sur l'appetit bestial: & au parauant qu'on puisse bien commander aux autres, il faut apprendre à commander à soy-mesme, rendant à la raison la puissance de commander, & aux appetits l'obeissance: & en ceste sorte chacun aura ce qui luy appartient, qui est la premiere & la plus belle iustice qui soit: & ce que les Hebrieux disoyent en commun prouerbe, commencer charité par soy-mesme, qui n'est autre chose, que rendre les appetits ployables à la raison, c'est le premier commandement que Dieu a establi par edict expres, parlant à celuy qui premier tua son frere. C'est le commandement qu'il auoit donné au parauant au mari par dessus la femme, porte double sens, & double commandement: l'vn, qui est literal, de la puissance maritale: & l'autre moral, qui est de l'ame sur le corps, de la raison sur la cupidité, que l'escriture saincte appelle quasi tousiours femme, & principalement Salomon, qui semble à beaucoup de persones estre ennemi iure des femmes, ausquelles il pensoit le moins quand il en escriuoit, comme tresbien a montré le sage Rabin Maymon. Or nous laisserons aux Philosophes & Theologiens le discours moral, & prendrons ce qui est politiques, pour le regard de la puissance du mari sur la femme, qui est le source & origine de toute societé humaine. [26]

In this last sentence Bodin emphatically states that the political subject of the *République* precludes his dealing at length with moral philosophy but the moral foundations of political thought are as fully exposed here as in the first chapter. In due course the king will come to be described as the political expression of the rule of reason while the passions will find their concrete counterparts in the social and political world in the subjection of women to fathers and husbands and the similar subjection of all corporations within the state to the king.

The *République* demonstrates the role of virtue in Bodin's theory of the state and of justice and confirms the less precise formulations of the *Oratio* and *Methodus*. From these three works we may understand how Bodin envisaged the origin and growth of the state as a vital component of the moral evolution of man. It is in the state that man fulfils his moral and religious nature. [27]

---

[26] *République*, pp. 19-20. Note the similarity of phrasing to *Methodus*, p. 123AB (pp. 38f) quoted above. Cf. note 10.

[27] For the theoretical superiority of the isolated contemplative life see *République*, pp. 7f, 586, noted above.

So rooted in virtue and religion, Bodin's republic, far from being the secular state of Hobbes, is in its essence a theocracy. [28]

*
**

In both the *Oratio* and the *Methodus* Bodin was moving away from Greek ethics towards a distinctly Judaised concept of justice, one influenced predominantly by his reading of Philo it would appear. The *Methodus* had preferred Philo's idea of justice to that of Plato even though both philosophers had proclaimed the command of reason over the passions. But Philo's justice escaped the narrow rationalism of Plato by appealing more fundamentally to the Jewish notion of righteousness or charity — "that justice which is nothing else than a certain rectitude and integrity... each man initiates charity in himself". [29] When Bodin came to re-write this passage for the *République* he stressed even more his agreement with the Jewish concept of justice as charity or righteousness, praising "the first and most beautiful justice there is, which the Hebrews call in their proverb 'beginning charity in oneself'". [30] This reduction of the pre-eminence of reason in ethics in favour of righteousness had a corollary of the most capital importance — the exaltation of the will. As early as the *Methodus* Bodin was accepting the critical role attributed in Jewish ethics and religion to the will in seeking righteousness. [31]

Bodin's new awareness and understanding of justice, righteousness and the supremacy of the will meant that the Judaisation of his political and ethical thought was well under way by the time he composed the *Methodus* and the *République*.

[28] One must disagree for instance with the opinion of Ernest Barker, *The Political Thought of Plato and Aristotle* (rev. ed., New York, 1959), p. 519, that Bodin abandoned the ethical foundations of political philosophy for a legal approach.

The neo-Stoic political philosophy of the sixteenth century was generally founded on ethics and may have influenced the youthful Bodin as it did his friend Pibrac. (See below Chapter IV). (Certainly Bodin was a powerful influence on the political philosophy of Justus Lipsius. See G. Oestreich, *Geschichte und Gestalt des frühmodernen Staates* (Berlin, 1969)).

[29] See above, note 10. See below Chapter IV for the place of Philo in Jewish ethics.

[30] See above, note 26. Bodin here also Judaises his early suspicions of women in the *Oratio* by adducing Maimonides as authority for his prejudice.

[31] See Chapters IV and V for the role of free will in Jewish thought and in Bodin respectively.

CHAPTER III

MORAL WISDOM IN BODIN'S LATER EDUCATIONAL WRITINGS

During the 1580's Bodin wrote a trio of short pedagogic texts which represent a major advance on the educational and moral thinking comprised in his earlier work in that *genre*, the *Oratio* of 1559.[1] These treatises saw a change of emphasis from social and political virtue to concern with a more private morality and they announced new themes and perspectives which Bodin was to develop in his last works, the *Paradoxe*, the *Theatrum* and the *Heptaplomeres* written in the years around 1590.

a) Epître à son neveu [2]

Dated 9 November 1586 this letter was written by Bodin to his nephew who had requested information on how Bodin had educated his children so that the nephew might instruct his own in the same fashion.[3] Bodin's plan of instruction consists of an attempt to acquire an encyclopaedic understanding of the world in the course of learning Latin. The first step in the education of his two small children, says Bodin, had consisted in their being taught to name in Latin those everyday objects which they saw such as nuts and cherries. But Bodin was scarcely content to let matters stay on this mundane level. Seeing the children's aptitude for the word-game Bodin soon expanded his simple language instruction into a scheme to understand the universe by means

---

[1] The existence of these texts was first properly noticed by A. Garosci, *Jean Bodin. Politica e diritto nel rinascimento francese*, Milan, 1934, p. 61.

[2] A copy of the text is to be found in Bibliothèque Nationale, Paris, Ms. Latin 6564, fols. 483-485. It is printed by G.E. Guhrauer, *Das Heptaplomeres des Jean Bodin*. Berlin, 1841 (reprint, Geneva, 1971), pp. 254-256 (cf. p. lxxv) and appears in part in H. Baudrillart, *Jean Bodin et son temps*, Paris, 1853 (reprint, New York, 1969), pp. 130f.

[3] On the duty of fathers to educate their children in virtue and letters see François de la Noue, *Discours politiques et militaires*, ed. F.E. Sutcliffe, Geneva, 1967, p. 42.

For another letter written by an uncle (the Venetian senator Francesco Barozzi) to a nephew on studies see P.L. Rose, "A Venetian Patron and Mathematician of the Sixteenth Century: Francesco Barozzi (1537-1604)", *Studi Veneziani*, N.S. I, 1977, 119-178, Appendix 5.

of nomenclature. Memorisation was not a simple mechanical process but rather a phenomenon to be based on the structure of the universe itself. [4] "Le plus beau secret de leur faire la mémoire et le jugement assuré, c'est de leur apprendre toutes choses belles et par ordres". [5] The first order of the world is that of the spirits and Bodin provides for his pupils the names of the angels, "the darknesses and the lights." Then the world and its age (5534 years) are identified in Latin, followed by the heavens, stars and planets together with their movements, and then the elements. Mountains, fields, forests, rivers and seas come next and after them the names of the birds and animals. After naming the various artefacts of man — his towns, houses, furniture and clothing — man's own external and internal parts are indicated in Latin. Bodin then returns to the order of natural philosophy and names in turn the six sensible qualities, the six tastes, the six musical intervals, the six perfect geometrical bodies, the six simple metals, the six natural motions and the differences of place. Finally come the seven main virtues and vices.

Bodin's teaching of Latin therefore encompasses a rapid tour through the whole encyclopaedia of knowledge and two points should be noted in this context. The first is the Ramist character of the instruction. Rather than teaching Latin in a purely philological and humanist fashion Bodin resorts to a Ramist approach recognising the direct relation of words to reality. Words do pertain to real things and to real life and accordingly languages should be taught in the light of this relationship. [6] In the second place, one should beware of taking Bodin's encyclopaedism for some highly diversified curriculum lacking a solid central focus. In fact French educational encyclopaedism of the sixteenth century — Bodin's included — was securely anchored in the primacy of ethics: as in Greek educational thought, the encyclopaedia connoted the moulding of a well-rounded mind rather than the mere training of the mind in all the various liberal arts and sciences. [7]

The central place of ethics in Bodin's encyclopaedia is to be clearly seen in the next stage of his Latin curriculum. Once the nomenclative function of Latin has been established Bodin turns his pupils' attention to the declensions

---

[4] The universe described here by Bodin was represented in Coronaeus' *pantotheca* at Venice which Bodin in the *Heptaplomeres* imagines as containing models or reproductions of all the "orders" and species. See *Colloquium Heptaplomeres*, ed. L. Noack, Schwerin, 1857 (reprint Stuttgart, 1966), p. 2. For these "universes" in general see Frances Yates, *The Art of Memory*, London, 1966.

[5] Text in Guhrauer, *Das Heptaplomeres*, p. 256.

[6] See K.D. McRae, "Ramist Tendencies in the Thought of Jean Bodin", *Journal of the History of Ideas*, XVI, 1955, 306-323; "A Postscript on Bodin's Connections with Ramism", *ibidem*, XXIV, 1963, 569-571. The only known surviving book from Bodin's library is a compilation of Ramist treatises, described by G. Barber, "Haec a Joanne Bodino lecta", *Bibliothèque d'Humanisme et Renaissance*, XXV, 1963, 362-365.

For Bodin's early sarcasm towards the pettiness of those *grammatici* who lacked philosophy see *Methodus* in *Œuvres philosophiques*, ed. P. Mesnard, Paris, 1951, I, 109, 141.

[7] A.H.T. Levi, "Ethics and the Encyclopedia in the Sixteenth Century", and A. Stegmann, "Un thème majeur du second humanisme français (1540-70): l'orateur et le citoyen. De l'humanisme à la réalité vécue", both essays in *French Renaissance Studies 1540-70*, ed. P. Sharratt, Edinburgh, 1976, pp. 170-184 and 213-233 respectively. For Plato of course ethics was also the essence of education but Bodin differed from the philosopher in his religious conception of ethics.

and conjugations, knowledge of which will enable his children to understand the meaning of sentences as opposed to words and things. As a model sentence for parsing Bodin recommends a maxim which will promote religious as well as linguistic understanding: "Ego cupio vehementer laudare Opificem mundi optimum et potentissimum omnium pro dignitate". In urging this sentence upon his family Bodin could well feel that he was following Judaic tradition and obeying the injunction of Deuteronomy VI, 7, that parents should teach their children the love and worship of God.

Thanks to this training Bodin's children could soon speak Latin just as well as French and were then able to proceed to memorise a few at a time the collection of three hundred *sentences morales* in French and Latin which he had extracted from the "best authors". Bodin's collection of these sentences fortunately appears to have survived in print as the *Sapientiae Moralis Epitome* and reveals graphically how his concept of ethics was rooted in religion. In the *Paradoxon* Bodin was to examine more systematically this primarily moral aspect of his educational practice but he was also to take the nomenclative aspect of education much further in another major work. The present *Epître* alludes not only to the three hundred *sentences morales* but to another "600 questions en latin sans françois de toute la beauté de nature". These *sentences naturelles* we may now recognise in dialogue form in the *Theatrum Naturae* of 1596 which presented a comprehensive account of the natural and spiritual universe, a universe very much the same as that which Bodin described in the *Epître*.

Bodin's *Epître à son neveu* therefore suggests two of the major directions that his religious interests were taking in the 1580's; in the one case his tendency to approach religion through moral philosophy was to culminate in the *Paradoxon* while in the other his attempt at a naturalistic understanding of religion found its fulfilment in the *sentences naturelles* of the *Theatrum*.

b) Consilium de institutione principis

Before coming to the collection of *sentences morales* which makes up the *Sapientiae Moralis Epitome* we should first notice a neglected but important work in which Bodin amplified the views put forward in the *Epître* while adapting them to the education of a prince rather than a member of his own family. Bodin's *Consilium de institutione principis aut alius nobilioris ingenii* was published in an obscure collection entitled *Consilia Iohannis Bodini Galli et Fausti Longiani Itali de principe recte instituendo* (Weimar, 1602), edited by the German scholar Johannes Bornitius. A further edition appeared in 1603 at Erfurt and it is to this second edition that all page references given here pertain. [8] Bornitius' dedication to the Saxon princes states that his uncle had been given an unpublished French manuscript of the text by an un-named

[8] All references are to the 1603 edition, copies of which exist in the British Museum Library, Harvard University Library, the Bibliothèque Mazarine at Paris, and various German libraries. Copies of the 1602 edition are held by the Biblioteca Nazionale, Rome and at Gotha, Munich and Berne.

(I am grateful to Professor Roland Crahay of the Université de Mons for forwarding

gentleman at the Saxon court. This gentleman had testified that the manuscript had been handed to him personally by Bodin himself.

Presumably the Latin translation which is now the sole known version of the *Consilium* was done by Bornitius.

Can a date be fixed for the composition of the *Consilium*? In the *Consilium* (sig. B2rv) Bodin recommends as a text for study the *versiculi morales* (i.e. the *Quatrains*) of his friend Pibrac du Faur. This prescription of Pibrac may suggest a dating for the *Consilium*. In his *Epître* of 1586 Bodin referred to his own *versiculi morales, viz.*, the *Sapientiae Epitome,* as a suitable text; no mention was made of Pibrac's work. Now if Bodin had written the *Consilium* after November 1586 (the date of the *Epître*) he would have been able to prescribe for study his own work rather than Pibrac's, just as he did in the *Epître*. One may conclude, therefore, that the *Consilium* was written before November 1586. Furthermore, if Bodin is referring in the *Consilium* to the printed edition of Pibrac's *Quatrains* (first published in 1574) that would give us 1574 as the earliest possible year in which the *Consilium* was written. The *Consilium* may, therefore, be ascribed to the period 1574-86, and most likely, in view of its remarks on ethics and religion, to the latter part of that period.

The *Consilium* concerns the education of a prince and follows in a long line of Renaissance treatises on princely education, the most pre-eminent of which had been Erasmus' *Institutio principis Christiani*. [9] Bodin's interest in the particular subject dated from some years before he wrote the *Consilium*. In the *Methodus* of 1566 he had urged that the education of a prince must be fundamentally religious rather than merely academic in character.

> The best teachers and guides to learning should be won over by great rewards to the education of the prince, not to imbue the flexible mind of the young prince with a foreign language ... but with true religion (*religio vera*). Of all topics of discussion about the laws and government, none is greater or more worthy of zeal and study than that the prince should understand that he has come into this world for the true worship of God. In this alone consists the supreme safety of the state and of all the laws. [10]

me the information on these locations which has been gathered by his Séminaire de Bibliographie Historique.)

The *Consilium* was cited by Pierre Bayle in his life of Bodin (reprinted in Bodin, *Œuvres philosophiques,* ed. Mesnard, p. xxvi) and more recently by Garosci, *Jean Bodin,* p. 323. It is something of a surprise to find no reference to the *Consilium* in P. Mesnard, "Jean Bodin devant le problème de l'éducation", *Revue des travaux de l'Académie des Sciences morales et politiques,* 1959, 217-228 which otherwise gives a good account of Bodin's educational writings.

[9] Desiderius Erasmus, *The Education of a Christian Prince* (trs. L.K. Born, New York, 1936).

[10] *Methodus,* ed. Mesnard, p. 223A (trs. p. 289) : "consequens est ad unius Principis institutionem optimi sapentiiae magistri ac moderatores, maximis propositis praemiis conquirantur: non qui peregrina lingua ... sed qui religione vera molles Principis animos leniter imbuant. nam omnium quae de legibus & Repub. disputantur, nihil majus est, aut majore studio dignum, quàm ut Princeps intelligat se ad verum Dei cultum in hanc lucem venisse. in eo solo versatur Reipublicae ac legum omnium suprema salus."

Cf. Ronsard's "Institution pour l'adolescence du roi très-Chrestien Charles IXe de ce nom", part of the *Discours des misères de ce temps,* in Pierre Ronsard, *Œuvres complètes,* ed. G. Cohen, Pléiade ed., Paris, 1958, II, 560 ("Un roy sans la vertu porte le sceptre en vain... Il faut premièrement apprendre à craindre Dieu"). Cf. R. Bady, *L'homme et son institution de Montaigne à Bérulle (1580-1625),* Paris, 1964, chapter 13.

If the king is educated in *vera religio* then the state will be preserved securely. In expounding the religious basis of such a royal education the *Consilium* effectively strengthens the whole moral and theocratic complexion with which Bodin endowed the state in his political writings.

> Et qui fut onques le prince pareil à Salomon en sagesse? Nous lisons toutesfois que la seule prière qu'il fit a Dieu, fut pour obtenir sagesse, à fin de bien juger son peuple (*République*, pp. 612f).

This wisdom, as we shall, see, is not just learning but rather one of the highest religious virtues.

Where Bodin's *Epître* had been content to recommend for Latin parsing a religious sentence praising God, the *Consilium* firmly establishes at the outset the claim of religion to be the foundation of education. To inculcate the fear of God must be the first concern of the prince's instructor for all else flows from that — wisdom, knowledge, judgement, memory, happiness and health (sig. A4). Prayer is the foremost means of attaining to respect for God and Bodin's elucidation of prayer here is wholly in keeping with his description of inner divine worship in the *Démonomanie* and his other religious writings. There is no mention of Christ in the prayers recommended by Bodin to his noble pupil but they should, he says, follow the model of the *orationes sanctorum prophetarum* in their brevity (an indication of Bodin's prophetic religion) (A4v). Insincere prayers avail nothing except to bring down execration and since casual prayers simply jest with God Bodin insists that prayer be offered on bended knees with lowered face as holy men do.

Prayer itself may be divided into four activities and, as we have come to expect in Bodin, none of these concerns the begging of redemption whether through Christ or not. The first activity is the begging of divine forgiveness of sins. Next is the invocation of God's gift of light and wisdom (*sapientia*) and the supplication that He will infuse our souls with fear and love and through His good angel draw us to obedience of His highest laws, an obedience that protects men from both seen and unseen enemies (A5). In its insistence on man's dual feelings of fear and love towards God, on obedience and the idea of the mediating angel, this passage is entirely characteristic of Bodin's later Judaised religion which will be described in subsequent chapters.[11] The third activity which constitutes prayer is the giving of thanks for the benefits received from God, the fourth the singing of psalms in His honour. Bodin then concludes his religious introduction by proclaiming blasphemy and contempt of the divine name to be the worst form of impiety and deserving of death (A5v).

The next portion of the *Consilium* pronounces some general opinions on the prince's education: he should have one or two studying companions so as to encourage competition in learning; he should sleep only six or seven hours so as to promote alertness; and his food should be prepared without condiments for the sake of his health (A6-A7).

In the ensuing section (A7v-11) Bodin largely repeats with additional detail the scheme of learning Latin which he had sketched in the *Epître*. Latin, he

[11] See Chapters V and VIII for Bodin's later religion.

56

says, is best learnt by being taught "vocabula latina secundum naturae ordinem", beginning with God himself and proceeding to "the darknesses, light, spirit, angel, form, material, body, earth, heavens, stars and planets..." The schematic listing of the *ordo naturae* which follows is rather more rigorous than in the *Epître* and reflects the more formal character of the *Consilium* as compared to the *Epître* which was after all merely a private letter.

Bodin first lists the heavenly bodies and various meteorological phenomena. Then he moves on to the names of the trees and herbs ("of which there are 1200 species"), metals and minerals. Animals come next classified into birds (120 species), fish, insects and quadrupeds, with the various subdivisions of these classes being indicated.

Man is seen as a unique phenomenon and Bodin urges that the greatest attention be given to distinguishing and naming each of his parts, first the parts of the soul then of the body. It is in the context of man that Bodin goes on to treat the various accidents of substance, seeing quantities and qualities in the light of how they are perceived by man.

Colours are the object of sight, musical intervals the object of hearing, heat and cold the object of touch; even motion is seen in terms of man's movement and location. This classification in human terms has the general effect of reducing natural philosophy to an entirely man-centred study in accordance with man's unique relationship with the creator of nature (A9v).

Finally in this account of man come the virtues and vices which Bodin divides into intellectual and moral categories. The intellectual virtues are represented by the liberal disciplines, the mechanical arts and prudence, while the moral virtues include the Aristotelian virtues of temperance, magnanimity and liberality. But Bodin does not give much attention to these specific virtues, presumably because his theory of "true virtue" is essentially religious and as such has already been dealt with in the introductory section of the *Consilium*. It is precisely this Judaised religious feeling which sets Bodin's moral philosophy radically apart from Aristotle's and sharply distinguishes his educational thought from the ideas of both Plato and Isocrates even though Plato had also founded his idea of education on ethics. [12]

After the encyclopaedic course of instruction by means of Latin nomenclature has been completed a new series of higher studies is embarked on covering history, music, mathematics, geography and astronomy (A12v-B2). At the same time the student is to be taught the Latin declensions and conjugations which will not only enable him to read Cicero and Virgil but also serve both to train his memory and set him on the path to virtue (A11rv). In connection with this second cycle of studies Bodin recommends two significant texts. The first is Ramus' *Dialectica* which is the best of logics in that it "makes the mind capable of varied arguments". This, the only mention of Ramus by name in Bodin's works, corroborates the distinctly Ramist tendency already noted in the *Epître*. [13] The second text is the *versiculi morales* of Pibrac which Bodin

---

[12] Cf. Plato, *Republic,* books VI and VII. For Greek educational ideas including those of Isocrates on the education of a prince see W. Jaeger, *Paideia,* 2nd ed., Oxford, 1939-45. For French Christian modifications see Bady, *L'homme et son institution.*

[13] McRae, "Ramist Tendencies", p. 320.

here prescribes in place of his own *sentences morales* (B2rv). Pibrac had been a close friend of Bodin's since their early days together at Toulouse in the 1550's and it was to him that the *République* was dedicated. The *versiculi morales* which Bodin had in mind must have been the well-known *Quatrains moraux* which bear many resemblances to Bodin's own *Sapientiae Epitome*.[14]

In order to round out his education Bodin would send his noble pupil to the German and Italian universities to learn the royal science of law; finally the prince should become acquainted with various regions and cities and also should have examined the state of the *respublica* and its offices and the laws, customs and natures of various peoples. For it is in this wide experience of practical affairs that prudence consists: "Vera prudentia, dux et lux virtutis" (B3).

The closing pages of the *Consilium* return to the consideration of virtue and religion. Punishment of the pupil should not be so harsh as to provoke the vice of hatred; rather the punishment must induce repentance and a will to learning and virtue. Here Bodin's pedagogical conception of punishment faithfully reflects his religious and moral philosophy (B4-5v).

In its conclusion the *Consilium* brings us to the heart of Bodin's Judaised religion in terms directly reminiscent of the *Démonomanie*.

> Because God is the master of all science and of all the virtues, and human effort lacking His help is in vain, let the student pour out prayers to God from Psalm 143 each morning:
>
> "Teach me, O Lord, Thy will..." (B5v).

It was, as we shall see, the invocation of this same psalm and those same words which had brought Bodin to the first stage of his conversion to *vera religio* in the 1560's.[15] And the desired result of the prayer here, as in the experience recounted in the *Démonomanie,* is the same: this prayer will cause the years to pass happily and God will assign a guardian-angel to counsel the student in dreams and visions what to do and what to avoid (B5v-6). "The beginning of wisdom is the fear of the Lord", a motto, says Bodin, that should be inscribed within the prince's abode in Hebrew, Greek and Latin letters.

c) Sapientiae moralis epitome

In 1588 Bodin's customary printer, Jacques Dupuys of Paris, brought out a collection of moral *sentences* under the title *Sapientiae Moralis Epitome* with

---

[14] For Pibrac see above Chapter I. In a letter of 1555 he had lamented that "fathers now educate their sons not in virtue but in buying office" (quoted by A. Cabos, *Guy du Faur de Pibrac. Un magistrat poète au XVIᵉ siècle* (Paris, 1922, pp. 36ff).

[15] *Consilium*, sig. B5v: "Et quia Deus sapientiae omnisque scientiae et virtutum magister, omnisque labor humanus absque ejus auxilio frustraneus est, ideo singulis diebus mane ex Psalmo 143 ad Deum preces fundat: 'Quid facto sit opus ... iussa voluntatis, me Deus alme doce'." For the role of this psalm in Bodin's conversion see Chapter VIII, note 61.

the authorship attributed to one Elie Bodin.[16] The dedication "ad juventutem Laodunemsem", dated 29 August 1587, states that the author had not intended printing this pedagogic work but had been forced to establish a proper listing by the fact that several inaccurate versions were circulating at Laon. Since Elie, who was Bodin's son, was then only twelve years old it seems reasonable to assign the authorship of the *Sapientia* to Bodin himself, particularly as the style and content of the dedication and the *sentences* themselves share the characteristics of Bodin's other philosophical and educational writing.

The compilation consists of a series of moral maxims in Latin drawn mainly from verses by Ovid, Horace, Juvenal and Lucretius accompanied by a parallel free translation in French verse on the facing page. The French verse recalls the model of Pibrac's famous moral *Quatrains* which Bodin in his *Consilium* had recommended as a suitable teaching text.[17]

Numbering 210 in all (a product of the significant Pythagorean numbers $3 \times 7 \times 10 = 210$) the maxims are arranged into groups of seven sentences, each group beginning — except the first sentence of the whole collection — with Bodin's own comparative sentence announcing the topic of the group.[18] Sentence 8, for instance, "Praestat natura doctrinae", summarises the argument of sentences 8-15. These comparative sentences amount to a graphic listing of Bodin's priorities and preferences, exposing the structure of his mind in an almost geometrically schematic fashion. "Liberty", for example, "is better than slavery" (sentence 113), but "Slavery is better than anarchy" (120). Or, fundamentally, "True religion is better than superstition" (189), but "superstition is better than impiety" (182). We see here ranged in strict order of preference *vera religio,* superstition (including one presumes the various rites of the confessional churches) and impiety (including atheism). Bodin may be prepared to put up with the superstitious diversity of the various positive religions, but impiety and atheism are not to be tolerated.

The first half of the *Sapientia* consists mainly of generalities insisting on the necessity of honour, truth, charity and virtue. This leads to two sets of sentences on the moral status of war in which Bodin explains those moral prejudices which were two years later to lead him into a temporary and condit-

[16] The existence of this rare text was noticed by Garosci, *Jean Bodin,* p. 323, and an analysis given by Mesnard, "Bodin devant le problème de l'éducation". There is a copy in the Bibliothèque Nationale, Paris and Prof. Crahay has kindly informed me of another copy in Lambeth Palace Library, London.

[17] *Consilium* (1603), sig. B2v. For Pibrac see the beginning of Chapter I above. Also A. Cabos, *Guy du Faur de Pibrac. Un magistrat poète au XVIe siècle (1529-84),* Paris, 1922. The *Quatrains* were first published in 1567 and have been edited by H. Guy, "Les *Quatrains* de Pibrac", *Annales du Midi,* XV, 1903, 449-469: XVI, 1904, 65-80, 208-222.

R. Chauviré, *Jean Bodin, auteur de la République,* Paris, 1914, p. 92, (reprint, Geneva, 1969), being unaware of the *Sapientia,* thought that the *Quatrains* comprised most of the actual *sentences morales* to which Bodin refers in his *Epître à son neveu.*

[18] Mesnard, "Bodin devant le problème de l'education", believed there were only 209 sentences and that the final missing sentence was to be supplied by the idea of God. In fact there are 210 sentences in all; although the last sentence is numbered as "209", a printer's error earlier on had labelled two separate consecutive sentences as "178" (fol. 14v).

ional support of the League's war against Henri III. [19] It is better, says Bodin (sentence 99), to prevent contumely than to invite it and defence by war is honest. For all that, war causes faith, piety, God and law to be forgotten and opens the world to the wicked (106-112). Grievous as it may be to serve a proud enemy, slavery and even subjection to women are preferable to anarchy since without authority all ills will reign. Let the safety of the people be the supreme law, says Bodin — a legal maxim he was to cite again in 1589-90 as the basis for his support of the League (120-126).

This discussion of conflict and authority leads to Bodin's considering the major problems of his moral philosophy. The first requirement for happiness is that the ordinary virtues must rule the passions (134-147) and then that prudence — "la prudence (qu') après Dieu nous guide" — should in turn govern the virtues (148-154). But above prudence itself rules justice and above justice there is *caritas* (155-168). [20] Finally charity itself is subject to wisdom (169-175);

> La charité passe science
> Et sur les deux est sapience.
> De toutes vertus la maistresse,
> A bon droit on nomme sagesse (169-179).

Wisdom emerges here as an entirely religious phenomenon:

> Qui de sagesse a le vray tître
> Est du bien et du mal arbitre.
> Sage est celuy qui a emprainte
> En son cueur, du grand Dieu la crainte (173-74)

The pursuit of moral wisdom has therefore led Bodin away from conventional Platonic and Aristotelian ethics into the domain of religion; the rest of the *Sapientia* provides a succinct summary of Bodin's mature religious thought.

Contemplation is the surest route to the heart of Bodin's religion:

> Les contemplations sacrées
> Faut voir des choses plus cachées.
> L'athéiste de Dieu moqueur
> A contempler change son cueur.
> C'est la ravissement des sages
> Et la mort des saints personnages (179-181).

In the group of sentences beginning "Beaucoup pire est l'impiété, Que des Dieux la pluralité", Bodin denounces atheism and impiety, preferring even paganism (182-88). Bodin's abhorrence arises out of the atheist's blasphemous denial of his Creator ("Du grand Dieu la maiesté pure, Se monstre en toute

---

[19] For Bodin's support of the Catholic League as being consistent with his general religious and philosophical attitudes see P.L. Rose, "The Politique and the Prophet: Bodin and the Catholic League 1589-1594", *The Historical Journal*, XXI, 1978, 783-808. P.L. Rose, "Bodin and the Bourbon Succession to the French Throne 1583-1594", *Sixteenth Century Journal*, IX, 1978, 75-98. (See Chapter IX, note 16.)

[20] No. 166: "Souvent la damnable cité / Est sauvée par charité". This theme reappears in Bodin's League letters in his admonition to Paris to save herself by turning to charity. See Rose, "The Politique and the Prophet", p. 787. (Below, Chapter IX.)

créature" (188)). Nevertheless, true religion is to be preferred to the super-
stitions of paganism and, it is implied, to such positive religions as Christianity (189-195). The central Bodinian — and Philonic — idea of prayer as
voluntary sacrifice figures prominently here:

> C'est à Dieu plaisant sacrifice,
> Foy, louange, oraison propice (191) .
>
> Servir Dieu hors la créature,
> C'est vrayment religion pure (195).

Religion pure for Bodin is a matter of man's internal purity and devotion.
But even this kind of religion is of a lower order than God's own law which
manifests itself through grace (196-202).

> Sus la religion a place,
> De Dieu la sainte loy de grace (196). [21]

Here we see clearly how Bodin, while in some respects advocating a form
of natural religion, is insistent that it must be restricted by the intervention
of divine will and grace; the law of God provides a revelation which nature
often conceals.

> La loy de Dieu entière et pure,
> Est plus que patron de nature.
> La Loy de Dieu souvent découvre,
> Les trésors que nature couvre (197-98).

One should note here how Bodin's French translation converts classical and
Stoic maxims into Judaised religious notions. The Latin originals of the lines
just quoted are "Naturae archetypus, lex est, sed latius exit. Ardua lex aperit
thesauros saepe latentes". This religious transformation is also evident in the
last sentence of this particular set:

> La loy de Dieu nous éclaire,
> Si sa lumière éclaire (202). [22]

Although the Stoic original reads simply "Nemo capit legem, nisi lux effulserit
illi", it would still be possible to take Bodin's French translation as Stoic in
meaning were it not for the fact that he has just explained that the law of
God is *above* nature (197) and that this law is enacted by God's grace, that
is by God's will. Such notions as divine will and grace, and the transcendental
separation of God from nature are alien to Stoicism and reveal Bodin's profoundly religious commitment.

In the *Heptaplomeres* Bodin later asked "What shall be the subject of
moral wisdom" (*sapientia moralis*)?" and answered: "The disposing of man for

---

[21] Grace is eliminated from the vocabulary of Bodin's own religion in his later
works but still occurs in *Démonomanie*. See Chapter VI, note 28.

[22] For Bodin's doctrine of illumination see Chapters V and VI.

happiness (*homo beandus*)". [23]   In the *Sapientia* we have found Bodin already asserting that moral wisdom depends ultimately on a religious understanding of God.   To base moral philosophy on such a religious principle meant rejecting the main traditions of Greek ethical thought, whether Platonic, Aristotelian or Stoic.   No matter how classical in origin were Bodin's Latin sentences his own free French translation shows how remote from their original meaning was Bodin's understanding of Greek and Roman beliefs about "God", nature and virtue. [24]   Nor should it be thought that Bodin's view of moral wisdom and virtue was any more Christian than it was Stoic.   Certainly faith and charity appear in the *Sapientia* but they are no longer the supernatural theological virtues of Christianity.   Faith now appears simply to mean voluntary belief in God without dependence on rational arguments. [25]

> Captiver sa raison soubz foy
> C'est le plus haut point de la loy (190).

As in the later *Paradoxe* faith is now seen as one of a group of naturally willed virtues which are attainable by man's natural powers.

> C'est a Dieu plaisant sacrifice
> Foy, louange, oraison propice (191).

The same may be said for charity in the *Sapientia*.   Charity is no longer Christian charity but rather a slightly inferior form of wisdom. [26]   Indeed in their general hierarchy of natural virtues the *Sapientia* and the *Paradoxe* are in general agreement; — prudence, justice, science, faith, charity, wisdom form Bodin's divisions of the virtues rather than either the Greek scheme of moral and intellectual virtue or Christian theological and natural virtue.

The *Consilium* and *Sapientia* reflect the accelerating pace of Bodin's Judaising, a tendency which brings them closer to the *Démonomanie* and the *Paradoxe* than to the religious and moral ideas in Bodin's previous works. Concepts of prayer, repentance and the fear and love of God present in these educational writings correspond closely to ideas found in Bodin's later books, ideas which can be traced back to Jewish traditions of thought.   Take for

---

[23] *Heptaplomeres*, ed. Noack, p. 189 (trs. p. 247).   Repeated in *Paradoxon*, p. 20 (*Paradoxe*, p. 10).   See Chapters V, note 16, and VII, note 7.   Note that the subject of normal philosophy is the disposing of men to receive happiness; it is not happiness itself which is the subject of theology since true happiness comes only with divine illumination and prophecy.

[24] For the Stoic view that virtue and wisdom conformed to a natural order see E.F. Rice, jr., *The Renaissance Idea of Wisdom*, Cambridge, Mass., 1958.   W.J. Bouwsma, "The Two Faces of Humanism: Stoicism and Augustinianism in Renaissance Thought", in *Itinerarium Italicum*, ed., H. Oberman, Leiden, 1975, pp. 3-60.

Bodin's order, it should be remembered, was religious, not natural.

[25] Cf. *Paradoxe*, pp. 90ff.   See Chapter V.

[26] Cf. *Paradoxe*, pp. 88ff.   See Chapter V.

example Philo's idea of prayer as the willing sacrifice of the soul. This notion is alluded to at the end of the *Sapientia* (191) and also appears in the *Démonomanie* where Bodin assigns it a crucial role in the narrative account of his own conversion to true religion. [27] Similarly guardian angels originating in Maimonidean prophetic theory appear in both the *Consilium* and conversion narrative of the *Démonomanie*. [28] These educational writings of the 1580's indeed look forward to the *Paradoxe*. The *Sapientia*, for instance, hints at a theory of illumination later elaborated in the *Paradoxe* and both works have in common a Judaised, non-Christian structure of natural virtue ranging from prudence through justice, science and *non-Christian* faith and charity to the culminating virtue of wisdom. It is this unusual system of moral philosophy to which we now turn our attention in order to analyse the extent to which Jewish concepts dominated Bodin's ethics and religious beliefs.

[27] See Chapter VIII.
[28] See above and Chapter VIII.

PART B.

BODIN'S JUDAISED RELIGIOUS ETHICS

CHAPTER IV

FROM PHILO TO THE ACADÉMIE DU PALAIS. CHRISTIAN AND JEWISH ETHICS AND THE PROBLEM OF THE "HEPTAPLOMERES"

From his earliest writings Bodin had sought to unite virtue with knowledge to form wisdom (*sapientia*). In the *Oratio* Bodin had averred that "true wisdom is a conflation of virtue and knowledge (*scientia*)" and had generally argued for the unification of *virtus* and *doctrina*. Some years later the *Methodus* had pointed up the religious content of this notion of wisdom by claiming that "from the virtues prudence, knowledge (*scientia*) and religion together is created true wisdom".[1] In his later writings, above all in the *Paradoxe,* Bodin was to deepen his understanding of virtue, knowledge and wisdom, and to present his idea of their unity in a fully elaborated and profoundly religious form.

In his remarkable book *The Renaissance Idea of Wisdom* Eugene Rice has interpreted the idea of wisdom in the sixteenth century as an evolution from a Christian to a naturalistic and secular conception, a process shared in by the closely associated idea of virtue. In the early part of the century wisdom was often seen to be based on the theological virtues of faith, hope and charity; it then went through various transformations to become a reflection of intellectual virtue, wisdom being conceived as a contemplative knowledge of the divine and human. Finally, there emerged a moralised understanding of wisdom which understood *sapientia* as essentially the pursuit of active moral virtue. While Rice's elegant analysis may enable us to understand more precisely the mass of sapiential writing produced by the sixteenth century, one drawback to his rather schematic approach has been a tendency to lose sight of the religious content of some of the reputedly more "secular" theories of moral and intellectual wisdom.

Bodin, for instance, is difficult to fit into this classification, cutting as he does across the boundaries and categories with which Rice works. For Bodin advances an idea of wisdom which is both intellectual and moral, being based on virtue *and* knowledge. At the same time, despite its moral content, Bodin's theory of wisdom is scarcely a secular or naturalistic one but rather permeated with religion. Furthermore, Bodin's religion is not Christian, with the con-

---

[1] *Oratio*, ed. Mesnard, p. 14; *Methodus,* ed. Mesnard, p. 114B. See above Chapter I, note 26 and Chapter II, note 1.

sequence that his wisdom is not based like other religious ideas of wisdom on the Christian theological virtues but rather is nourished on Hebraic and Jewish virtue. It is difficult indeed for such a unique fusion of moral, intellectual and theological virtue as this to find a place in a linear history of wisdom in the Renaissance. Bodin's theory of wisdom is very much *sui generis* and must be understood on its own terms even though it was born out of those ancient and contemporary debates on wisdom and virtue to which we now turn.

*
**

Plato, Aristotle and the Stoics supplied much of the framework for the sixteenth century debate on virtue.[2] In book IV of the *Republic* Plato had advanced a unified theory of virtue seeing it as indivisible and ideal. Virtue was in fact knowledge and the winning of virtue was the gradual disclosing through philosophy of an innate quality in man. For Plato therefore all the specific virtues were intellectual; the four cardinal virtues, or qualities, which he named wisdom, courage, temperance (or prudence) and justice, were all manifestations of the central ideal of virtue, which was knowledge. Among the four cardinal virtues, however, justice occupied a determining place in that it signified that proper harmony of the parts of the soul which knowledge and philosophy sought to establish. Where reason was lacking, however, the passions overran their proper bounds and a state of psychic war reigned. In Plato, therefore, we find a theory of virtue which explained all virtue — including the moral virtues — in intellectual terms, treated virtue as an absolute, and saw the task of reason as the control of the passions.

Where Plato had seen ethics as a certain and exact science Aristotle adopted a pragmatic approach. Virtue was not absolute but based rather on the mean between two vices, a mean which man learned to recognise empirically through sense-knowledge in contrast to Plato's view that the acquisition of virtue was a process similar to recollection rather than invention. Rejecting the opinion that all virtue was intellectual Aristotle divided virtue into two main categories, moral and intellectual, corresponding to the divisions of the soul. The moral virtues were the results of choices made by the appetite and will and included such specifics as liberality, temperance, courage and magnanimity. Among the intellectual virtues, which arose out of the rational search for truth, were art, science, prudence, intelligence and wisdom. Prudence signified the intellectual ability to choose the right principle of conduct and so although it belonged among the intellectual virtues it was also closely bound up with moral choice. The determining virtue in Aristotle's system, as with Plato, was justice but Aristotle saw justice not as an intellectual quality but rather as a permanent disposition of the soul towards the mean. As such, justice represented not just a part but rather the whole of virtue and hence refuted Plato's intellectualistic theory of virtue. Finally, to complete this general revision of Plato, Aristotle introduced a more independent conception of the will, asserting that both good and evil may be willed whereas Plato's exclusively intellectual philosophy had led him to conclude that no one could knowingly will evil.

[2] For Greek views of virtue see W. Jaeger, *Paideia* (3 vols., Oxford, 1939-45). Cf. Plato, *Republic,* IV. Aristotle, *Ethics,* I, II.

It was left to the Stoics to attempt a naturalistic theory of virtue which included elements of the earlier views of Plato and Aristotle. Stoic virtue meant living according to nature and this required that one first understand both the natural law of the universe and one's own nature. Once he had perceived the harmonious and rational character of the universe as it had been well ordered by Providence, then a man might attune himself to it and so achieve the supreme good of virtue and happiness. The main obstacle to man's understanding of universal reason and his conformity to it lies in his passions. Vice is essentially false judgement and arises out of lack of restraint of the immoderate passions originating in the irrational part of the soul, passions which unlike the moderated affections of the rational soul are incompatible with right reason. It was the function of the will to reduce the passions to obedience to right reason; but the will was not an independent faculty, being merely a mechanical servant of the intellect. The Stoics were therefore able to come close to Plato in declaring that to know the good is to do the good, the will being not the potential impediment it was in Aristotle.

Ethical discussion in the Greek world revolved therefore around such problems as the relative powers of intellectual and moral virtue, the restraint of the passions by reason, and the question of whether virtue was a mean or an absolute. The coming of Christianity, however, revolutionised the debate by introducing two new themes. One of these was the relationship of theological virtue and religion to the other virtues. The other novel problem was whether virtue was natural or divine in origin.

Where the Stoics had envisaged a divinity that was entirely immanent in the universe and so had averted any possible clash between the divine and the natural, Christian theology revolved around the transcendental separation of God and nature, a rift healed only by the redemption of Christ. This transcendentalism or supernaturalism had immediate repercussions for the idea of virtue. Augustine, for example, allowed the existence of a pagan natural virtue, manifested in the four cardinal virtues prudence, fortitude, temperance and justice.[3] But these natural virtues were but imperfect remnants of that true virtue lost at the Fall. They are in any case bestowed on human nature by God's original grace. More important still is the fact that these vestiges of natural virtue are completely incapable of enabling man to transcend the natural world and seek that reconciliation with God which Augustine saw as the true purpose of virtue. Only grace may effect this restoration and it was therefore those higher theological virtues which arise exclusively out of the receipt of grace (unlike the natural virtues) which constitute true virtue. Faith marks the beginning of grace in man while charity — the love of God — presupposes all the other virtues and is the greatest gift God can bestow. For love is the essence of all the virtues, whether cardinal or theological. Through grace the will is made receptive and purified to become love and it is this good disposition

[3] See E. Gilson, *The Christian Philosophy of St. Augustine* (London, 1961), pp. 131, 136-41, 152, 166. G. Leff, *Medieval Thought* (London 1958), pp. 41ff.

of the will — the "ordering of love" — which for Augustine defines all virtue. The chief distinction between the cardinal moral virtues and the theological is that the objects of love of the former are earthly while the latter have as their object of love the highest good, God Himself.

For Augustine, then, grace is the condition *sine qua non* of all virtue. It perfects the natural moral virtue inchoately present in man and at the same time engenders the theological virtues of Christianity.

But the moral power of nature in man was so weak, according to Augustine, that it was unable even to accept the bestowal of grace and so the efforts of the Pelagians to argue that not only might nature accept grace but even demand grace as the reward for its own natural goodness met with Augustine's bitterest denunciation. The Augustinian campaign against Pelagius' idea of natural virtue was so effectively conducted and intellectually established that it was even to obstruct those Christian humanists of the Renaissance who sought to reconcile their optimistic belief in natural virtue with their Christian ideals. [4]

It was on this Augustinian foundation that Aquinas built his own theory of natural and theological virtue adding to it various materials mined from Aristotle. [5] Aquinas of course adopted much of the Aristotelian teaching on virtue as a mean, but more fruitfully he took Aristotle's idea that the virtues were properly good habits and expanded it in the light of Christian belief in original sin. The virtues aimed at repairing the harm done by the Fall and remedying the subsequent weakness of nature. It was the task of the intellectual virtues to predispose reason to the good while the four Aristotelian moral virtues bent the will to act in accordance with right reason. Prudence, though an intellectual virtue, was bound up with the moral virtues since it directed them to the right means to the good. For Aquinas these virtues may all be present in inchoate form in the natural man but their *perfection* depended on an infusion of divine grace. "Grace does not abolish nature but perfects it". Most importantly, divine grace brings with it the infusion of a higher form of theological virtue. "Faith, hope and charity transcend the human virtues" and allow man to rise to supernatural communion with God.

Aquinas' distinction between natural and theological virtue and his distinction between true and perfect virtue require some explanation here since they are important for an understanding of how far Bodin departed from Christian thinking on virtue. "True", or authentic, virtue may for Aquinas, as for Augustine, exist in the natural man but does so in an imperfect form. To perfect this natural true virtue the presence of the theological virtues and above all of charity is needed in token of the fact that grace is necessary for the perfection of natural virtue and wherever there is grace there is the theological virtue of charity. For Aquinas, then, true moral virtue may exist in a pagan without Christ or Christianity. But perfect moral virtue demands for its perfection that a man also be a Christian and in receipt of divine grace. As we shall see Bodin eschewed Aquinas' view that Christianity is indispensable for

---

[4] A. Levi, *Pagan Virtue and the Humanism of the Northern Renaissance* (Society for Renaissance Studies, Occasional Paper 2, London ,1974).

[5] F. Copleston, *Aquinas* (London, 1955), pp. 204-11. E. Gilson, *The Christian Philosophy of St. Thomas* (London 1957), pp. 259-64, 333-47. See *Summa Theologiae*, Ia-IIae, Q. 58 and 63 etc.; IIa-IIae, Q. 81ff.

the perfection of virtue and instead linked virtue with a Judaised *true religion*, a term which signifies something quite different from Aquinas' use of the phrase.

Aquinas had classified *religio* as a moral rather than a theological virtue. Like the other natural virtues religion was a true but imperfect virtue. It signified justice towards God rather than towards man and while having God as its end, had homage and worship — a human act attainable by natural virtue — as its object. This is all in contrast to the theological virtue of faith which has God not as its end but as its object, attainable only by supernatural virtue. By placing religion among the natural moral virtues Aquinas allowed piety and religion to pagans but he insisted that like the other natural virtues religion was inchoate and required for its perfection the theological virtues and grace which were mediated through Christianity alone. Aquinas therefore saw "true religion" as a virtue which in its origin was natural rather than infused. Bodin's idea of virtue (as we shall see in the next chapter) was radically different from this Christian view. True religion, according to Bodin, signified an already perfected religious virtue, namely the worship and recognition of God. True religion, furthermore, was achievable by man's natural powers alone; it was the product of human free will and had no need of divine grace. The only role allotted to grace in Bodin was in illuminating man with the prophetic spirit, which was an arbitrary gift of God and not the result of natural ethical goodness. Prophecy alone was "infused" and in this belief Bodin followed Maimonides and Jewish tradition, not Aquinas. Despite Bodin's use of the Thomist terminology of true religion, free will, infusion and grace, his mind was working along lines which denied the entire religious philosophy of Christianity.

The basic conception which occasioned this staggering divergence between Aquinas and Bodin was original sin. Aquinas was led by the idea of original sin to insist on the indispensability of Christ's Incarnation to redeem men who were unworthy of redeeming themselves. This attitude generated the Christian theory of grace and theological virtue. Bodin, however, following Jewish thinkers, did not recognise original sin and consequently felt no need to believe in the Incarnation of Christ: neither Christ, nor the theological virtues which Christ generated were therefore necessary for the redemption of man and the restoration of man to God. Man's natural free will alone sufficed for redemption and the theological virtues of Christianity were wholly superfluous in Bodin's eyes. Free will, not grace, led to true religion, and Christ was not essential to that religion. It was only as a prophet infused with divine grace that Christ was significant for Bodin (see Chapters VII and VIII).

Aquinas' theory of grace and theological virtue was to meet with one major refutation from within Christianity. In discussing grace Duns Scotus' preference for contingency over necessity expressed itself in doubts voiced about the efficaciousness of grace; Duns for example argued that God might save man without the operation of grace and theological virtue. This, together with Duns' semi-Pelagian insistence on the power of free will to prepare man for grace, undermined Aquinas' entire moral theology including his concept of theological virtue. Not surprisingly Bodin with his distaste for necessity and determinacy and his doubts about theological virtue found Duns a rich source with which to deck out his own non-Christian writings with solid Christian citations. One should be cautious, nevertheless, of seeing in Bodin's rejection of Thomist grace and theological virtue anything more than a mere echo of the Scotist position. [6]   Indeed to treat Bodin as a Scotist is in some ways like making Hume into one on account of his scepticism about reason and the validity of rational discussion of divine attributes.

The most basic difference between Duns and Bodin was that Duns, in accepting the New Testament as a positive revelation which controlled his theology, believed that Christ was the true redeemer. This recognition of Christ dominated Duns' whole mind. One finds, therefore, in Scotus the principle that the positive revelation of the New Testament must be heeded, a revelation which establishes that God has declared the man infused with grace and charity to be worthy of eternal life. So despite Duns' apparent attack on moral theology one finds him fundamentally committed to the reality of infused theological virtue. Moreover, it is important to remember that for Duns in the *normal* situation (i.e. the situation governed by God's *potentia ordinata*) it is grace which saves just as it is for Aquinas. Duns only raises the possibility of a man being saved by God without charity or ordinary grace to illustrate the extraordinary power of God (*potentia absoluta*) to overrule convention and necessity. For Bodin, on the other hand, grace has no power to justify or save men in normal circumstances. According to Bodin (following Jewish tradition) man is usually saved by exercise of his free will to choose good and live (as the Deuteronomic formula has it). The Old Testament represented a divine promise that the righteous man who obeyed the commandments would be saved and there was no indication there that God would renege on this guarantee of salvation unless man first broke the covenant.

The strange case of Duns goes to show that as long as men accepted Christ as the redeemer the concept of theological virtue remained valid and was bound to dominate European thought. Among religious writers of Bodin's time we find St. François de Sales, for instance, extolling charity as the virtue of virtues and the theological virtues set high above the moral and intellectual. The theological virtues link God and man and St. François holds that this *convenance* (or as Bérulle has it, *capacité de Dieu*) may be accorded to man as a fact of his nature but still requires divine grace for its realisation. [7] There was indeed little questioning even among sixteenth century French "secular" moralists of the supremacy of the theological virtues. But there had nevertheless emerged a revival of the classical manner of writing on ethics which, while not denying the theological virtues, conveniently put them to one side in discussions of intellectual and moral virtue.

The conspicuous, but excusable, absence of theological virtue from such treatises creates the impression of a secularised concept of virtue; they may indeed have contributed to the creation of such an idea, but in virtually all

[6] M. Isnardi-Parente, 'Le Volontarisme de Jean Bodin: Maïmonide ou Duns Scot?', in *Verhandlungen der internationalen Bodin Tagung in München*, ed. H. Denzer (Munich 1973), pp. 39-51, while usefully listing Bodin's citations of Maimonides and Duns, seems to me to lose sight of the fundamentally non-Christian belief of Bodin which greatly limited his debt to Duns. The Scotist citations seem to me a polemical stratagem although they may also reflect Bodin's belief that all positive religions contain elements of *vera religio*.

[7] R. Bady, *L'Homme et son institution de Montaigne à Bérulle (1580-1625)* (Paris 1964), pp. 144ff, 535ff.

these secular theorists a basic Christian element remained, even if unacknowledged explicit and sometimes implicitly contradicted by the very discussion. As long as a writer remained a Christian it is difficult to see how he could have finally rejected the existence of theological virtue no matter how far he might have gone in appearing to analyse intellectual and moral virtue in naturalistic terms. True natural virtue could only appear when one had ceased to be a Christian and there were very few who were prepared to go as far as Bodin in renouncing belief in Christ the saviour. This we should bear firmly in mind when we turn to look as those friends and contemporaries of Bodin who participated in the debates on virtue held in the Académie du Palais in the 1570s and after.

***

From February 1576 the gathering known as the Académie du Palais met in the cabinet of the king in the Louvre and its meetings were continued at Blois and elsewhere until 1579. [8] Although Guy du Faur Pibrac (whom we have already met in the previous chapter) has been described as the "author of the enterprise" it was most likely Henri III himself who instigated the meetings to instruct him in philosophy. Its members included Ronsard, Jean-Antoine de Baif, Pontus de Tyard, Guy Le Fèvre de la Boderie, Amadis Jamyn and Bartolomeo Del Bene and their meetings for the most part pursued debates on intellectual and moral virtue. Although it has not been suggested in any of the current accounts of the Académie it seems certain to me that Bodin was a member of it.

Bodin had been a close friend of Pibrac since their youthful days at Toulouse and the two had remained associated at the Paris bar in the 1560s and 1570s; indeed Bodin dedicated the *République* to Pibrac in 1576, the year of the Académie's institution. [9] This connection renders it highly probable that Bodin participated at the Academie's meetings in Paris. Nor was Pibrac the only friend of Bodin's to have been active in the Académie; it seems that Pierre Ayrault, Christophe de Thou and Barnabé Brisson were also involved. [10] A second major piece of evidence for Bodin's membership of the Académie was that Bodin is known to have participated in dinner discussions at Blois in late

---

[8] R.J. Sealy, 'The Palace Academy of Henry III', *Bibliothèque d'Humanisme et Renaissance,* XL (1978), 61-84. E. Fremy, *L'Académie des derniers Valois 1570-85* (Paris 1887), pp. 162ff. Frances Yates, *The French Academies of the Sixteenth Century* (London 1947), pp. 31f, 108ff. Bady, *L'Homme et son institution,* pp. 133ff. A. Levi, *French Moralists. The Theory of the Passions 1585 to 1649* (Oxford 1964), pp. 63ff. Sealy, p. 82, dates the activity of the Académie between 1576-79 and rejects Fremy's view that the group continued to meet until the death of Pibrac in 1584.

[9] Bodin seems to have been well informed about — and may have been involved in — two earlier academies which have been linked with Pibrac's name: the Académie de Musique of 1567 and the Académie de Poésie et Musique of 1570. See F. Secret, 'La première académie française de musique selon les témoignages de Genebrard et de Jean Bodin', *Bibliothèque d'Humanisme et Renaissance,* XL (1978), 119-120.

[10] For Brisson, de Thou and Ayrault respectively see Fremy, *L'Académie,* pp. 145, 146, 157. Yates, *French Academies,* p. 108, cites a manuscript *Discours des vertus morales en général* (Bibliothèque de l'Arsenal, Paris, MS 4117/2), perhaps delivered to the Académie by Brisson.

1576 and early 1577 with the king.[11]   This was the very time and place at which the Académie seems to have been holding its sessions at Blois in the form of conversations at the king's dining table on "diverses questions de philosophie morale".[12]   It may be assumed therefore that Bodin's discussions at table with Henri III at Blois were part of the activity of the informal Académie du Palais. (Bodin incurred Henri's displeasure as a result of his leading the opposition in the Estates to the anti-Huguenot policy of the king; this no doubt enforced Bodin's absence from later meetings of the Académie which in any case seems to have been depleted in membership after 1577).

Henri III himself set the philosophical tone of the Académie by putting to its members the question: "Are the moral virtues more worthy of praise, more necessary and more excellent than the intellectual virtues?".   This particular question evoked five extant *discours* but all the available speeches turned on the relationship of the passions and the will to reason and the intellect.   The root of the problem was the opinion that the intellectual virtues were cultivated in the rational soul of man whereas the moral virtues seemed to be acquired habits impressed on the irrational soul to curb its passions.   Most of the participants in these debates took the line that the rational intellectual virtues had priority, shaping as they did both the passions and the will, Pibrac, for example, argued that the passions should be transformed and elevated by reason. "Les passions, quand elles secondent la raison, servent à roidir les vertus".[13]   In describing virtue as a mean Pibrac followed the customary Aristotelian opinion, but the concluding appeal in his *Discours* for concord and peace reflects already the manner in which the peculiar circumstances of French political life were beginning to shape a more original and unique moral philosophy in the last decades of the century.

Unlike the other members of the academy Ronsard came down heavily in favour of the intellectual virtues.   Since action eliminates contemplation and *vice versa*, Ronsard argued, it was impossible to combine the two kinds of virtue associated with these ways of life.   If one species of virtue alone should be sought then it should be moral virtue which teaches man how to live well. Man was in any event incapable of true knowledge of the divine — all the sciences were uncertain and subject to error — and he was better advised to seek to manage and govern his unstable passions, an accomplishment within his grasp.   "Since the moral virtues make us more charitable, humane, just, moderate, firmer, more sociable and obedient to our superiors, they are to be preferred to the intellectual".[14]   Against this extreme view other debaters such

[11] Jean Bodin, *Recueil de tout ce qui s'est negotié en la compagnie du Tiers Estats de France... en la ville de Blois, au novembre 1576* (s.l., 1577), p. 59.

[12] Sealy, 'Palace Academy', p. 72.

[13] Pibrac, *Discours de l'ire et comme la faut modérer*, printed in Fremy, *L'Académie*, pp. 279ff.   Cf. Bady, *L'Homme*, pp. 11f, 160ff.

[14] Pierre Ronsard, *Des Vertus intellectuelles et morales*, in his *Œuvres complètes*, ed. G. Cohen (Pléiade ed., Paris ,1950), II, 1030ff.   Cf. Bady, *L'Homme*, pp. 133ff.   Levi, *French Moralists*, pp. 63f.   E.F. Rice jr., *The Renaissance Idea of Wisdom* (Cambridge, Mass., 1958), pp. 154f.   Montaigne also generally preferred the will to the intellect as a guide to virtue.   But although he felt man to be incapable of knowing for certain either the good or the true Montaigne accepted reason as a brake on passion, acting through the intellectual virtue of prudence.   See *Essais*, I, 29; II, 12 and 29.   Cf. Bady, *L'Homme*, pp. 136ff.

as Philippe Desportes insisted that the intellectual virtue of prudence governed the moral virtues in Aristotelian style and that the intellect reflected the divine while human morals were uncertain. Amadis Jamyn too pointed out that intellectual and moral virtue could not be separated as Ronsard thought. [15]

*
**

Notwithstanding this apparently secular Aristotelianism there was already among the members of the Académie the beginnings of a trend towards a more religious interpretation of virtue, best seen in Pibrac's *Discours* and his *Quatrains*. This trend was to be intensified in the late 1570s as the religious wars flared, producing a deeper religious awareness of evil and good which expressed itself in the Christian Neo-Stoicism of the last decades of the century. The connection between the internal psychic condition of man and the state of the outer world was clearly perceived in the political and moral writings of this school and indeed the political thought of many of the so-called *politiques* must be seen in terms of moral philosophy and religion. To these Christian Neo-Stoics (who were for the most part synonymous with those usually classified nowadays as *politiques*) it seemed indisputable that if a man's psyche were at peace, his virtue prevailing over vice, then the political sphere would reflect that individual inner concord. On the other hand, the miseries of religious strife suggested only too vividly that psychic anarchy dominated man. Warfare, both of the physical and spiritual kind, arose out of moral disorder and a defect of virtue. [16]

The most famous Neo-Stoic was of course Justus Lipsius who chose philosophy in consolation for the disruption of his personal life by the wars which kept him continually in flight (unlike Descartes who set off to war to find certainty and inner peace!). [17] In his *De Constantia* of 1584 (which went through 80 editions in Latin alone) Lipsius expounded a Stoic view of peace and harmony as the natural condition of the universe, a peace reflecting the order of nature. But then, setting aside the pure immanence of the Stoics, Lipsius introduced a transcendent God, so dividing God from nature. Divine love too came in to modify the austere Stoic idea of dutiful submission to the law of nature, while Christian revelation completed this transformation of Stoic concepts of natural law, knowledge and virtue.

[15] Speeches printed in Fremy, *L'Académie*. See also Yates, *French Academies*, pp. 108ff.

[16] On this see C.R. Baxter, 'Problems of the Religious Wars', in *French Literature and its Background*, ed. J. Cruickshank (Oxford 1968), I, 166-85. Also the excellent books of Frances Yates, particularly *The Valois Tapestries* (2nd ed., London 1975) and *Astraea* (London 1975).

[17] J.L. Saunders, *Justus Lipsius. The Philosophy of Renaissance Stoicism* (New York 1955). W.J. Bouwsma, 'The Two Faces of Humanism: Stoicism and Augustinianism in Renaissance Thought', in *Itinerarium Italicum* (for *P.O. Kristeller*), ed. H. Oberman (Leiden 1975), pp. 3-60, especially pp. 29ff, 59. Levi, *French Moralists*, pp. 67-73. Bady, *L'Homme*. L. Zanta, *La Renaissance du Stoïcisme au XVIe siècle* (Paris 1914). G. Oestreich, *Geist und Gestalt des frühmoderne Staates* (Berlin 1969), pp. 11-156. G. Abel, *Stoizismus und frühe Neuzeit. Zur Entstehungsgeschichte modernen Denkens im Felde von Ethik und Politik* (Berlin 1978). J. Jehasse, *La Renaissance de la critique* (St-Etienne, 1976), pp. 614ff.

In France Lipsius' Neo-Stoicism was developed above all by Guillaume Du Vair (1556-1621) and Pierre Charron (1541-1603), both of whom moved in the same circles as Bodin although we have no definite evidence of their meeting. Du Vair and Bodin were both members of the court of the duke of Alençon and belonged furthermore to the circle which gathered around Christophe de Thou, president of the Parlement of Paris.[18] Charron, too, it appears, knew de Thou and was also acquainted with Bodin's friend of long-standing, Pibrac; as a member of the Paris bar it seems more than likely that Charron would have come into contact with Bodin himself on many occasions.[19]

In his tracts of the 1580s Du Vair outlined a Christian ethics built on the fact of revelation but he incorporated some Stoic ideas.[20] In his *De la Constance,* probably written in 1591, however, the full impact of the wars of religion on Du Vair became plain. *De la Constance* was intended to offer concrete advice on the management of the manifold evils bred by the religious wars. Prudence should, Du Vair recommended, guide the good man to "retard and slacken cunningly the cause of violence which he may not altogether stop". Moderation, rather than excessive zeal, in justice is advocated; injustice may be tolerated to avoid yet greater injustice. While a man's public duty consists in consulting the public interest his private duty is to lead a good virtuous life of charity. The private man's first happiness is the avoidance of evil, his second happiness to bear evil with constancy. Man therefore is not obliged to seek a virtue that is harsh and bitter.[21]

In many respects Du Vair's reaction to the civil war of 1589-94 was rather similar to that of Bodin who, though discerning in these wars the hand of divine retribution, was prepared to bend rather than break before the onslaught of the Catholic League.[22] The gathering storm had, however, been observed long before by men of Bodin's circle, as Du Vair illustrates in the concluding section of *De la Constance* which consists of the *Remonstrance* of Christophe de Thou. This purports to be the record of de Thou's words in a discussion held the day before his death in 1582 on the relationship between virtue and the civil wars; de Thou, says Du Vair, had proclaimed Christianity to excel over Stoicism on account of the Christian vision of the immortality of the soul and its significance for the validity of virtue. It was in the future life that man's virtue would be rewarded and this provided a guarantee of the worth of virtue that was notably lacking in pagan Stoic thought. The immortality of the soul, therefore, vindicated the unproven Stoic assertion that Providence was just. But in the short run de Thou foresaw a time of trial

---

[18] R. Radouant, *Guillaume Du Vair. L'Homme et l'orateur jusqu'à la fin des troubles de la Ligue (1556-96)* (Paris 1907), pp. 34, 38, 41, 45, Levi, *French Moralists,* p. 94.

[19] Levi, *French Moralists,* p. 97.

[20] Radouant, *Guillaume Du Vair,* and the revised datings by G. Michaut in his edition of Guillaume Du Vair, *De la Sainte Philosophie: Philosophie morale des Stoïques* (Paris 1945), who places *Sainte Philosophie* earlier than *Philosophie morale* and assigns both to before 1585 although the former was published only in 1588. See also the introduction by R. Kirk to the English translation of *The Moral Philosophie of the Stoicks* (New Brunswick 1951).

[21] G. Du Vair, *De la Constance* (2nd ed.), (Lyons 1595), pp. 335, 359-64, 267-70.

[22] See P.L. Rose, 'The *Politique* and the Prophet: Bodin and the Catholic League 1589-94', *The Historical Journal,* XXI (1978), 783-808.

for his friends when France would succumb to the greatest miseries. In the face of this imminent violence and tempest de Thou urged constancy and adherence to right and reason, but in conformity with prudence. "Follow destiny, without forsaking virtue" was de Thou's advice to his friends among whom surely must be included Bodin. [23]

Pierre Charron's *De la Sagesse* (completed in 1599 and published in 1601) is probably the most famous product of French Neo-Stoicism. [24] The second edition of *Sagesse* (1604) borrowed extensively from Bodin's *Theatrum Naturae* and the *Paradoxe,* but although Charron shared Bodin's programme of reducing the superstition prevalent in positive religion he never abandoned his essential belief in Christianity. It cannot be said, therefore, that Charron was truly a disciple of Bodin though it seems that the latter's rejection of virtue as a mean influenced the similar position taken in *Sagesse.* [25]

For Charron prudence was the chief virtue and included within it all the moral virtues. Virtue, in Charron's apparently Stoic formulations, consisted of obedience to the law of reason and nature. "The law of nature is a light within us...a natural illumination inspired by God". "Wisdom must spring from nature, from that law and light which God has put in each of us at his creation". [26] This stress on the innateness of prudence and virtue in man and the Stoic phrases have sometimes created an impression that he was advocating a purely secular and naturalistic theory of virtue quite divorced from religious belief. A caveat must be lodged against any such modernising interpretation.

Although it is true that Charron makes an important theoretical separation between virtue and religion, one cannot describe this as a "secularisation" of virtue except in the most formalistic ground of definition. Formally, for Charron, virtue is possible without religion, but the two are in reality inter-related. Virtue, as he insists, is part of "the road to religion". [27] For a Christian like Charron it would be psychologically impossible — however logically feasible — to believe in a purely secular virtue which had no need of religion. A Charron who believed in secular virtue in the modern sense would not be a historical Charron and one must be wary of introducing such anachronistic modern-day "humanism" into a fundamentally Christian thinker. For Charron — "religieux, conscientieux, et (craignant) Dieu", and accepting the

[23] Du Vair, *Constance,* pp. 423f, 433ff.

[24] By far the best account is R. Kogel, *Pierre Charron* (Geneva 1972). See also Levi, *French Moralists,* pp. 95-111. Both Kogel and Levi stress the religious content of *De la Sagesse* whereas the secular and naturalistic aspects of the work are emphasised — to my mind a little too much so — by Rice, *Renaissance Idea of Wisdom,* Ch. 7; and M.C. Horowitz, 'Natural Law as the Foundation for an Autonomous Ethic: Pierre Charron's *De la Sagesse', Studies in the Renaissance,* XXI (1974), 204-227.

[25] See J.-B. Sabrié, *De l'Humanisme au rationalisme. Pierre Charron (1541-1603)* (Paris 1913), pp. 262-67. Kogel, *Charron,* Chapter 4 on religion. Curiously enough Charron like Bodin (Levi, *French Moralists,* p. 97) belonged for a short time to the Catholic League although he later attributed his membership to a surge of passion rather than conviction which had for the most part governed Bodin's behaviour. (See Rose, *'Politique* and Prophet').

[26] Extensive quotations are given in Kogel, *Charron,* and Rice, *Renaissance Wisdom,* especially pp. 192ff.

[27] Kogel, *Charron,* pp. 59, 76ff.

need for grace as the perfection of virtue [28] — natural secular virtue was a mere hypothesis, not an existential possibility.

Charron's religious sensibility therefore should warn us against describing his theory of ethics as secular or autonomous. And this warning is further confirmed by the particular manner in which Charron phrases his comments on natural virtue. For in the quotations given above Charron starts off with what appears to be a typically Stoic naturalistic statement but then in a complementary sentence introduces a Christian religious idea which annuls the apparent Stoicism and naturalism. Virtue and wisdom spring from nature, says Charron, but then he immediately affirms that these instincts have been placed in man by God's original illumination. Now if Charron's God were the immanent God of the Stoics then one might say that his statement amounts to a naturalistic theory of virtue. But Charron's God is a transcendent, creating Christian diety. True natural virtue may be possible in a Stoic universe but in the Christian world virtue, no matter how instinctive it may be, is always affected by a religious conception and is never exclusively natural. God's grace instills the tendency to virtue in the first place, and God's grace continues to perfect that virtue. So, although Charron does indeed make a formal separation between virtue and religion, this does not mean that he ever conceived of virtue as properly natural, but rather always as a mixture of the natural and the divine.

Neo-Stoicism represents one of the most ingenious attempts of the Renaissance to Christianise a body of ancient thought which was by its very nature intractable. Where Stoicism had propounded an intrinsically static universe and demanded submission to the eternal order of nature, the Neo-Stoics expounded a dynamic order; Christ had liberated men from helpless obedience to nature while divine grace enabled men to transcend the natural order of things. The internal contradictions of the Stoic revival were, however, to produce within a short time two irreconcilably opposed traditions. On the Christian side there occurred a shift towards a more intensely religious, even mystic, idea of virtue, represented in the writings of Bartolomeo Del Bene, Jacques Davy Du Perron and Honoré d'Urfé. Some of these advocated a mystic ideal of the ascent of the soul to the divine by means of theological virtue which subsumed the intellectual and moral virtues. Within this current discussions of philosophy developed more and more into analyses of religious piety. [29] In the other direction, however, the more naturalistic tendencies of the Stoic revival led to the gradual extinction of its Christian content. Originally harnessed to form part of a Christian apologetic, the Stoic ideas of nature and reason were soon freed from such restraints and, in de-Christianised form, adapted to the arsenal of later libertine thinkers. Some of the earlier religious opinions about natural virtue, such as Charron's, were to have a great influence on the libertine tradition proper, but it should always be remembered that originally the writings of nearly all the sixteenth century "libertine" or "natu-

---

[28] *Ibidem,* p. 24. Levi, *French Moralists,* p. 111.

[29] See, e.g. Bene's *Civitas veri sive morum* (Paris 1609); Du Perron's *Traité des vertus morales* in his *Diverses œuvres* (Paris 1622); and d'Urfé's *Epîtres morales* (Lyons 1598).

ralistic" writers — including Bodin — were part of a religious matrix and never truly naturalistic. [30]

*
* *

We have so far sketched the philosophical and Christian background to Bodin's idea of religious virtue so as to illustrate presently just how far Bodin departed from the general run of sixteenth century thought. But before examining the *Paradoxe* in detail we must first describe two particular traditions which moulded Bodin's unique understanding of virtue. One of these was connected with Bodin's youthful membership of the Carmelites, a religious experience perhaps as significant for Bodin as Rabelais' years in the Franciscans were for the satirist. [31] The other tradition was the Jewish ethics of Philo and Maimonides.

According to the documentary evidence assembled by Ponthieux Bodin spent some years in studies at the Carmelite monastery in Paris. It is possible to reconstruct some of the likely circumstances surrounding this time of Bodin's as a Carmelite student. In the sixteenth century the Parisian monastery of the order at Place Maubert was the main *studium generale* of the Carmelites in France. Under the energetic prior-generalship of Nicholas Audet (prior-general 1523-62) reforms had been carried out between 1530-32 with the intention of making Place Maubert into an international house of study. The strictest requirement was laid upon each of the various priors of the order to send at their monastery's expense at least one student to a *studium generale* of the order. [32]

By 1540 there were at least 15 students from other monasteries attending the courses at the Paris *studium* and it seems very likely that when Bodin arrived a few years later at the Carmelite monastery at Place Maubert he was there as the nominated scholar from the order's house at Angers. [33] In 1548 Audet reiterated that it was the duty of priors on pain of suspension to send scholars to Paris and at the same time set out stringent regulations on the teaching and examining of students in arts. From these it appears that

[30] Cf. *Aspects du libertinisme au XVIᵉ siècle*, ed. J. de Boisset and A. Stegmann (Paris 1974). J. Wirth, "'Libertin' et 'Epicuriens'. Aspects de l'irréligion au XVIᵉ siècle', *Bibliothèque d'Humanisme et Renaissance*, XXXIX (1977), 601-627. R. Pintard, *Le Libertinage érudit dans la première moitié du XVIIᵉ siècle* (Paris 1943). A. Tenenti, 'Libertinisme et hérésie', *Annales ESC*, XVIII (1963), 1-19. S. Mastellone, 'Gallicani e libertini', *Il Pensiero Politico*, VI (1973), 249-253.

[31] For Bodin as a Carmelite — a fact attested by de Thou, Postel and explicit documentary evidence — see Chapter VIII. On Rabelais see A.J. Krailsheimer, *Rabelais and the Franciscans* (Oxford 1963).

[32] The statute of 1532 is printed in B. Zimmerman, ed., *Acta Capitulorum Generalium Ordinis Fratrum B.V. Mariae de Monte Carmelo* (Rome 1912), I (1318-1593), 393, 395. (=ACG). Cf. J.A. Smet, *The Carmelites. A History of the Brothers of Our Lady of Mount Carmel, ca. 1200 AD until the Council of Trent* (privately printed, Illinois 1975), pp. 36ff, 187, 194, 203. A. Staring, *Der Karmelitengeneral Nikolaus Audet und die katholische Reform des XVI Jahrhunderts* (Rome 1959), p. 235.

I am most grateful to Father B. Pitman, O. Carm. of Whitefriars, Donvale, Victoria, for his help in obtaining materials on the Carmelites.

[33] For the 1540 figure see Staring, *Audet*, p. 241. Bodin is not mentioned in any of the Carmelite sources I have seen.

candidates for the bachelor of arts were to spend a first year studying logic and the next two years on physics and moral philosophy before proceeding to a two year course of theology. [34] But Bodin's main debt to the Carmelites probably lay not so much in his philosophical education as in the peculiar spirituality to which he was exposed.

The founding Rule of St. Albert (1206-14) placed great store on prayer, meditation and purity of heart as the foundation of Carmelite spitituality. "Many are the ways which the Holy Fathers have instituted for following Christ and serving him faithfully with a pure heart and good conscience". [35] The Rule prescribed solitary meditation by day and night on the Law of the Lord and watching in prayer; at the same time it instituted communal penitential practices centered on fasting and continual prayer. One is reminded at once of Bodin's immersal in prayer in order to purify his heart before his final conversion in 1567-68. [36] This emphasis on purification by prayer was expounded in detail in what was by far the most influential handbook of Carmelite spirituality before the great reform of the later sixteenth century. This was the *Institutio primorum monachorum,* written about 1370, and widely available in the monasteries of the order. [37] The *Institutio,* however, divided the Carmelite's pursuit of holiness into two spheres, the way of purification and the way of illumination.

> The goal of this life is twofold. One part we acquire, with the help of divine grace, through our efforts and virtuous works. This is to offer God a holy heart, pure from all stain of actual sin. We do this when we are perfect and in Carith, that is, hidden in that charity of which the wise man says "Charity covereth all sins". (Proverbs, X, 12). God meant Elijah to advance this far when He said to him *"Hide* thee in the torrent of Carith". (I Kings XVII, 3).
>
> The other part of the goal of this life is granted to us as the free gift of God, namely to taste somewhat in the heart and to experience in the soul, not only after death but even in this mortal life, the intensity of the divine presence and the sweetness of the glory of heaven. This is to *drink* of the torrent of the love of God. God promised it to Elias in the words "And there thou shalt drink of the torrent". [38]

[34] Zimmerman, *ACG,* pp. 427-29. Staring, *Audet,* p. 238. The Carmelites were not particularly prominent among the humanists of the early sixteenth century although they included among their number the well-known Arnoud Bostius of Ghent (1445-99). See B. Zimmerman, 'Les Carmes humanistes', *Etudes Carmélitaines,* XX (1935), 19-93.

[35] Quoted by Smet, *The Carmelites,* pp. 7ff. There is a recent translation by B. Edwards, *Rule of St. Albert* (Aylesford 1973). On Carmelite spirituality see Smet, *Carmelites,* and the *Dictionnaire de spiritualité ascétique et mystique* (Paris 1932), ed. M. Viller et. al., II, 156ff. J. Dagens, *Bérulle et les origines de la restauration catholique (1575-1611)* (Bruges 1952).

[36] *Démonomanie* (Paris 1580), f. 10v. See Chapter VIII, note 62.

[37] Allegedly written by John the 44th bishop of Jerusalem. It was first publicised by Philip Ribot in 1370. A Latin text was published in the *Speculum Ordinis Carmelitanum* (Venice 1507) and in several later Latin collections. For the Latin texts of the important sections discussed here see Fr. Gabriel Wessels, 'Pars ascetica Regular Iohannis 44', *Analecta Ordinis Carmelitarum,* III (1914-16), 346-67. English chapter summaries are in Fr.N. Werling, 'The Book of St. John 44', *The Sword,* III (1939), 293-304; and an English version of the mystical Chapters 1-9 is given in the same author's 'The Book of St. John 44', *The Sword,* IV (1940), 20-24, 152-160, 309-320. For the history of the text see Smet, *Carmelites,* pp. 63ff.

[38] *Institutio primorum monachorum,* Chapter 2.

The way of purification — "the hiding of oneself in the torrent" — demanded the penitent's absolute love of God and the Crucifixion and was achieved by four steps, again deduced allegorically from the Biblical account of Elijah's sojourn in the wilderness of Carith.

> God says 'Get thee hence', namely from the perishable and transitory things of earth — 'and go towards the east', that is against the original cupidity of the flesh — 'and hide by the torrent Carith', do not dwell in cities with multitude — 'which is over against the Jordan', that you may be cut off from sin by charity. Ascending these four steps to the peak of the prophetic perfection, 'there thou shalt drink of the torrent'. [39]

It is in "drinking of the torrent" that the Carmelite finally attains illumination and prophetic perfection.

> Wherefore because of the love of God you should leave the world and the companionship of men in order that you may cling to God with a pure heart; you shall merit to enjoy abundantly divine conversation, so that hidden and even future things will be revealed to you by God. Then thou shall abound in inexpressible delights and shall gladly lift up the face of thy mind to contemplate God. [40]

The mystic ascent to God therefore passes through the various stages of love of God, knowledge of God and contemplation of God before arriving at the highest ecstasy of joy of God. But none of these is possible without the benefit of divine grace.

For the Carmelites this process of illumination by grace is actually identical with the bestowal of prophecy upon men and Carmelite mystical feeling in the *Institutio* explicitly takes the form of a quest for prophetic perfection. The order was reputed to have been founded by the prophet Elijah and the sojourn of Elijah in the wilderness of Carith — traditionally depicted in paintings in Carmelite monasteries — was the central allegory embodying the order's vision of purification, illumination and prophecy.

> This prophet of God, Elias (Elijah), was the chief of the monks from whom the holy and ancient order took its origin. For it was he, who, desirous of achieving progress in the pursuit of divine contemplation, withdrew far from the cities (and) ... was the first to adopt the holy and solitary life of a prophet ... In a vision God ordered him to depart ... and hide himself in the desert..." And the word of the Lord came to him saying: 'Get thee hence, and go towards the east and hide thyself by the torrent Carith which is ever against the Jordan, and there thou shalt drink of the torrent; and I have commanded the ravens to feed thee (I Kings, XVII, 2-4)'." These salutary commands ... should be meditated upon by us hermit monks word for word, not only historically by mystically and with the greater application since the Order is fully comprehended in them, that is, the rule for arriving at the perfection of the prophets and the goal of the eremitic religious life. [41]

---

[39] *Ibidem.*

[40] *Ibidem,* Chapter 7.

[41] *Ibidem,* Chapter 2. Cf. P. Elisée de la Nativité, 'Les Carmes imitateurs d'Elie (1370-1668)', in *Elie le prophète* (Etudes Carmélitaines, 35, Bruges 1956), II, 82-116. B. Botte, 'Le Culte de prophète Elie dans l'Eglise Chrétienne', *ibidem,* I, 208-218.

In view of this close association with Elijah or Elias with the Carmelites it is little wonder that Postel referred to Bodin as a renegade "Elian" meaning a Carmelite (*instituti Eliani aliquando sectator*). [42] The term "Elian", however, might have been applied to virtually any adherent of the prophetic current of sixteenth century religion including Postel himself [43] and the *libertins spirituels*. [44] It might also refer to the Jewish idea of an Elian prophecy of the "world-week" to which Bodin himself alludes in the *Methodus*. [45] Any and all of these beliefs and heresies might have been encountered by Bodin in the monastery at Place Maubert since in the late 1540s, it seems, there was a sudden growth of heresy within the Carmelites when for instance the works of Tauler began to penetrate the order. [46] But however this may be, it is

[42] See Chapter VIII, note 2. The Carmelites were known as *Elianus ordo,* as in Fr. Daniel a Virgine Maria's collection *Speculum Carmelitanum sive historia Eliani ordinis fratrum Beatissimae Virginis Mariae de Monte Carmelo* (Antwerp 1680).

[43] See W.J. Bouwsma's fine study, *Concordia Mundi. The Career and Thought of Guillaume Postel (1510-81)* (Cambridge, Mass. 1957), pp. 163ff, 281ff, on Elian prophecy. F. Secret, 'L'Emitologie de Guillaume Postel', in *Umanesimo e Esoterismo,* ed. E. Castelli, (Archivio di Filosofia 2-3, Padua 1960), pp. 381-437, esp. p. 407-16; Idem, 'De quelques courants prophétiques et religieux sous le règne de Henri III', *Revue de l'Histoire des Religions,* CLXXII (1967), 1-32. The theme of Elian prophecy (related to the Joachite idea of the three ages) is to be found particularly in Postel's compilation *Restitutio rerum omnium conditarum per manum Eliae profetae* (by pseudo-Abraham) (Paris 1552) and his *Le Thrésor des prophéties de l'univers,* ed. F. Secret (Archives Internationales d'Histoire des Idées, 27, The Hague 1969), pp. 171-73. Cf. F. Secret, *Guillaume Postel (1510-81) et son interprétation du Candélabre de Moyse* (Nieuwkoop 1966). Elias Pandochaeus (i.e. Postel), *Panthenosia* (Basle 1547), pp. 70ff. Postel also wrote a manuscript treatise entitled *De formidando Eliae adventu nunc in spiritu futuro* (according to F. Secret, *Bibliographie des manuscrits de Guillaume Postel* (Geneva 1970), p. 41, perhaps to be identified with his *Restitutio rerum* (ibidem, p. 46).
It is difficult to establish the extent of Bodin's debt to Postel; it must certainly be limited by Postel's essential Christianity which would have rendered him incapable of writing the *Heptaplomeres* (despite recent suggestions that Postel was the author). I would, however, think it almost certain that Bodin was acquainted with Postel's writings and may even have been among the many influential persons (including Charles IX) who found their way to the priory where Postel spent his last two decades under light arrest. Cf. A. Lefranc, 'La Détention de Guillaume Postel au prieuré de Saint-Martin-des-Champs (1562-81)', *Annuaire-Bulletin de la Société de l'Histoire de France,* XXVIII (1891), 211-230.

[44] See G. Demerson, 'Un Mythe des libertins spirituels: le prophète Elie', in *Aspects de libertinisme au XVI⁰ siècle,* ed. de Boisset and Stegmann, pp. 105-120. H. Busson, *Le Rationalisme dans la littérature française de la Renaissance* (2nd ed., Paris 1957), pp. 296-317. C.G.A. Schmidt, *Les libertins spirituels. Traités mystiques écrits dans les années 1547 à 1549* (Basle 1876). A. Jundt, *Histoire du panthéisme populaire au moyen âge et au seizième siècle* (Paris 1875).

[45] *Methodus,* ed. Mesnard, pp. 154B, 241A (trs. pp. 122, 333). Bodin regards the Elian prophecy of the world-week and the age of the earth as impious. The source of his knowledge seems to be the Talmud. See *The Babylonian Talmud,* trs. I. Epstein (34 vols., London 1935-48), volumes entitled *Sanhedrin,* pp. 656ff and *Idolatry* (*Abodah Zarah*), pp. 42ff.

[46] Zimmerman, *ACG,* p. 426. Cf. Dagens, *Bérulle,* pp. 308-16. Staring, *Audet,* pp. 322ff. P. Imbart de la Tour, *Les Origines de la Réforme* (4 vols., Paris 1915-35), IV, 231f. In a letter of 7 November 1545 Calvin refers to a Carmelite of Lyons who was associated with the *libertins spirituels.* See John Calvin, *Opera omnia* (Corpus Reformatorum 40, Brunswick 1863-97), XII, 210. Cf. his *Contre la secte phantastique et furieuse des libertins qui se nomment spirituels* of the same year in *Opera,* VII, 145ff, 341ff (CR 35). Unlike Bodin the *libertins spirituels* were Christians despite some of Calvin's aspersions.

scarcely in doubt that Bodin's membership of the Carmelites introduced him to that prophetic awareness and sensibility which is so characteristic of his own *vera religio*.

Between the main trends in Carmelite spirituality and mysticism and Bodin's religion there are some remarkable similarities. First of all Bodin observes the Carmelite division of spirituality into the way of purification and the way of illumination. On the one hand Bodin advocates prayer and the cultivation of the "pure heart" so essential in Carmelite religion; but he also preaches the mystic and prophetic approach to God culminating in the joy of God, an illumination granted by divine grace alone. If we recall Bodin's narrative in the *Démonomanie* of his own conversion of 1567-68 (Chapter VIII below) there is a striking parallel between the Carmelite two-fold goal and the process of Bodin's own conversion of 1567-68. First Bodin purified his heart by constant prayer and meditation; then the prophetic illumination came upon him. It seems difficult to escape the conclusion, therefore, that Bodin's Carmelite training must have had a powerful psychological impact upon him which was to determine the contours of his later conversion. Nevertheless it should be emphasised that Bodin's religion was at root completely opposed to the Christianity of the Carmelites. Purification, illumination and prophecy for him utterly lacked the Christian context in which they were fixed by his former brothers. And so we find a critical difference between the ideas of the Carmelites and Bodin on how purification is actually achieved. The Carmelites, believing as Christians in original sin, insisted on the necessity of divine grace to aid human virtues in man's efforts to purify his soul: [47] but Bodin saw no need for divine grace in the sphere of purification for, following Jewish tradition, he saw human free will as being in itself capable of achieving virtue and purity. Grace, for Bodin, was only essential in the second sphere of illumination and prophecy.

A second major resemblance between Bodin and Carmelite thought is to be found in the mystic language used in discussing illumination. In both cases we find a similar progression from love though knowledge and contemplation to joy of God. (Our analysis of the *Paradoxe* will make this plain in the next chapter).

Prophecy represents the third main area of similarity. Bodin and the Carmelite author of the *Institutio primorum monachorum* both accept the central role of prophecy in religion, seeing it as a special gift of God which is independent of human will although the properly disposed and purified soul will often be rewarded with it. Prophecy has two main functions. The first of these is to convey the illumination which God grants to the soul and both Bodin and the Carmelites are agreed on this. Secondly, prophecy is the communication of God's revelation through the prophets. Bodin's letter to Bautru and the *Institutio* both affirm that the prophets have been sent by God to recall men from evil to good. Yet here again a significant departure from Christian thought arises out of Bodin's novel religious ideas. Where the Carmelites see the evil in man as original sin which can be redeemed

---

[47] For Carmelite thought — coloured by a strongly Augustinian tinge — on natural virtue and grace see Smet, *The Carmelites*, pp. 67ff. Dagens, *Bérulle*, pp. 282f, 335, 350.

only by Christ, Bodin believed that the evil in men may be set right by free will and purification. [48]

As a final, though tentative, example of the marks which a youthful exposure to Carmelite spirituality left upon Bodin, one might point to the aversion to cities shown by the *Institutio* which devotes a chapter to arguing that cities produce lust and avarice and compel the innocent to suffer the wars of others. In Bodin's letters on the Catholic League of 1589-90 a similar revulsion surfaced in his condemnation of the luxury and silver trafficking at Paris which he sees as producing the current civil wars. [49]

We may well say, therefore, that Carmelite teachings provided Bodin with much of the mystic and prophetic sensibility which permeates his mature *vera religio*. But, it must be emphasised, the Christian spirit of this approach limited its appeal for Bodin; Carmelite spirituality could scarcely remain persuasive or sufficient in the light of that dominating universalism which pervaded Bodin's religious thought from at least 1559 and was perhaps the most salient feature of his mind. [50]

*
**

There was, however, one religious tradition which incorporated much of the substance of Carmelite spirituality — prayer, purification, illumination and prophecy — and yet was not tied to Christian beliefs about original sin, the incapacity of natural virtue and the redemptive power of Christ. Judaism, for Bodin, held out the double advantage of reinforcing Carmelite spirituality and at the same time rescuing that spirituality from the particularity of Christianity; the spiritual feeling of the Carmelites might in this way be brought into philosophical agreement with Bodin's universalising cast of mind. In this sense, Judaism might be said to be the catalyst of Bodin's conversions.

Our final chapter will investigate the impact of Philo and Maimonides on the religious conversions of Bodin. There are indeed many striking resemblances between the theological ideas of the Jewish writers and of Bodin — one may cite their common understanding of the relationship between natural and revealed religion, or their shared concepts of creation, of transcendence and immanence, of divine will and miracles. Further similarities with Bodin's religion are to be found in Philo's and Maimonides' idea of spirit and the pneuma, in their theory of the soul as spirit, in their angelology and demonology, in their

---

[48] See *Institutio primorum monachorum*, Chapter 8 (Latin text in *Analecta Ord. Carm., loc. cit.*; Eng. trs. by Werling in *The Sword*, loc. cit.): "'I shall send the ravens to feed thee'. By the word raven is rightly to be understood the holy prophets whom I have sent you as an example ... to lead man to the hidden food of my love ... warning them ... to contrition." For the letter to Bautru see below, Chapter VIII.

[49] *Institutio*, Chapter 5. For Bodin's attack on Paris in the printed letters of 1589 and 1590 see Rose, 'The *Politique* and the Prophet', pp. 787ff.

[50] The Carmelites with their interest in Hebrew may heve sponsored Bodin's drift to Judaising. The converted Italian Jew Jean-André (Giovanni Gelida) de Padoue lectured on Hebrew at the Carmelite refectory in Bordeaux, lectures later transferred to the Collège de Guyenne which was regarded as a Judaising centre in the hands of the *conversos*. See F. Secret, 'Notes sur les Hébraïsants Chrétiens', *Revue des Etudes Juives*, CXXIII (1964), 141-168, at pp. 153f. S.W. Baron, *A Social and Religious History of the Jews* (2nd ed. rev., New York, 1952-   ), XV, p. 77.

theory of prophecy — in sum, in their whole vision of a moral universe of spirits. Above all there is the significance of Philo's ideas of true religion, conversion and the sacrifice of the purified soul for Bodin's own momentous conversion to prophetic religion in 1567-68. [51] But our present examination of the influence of Philo and Maimonides is confined to those Jewish theological ideas which specifically affect ethical thought.

In Judaism free will represents a religious choice rather than the naturalistic idea it is in Aristotle (*Ethics*, III, 2). (One might point out that in view of this it is somewhat futile for modern philosophers to attempt to prove or disprove free will by rationalistic argument — as Voltaire well recognised). The roots of the Jewish idea are of course to be found in Scripture and sapiential literature, but it was first fully formulated in the works of Philo. Free will is a central element of Jewish theodicy for it is envisaged as an essential part of divine justice which rewards good: evil arises not out of God's immanence but rather of man's free will choosing to do evil. Since original sin is not present in man, free will in Jewish tradition suffices for salvation through the attainment of true religion. There is no need for saving grace or the infusion of virtue. [52]

Grace therefore loses the essential connection with virtue which it has in Christian thought. Grace does exist in Jewish theology but it is *necessary* only for extraordinary purposes, e.g. for the infusion of prophecy, or for the performance of miracles. In these cases grace is a manifestation of God's will and command. Hence human free will does not contradict either the Jewish or Bodin's idea of grace since free will can also be overruled by God's command or grace. This may seem to be much the same as the Christian idea of grace but in fact the whole structures of thought concerning grace in Jewish and Christian theology are radically different. This is revealed most obviously in the terminology. The Hebrew terms for grace — *hesed* and *hain,* translated respectively as lovingkindness and favour — refer both to the good bestowed by God and His love without cause for humanity. In their Old Testament contexts these terms for grace do not refer to the theological problem of nature versus grace which,

---

[51] For the influence of Philo and Jewish concepts on Bodin's "conversions" see Chapter VIII.

I hope to deal in detail with the appearance of these Judaised ideas in the *Démonomanie, Theatrum* and other works in a fuller study of Bodin. But for a few remarks in the interim see Chapters VI-VIII.

[52] See for example the relevant articles in the *Encyclopaedia Judaica* (London-Jerusalem, 1971) and I. Epstein, *Judaism. A Historical Presentation* (Harmondsworth, 1959). The *Zohar* treats grace along with judgement and mercy as the three creative attributes (*sefirot*) of God. Grace softens the harsh effects of God's judgement or anger. See G. Scholem, *On the Kabbalah and its Symbolism* (New York, 1969), pp. 79, 144.

On Philo's ethics and moral philosophy see H.A. Wolfson, *Philo* (Cambridge, Mass., 1947), I, 424-461; II, 165-321. E.R. Goodenough, *An Introduction to Philo Judaeus* (2nd ed., Oxford, 1962), pp. 112-123, which, however, overstates the Hellenism of Philo's ethics. E. Bréhier, *Les Idées philosophiques et religieuses de Philon d'Alexandrie* (3rd ed., Paris, 1950), pp. 272-295, perhaps reads a few too many Stoic and Christian attitudes into this quintessentially Jewish philosopher. J. Giblet, 'L'Homme image de Dieu dans les commentaires littéraux de Philon d'Alexandrie', *Studia Hellenistica*, V (1948), 93-118, demonstrates that for all his Platonic and Stoic terminology Philo's ethics are peculiarly un-Greek. For the influence of Old Testament sapiential literature on Philo see J. Laporte, 'Philo in the Tradition of Biblical Wisdom Literature', in *Aspects of Wisdom in Judaism and Early Christianity*, ed. R. Wilken (Notre Dame, Indiana, 1975), pp. 103-141.

as one of the foundations of Christianity, appears only in the New Testament. In the latter the Hebraic idea of grace is denoted by the Greek *charis,* whereas the novel Christian concept of grace is called *agape.* Again, Jewish tradition holds that for those who of their own free will keep the divine commandments God's love or grace is a possession for ever. Grace is therefore the reward of merit whereas in Christianity it is essentially unmerited since original sin has perpetually rendered man incapable of religious virtue by his own natural effort. When Bodin uses the term "grace" to express his own beliefs it is generally in the Old Testament sense of God's love and will; and indeed in the *Heptaplomeres* Bodin openly argues that the entire Christian débate on nature and grace is misconceived and futile. [53]

Some conceptions of charity are common to both Jews and Christians, for example the idea of charity as love of the highest good (i.e. God) or as the pursuit of the vision of God. But the central Christian view of charity sees the love of God as a theological virtue which is supernaturally infused by grace and made possible in its completeness only by the Incarnation and Cruci-fixion of Christ. In contrast the Jewish notion of charity is represented in the use of the word *zedakah* (*tsidoco*) or "righteousness" to denote charity. *Zedakah* or charity is achieved by free will alone aspiring to love of God. Aquinas, it will be remembered, would have regarded this sort of charity as an imperfect natural virtue since it exists without the need for grace.

Righteousness is the essence of the Jewish idea of virtue and indeed is the governing principle of all Jewish ethical thought. It makes for a unique theory of virtue since, unlike the virtue of either Aristotle or Aquinas, righteous-ness is a combination of the religious and the natural, being neither wholly one nor the other. Moreover, where Greek and scholastic philosophy had defined the various virtues systematically, in Jewish tradition there was only a loose general notion of virtue as righteousness, love of God and the performance of good deeds out of love of God. Consequently, the Jewish positive virtues included contentment and humility, joy and faith in God, and fear and love of God.

Most of these traditional elements of Jewish ethics are to be found decked out in Greek philosophical vocabulary in the works of Philo. [53] Bodin had in the *Methodus* alluded to Philo's moral philosophy and in the *Démonomanie* he commended it saying that "Philon Hébrieu est admirable en ses interpré-tations pour le moral, et Léon et Maymon (*Maimonides*) pour la nature, et le livre du Zoar...pour tous les deux". [54] Bodin's conformity to Philo's general ethical position is well illustrated by his detestation of atheism as the greatest of crimes. For Philo and Bodin God was the author only of good and moral evil arose out of man's free choice to do good or evil. Philo saw moral evil as essentially a distancing of oneself from God. Hence, atheism — the farthest one could be from God — was the extreme of evil. Atheism was born when the passions overcame man's desire for virtue and for God; so, far from being

[53] See Chapters V-VII. In the *Heptaplomeres* Bodin twice uses the term *gratia* in a context where it has the Jewish meaning only (ed. Noack, pp. 311, 323). It cannot be taken here in the Christian sense since these passages are denying original sin and the need for a redeemer.

[54] *Démonomanie,* f. 66. *Methodus,* p. 123AB (trs. p. 38). See Chapter II, note 10.

an intellectual and scientific attitude as its adherents claimed, atheism was actually the exemplar of evil passions and the immoral. [55]

The basic corrective to atheism is moral conscience (a concept first defined by Philo) which enables man to progress morally. Moral conscience urges man to the virtues of repentance and hope and causes the soul to feel the majesty of all the virtues. [56] In enumerating the specific virtues Philo cites various virtues from the lists of Plato, Aristotle and the Stoics such as prudence, graciousness, courage and self-mastery, but his central idea of virtue is based on Hebraic religion: although the trees and rivers in the garden of Eden may represent particular virtues the tree of life signifies "reverence towards God, the greatest of the virtues, by means of which the soul attains to immortality". [57] (Where Plato had believed that the soul derived its immortality from being part of the divine soul, Philo's soul was conceived as a created entity and not the same substance as God but rather formed of a different *pneuma* or spirit). [58]

For Philo the purification of the soul by virtue was allegorically represented by the Biblical precepts concerning the Temple sacrifices. Instead of taking these texts literally Philo interpreted them as allegories of an inner personal purification, an interpretation cited approvingly by Bodin in both the *Démonomanie* and the *Heptaplomeres*. [59] Bodin would have completely agreed with Philo's remark that "the mind is cleansed by wisdom and the truths of wisdom's teaching which guide its steps to the contemplation of the universe and all that is therein and by the sacred company of the other virtues". [60] Again, "the priest is bidden to take such a soul... to offer the best of sacrifices, even the whole soul, brimful of truths of all sincerity and purity — a soul rich with fatness, gladdened by light divine and perfumed with the breath exhaled from justice and the other virtues". [61] "Sacrifice consists not in the victims but in the offerer's intention and zeal... derived from virtue". [62] "The true altar of God is the thankful soul of the sage, compacted of perfect virtues". [63]

The pursuit of those virtues which purify the soul for sacrifice is something of which natural man using his free will is capable without the necessity of grace. [64] But Philo does admit the need for grace in some other respects.

---

[55] See the Loeb edition and translation of Philo edited by F.H. Colson *et al.* (London-Cambridge, Mass. 1929-62) for translated passages from *Legum Allegoriae* III, 7 and 13; *De Confusione Linguarum,* 114 . Cf. Bréhier, *Idées,* pp. 297ff. (See also Chapter VIII for other aspects of Bodin's use of Philo).

[56] Philo, *De Virtutibus,* 178ff. (Cf. Bréhier, *Idées,* pp. 302ff).

[57] For Philo's allegory of the rivers and trees of Eden as virtues see *De Opificio Mundi,* 154; *Legum Allegoriae,* I, 48-99.

[58] A. Laurentin, *Le Pneuma dans la doctrine de Philon* (Analecta Lovaniensia Biblica et Orientalia, ser. II, fasc. 25, Louvain-Bruges, 1952). Giblet, 'L'Homme image'. One of Philo's major allegories for the history of the soul is the *Song of Songs.*

[59] *Démonomanie,* f. 11. *Heptaplomeres,* ed. Noack, p. 146 (trs. Kuntz, p. 189), citing Philo on the sacrifice of *mentes puras.* See Chapter VIII, sections B and D.

[60] *De Specialibus Legibus,* I, 269. Cf. Bréhier, *Idées,* pp. 228f.

[61] *De Somniis,* II, 74.

[62] *De Specialibus Legibus,* I, 290.

[63] *Ibidem,* 287.

[64] Wolfson, *Philo,* I, 424-61 especially pp. 446 ff for the Jewish combination of "grace" and absolute free will. Laurentin, *Pneuma,* p. 422.

Grace is required for the original creation of the soul, for the revelation of God's purpose to man, and to give man *perfect* happiness. For the perfection of happiness accompanies only the ecstatic vision of God and that vision depends on God's granting an individual man the gift of the prophetic *pneuma* which is quite different from that of the soul. [65] This is precisely the mystical position adopted by Bodin in his treatment of illumination and the vision of God in the *Paradoxe* (as we shall see in Chapter V).

Philo sees in the progress of the virtuous man seeking happiness a series of stages, one of the major allegories for this natural history of the soul being the *Song of Songs* (as it was for Bodin). [66] These stages, which are also adopted by Bodin in the *Paradoxe,* begin with the direction of man to God by nature and reason; this is followed by the love and knowledge of God which culminates in the joy of the ecstatic vision of God. Philo's ecstasy, like Bodin's, is quite unlike that of Plato in that it is identified with the influx of the prophetic *pneuma* or spirit. [67] We shall see in the *Paradoxe* how closely Bodin follows these ideas. (There are also echoes of Philo in the discussion of ecstasy in the *Theatrum* but it should be noted that the ecstasy treated there is a "natural" ecstasy rather than an illuminated prophetic one:

> Car Philon Hébrieu interprète ainsi élégamment ces parolles de l'escripture Saincte: Et Abraham sortist avec toute sa substance: c'est à dire, qu'il s'en alla de son corps avec toute ses sciences et vertus.) [68]

Throughout their discussions of psychology and pneumatology Philo and Bodin resemble one another in their advocacy of a theory of the soul which appears to be naturalistic but is in fact at the same time deeply religious. So too does Bodin agree with Philo that morality becomes religion when the good man offers his soul purified by natural virtue as a sacrifice to God. [69]

Just as Philo had reconciled religious and natural elements in a Platonic guise, so Maimonides integrated the natural and the religious in a superficially Aristotelian framework. The main attraction of Maimonides for Bodin was his argument that natural philosophy was compatible with religion. Maimonides argued against the Aristotelian doctrines of necessity and the eternity of the

---

[65] Laurentin, *Pneuma,* p. 422. G. Verbecke, *L'Evolution de la doctrine du pneuma du Stoïcisme à Saint Augustin* (Paris-Louvain, 1945), p. 259. E. Vanderlinden, 'Les Diverses modes de connaissance de Dieu selon Philon d'Alexandrie', *Mélanges de science religieuse,* IV (1947), pp. 285-304, at p. 296. L. Feldman, *Scholarship on Philo and Josephus (1937-1962)* (Studies in Judaica, I, New York, 1963), p. 18. Bréhier, *Idées,* pp. 101ff.

[66] Vanderlinden, 'Diverses modes'. See the discussion below of the *Paradoxe.*

[67] Verbeke, *L'Evolution,* pp. 259f. Bréhier, *Idées,* pp. 196f.

[68] Bodin, *Théâtre* (Lyons, 1597), p. 730. *Theatrum* (Lyons, 1596), p. 506. The reference appears to be to Philo, *Legum Allegoriae,* II, 59 which cites Genesis XII, 1 instead of XII, 5 for the actual Biblical quotation. But the context is correct even if Bodin has slipped a little. Bodin here cites several authorities including Plato and Léon Hébreu but the only author whose views are almost completely compatible with Bodin's is Philo. P. Mesnard, 'The Psychology and Pneumatology of Jean Bodin', *International Philosophical Quarterly,* II (1962), 244-264, at p. 259, draws attention to the passage quoted but underestimates the importance of Philo and prefers to see Philoponus (p. 261) as the main influence on Bodin's pneumatology. (See Chapter VIII D).

[69] E.g. Bréhier, *Idées,* p. 229 and above.

universe and so preserved intact the omnipotent freedom of God to act as He will as creator. [70] In other respects too Maimonides proved congenial to Bodin, particularly for his theory of prophecy as infused spirit. [71] So also many parallels may be drawn between Maimonides' and Bodin's ideas of natural law as the result of a positive command of God. Maimonides rejected the notion that the Noachite laws and moral law were "natural" in the sense that they were founded on reason and both writers preferred to see moral laws, not as rational ideas, but rather as "propositions (*established by God*) which are known and require no proof for their truth". [72]

In keeping with his general approach to Aristotle Maimonides in the first instance accepted the Greek philosopher's view of virtue as a mean but quickly transformed it from a systematic principle into the Hebraic ideal of moderation in personal conduct. [73] Maimonides then departed further from Aristotle by asserting that free will to obey God's law led to salvation and he attempted to reconcile free will with Providence by arguing that Providence took men under its care and that its effect varied according to the moral condition of man. Without both free will and Providence, said Maimonides, "all the moral and intellectual virtues of man are destroyed". [74]

As in Jewish tradition Maimonides also identified virtue and charity with righteousness (*zedakah*). "When we walk in the way of virtue we act righteously towards our intellectual faculty and pay what is due to it. And because every virtue is thus *zedakah,* Scripture applies the term to the virtue of faith in God". [75] Like Bodin's theory of virtue Maimonides' was ultimately intellectual for it saw the height of virtue as the pure knowledge of God. This is clearly put in the last chapter of the *Guide for the Perplexed* where Maimonides describes the four perfections of man. Firstly there is acquisitive perfection which leads to wealth and property, and secondly, physical perfection resulting in health. The third perfection is moral, being that "highest degree of excellence in man's character" which promotes virtue. "But the fourth kind is the true perfection of man, the possession of the highest intellectual faculties; the possession of such notions which lead to true metaphysical opinions as regards

[70] M. Isnardi-Parente, 'Le Volontarisme de Jean Bodin: Maimonide ou Duns Scot?', in *Verhandlungen der internationalen Bodin Tagung in München,* ed. H. Denzer (Munich, 1973), pp. 39-51. P. Mesnard, 'Jean Bodin et le problème de l'éternité du monde', *Bulletin de l'Association Guillaume Budé,* ser. 3, v. I (1951), 117-131. (Bodin probably used the Latin version of the *Guide; Dux seu director dubitantium* (Paris, 1520).

[71] J. Guttmann, 'Jean Bodin in seinen Beziehungen des Judentums', *Monatsschrift für Geschichte und Wissenschaft des Judentums,* XLIX (1905), 315-348; 459-489, especially pp. 477-89. G. Roellenbleck, *Offenbarung, Natur und jüdische Überlieferung bei Jean Bodin* (Gütersloh, 1964), p. 121. See Chapter VIII.

[72] See M. Fox, 'Maimonides and Aquinas on Natural Law', in *Studies on Maimonides and St. Thomas Aquinas,* ed. J. Dienstag (New York, 1975), pp. 75-106, at pp. 85ff.

[73] D. Rosin, *Die Ethik des Maimonides* (Breslau, 1876).

[74] Maimonides, *Guide for the Perplexed,* trs. M. Friedländer (2nd ed., London, 1904), p. 288 (III, chapter 17). There is also an excellent translation by S. Pines, *The Guide of the Perplexed* (Chicago, 1963), marred unfortunately by a perverse introduction by L. Strauss which invents mysteries and deviousness where there are none. A good introduction to Maimonides is L. Roth, *The Guide for the Perplexed: Moses Maimonides* (London, 1948).

[75] *Guide,* trs. Friedländer, p. 393 (III, ch. 53).

God. With this perfection man has obtained his final object... Wisdom (*hokhma*) denotes the highest aim of man, knowledge of God". [76]

A somewhat less orthodox Judaism is represented by Léon l'Hébreu (Leone Ebreo, 1465-post 1521) whose *Dialoghi d'Amore* (first printed in Italian 1535) was even more strongly Platonised than were Philo's works. [77]   Through the fifteen editions of its French translation between 1551 and 1595 the *Dialoghi* exercised a major influence on French Platonism and moral thought and was well-known to Bodin. [78] Léon saw two roads to happiness, one the moral life and moral virtue, the other the cultivation of intellectual virtue leading to the knowledge of God. Active moral virtue had as a determining principle moderation and so might be understood in the light of the Aristotelian doctrine of the mean. But contemplative intellectual virtue was an extreme and not a mean.

> Bien est il vray (comme le confessent mesmes les Péripatétiques) que la cure et sollicitude des choses utiles, et le désir des délectables, en quelque sorte que ce soit, soit aux extrémitez de beaucoup et de peu, voir à la médiocrité est réputée pour vice à ceux qui suyvent la vie contemplative et intellectuelle, en laquelle consiste le comble de l'extreme félicité.... Tellement que quant à la vie Morale la vertu consiste en la médiocrité et milieu de l'utile et du délectable; et quant à la Contemplative, la vertu consiste en l'extrémité de peu. En la vie Morale les deux extrémitez sont vicieuses ; et en la Contemplative le trop est seulement vicieux. [79]

The highest goal of man is love of God and in Léon's religion love is the knowledge of God reached by the exercise of the intellectual virtues which include prudence and wisdom. [80]   Finally through illumination by the Active Intellect (apparently God Himself) man enjoys his highest happiness in the intellectual vision of God which comprehends His essence and permits a perfect union with God. [81]   Bodin, like Philo and Maimonides, would have thought this perfect knowledge of the divine essence together with actual union of the soul with God an impossibility for the human race, given the absolute transcendence of God. Léon's exaggerated Platonic mysticism indeed muted in a fundamental

[76] *Ibidem*, pp. 395f (III, ch. 54).

[77] Leone Ebreo, *Dialoghi d'Amore* (Rome, 1535), written in Italian ca. 1501-02. My references are to Léon l'Hébreu, *Dialogues de l'Amour. The French Translation attributed to Pontus de Tyard and published in Lyon 1551,* ed. T.A. Perry (Studies in Comparative Literature, 59, Chapel Hill, N. Carolina, 1974). Although some early editions of the *Dialoghi* claimed Léon as a convert to Christianity it seems rather that he remained Jewish. See C. Roth's introduction to Leone Ebreo, *The Philosophy of Love,* trs. F. Fredeberg and J.H. Barnes (London, 1937). In general see S. Damiens, *Amour et intellect chez Léon l'Hébreu* (Paris, 1971). W. Melczer, 'Platonisme et Aristotélisme dans la pensée de Léon l'Hébreu', in *Platon et Aristote à la Renaissance* (De Pétrarque à Descartes, 32, Paris, 1976), pp. 293-306.

[78] P. Mesnard, 'Le Platonisme de Jean Bodin', *Actes du Ve Congrès de l'Association Guillaume Budé* (Paris, 1954), pp. 352-361, for Bodin's knowledge of Léon. A.J. Festugière, *La Philosophie de l'amour de Marsile Ficin et son influence sur la littérature française au XVIe siècle* (Etudes de Philosophie Médiévale, 31, Paris, 1941). Cf. P.O. Kristeller, 'A Thomist Critique of Marsilio Ficino's Theory of Will and Intellect', in *Harry Austryn Wolfson Jubilee Volume* (Jerusalem, 1965), II, 463-494.

[79] Léon l'Hébreu, *Dialogues de l'Amour,* ed. Perry, p. 49.

[80] *Ibidem,* p. 57.

[81] *Ibidem,* p. 63. (Cf. Perry's introduction, p. 15). Damiens, *Amour,* p. 158, for the mystic union.

way his influence upon Bodin even though the latter approvingly quoted Léon's opinions given elsewhere in the *Dialoghi d'Amore* on the relationship of God and nature and on the problem of unity and diversity within the created universe. [82]

*
**

Enough has been said in passing in the course of this survey of Jewish ethics to justify regarding Bodin as one of the curious company of sixteenth-century "Judaisers". But two kinds of Judaising should be distinguished in the sixteenth century — that of Servetus who availed himself of Jewish concepts in order to reform and restore Christianity; [83] and that of Bodin who Judaised in order to weaken the claims of Christianity to be the sole (or at least the highest) true religion and to downgrade it to being merely one variation of positive religion — and one inferior to Judaism at that. [84] The differences between

[82] Mesnard, 'Platonisme' and Isnardi-Parente, 'Volontarisme', to my mind seem to exaggerate the influence of Léon while under-estimating that of Philo as a Platonic influence on Bodin. (For Léon love was the principle defining the relationship between the Creator and His creation.)

[83] L.I. Newman, *Jewish Influence on Christian Reform Movements* (New York, 1925). F. Secret, 'Un Cheval de Troie dans l'Eglise de Christ: La Kabbale Chrétienne', in *Aspects du Libertinisme*, ed. de Boisset and Stegmann, pp. 153-166 ter. J. Friedman, 'The Reformation and Jewish Anti-Christian Polemics', *Bibliothèque d'Humanisme et Renaissance*, XLI (1979), 83-97.

On Servetus see now J. Friedman, 'Michael Servetus. The Case for a Jewish Christianity', *Sixteenth Century Journal*, IV (1973), 87-110. Idem, *Michael Servetus. A Case Study in Total Heresy* (Travaux d'Humanisme et Renaissance, 163, Geneva, 1978). R.H. Bainton, *Hunted Heretic. The Life and Death of Michael Servetus (1511-53)* (Boston, 1953). The Judaising charges against Servetus are to be found in *Registres de la Compagnie des Pasteurs de Genève au temps de Calvin*, ed. R.M. Kingdon, J.-F. Bergier and A. Dufour (Geneva, 1962-), II.

Judaism represented for Servetus a liberation from the tyranny of Christian Trinitarian concepts about the Godhead. Servetus felt that traditional Christianity lacked the proper terminology for expressing his modalist ideas which saw God as a unity of substance while accepting the Son and the Holy Spirit as adjectives, aspects or modes of the Father. These divine modes vary according to the Father's expression; for instance in creating He expresses himself as the Holy Spirit, in redeeming as the Son. But these modes being adjectival are non-eternal and non-substantial and hence are alien to traditional Christian thinking which sees the Holy Spirit and Christ as substantial.

As far as I can discover Bodin does not mention Servetus' name in any of his works. But he did condemn the Judaising of Pico and the Hermetists for having perverted the Cabala to magical ends. (*Démonomanie*, I, Ch. 5). Bodin was quite ready to admit the Cabala understood religiously and morally as a guide to divine justice as is revealed by his praise of the *Zohar* in *Démonomanie*, f. 66, quoted above in footnote 54. (Curiously enough Servetus, like Bodin, used Philo as a bridge between philosophy and religion. See Friedman, *Servetus*, p. 55).

For the Judaising of a later reader of the *Heptaplomeres* see K. Cohen, *The Throne and the Chariot. Studies in Milton's Hebraism* (The Hague, 1975). Miss Cohen does not seem to be aware that Milton owned a copy of the *Heptaplomeres* but see L.I. Bredvold, 'Milton and Bodin's *Heptaplomeres*', *Studies in Philosophy*, XXI (1924), 399-402.

[84] On Bodin's Judaising see C.R. Baxter, 'Jean Bodin's Daemon and his Conversion to Judaism', in *Verhandlungen der Bodin Tagung*, ed. Denzer, pp. 1-21. P. Mesnard, 'Jean Bodin et la critique de la morale d'Aristote', *Revue Thomiste*, LVII (1949), 542-562 at pp. 558ff. F. Bezold, 'Jean Bodin als Okkultist und seine *Démonomanie*', *Historische Zeitschrift*, CV (1910), 1-64 at pp. 50ff. Roellenbleck, *Offenbarung*. Guttmann, 'Bodin in seinen Beziehungen des Judentums'. H. Busson, *Le Rationalisme dans la littérature française de la Renaissance (1533-1601)* (2nd ed., Paris, 1957), pp. 550ff.

these two currents is summed up perhaps in the contrasting attitudes of the Judaisers towards the Jews: Pico and Servetus sought to convert the Jews, Bodin did not.

The bite of Bodin's critique of Christianity comes across most incisively in the speeches of the Jew Salomon in the sixth book of the *Heptaplomeres*. Salomon seeks to put an end to pages of theological wrangling over the nature of redemption by stating bluntly that the whole notion of original sin is a Christian fiction.

> All this discussion about the original Fall, which I think is no Fall, has its beginning in the leaders of the Christian religion.... They established that the sin of Adam which resided in himself was propagated into infinite posterity and for this sin eternal punishments which bind all are due. Hence the seeds of errors began to creep far and wide through men's minds, because they decided that all mankind had been corrupted by that Fall of uncleanness so that no one could do or even think rightly nor obtain any part of justice. [85]

Salomon prefers instead to understand the Fall as an "elegant and divine allegory", a parable of punishment and repentance leading to salvation (an interpretation openly derived from Philo's *Legum Allegoriae*).

> Thus it happens that even if we wander from the straight path and immerse ourselves in the filth and defilement of pleasures, finally we at some time rise up from the filth and return to the straight path of salvation... God did not henceforth condemn Adam to eternal death. [86]

Since original sin presents no impediment, free will, insists Salomon, is sufficient to achieve salvation.

> Moses in the assembly of the people ... said: "Choose life that you may live...." Why would the people choose life if they had been destined for eternal punishment, or if they had no power for choosing salvation (*salutis potestas*)? [87]

---

[85] *Heptaplomeres*, ed. Noack, p. 306 (trs. p. 404): "Tota haec disputatio de originis labe, quae nulla esse mihi videtur, a primoribus christianae religionis initium duxit ... posuerunt, Adami peccatum, quod in ipso resedit, in infinitam posteritatem propagari eique poenas sempiternas deberi, quibus omnes in solidum tenerentur. Haec errorum semina longe lateque per hominum mentes serpere coeperunt, quia totum hominem ista contagionis labe corruptum fuisse judicabant, ut nec recte quisquam agere ac ne cogitare quidem, aut ullam justitiae partem posset adipisci." For Jewish ideas in this work see Roellenbleck, *Offenbarung*, pp. 97-113. In general Jewish polemicists regarded original sin as inconsistent with God's justice. The concept of original sin was not entirely foreign to Judaism but even those who did admit it believed that man's free will was sufficient with divine "aid" to achieve redemption. (This was similar to Bodin's view of divine "aid" and free will in the *Paradoxe*. See Chapter V). See D.J. Lasker, *Jewish Philosophical Polemics Against Christianity in the Middle Ages* (New York, 1977), pp. 107, 226f.

[86] *Heptaplomeres*, ed. Noack, p. 306 (trs. p. 405): "Sic nobis accidit, eum aberrantes a recta via, in sordibus ac coeno libidinum immersi, tandem aliquando emergimus et in rectam salutis viam regredimur. Ac tametsi Deus Adamo ... non praeterea tamen aeterna morte damnavit."

[87] *Ibidem*, pp. 314ff (trs. p. 415): "Moses enim, coacta populi concione, contestatus est coelum ac terram, se populo vitam et mortem proposuisse. Elige, inquit, vitam, ut vivas .... Ad quid populus vitam eligeret, si ad sempiternum supplicium destinatus esset, aut si nullam eligendae salutis potestatem haberet?"

... Isaiah shows that each one must be content with his own situation which was granted to him by God, since the door of salvation lies open to every age, to every order, to every sex, since God embraces not only men, whom He placed in charge of the world, but also all creatures, with supreme love ... Moses Rambam (Maimonides), in the letter which he wrote against the astrologers, said: "All the theologians confirm that man has a will free for salvation." [88]

When the question turns from salvation to justification Salomon is equally destructive of Christian theology.

> That justice is obtained for any mortal by Christ's death or cruelty towards Him, is so far removed from the truth that this Christian belief is most distant from true religion (*vera religione*). Very close to this error is the fact that all Christian and Agarenian theologians think that justification is possible from acts of virtues or faith or both, not only among men but also with immortal God... God clearly says: "No one of the living shall be justified before me" (Psalm 53). [89]

In Salomon's eyes the Christian argument about justification is misconceived. For man to be justified he would have to be as pure as God. It is not original sin but rather the transcendent goodness of God which renders justification impossible and indeed meaningless.

> If Adam had remained in his God-given integrity and innocence as great as is possible in man, he would not even for that reason be considered just before God... If no one is upright, if nothing is pure, nothing clean, if the sun itself and the angels who are closest to the divinity of immortal God are not bright, that whole discussion about the justification of man, whether it stems from faith or honourable actions or both, or from the grace of God alone, is completely empty, since justification cannot belong to man. [90]

In place of the Christian idea of justification Salomon presents the Jewish Philonic notion of "blessedness" or beatitude (viz. "happiness").

> I grant that no one is made just by actions, no matter how worthy they may be, much less by an empty belief in a dead Jesus. Rather each man is blessed (*beari*) by eternal God according to honourable actions, and the more justly and

---

[88] *Ibidem*, p. 317 (trs. 418): "Hoc enim sermone Esaias docet. sua quemque conditione, divinitus sibi concessa, contentum esse oportere. At cum omni aetati, omni ordini, omni sexui patet porta salutis, quoniam non tantum homines, quos orbi terrarum praefecit, verum etiam creaturas omnes, complectitur summa caritate .... Moses Rambam in epistola, quam adversus astrologos scripsit: Omnes, inquit, theologi confirmant, hominem liberum salutis arbitrium habere."

[89] *Ibidem*, p. 322 (trs. p. 424): "Ac tantum abest, ut supplicio Christi aut crudelitate erga eum justitia mortali cuiquam parta sit, ut ea fide Christianorum quam longissime a vera religione discedatur. Huic errori proximum est, quod omnes theologi Christiani et Agareni actionibus virtutum aut fide aut utrisque justificari posse opinantur, non modo apud homines, sed etiam apud Deum immortalem.... Sed ut Deus ... clara voce contestatur: Nemo viventium, inquit, coran me justificabitur."

[90] *Ibidem*, p. 323 (trs. p. 425): "At ne Adamus quidem, si in collata sibi divinitus integritate ac innocentia, quanta maxima in homine esse potest, perstitisset, propterea justus apud Deum haberetur. Deus solus, inquit ille, justus est, ac praeter eum alius nemo. Si nemo integer, nihil purum, nihil mundum, non sol ipse, non angeli, qui proxime ad immortalis Dei numen accedunt, nitidi sunt, tota illa de hominis justiifcatione disputatio, an a fide pendeat, an vero ab actionibus honestis, an ab utrisque, an etiam ab unius Dei gratia plane inanis est, cum in hominem justificatio cadere non potest."

honourably each man has lived, the more blessed (*beatiorem*) and the more pleasing he will be to immortal God.

All creatures and indeed all demons are blessed more or less in accordance with the goodness of the giver or the capacity of the deceiver or the unworthiness of him who rejects the abundant light brought to them. Indeed it is one thing to be blessed, another to be justified. Christian theologians have confused these issues or understood them too little, and in this discussion they have produced serious obscurities and errors. For if no one except the just is blessed, no one would ever be blessed. Yet all creatures are blessed, although no one is justified, and none is free from stain or impurity. [91]

In these passages we find Bodin unabashedly voicing Jewish attitudes towards Christianity — he rejects belief in original sin (though accepting human impurity compared to the pureness of God), denies Christ to be the redeemer, and regards as misconceived the theological virtues and the Gospel's idea of grace.

But the question then arises: do the views put into Salomon's mouth in the *Heptaplomeres* faithfully represent what Bodin himself believed? [92] Here we encounter the fundamental problem of how to interpret any work written in dialogue form such as the *Heptaplomeres*. Of course the vision of true religion unfolded in this work comprises all the religions of the participants, but if Salomon's charges against Christian theology are allowed to stand then they effectively destroy a great deal of the essence of Christianity and certainly discredit the claim of Christianity to be the highest expression of religious truth. Salomon indeed seems to have the last word and it is a word which Bodin does little to qualify. Yet how can Bodin's sympathy with the Jewish position be demonstrated in a conclusive manner?

Since the ambiguities of dialogue and colloquy form are notorious the best way out of the dilemma may well be to resort to external controls. One way of settling the question would be to examine Bodin's published works — particularly the *Paradoxe* — and discover whether they contradict the Jewish ideas of the *Heptaplomeres*. For obvious reasons one would not expect to see in these published writings any openly pro-Jewish critique of Christianity; the treatment of Servetus would have deterred Bodin from such rashness. But if the general structure of thought in the *Paradoxe* and Bodin's other writings corresponds to that of Salomon's Judaism and if the *Paradoxe*, while not overtly

---

[91] *Ibidem*, pp. 324f (trs. p. 427): "Concedo illud, ex actionibus, quantaecunque sint dignitatis, justum fieri neminem, multo minus ex inani credulitate in Jesum mortuum, sed ex honestis actionibus ab aeterno Deo quemque beari, et quo quis justius et honestius vixerit, eo beatiorem et immortali Deo fore gratiorem. Omnes enim creaturae ac daemones quoque beantur plus minusve pro largientis effusa bonitate, aut suscipientis capacitate, aut respuentis oblatam lucis affluentiam indignitate. Aliud est enim beari, aliud justificari, quae, a theologis christianis confusa aut parum perspecta, graves in has disputatione tam obscuritates quam errores pepererunt. Nam si nulli nisi justi bearentur, nemo bearetur unquam. At omnes creaturae beantur, nulla tamen justificatur, nulla tamen caret immunditia ac impuritate." For "happiness" see below Chapter V, section b.

[92] The problem of the sincerity of the Jewish arguments in the *Heptaplomeres* is raised — but not resolved — by Busson, *Rationalisme*, pp. 552ff.

Roellenbleck, *Offenbarung*, properly integrates the text with the published *Theatrum*.

One should remember that Bodin had published elsewhere hints as to his Jewish sympathies, e.g. *Methodus*, ed. Mesnard, p. 253A (trs. 363): "It may seem even more remarkable that from the Jews flow as from a fountain all the religions which are accepted by the whole world." (See Chapter VIII).

supporting Jewish ideas, nevertheless does not contradict or condemn them, then one has good reason to believe that Bodin's apparent inclination to Judaised concepts in the *Heptaplomeres* was indeed true and real. I hope to show in the following chapter that in the *Paradoxe* the Jewish opinions of Salomon appear in a muted form which may apparently soften the cutting edge of their refutation of Christianity but does not by any means weaken their force. [93]

[93] For the Judaising tendency of the *Theatrum, Démonomanie* and Bodin's other writings see Chapter VI. References may also be found in Roellenbleck, *Offenbarung*, pp. 92-113, and U. Lange, *Untersuchungen zu Bodins Démonomanie* (Frankfurt, 1970), pp. 77-91.

CHAPTER V

THE JUDAISED ETHICS OF THE "PARADOXE"

> Everything requires God's help. Even with free choice the grace of God is necessary. Even free will is mercy.
>
> I.B. Singer, *The Estate.*

The civil wars of the last decades of the sixteenth century were critical for the development both of Bodin's religious and his political ideas. Distressed like the Neo-Stoics by the mounting disasters of war Bodin had sought to understand the reason for these afflictions of France and concluded that the wars were in essence a divine punishment for moral and religious evil, a working out of divine justice. It was a common hope among many of Bodin's Christian Neo-Stoic contemporaries that such moral and physical evil might be remedied by men themselves through the cultivation of ethics and true religion so as to avert God's chastisement.[1]

For this reason Bodin's *Paradoxe* is not, as it might seem, an escape from war and politics into the abstract realms of philosophy. It is rather an attempt to comprehend the current problems of war and politics by investigating the moral and religious constants of human nature.[2] Politics, as it were, is merely the superstructure of morality and religion. We might therefore say that Bodin's *Paradoxe*, far from being escapist philosophising, is a search for the foundations

---

[1] Paul Lawrence Rose, 'The Politique and the Prophet: Bodin and the Catholic League 1589-94', *The Historical Journal*, XXI (1978), 783-808 (cf. Chapter IX below). See also Pierre Bellier's dedication to his French translation of Philo (*Les Œuvres de Philon Juif* (Paris, 1575)) for the theme of war as God's retribution for blasphemy (reprinted in English in E.R. Goodenough, *The Politics of Philo Judaeus* (New Haven, 1938), pp. 121ff).

For other reactions to the wars see above and R. Bady, *L'Homme et son Institution de Montaigne à Bérulle (1580-1625)* (Paris, 1964), passim. C. Vivanti, *Lotta politica e pace religiosa in Francia fra cinque e seicento* (Turin, 1963). C.R. Baxter, 'Problems of the Religious Wars', in *French Literature and its Background*, ed. J .Cruickshank (Oxford, 1968), I. 166-185.

[2] See Chapter II.

of politics and represents the culmination of those tendencies which we have seen adumbrated in the discussion of virtue in the first chapter of the *République*.

First published in Latin in 1596 it might seem that the *Paradoxe* was written after the civil wars had more or less come to a halt; the Latin version (*Paradoxon*) was published in 1596 and followed two years later by a French translation (*Paradoxe*) done by Bodin himself from which most of the citations in this description have been drawn. [4] (There was a further French translation entitled *Paradoxes* done by Claude de Magdaillan in 1604.) [5] But the fact is that Bodin had been at work on the *Paradoxon* at the height of the civil war and had finished it in August 1591. This we know from the colophon to Bodin's Latin *Paradoxon* which was not retained in his French translation.

> Hunc libellum flagrante Gallia civili bello scripsit Ioannes Bodinus Regius apud Veromanduos Procurator A.D. III. Cal. Septembr. anno M.D.XCI. [6]

In the preface to the Latin edition of 1596 (also subsequently omitted from his French version) the urgency of Bodin's awareness of the evil of civil war and of the need for spiritual and moral repentance comes across strongly. Bodin saw from the first that the war concealed a multitude of quarrels — between the soldiers and the plebs, the people and the clerics, the clerics and the nobles, the nobles and the magistrates and so forth — and that this would make the conflict a protracted and a deadly one. Some had even said (remarked Bodin) that God had deserted man and that all was in the hands of fortune but this was the greatest impiety and contumely towards God imaginable, for God rules over a moral universe in which war represents His retribution for evil acts. God indeed now occupies the tribunal of justice which has so disgracefully been abandoned by the princes and He enquires not only into crimes committed but also those hidden in the hearts of the wicked. And the punishment is harsh. Flourishing cities are now gone from luxury to madness; dogs and viscera are eaten and many are the deaths inflicted by plague and sword, fire and massacre. Then, in counterpoint to this gloomy theme of war as divine vengeance, Bodin announces the motif of moral philosophy.

> Since I saw that no place remained for either city magistrates or military discipline, I have betaken myself from legal studies to this genre of writing, in order that if I might avail less in writing laws and giving judgments I might publish something for the shaping of men's morals. I have done this the more willingly not only because age weighs upon me and I have thought this peaceful manner of writing more suitable for my years, but also because of all the disciplines

---

[3] Jean Bodin, *Paradoxon quod nec virtus ulla in mediocritate nec summum hominis bonum in virtutis actione consistere possit* (Dionysius Duvallius, Paris, 1596).

[4] *Le Paradoxe de Jean Bodin Angevin qu'il n'y a pas une seule vertu en médiocrité, ny au milieu de deux vices. Traduit de Latin en François et augmenté en plusieurs lieux* (Denys du Val, Paris, 1598). Bodin's own translation according to p. 99: "Cet œuvre a esté achevé de traduire par l'autheur le second jour de Janvier 1596."

[5] *Paradoxes de M. J. Bodin, doctes et excellents discours de la vertu... traduit du Latin en François par Claude de Magdaillan* (T. Du Bray, Paris, 1604).

[6] *Paradoxon* (1596), p. 100. P. Mesnard, 'Jean Bodin et la critique de la morale d'Aristote', *Revue Thomiste*, LVII (1949), 542-562, at p. 543 slipped in dating the composition of the *Paradoxon* to 1594.

none is more profitable or fruitful than that which concerns the virtues and the ends of goods and ills, yet at the same time none is less understood or explained. [7]

The juxtaposition in the preface of the twin themes of war and moral philosophy should warn one off the temptation to see in the succession of Bodin's writings a shift from an "active" political attitude to a "contemplative" religious disposition. Bodin's religious and moral convictions remained strong from his early writings until his death and so too did his resolution that religious and moral values must be applied to the active world of politics. To attempt to discern a radical change from the active to the contemplative in Bodin's character in his later years is to lose sight of the steadiness with which he defended the connection between religion, moral philosophy and politics throughout his career. [8]

Far from being the confused and amorphous compilation which some commentators have found it, the *Paradoxe* is a well-constructed treatise which falls into five main sections. After some introductory material the first main section discusses the problem of good and evil and divine justice (pp. 6-15). The second section comprises a series of distinctions between the sovereign good, the end and good of man, and the happiness of man — distinctions worked out at considerable length as forming the basic structure of Bodin's moral philosophy. For Bodin moral philosophy (which deals with those virtues attainable by man's free will) is quite separate from theology which treats of prophecy and illuminated virtue. Nevertheless, for all its lying within the boundaries of nature Bodin's moral philosophy is a thoroughly *religious* subject, embodying an ethics which is at once natural and religious. These two categories — the natural and the religious — may seem antithetical to modern eyes but Bodin was working with a set of Judaised categories peculiarly his own; the fact that Bodin's categories mix apparently conflicting concepts has proved disconcerting to both Christian and secular theorists who have generally taken his thinking to be hopelessly confused rather than recognising the logical consistency it assumes when read in Judaised terms.

Relying on his armoury of Judaised categories Bodin enters into a fundamental discussion of the roles of grace and free will in the achievement of virtue and reaches conclusions remote from Christian understanding. Divine light is needed for man to receive the gift of prophecy and the supernatural mystic love and vision of God associated with the prophetic spirit. These "theological virtues" — supernatural knowledge, love, joy and vision — are all the result of divine illumination and beyond the capability of human free will.

---

[7] *Paradoxon* (1596), p. 5: "Cùm autem ne magistratibus urbanis ullum nec militari disciplinae locum relinqui viderem, me à forensibus literis ad hoc scriptionis genus contuli, ut si minùs legibus scribendis ac iudiciis exercendis possem, moribus hominum conformandis utcunq. prodessem: quòd eò libentius feci, quod cùm aetas ingrauescat iam mea, tranquillum hoc scribendi genus huic aetati aptius esse existimavi, tum etiam quòd ex omnibus disciplinis nulla magis frugifera ac fructuosa quam quae est de virtutibus ac finibus bonorum ac malorum, nulla tamen minus cognita minusque explicata mihi visa est."

[8] Bodin's firm belief that the active and contemplative worlds were inexplicably connected is evident in the *Oratio* and the *Methodus* (e.g., *Œuvres*, I, p. 120A; trs. Reynolds, p. 30.)

But all other virtues, including wisdom and the non-mystical love of God, may be attained by that free will rooted in human nature and without divine illumination. In this thoroughly Judaised discussion Bodin depicts a universe that is at the same time moral and natural; free will is seen as part of the order of nature (pp. 15-44).

In the third section we come to an investigation of the particular virtues and vices with emphasis on their natural origin. Here Aristotle's doctrine of the mean is refuted together with his division between moral and intellectual virtues. The extensive critique of Aristotle here is grounded on Judaised concepts of intellect and will. All virtue is redefined as intellectual and yet is subject to Bodin's Judaised free will which is naturally capable of generating virtue by commanding the intellect to seek the good. We are indeed a long way from either Greek or Christian ethics (pp. 45-64).

The fourth section proposes a group of prudential virtues comprising prudence, magnanimity, temperance and justice. Although prudence acts theoretically like an "intellectual' virtue Bodin's argument reveals that he regards it in effect as a "moral" virtue. But by "moral" Bodin does not mean that prudence is a moral virtue in Aristotelian terms; for Bodin's "moral" virtue has taken on an entirely novel Judaised significance in which the will and the intellect act together to produce a species of natural virtue which combines elements of the moral and the intellectual (pp. 65-88).

In the final section Bodin (pp. 88-99) discusses wisdom and charity or love of God as the highest natural virtues in his scheme. He first refutes the Christian concept of theological virtue which made charity together with faith and hope supernatural virtues depending exclusively on infusion by divine grace. Then Bodin explains how there is indeed often some divine aid involved for God, in granting the good prayerful man charity, draws or snatches him (ravir) closer to Himself. Bodin's conceptions of charity and the character of the divine aid "without which charity is *almost* impossible" are both completely Judaised, although this is obscured by his mystical vocabulary here. But *ravissement* is not the same as the *illumination* discussed in the second section. *Illumination* pertains to the receipt of prophecy and the higher mystical love and vision of God which is wholly God's gift and independent of man's will. *Ravissement* on the other hand lies mostly within the domain of man's will because if a man willingly prays to God then God will draw him near; thus will the worshipper acquire wisdom or the natural love of God which is charity. This is essentially a Solomonic idea of charity or wisdom and one radically opposed to Christian charity. Needless to say Bodin in a published work could not be frank in his Judaised refutation of Christianity but still the directness of his criticisms of the traditional concept of theological virtue is for the period very startling indeed.

Why was this not recognised as stark heresy at the time? Possibly because of the smokescreen created by Bodin's rather opaque discussion of *ravissement*. A trusting reader might well have assumed that by this term Bodin really meant infusion by grace and might have been able to reconcile Bodin's admittedly curious remarks with the Thomist position on good works and grace (pp. 88-99).

To any reader unaware of Bodin's Judaised orientation the whole of the *Paradoxe* might indeed be taken for a blurred, confused and idiosyncratic attack from some strange sort of Christian viewpoint on Aristotle's ethics; and no doubt Bodin hoped that the polemic against Aristotle would conceal the far more radical undercurrent of the book. Certainly the work is very much a *Paradoxe* in the sense paradox has of being a contradiction of received opinion, in this case the Aristotelian opinions that virtue consists in moderation, that virtue is a mean between two vices, and that the sovereign good of man depends on the action of virtue. At the same time the falsely Christian aura is enhanced by well-placed references to Scriptural and patristic authority in the text and margins, admirably chosen to allay the incipient anxieties of any Christian reader. Yet any Christian (or for that matter secular) reader who fails to recognise Bodin's Judaising strategy is sure to come away from reading the *Paradoxe* with the conviction that Bodin was a hopelessly confused moral philosopher who repeatedly contradicts himself in his exposition of Christian moral theology. Indeed, read as a "Christian" treatise the *Paradoxe* contains the most absurd errors on grace, free will and virtue (as some of its less perceptive critics in recent times have been delighted to point out). [9]

a) Good and Evil in the Moral Universe

What is the good, asks Bodin? "It is that which is profitable or useful to whomever has the enjoyment of it". What is the greatest good? "That which is the most useful and the most necessary to every creature which may be imagined — it is God from whom all the sources of good issue and nothing evil... good in Himself and alone good". And to give a Christian gloss to this statement Bodin quotes in the margin Matthew, XIX, 17: "Why callest thou me good? There is none good but one, that is, God". [10] Bodin characteristically suppresses the Hebraic ending of the verse: "but if thou wilt enter into life, keep the commandments". It will readily be seen that Bodin has here quoted one of the "Jewish" verses of the New Testament which tends to weaken the Christian interpretation of Christ as God and whose unquoted continuation alludes to the Deuteronomic injunction to choose life and salvation through obedience of the commandments of God.

Again, when it comes to defining evil Bodin, rather than quoting a Jewish source, makes obeisance to a Church Father: "The definition of evil as due to

---

[9] Among those critics who have failed to understand the Judaised character of the *Paradoxe* the most notable is T.N. Tentler, 'The Meaning of Prudence in Bodin', *Traditio*, XV (1959), 365-384, whose entire analysis seems to me to be without value as a result. Cf. also R. Chauviré, *Jean Bodin, auteur de la République* (Paris, 1914), p. 95.

Mesnard, 'Bodin critique d'Aristote', pp. 558-62, on the other hand saw how radically different was the *Paradoxe* from Christian moral philosophy and theology and recognised its Judaised structure. But in maintaining that it followed "un ordre très subtil et fort Platonicien" (p. 545) Mesnard somewhat underrated the influence in this work of Philo, Maimonides and traditional Jewish ethics — and consequently of the Jewish aspects of Bodin's concept of grace. See below for details.

[10] *Paradoxe* (1598), p. 6.

the privation of good is owed to St. Augustine".[11] (Philo might have been a more authentic allusion.)[12] Aristotle was mistaken that evil was a contrary principle to good and also erred in thinking the good to be finite, evil infinite and evil to proceed from matter. If evil were an actual principle, argues Bodin, then a thing or man might be good and evil at the same time, thus giving rise to a contradiction of nature. But more importantly "God the author and inexhaustible source of all good would be the cause of all evil — an idea which ought not to enter the man of man". Murderers are according to Bodin evil in so far as they depart farther than others from the sovereign good: evil has no essence or substance or place in nature and hence cannot stem from matter which is "created by God and participates in his goodness". Again, if evil were infinite and good finite as Aristotle held, then God would be overcome by evil and "His finite bounty extinguished and exhausted and the order of the universe overturned". Against this impiety Bodin quotes the sapiential books of the Old Testament to the effect that malice will never exceed goodness, the sovereign good being so great and powerful that it defeats evil. As to the Manichaean opinion that evil was a rival principle or power, Bodin observes that it "is no less impious than absurd." The universe could hardly exist in a contest between two equal and opposed principles. God has established an accord between the heavens and the angels by His infinite power (*Paradoxe,* pp. 8-11).

Deprivation of God's goodness is the fundamental explanation of physical evil: "We see ruination, calamities, wars and mortalities occurring when God withdraws His bounty". But in an effort to explain the actual mechanics whereby the withdrawal of divine favour brings about war and disaster Bodin now invokes the demonological machinery familiar to us from his other writings. God has set up guardian angels to tend to cities, families and individuals. Subordinate to the angels are the demons "which derive their essence from God, reason and will and are not bad in their own nature". Nevertheless while God produces and conserves, demons destroy. "The duty of demons (*diables*) is to damage, ruin and corrupt by means of war, plague and famine". But in doing this work they always require the express command of God or the celestial powers. "In this way even calamities, plagues and famines are good and useful inasmuch as they proceed from the will and justice of God. Indeed the most dangerous threat God may make to men is to say that He will no longer punish them" (*Paradoxe,* pp. 12 f). (Little wonder that Bodin saw the League Wars of the 1590's as divine retribution, as "religious wars" in the deepest sense).[13]

These positive instructions from God to the demons to work evil might seem to contradict Bodin's basic premise that evil is simply the privation of good. But in fact the demons are a necessary logical link between the withdrawal of divine favour and the production of physical evil. If Bodin had subscribed to the Christian doctrine of original sin there would have been no

---

[11] *Ibidem.*

[12] Philo stresses repeatedly that only good can come from God. Cf. E.R. Goodenough, *By Light, Light* (New Haven, 1935; rep. 1969), pp. 53f.

[13] See Rose, 'The Politique and the Prophet'. And below, Chapter VIII.

need for the demons since man's own naturally evil inclinations would have been sufficient to produce war and misery. It is because of Bodin's Judaised concept of man as free from original sin that he was obliged to invent the avenging demons and inflictors of evil. Moreover, in Bodin's mind there was no contradiction of divine omnipotence involved since he was clear that God's just anger came first as the moving principle, while the ensuing creation of evil through the demons was merely a matter of the mechanics of punishment rather than amounting to a conception of evil as an independent principle. There is, it might be suggested, a close resemblance between Bodin's ideas and the theodicy of Leibniz in that both seem to regard evil as a disguised variation of good. (Curiously enough although Leibniz as a young man refuted the *Heptaplomeres* he came in later life to have a high opinion of the work.) [14]

Bodin's explanation of good and evil constructed a vision of the relationship of God and creation expressed in his formula "the Great God of Nature". In Bodin's moral universe, governed by divine justice and ordered in universal harmony, war and suffering exist but they are not intrinsic to nature. War is rather the result of divine retribution for human disobedience, a punishment administered through the agency of demons. What is intrinsic to nature is not evil but rather decay and degeneration. In nearly all of Bodin's writings, particularly the *Theatrum,* one finds the notion of the conserving power of God as legislator set against the natural degenerative tendency of the universe and society; the order of the world depends on an all-powerful, benevolent God, the [Great God of Nature. Yet even if degeneration is intrinsic to nature, it is not in itself evil and it is in this respect that Bodin departs from a great deal both of Greek and Christian thought.

b) Moral Philosophy, Religion and Theology: Judaised "Grace" and Free Will in the Moral and Natural Universe

The next section of the *Paradoxe* (pp. 15-44) consists of an attempt to define the subject of moral philosophy and is pursued through successive definitions of the sovereign good of all things, the end of man, the good of man and the happy life. These distinctions, far from being senseless as some critics have alleged, are designed to preserve the disciplinary separation of moral philosophy from theology while at the same time putting forward a view of moral philosophy which is essentially religious. [15]

Aristotle and Aquinas had treated the end and good of man as identical. But Bodin's separation of moral philosophy from theology demands he distinguish between end and good. The end of man (which must lie outside man) is the glory of God, while the good of man consists in his leading a happy

---

[14] G.E. Guhrauer, *Das Heptaplomeres des Jean Bodin* (Berlin, 1841), pp. lxxxff.

[15] Tentler, 'Prudence in Bodin', p. 373, entirely misses the point of this section and finds Bodin's critical distinctions to be without "meaning" and animated solely by a desire to be combative towards Aristotle. Contrast Mesnard, "Bodin critique", pp. 547ff, who grasps Bodin's strategy.

life. The glory of God, indeed, is the end of all created things, just as God Himself is the sovereign good (*Paradoxe,* pp. 15-17). Armed with these definitions Bodin is able to make a formal separation between moral philosophy (which has as its subject not the happy man himself, but "l'homme disposé à recevoir la félicité humaine") and theology whose subject is the sovereign good, God Himself (pp. 19 f). [16]

It might seem that in so separating moral philosophy from theology Bodin is introducing an ethics which is wholly secular or natural. But he now starts to sketch an intrinsically religious theory of moral philosophy, arguing that virtue entails obedience of God's commands and that happiness is a supernatural gift bestowed by God. While virtue lies within the natural power of man, happiness does not. Happiness may be "le souverain bien de l'homme", and "le plus grand et dernier bien" but it is not to be acquired by man's freely-willed actions and remains therefore outside the ambit of Bodin's domain of moral philosophy. This emerges from Bodin's discussion of "le souverain bien de l'homme": "(Cela gît) en une trèslongue et trèsheureuse vie", says Bodin, quickly adding that *vie* is not to be taken in the sense of our earthly life alone but rather to mean both the present and future life as the Hebrew usage of *hayyim* or *lives* indicates (p. 21). And what makes for a happy life? "C'est le plus grand plaisir et plus durable de tous". This resides not in physical pleasure but rather "en la pleine et parfaite jouissance de la plus belle et plus excellente chose de toutes, qui est la fruition de Dieu, qui ne se peut avoir que par réflexion; en cela gît la plus grande félicité humaine" (p. 23).

Bodin cannot emphasise enough that this divinely granted happiness, this sovereign good of man, is not the subject of moral philosophy. Bodin cannot admit it as such because to do so would wreck his Judaised conception of moral philosophy as being rooted in righteousness and free will; if happiness were indeed the subject of moral philosophy then man's free will would have nothing to do with moral philosophy — an unthinkable horror for Bodin. We may now begin to see the point of Bodin's apparently sterile insistence that the subject of moral philosophy is not happiness itself or the happy man, but rather the readying of man to receive happiness, a self-readying that depends on the exercise of free will.

Man's own natural power of free will suffices, according to Bodin, to dispose him to receive happiness which is God's gracious gift alone; he does this by obeying the commands of God and leading a virtuous life. [17] Such preparation by and for virtue constitutes the realm of moral philosophy. Happiness itself, however, is a purely religious and even theological concept, identical, as will emerge, with the gift of prophecy and the vision of God. And from Bodin's other writings we know that he believed that while man's natural free will is critical for the obedience of God's laws and the pursuit of virtue, it is quite unavailing in the procurement of prophecy and the divine vision. In sum, ethics and virtue lie within man's natural grasp, but happiness is a

---

[16] More tersely phrased in the *Paradoxon* (p. 20) and the *Heptaplomeres* as *homo beandus.* See Chapters III, note 23 and VII, note 7.

[17] As Philo also believes. Cf. S. Sandmel, *Philo of Alexandria. An Introduction* (Oxford and New York, 1979), p. 101.

supernatural gift of God. We have arrived now at a starting-point for a discussion of will and grace which is thoroughly Judaised in character and has little to do with grace in the Christian sense of the term (pp. 24-38).

Bodin's terminology itself reveals his desire to distinguish his Judaised ideas from the Christian doctrine of grace.[18] The *Paradoxe* never refers to "grace" except in describing Christian grace (as at p. 88, see below). Instead it speaks of *aide extraordinaire* (p. 35) or *effusion de lumière divine* (pp. 24, 29, 31, 42).[19] The general bias is in fact in favour of *illumination* or *éclair-cissement* and Bodin throughout the *Paradoxe* speaks of the mystical love and vision of God as being illuminated rather than "infused" in man. Where *infusion* belongs to the terminology of the Christian theological virtues (p. 88), *illumination* falls within the Platonising Jewish tradition of Philo and Léon Ebreo. But it is the influence of Philo which is manifested most strikingly in Bodin's theory of illumination. For Philo held that perfect happiness consisted in the ecstatic vision of God, a vision bestowed supernaturally by God through the medium of His illuminating lightstream.[20]

Bodin's purpose is to show how divine illumination is essential for the attainment of perfect happiness although man may, by the exercise of free will in the pursuit of virtue, prepare himself to receive that happiness. To the question of why the *jouissance* or enjoyment of God — the sovereign hapiness of man — is enjoyed only *par réflexion,* Bodin replies that it is because:

> ... le souuerain bien de l'homme ne git en action, ni en cótemplation simplement, comme plusieurs estimét, mais bien en vne certaine effusion de lumiere diuine qui aduient à l'homme quand il ha la vision de Dieu (p. 24).

[18] Mesnard, unlike Tentler, recognises that Bodin's idea of virtue and nature is not Christian and that the divine illumination described by Bodin is not the same as Christian grace. However, Mesnard does not fully discuss the Jewish origins of Bodin's concept of divine "grace" — or rather aid — and, by using the term "infusion" to analyse Bodin's idea of virtue, Mesnard obscures the philosopher's careful avoidance of Christian infusion in favour of a Judaised vocabulary of illumination. (Kogel, *Charron*, p. 66 also loosely speaks of Bodin's theory of "infused virtue").

This imprecision leads to some misunderstanding of what Bodin means by "love of God". Mesnard (p. 55), misled by Bodin's economical but ambiguous phrasing, fails to distinguish between Bodin's natural love of God (which arises out of the Deuteronomic choice) and the illuminated mystical love of God which is independent of free will (see below, note 30 etc.). Hence, Mesnard is forced to argue that the love of God is divinely infused but naturally cultivated, thus fusing Bodin's *two* loves of God into a single love. But this makes nonsense of Bodin's argument which holds that the supernatural love of God is divinely illuminated, the natural love of God naturally cultivated. Had Mesnard been alert to Bodin's preference for "illumination" over "infusion" with its Christian undertones, this misunderstanding might have been evaded. (Mesnard, p. 551, saw that the "divine effusion of light" discussed by Bodin was not identical with Christian grace but did not pursue the Jewish aspects of this illumination).

[19] *Opes divina* in the *Paradoxon*. See note 26 below: and Chapter VI, notes 15, 16, 28. (In the *Heptaplomeres* Bodin uses "grace" in the Jewish sense, see Chapters VI, note 32, and VII, note 35.)

[20] See below, note 54 and Chapter IV, note 65. Cf. Goodenough, *By Light, Light*. Sandmel, *Philo*, p. 101. The Jewish notion of happiness as the contemplation of a transcendent God is different from the Platonic view of happiness as the contemplation of a supernal world of forms. See A. Altmann, 'Ibn Hayya on Man's Ultimate Felicity', in *Harry Austryn Wolfson Jubilee Volume* (Jerusalem, 1965), I, 47-87.

To strengthen the Judaised sense of these words Bodin rules out the notion of some Platonists that the soul can unite itself to God and adopts instead a Solomonic mysticism which allows the soul to approach closely or even "adhere" to God but not to "unite" itself with a transcendent deity (p. 26).

Again Bodin takes pains to dissociate his Judaised ideas of knowledge and love of God from the *contemplatio* of Greek philosophy. Platonic or Aristotelian contemplation is an act of the intellect whereas Bodin's mystical reflection is passive in that it is produced by God's illumination of the soul (p. 29). In the course of this argument Bodin uses Maimonides' concept of the *active intellect* to describe the transmission of grace to men and supports it with Solomon's sapiential idea of happiness as *jouissance* born of knowledge of God (p. 39).

It will be remembered that Maimonides' *active intellect* instilled not only *jouissance* but also prophetic spirit in men's souls [21]; and indeed *jouissance* and prophecy appear as degrees in the scale of human happiness in Bodin's eyes.

> ... qui pouuons nous dire estre les plus heureux en ce mòde apres ceux la que vous auez dit estre tres-heureux? Ceux à qui Dieu à departi la lumiere de prophetie, & qui ont la communication du bon Ange, que les autres appellent l'intellect actuel, de la splendeur duquel les gens de bien sont instruits par songes & visions de tout ce qu'il faut suivre & fuir, & auertir les Princes & les peuples de la volôté de Dieu ... car les plus diuins personnages qui furêt onques n'ont iamais perceu ceste ioüissance diuine sinon en dormant: c'est pourquoy la felicité de l'hôme se parfait quand Dieu agit en luy par effusion de sa lumiere & vision de la beauté, qui n'auiêt iamais à l'homme veillant (p. 31)...

> ... il y a plusieurs degrez de felicité: l'homme riche ... l'homme prudent & modeste encore plus: & beaucoup plus celuy qui à l'ame pure & nette de passions turbulentes, prenant son plaisir à contempler les choses celestes: mais celuy se peut dire encore plus heureux qui ha la vraye sapience & cognoissance de la premier cause: & s'il ha le don de l'intellect actuei, que le philosophe Auerroes appelle l'intellect octroyé, qui est l'Ange de Dieu se cõmuniquãt a luy, il approche fort pres de la felicité souueraine, qui git en la ioüissance de la vision de Dieu (pp. 32 f).

Through an adroit fusion of Maimonidean and Solomonic ideas Bodin succeeds in presenting mystic knowledge, mystic love of God, prophecy, and the enjoyment of God as the hierarchy of supreme happiness, while at the same time allowing that some form of happiness is enjoyed by men at any stage of moral perfection. The love of God born of free will, for instance, secures happiness for man, although it is clearly not the same (as we shall see) as that mystical love of God which comes with the reception of divine illumination. [22]

---

[21] See Chapter VIII for Maimonidean prophecy and the theory of the active intellect. Philo also identifies the illuminated ecstatic vision of God with prophecy. See Chapter VII, note 22.

[22] *Paradoxe*, pp. 33, 37, referring to Matthew XI, 30 and Deuteronomy, XXVIII-XXX. See the end of this chapter. (Philo also uses apparently contradictory terminology so as to obscure a genuinely consistent argument. See Sandmel, *Philo*, p. 113.)

How does one prepare or dispose oneself to receive this highest mystical happiness? By free will, obedience of the divine commandments and the perfection of virtue. As with his illuminative idea of "grace" Bodin's theory of virtue and will is very much in the mould of Jewish thought. [23] The simple answer to the question of what man himself must do to reach the life of supreme happiness is the injunction: "Obey the commandments of God". This much lies within man's natural capacity of free will since God is not a tyrant but rather "ce grand Législateur de nature trèsbon et très-puissant, veu mesme ce qu'il dit, Mon fardeau est léger, et mon ioug aggréable" (p. 33) — another example of Bodin selecting a New Testament quotation to illustrate a moral position which is actually far closer to that of the Old Testament. [24] For Bodin this Judaised trust in the ability of man's free will to choose to obey the commandments is the source of all moral virtue; "ceux qui disent le contraire (that is, the Christian exponents of grace and the weakened free will which that concept entails) ne cherche autre chose que l'éversion de toutes les loix divines et humaines" (p. 33). For to diminish the freedom of the will means rendering illusory the rewards of the just and the punishment of the evil-doers, at the same time permitting the wicked to blame their crimes on God Himself.

This dominating emphasis on the will leads to Bodin's severely criticising both Plato and Aquinas — Plato for thinking that the will itself cannot err, Aquinas for holding that a defect of reason results in the erring of the will. To Bodin's mind sin occurs when the will submits to man's animal appetite; sin is not an error of reason, it is an intentional error of will (p. 35). [25]

Another argument which Bodin presents to refute the Christian notion of grace is significant for the light it throws on Bodin's understanding of the relationship between the divine and the natural, a relationship which plays a critical role in all of his writings. Here one of the interlocutors asks whether there is any sense at all in which one may be said to need God's will or special aid to obey the commandments.

> Ie n'enten pas seulement de son aide ordinaire qui procede des causes naturelles ainsi qu'elles sont ordōnees de Dieu en tout ce monde, ains aussi de son aide

---

[23] Mesnard, 'Bodin critique', p. 551, rightly observes that Bodin's theory of virtue, free will and grace is not Christian but, somewhat neglecting its Jewish character, prefers to describe it as "theological naturalism". Later in the same valuable article Mesnard does indeed emphasise the Judaising tendency and structure of the *Paradoxe*.

[24] See below, note 64.

[25] Having no inkling of its Judaised character Tentler, 'Meaning of Prudence', pp. 376f, cannot understand Bodin's emphasis on the will. He accordingly finds that "in ali of these arguments there is a lamentable carelessness" and remarks that "why Bodin took this voluntaristic position is difficult to say". And "Bodin's arguments seem to have two main sources; one, the Christian tradition, the other the desire to disagree with Aristotle". Consideration of the Jewish elements in the *Paradoxe* might have diminished Tentler's bewilderment.

Although there is some superficial resemblance — which Bodin plays upon — to the voluntarism of Duns, Bodin's rejection of the Christian theological virtues and grace is utterly alien to and destructive of the foundations of Scotist theology.

extraordinaire en disposant les hõmes, ou les Anges, ou quelques autres creatures à nostre secours (p. 35). [26]

This is of course really asking whether grace — in the form of the prophetic angels — is necessary in order to heed God's laws. But instead of repeating what he has said earlier to prove that free-will suffices for a man to obey God, Bodin now enters upon a discussion comparing free will to the eye; both may have been implanted originally in mankind as a gift of God but currently they operate within the natural order — the eye seeing naturally without God's special or extraordinary help, free will choosing good without that same special aid. "So the soul using the virtue and power which God has given it, using its natural reason, can flee evil and seek good (p. 35-6). Reason always has the power to command to passions, *par commandement seigneurial*" (p. 40). [27]

In a curious passage (pp. 37-38) Bodin for the sake of removing all obstacles to his argument allows that man may need God's extraordinary help to do good and be *juste et entier* rather than simply shun evil. But he yields this ground only in order to prove his major argument that man may lead a moral life by natural means, for, as Bodin says, "all agree that God never refuses His help to him who asks". The decision to ask God's help is made by the natural choice of free will. This is a crucial tenet of belief which Bodin resumes at the end of the *Paradoxe*. [28] There he states that although God's help is often required by the man who seeks the highest natural virtue of "wisdom" — that is, Bodin's Judaised "charity" — God will not withhold that help from him who chooses to pray and to obey. For the present Bodin remarks that God even gives His aid to those who do not ask, urging them in dreams and through angelic messengers to do good. It must be stressed that this concession by Bodin to the need for divine help in doing good, while it is in keeping with his prophetic theology, does not in the least diminish Bodin's certainty of belief in the power of natural free will to produce moral virtue. This is clear from Bodin's conclusion of the passage.

> ... il faut donc confesser que nous pourrons toutesfois & quãtes que nous voudrõs mettre en execution les cõmandemens de Dieu d'vne pure & franche volõté: car Dieu n'aime pas vne volonté forcée.
>
> Si la volonté est forcée, il me semble que ce n'est plus volonté (p. 38).

[26] As in all his writings Bodin preserves the power of God to intervene in nature and override the established natural order. Note here in the terms "extraordinary" and "ordinary" aid an echo of the Scotist distinction between the *potentia absoluta* and *potentia ordinata* of God. Together with Bodin's use of such Scotist terms as joy and fruition of God, this usage might suggest that Bodin was following the Christian nominalistic tradition. But it should be remembered that these terms have a quite different meaning when Bodin employs them. Duns believed that the will by itself could attain "enjoyment "of God within the ordinary natural universe. Bodin denies this; the will only readies man to receive happiness and enjoyment, while the enjoyment of God itself requires the *extraordinary* aid of God. Despite their similarities of terminology Bodin and Duns really hold fundamentally opposed positions on happiness and salvation. See E. Gilson, *Jean Duns Scot. Introduction à ses propositions fondamentales* (Paris, 1952), pp. 594ff.

[27] Resuming the idea of virtue as the command of the passions by reason, to be found in the *République*, I, i. See Chapter II above.

[28] *Paradoxe*, pp. 92, 95. See below, notes 54 and 58.

Bodin's distinction between God's *ordinary* and *extraordinary* aid to man to obey the commandments is of the greatest importance for it illustrates his whole conception of the divine and the natural. By *ordinary* aid Bodin means those natural means for pursuing virtue which God has implanted in mankind in general. The first of these means is of course free will; but Bodin also believes that God originally implanted in man a natural instinct to virtue (a belief also held by Philo). As he says later in the *Paradoxe*.

> ... mais tous les anciens Hebrieux & Academiques ont tenu pour chose asseurée, que nous auõs les ames parsemees d'vne semence diuine de toutes vertus, qui nous peuuêt conduire à peu près à la vie bien heureuse, si nous endurõs qu'elle prênent leur accroissement: & pour la preuue, nous voyons que les têdres esprits, qui n'ont iamais riê appris, concoiuent soudain les principes & fondemens de toutes sciences: & tout ainsi que la terre est enceinte naturellement d'vne infinité de plantes, metaux, mineraux, & pierres precieuses qu'elle produit sans semence & sans labeur, la mer les poissons, qui sont sustentez par les influences celestes: ainsi est il de l'ame qui est parsemée d'vne infinité de belle sciences & vertus, lesquelles estant arrousées de l'influence diuine produisent les doux fruits qui croissêt és arbres de prudence & de science (p. 65). [29]

Free will and the instinct to virtue are, therefore, for Bodin facets of nature, of the *ordinary* universe instituted by God. They allow man a natural capability to achieve *moral* virtue.

When it comes to God's *extraordinary* aid to man in the cultivation of virtue things are rather different. Here God acts extraordinarily in sending angels to help men to ascend the grades of prophecy, for as we have seen man's natural efforts made by means of the *ordinary* aid of God cannot achieve the possession of the prophetic spirit. God's *extraordinary* aid results, not in ordinary moral virtue such as love of God and obedience of the commandments, but rather in Bodin's supernaturally illuminated virtues — mystical beatitude and mystical love and joy of God. [30]

Bodin's implanted virtue therefore takes two forms. It may be an originally implanted instinct to moral virtue conjoined with free will; or it may be a supernaturally illuminated mystical virtue. In this two-fold conception of instilled virtue Bodin is neither Stoic not Christian; he is not a Stoic because while he accepts that man's natural seeds of virtue are sufficient to lead a moral life, he believes that they were originally instilled in the human race by a transcendent Hebraic God. Furthermore Bodin's higher religious virtues of mystical love and joy follow a supernatural path which is utterly alien to the pure naturalism of the Stoics. On the other hand Bodin's Judaised understanding of both natural and supernatural virtue sets him apart from Christian tradition.

---

[29] The belief in an originally implanted natural instinct is also apparent in Bodin's remarks in the *Paradoxe*, pp. 36, 88 and elsewhere. The phrasing may mislead readers into taking this opinion as Stoic in origin. But its true source is to be found in Philo, *De virtutibus* where a transcendental God plants these seeds rather than the immanent deity of the Stoics.

Cf. Bodin, *Le Théâtre de la nature universelle* (Lyons, 1597), p. 687: "Nous recognoissons que la semence de toutes les vertus et sciences a esté divinement esparse en noz âmes des leur premiere origine."

[30] For beatitude as an "effusion de la lumière divine", see *Paradoxe*, pp. 24, 29, 31, 42, 43, etc.

We may now see that Bodin's idea of the "natural" is not entirely natural-istic, but that it includes a substantial element of the "divine". Bodin is employing uniquely mixed categories which are neither Christian nor Greek but rather stem from Jewish traditions. To ask, therefore, whether Bodin advocates in the *Paradoxe* a "divine" or a "natural" ethics is to misconceive the matter at the outset since his thought does not properly admit the purely "natural" as an independent category; the divine always enters into Bodin's concept of the natural. "Ce grand Législateur de nature", Bodin calls the creator (p. 33) Who instils that natural faculty of free will which enables men to obey His laws. Just as moral free will is as intrinsic a feature of the natural world as are the oceans, so too is Bodin's natural universe at the same time an intrinsically moral one.

Because Bodin's moral and natural universes are congruent he is able to produce a hierarchy of religious happiness in which knowledge of the secrets of nature is part of *vera religio*.

> Qui est le point principal du seruice Diuin? C'est de l'aimer & loüer de tout son pouuoir, & rapporter tout son bien & fiance à luy seul...

> Qui sera celuy qui aimera Dieu plus ardēment, ou qui chãtera mieux ses louanges? Celuy qui plus approchera de sa vraye cognoissance.

> Qui est celuy qui plus approche de sa cognoissance? Celuy qui mieux entēd la puissāce, sa bōté, sa sagesse, ses faits, ses iugemens, & qui mieux cognoistra le grād chef d'œuure admirable de ce mōde, lordre, laccord, & l'vsage de chacune partie d'iceluy.

> Qui sera celuy qui mieux entendra toutes ces choses? Celuy à qui Dieu depar-tira plus de sa lumiere, & celuy plus en aura qui plus l'aimera (pp. 41f).

To many readers this might appear to be a very perplexing passage indeed. In the first place Bodin confusingly places "love" of God at the beginning and at the end of his hierarchy. But one should bear in mind the critical distinction made earlier in this section between natural free-willed love of God and the mystical love of God which comes from supernatural illumination. Then the "love and praise of God" with which the quotation begins may be taken as free-willed love of God, and the concluding reference to the man "who loves God most" understood as an allusion to illuminated mystical love of God.

Perhaps even more disconcerting, however, is the apparent suggestion that scientific knowledge of the natural universe is only possible to a man who has received divine illumination, "to whom God has sent most of His light". If this were so then Bodin would assume the position of believing that man is unable to achieve scientific knowledge by use of power of intellect. Note well, however, that this happy knowledge of the secrets of nature is no more the same as ordinary scientific knowledge than is illuminated love of God the same as natural love of God. Bodin never denied the ability of the rational intellect to investigate the facts of history, politics or the physical universe; such researches resulted in the production of a natural knowledge which is nonetheless at the same time religious in that it directs men to recognition of God. There exists on the other hand an illuminated knowledge of God and His works. The happiness of this illuminated *connaissance et science de ses œuvres et de ses loix*, [31] like the illuminated love of God, comes to the man prepared to receive it. Bodin has already shown that it is virtue which prepares man to receive the illumination and the theme is stated once more.

> Puis donc que la ioüissance du souuerain bien dépend de l'amour, & l'amour dépend de sa cognoissance, & la cognoissance d'iceluy dépend de la science de ses œuvres, de ses loix & iugemens, laquelle science prouient d'vne effusiõ de sa lumiere qui est d'autant plus grande en ceux la qui ont fait plus grãd amas de vertus, dites moy s'il vous plaist que c'est de vertu (pp. 43f).

Bodin's answer to this question takes up much of the remainder of the *Paradoxe*. First he will explain that all virtue is intellectual and yet depends on the will. Then he will distinguish various kinds of virtue, pre-eminently science, prudence and wisdom.

In the *Theatrum Naturae* Bodin investigated the secrets of nature whose unravelling constitutes the natural virtue of science; [32] prudence and wisdom —which he understands as Judaised virtues— form the domain of moral philosophy and are the subject of the last two sections of the *Paradoxe*.

c) The Judaised Critique of Aristotle's Mean: Intellect and Will in the Formation of Virtue

In this section (pp. 45-64) Bodin dispatches unceremoniously a stream of Aristotle's arguments on virtue and ethics, referring all the time to those Judaised ideas outlined in the preceding pages.

Virtue is immediately defined as "une qualité louable acquise à l'âme", vice as "un défaut de vertu". Vice is not an acquired habit as Aristotle thought; ignorance, for example, is not the acquisition of error but rather the lack of knowledge (pp. 44-5). Equally wrong is Aristotle's view that since contemplation is the *action* of the soul, all virtue is ultimately active. Bodin suggests that Aristotle may have expressed himself thus in order to preserve Plato's opinion that contemplation was the sovereign good of man while still putting forward an active conception of virtue. But, says Bodin, this dubious playing with words reduces Aristotle to the absurdity of identifying rest with movement. It is to escape the dilemma posed by asking which is the superior —action or contemplation— that Bodin proposes his highest Judaised virtues of *jouissance et fruition de Dieu* which altogether transcend both action and contemplation (pp. 45-48).

[31] Bodin's use of the terms *connaissance* and *science* might lead one to suppose that *connaissance* designates illuminated knowledge whereas *science* is natural knowledge. But it is clear from the quotation which follows that — *in this context* — Bodin regarded both *connaissance* and *science* as illuminated forms of knowledge. Elsewhere, as we shall see, *science* was treated as a natural virtue. The confusing use of a single term to designate two virtues, one illuminated and one natural occurs also, as seen above, with the term "love of God".

[32] See P. Mesnard, 'Jean Bodin à la recherche des secrets de la nature', in *Umanesimo e Esoterismo*, ed. E. Castelli (Archivio di Filosofia, 5, Padua, 1960), pp. 221-234.

Bodin still accepts a division of ordinary virtues into contemplative virtues such as "la sagesse et la science" and active ones like "la prudence et l'art" but his Judaised ideas have rescued him from the strait-jacketed discussion into which most writers on active and contemplative virtue had been forced by their adoption of Platonic and Aristotelian categories. However, when it comes to following another Aristotelian division of the virtues into moral and intellectual classes Bodin is far less tolerant. The very definition proposed by Aristotle is unsatisfactory because *all* the virtues are intellectual "inasmuch as the intellect alone is capable of virtue, as the Stoics have well said" (p. 49). How may this intellectualism be reconciled with Bodin's previous exaltation of the will? This is properly the subject of the next section but some pointers may be given now.

The idea of virtue as wholly intellectual is in accordance with Bodin's Judaised psychology of the unitary soul.

> Pourquoy ne mettrõs nous les vertus morales en l'ame inferieure, obeissant à la raison? Parce qu'il n'y a q'vne ame en l'hõme, a scauoir l'intellect, lequel suruiuant le corps sen vole, come nous estimons auoir clairemẽt demonstré au theatre de nature: les autres ames qu'on dit vegetatiue, sensitiue, raisonable, memoratiue, imaginatiue, &c. ne sont que proprietez & qualitez, comme Aristote mesme est l'auis en quelques lieux (p. 49). [33]

The intellectual soul commands and its various properties and qualities obey with no intrinsic virtue of their own; all virtues therefore are intellectual.

The separation of the properties of the soul is mirrored lucidly in Bodin's distinction between the appetite and the will, that will which is so important for both his moral philosophy and his religion. Appetite is a quality of the animal soul while "la volonté est l'acte de l'entendement, usant de son franc-arbitre" (p. 51). [34] Bodin loses no time in taking Aristotle to task for his confused thinking on the will; Aristotle is wrong to think that the *volonté* addresses itself only to virtuous and not vicious things. If that were so, reasons Bodin, there would be no free will and hence no sin. The will or *volonté* is greater than either *raison* or *entendement* and at this point Bodin cites Deuteronomy "XIII" (for XXX?) on the freedom of the will. Augustine's *De libero arbitrio* is also piously cited, but this is simply an instance of Bodin's giving a Christian gloss to what is essentially a Judaised argument, in this case an argument based firmly on the Deuteronomic choice.

> C'est pourquoy le sage legislateur apres auoir mis deuant les yeux d'vn chacun la vie & la fin des bõs & mauuis, il proteste qu'vn chacũn ha la vie & la mort, le bien & le mal en sa puissance, conuiant toute personne à choisir le bien & fuir le mal, autrement qu'ils periroyẽt miserablement (p. 51). [35]

Bodin is scathing too about Aristotle's opinion that the will is simply the appetite obeying reason. Reason judges what is true and false; the will

---

[33] Mesnard, 'Psychology of Bodin', *loc. cit.*

[34] The phrasing here is reminiscent of Rabelais' vocabulary. See A.J. Krailsheimer, *Rabelais and the Franciscans* (Oxford, 1963). For Bodin's early ideas of appetite and will see the discussion of the *Oratio*, above Chapter I.

[35] Bodin cites Deuteronomy XIII, proabbly a misprint for XXX (margin).

judges what is good and what is evil. That reason can override the will and reduce it to obedience, claims Bodin, is a pernicious doctrine.

> C'est biẽ laduis de quelques vns, mais il est reiette a bon droict: car en ce qu'ils disent qu'il n'est pas en nostre puissance de croire chose contre l'euidente preuue du sens commun, nõ seulement ils ruinent les fondemens de toute religion, ains encor ils aneantissent la force de la volonté (pp. 52f). [36]

Bodin now comes to the paradox which forms part of his title: a contradiction of Aristotle's opinion that each virtue is the mean between two opposed vices (pp. 53-64). [37] The starting point is Bodin's elimination of "moral virtue" (in the Aristotelian sense) in favour of an exclusively intellectual virtue in the domain of "moral philosophy".

> ... parce que toute vertu est intellectuelle: or il n'y a pas vne seule vertu intellectuelle en mediocrité, ni au milieu des vices: il s'ensuit donc qu'il n'y a point de vertu en mediocrité, ou bien au milieu de deux vices, nous auons cy dessus monstré par viues raisons & necessaires, que toute vertu est intellectuelle (p. 54).

The Aristotelians themselves had admitted that the doctrine of the mean applied only to the category of *moral* virtues. Yet even if such moral virtues existed, it would be as absurd to call someone "moderately good" as " moderately learned". Moral and intellectual virtue both demand extremes.

Again, how may one thing, such as a moral virtue, have two opposites, that is to say, the two extremes of vice between which it is placed? This would also have the dangerous consequence that vices would exceed virtues in number, and evil exceed good in the universe (pp. 55-6).

What of the Delphic admonition; "Nothing too much"? This, says Bodin, applied only to the curbing of desires. If otherwise, it would be better to be moderately rather than slightly vicious. But there are religious and naturalistic arguments, as well as logical ones, against the Aristotelian ideal of moderation. Moderation is contrary to nature; there are no half-fires or half-suns. Each creature uses all its force and with this naturalistic statement Bodin comes back to his Judaised conviction that in Moses' Law consists the whole of morality.

> ... si dõc les vertus sont conuenables à la nature, comme elles font, il faut qu'elles monstrent leur force à lextremité, & nõ point à demy. Aussi voyons nous que ce grand Legislateur au commandement le plus haut qu'il fit jamais, & le plus remarquable dit ainsi (Deuteron 6), Tu n'as qu'vn Dieu eternel, tu l'aimeras de tout ton cœur, & de toute tõ ame, & de toute ta puissance, & te ioindras a luy pour iamais. En quoy lon void que Dieu ne veut point d'amy a demy, & que la plus belle vertu du monde s'estend, non pas en mediocrité, mais en toute extremité, & en toutes les puissãces & facultez de l'ame: autãt peut on dire qu'il faut se fier en Dieu, non pas

---

[36] In the margin Bodin cites Pico and Duns. Duns does not oppose Aristotle's definition of the will as *appetitus rationalis* though he enters a proviso preserving the freedom of the will. See Gilson, *Jean Duns Scot*, p. 579.

[37] Several Catholics such as Honoré d'Urfé and Jacques Du Perron followed Bodin's critique of the mean, without of course accepting his Judaised rejection of theological virtue. See Bady, *L'Homme*, pp. 137ff, 218. R. Kogel, *Pierre Charron* (Geneva, 1972), p. 65.

à demy, ains de toute nostre puissance. Si donc c'est crime capital de poser vne mediocrité en l'amour & fiance qu'on doibt à Dieu, quelle apparence y a il de le faire és autres vertus, & soustenir qu'il ne faut pas estre d'vn cœur tresgenereux, ni fort modeste, ni tresiuste, ains qu'il faut estre à demy seulement? (p. 57).

Returning to his philosophical critique of Aristotle Bodin observes that the doctrine of the mean would render vices virtuous and virtues vicious. For Aristotle erred as a philosopher in treating his vices as "opposites" since he was really dealing with relativities. A dwarf and a giant are not truly opposite phenomena but rather relative in size to one another. So too are vices relative to one another and any virtue lying between them in the mean would also be relative and so share in their evil (p. 60).

Il falloit donc qu'Aristote, qui s'estoit departi de l'opinion de Platon, pour former vne nouuelle science morale, posast des principes certains pour asseurer le fondement de sa doctrine, & d'autant plus qu'il est question de faire chois du biē & du mal, en quoy git le pl'haut point de la prudēce (p. 61).

Before leaving the question of the mean and moderation Bodin considers the defence of Aristotle that he was proclaiming not a simple linear mean but rather a more complicated proportion which would place the virtue of liberality much farther away from the extreme vice of avarice than from that of prodigality. But even this defence is refuted by the philosophical principle that in the discussion of infinites (such as Aristotle believed vices to be) no mean, whether arithmetical or geometrical, may be found. "All the philosophers agree that it is impossible to have any science concerning infinites" (p. 62-3).

Finally, the greatest absurdities result from the Aristotelian mean: if all the virtues are means, then the sovereign good itself must be a mean. Aristotle, concludes Bodin, took refuge in the apparent poverty of the Greek language to argue his specious case for "ceste médiocrité vulgaire" (p. 64).

d) The Judaised "Moral" Virtues: Prudence and Justice

In treating the non-illuminated natural virtues Bodin's principle that all virtue is intellectual leaves one fundamental problem unanswered: if the will is stronger than the intellect, how is it that the natural virtues which depend upon the exercise of free will may be called intellectual rather than moral? Bodin had argued that Aristotle's justification of a separate category of "moral virtues" had been mistaken. But now he must come up with a proper justification of his own for claiming that such non-illuminated virtues as liberality are indeed intellectual.

Bodin's case is based on a statement enunciated already: "In the question of choosing between good and evil resides the main role of prudence" (p. 61). The significance of prudence is that it is a natural, intellectual, and non-illuminated virtue which functions as the servant of free will. Free will expresses itself through the operation of this intellectual virtue of prudence. Hence, Bodin's theory of prudence is able to reconcile his claims that all virtue is intellectual with his belief in the primacy of the will.

For Bodin, as we shall see, prudence is incorporated in a group of virtues consisting of justice, magnanimity and temperance, virtues which despite their intellectual foundation were regarded by Bodin as "moral" virtues of a sort. They were not, however, moral virtues in the Aristotelian sense; forced into Aristotelian categories they would, in being "prudences", be considered intellectual rather than moral. But Bodin's use of Judaised concepts permitted him to transcend traditional Greek and Christian habits of thought and to arrive at more idiosyncratic categories which fused the previously separated moral and intellectual virtues into a new compound. He was able to conceive an idea of prudence and justice which preserved the reality of both will and intellect.[38] Where Plato had in the end reduced the intellect to a sort of passion or will ("no one errs willingly") and Aristotle had finished by interpreting the will as a form of reason, Bodin's Judaised categories freed him from the paradoxes inherent in Greek philosophical systems.

Bodin starts the discussion by stating that "the soul is seeded with an infinity of good sciences and virtues" (p. 65).[39] But are the moral virtues included in these virtues?

> Comment donc entêdez vous ce qui est dit en lescripture sainte de Bezaleel, que Dieu le combla & enrichit de l'esprit diuin, de sapience, de science, de prudence, & de toutes sortes d'artifices, & n'est rien dit des vertus morales? (pp. 65f).

Bodin's answer is that all the virtues were included in this intellectual enrichment of Bezaleel by God and he regards the fivefold enumeration of gifts as representing the five qualities of virtue. The first of these, "divine spirit", represents the supernatural virtue of prophecy, "the most excellent gift a man may have in this world". Second comes the natural virtue of wisdom (*sapience*) which consists in the knowledge, love and pure worship of God; through wisdom one knows the difference between piety and impiety. Science comes third, "science which brings the knowledge of natural things and all the parts of the universe, the touchstone of what is true and false". The fourth quality of virtue is prudence, "princess of all the virtues, and mistress of human life, which judges between good and evil, between right and wrong". Lastly there is art, "which allows one to discriminate between the useful and the valueless". Bezaleel's five gifts were therefore prophecy, piety, truth, goodness (*la bonté*) and utility (pp. 66-7).

Bodin takes this five-fold order of the virtues as a firm hierarchy legitimated by his religious conception of the universe.

> Pourquoy met il la sapience premier que la science, & la science premier que la prudence? Parce que le plus haut point de toutes choses est d'aimer & seruir

---

[38] Tentler, 'Meaning of Prudence', pp. 380, finds Bodin "inconsistent" here. This incomprehension on Tentler's part is not surprising since he insists on interpreting Bodin in Christian terms of virtue, grace and free will.

Bady, *L'Homme*, pp. 137-140, 146, resumes Bodin's idea of prudence without attention to the nexus of Judaised concepts which sets Bodin apart from the other Christian critics of Aristotle treated in Bady's otherwise useful book.

[39] For the seeding of virtue see above, note 29. The "divine influence" which facilitates the growth of these seeds is the *ordinary* natural aid of God, not an *extraordinary* natural aid of God, not an *extraordinary* influence.

Dieu d'vn cœur entier, en quoy git la vraye loüäge de sagesse: le second git à considerer les œuures que Dieu ha crées d'vne varieté insatiable & plaisante à merueilles, afin qu'en icelles on puisse loüer la sapiěce, puissäce, & bõté de Dieu, en regardãt haut & bas la liaison des causes, & de leurs effects, auec vne entresuite de toutes choses tresbelle. or la sciěce est plus noble que la pruděce, d'autãt que la contěplation est plus noble ɋ l'actiõ: car la sciěce remarque ce qui est vray & faux en toutes choses naturelles, diuines, & principalemět és discours des mathematiques, que les anciěs ont posé entre les choses naturelles & diuines, & qu'ils ont proprement appelé sciences, pour leuidence & certitude d'icelles (p. 67).

This religious conception of wisdom is avowedly Solomonic in character:

> La prudence est vne vertu qui git du tout en actiõ, & au manimět des choses humaines: mais la science git à considerer les œuures du createur, pour paruenir à sa cognoissance: or les choses diuines surpassent les choses humaines, d'autant que Dieu est sans cõparaison plus excellent que l'hõme: c'est pourquoy le maistre de sagesse ayant suiui l'ordre du legislateur dit ainsi, Quand la sapiěce aura trouué place en ton cœur, & que tu auras pris plaisir à la science, alors la prudence te gardera: puis apres il adiouste, Di à la sapience tu és ma seur, & appelle la pruděce ta cousine: or nous sommes plus obligez d'affection à la seur que à la cousine: c'est pourquoy il appelle la sapice au mesme libure, le fruit de vie: & en autre lieu il dit, La maison est edifiée par sapience, & asseurée par prudence (p. 68). [40]

As with wisdom and science so too is Bodin's concept of prudence rooted in religious — and Judaised — conceptions. Prudence is not the traditionally simple virtue of Christian thought but rather a complex of virtues, comprising justice, magnanimity and temperance which are all so to speak "prudences". Plato had regarded *all* kinds of virtue as forms of prudence but prudence for Bodin designates only a separate quality or class of virtue. On the other hand, where Aristotle had seen prudence as an independent and separate governing virtue and one even shared in by the animals, Bodin clearly understands prudence as a complex and, *pace* Plato, does not allow it to govern his higher intellectual virtues (pp. 72-73); it is, moreover, unique to man insofar as free will is unique to man and does not exist in animals (p. 70). It is this foundation in the Judaised notion of free will which sets Bodin's idea of prudence so far apart from Greek conceptions, tending to place prudence, for all its intellectual quality, among the "moral" virtues which depend on the will rather than the intellect.

This notion of prudence as a Judaised "moral" virtue comes across very strongly in the ensuing distinction which Bodin makes between two different kinds of prudence.

> (Declairez moy s'il vous plaist les especes de pruděce). Il y en ha deux: la premiere git és actions touchant la vie & les meurs: l'autre git en l'exercice particulier ou pratique de toute doctrine qui peut se rapporter à l'action (p. 73).

---

[40] The allusions are to the Book of Proverbs. Bodin here gives a rehearsal of themes first evidenced in the *Oratio* and the *Methodus* (see above Chapter II) and treated in detail in the *Theatrum*.

On the following page (p. 69) there is an echo of the Hebraism of the letter to Bautru in the remark "et n'y eut onques mestier moins utile, et plus pernicieux que le mestier des images". (For this letter see Chapter VIII.)

The latter of these two sorts of prudence, "practical prudence", is to be found in the practical application of scientific knowledge and Bodin discusses the contributions made by the various disciplines to human affairs (pp. 73-75). But the former prudence — "moral prudence" — is Bodin's real concern here.

> En quoy git l'autre espece de prudence? en la reformation des meurs, & en ce qui est bien ou mal seant, honeste ou deshoneste: qu'an peut comprendre en deux especes, à scauoir magnanimité & temperance: ou pour le plus y adiouter la iustice, ce qui toutefois n'est point necessaire, car Platon a tresbien dit que la iustice n'est autre chose que l'accord melodieux de prudence, magnanimité & temperance: quand on donne la puissance de commander à la raison, & l'obeissance aux appetis de vengeãce & de plaisir: alors l'homme establit en soy mesme la vraye iustice, qui rend à chacune partie de l'ame ce qui luy appartiẽt (p. 76). [41]

These prudential virtues are in Bodin's eyes the real "moral" virtues and he openly points to the whole Judaising direction of his ethical scheme.

> Il n'y aura donc (à vostre aduis) que trois vertus morales, Prudence, Magnanimité & Temperance. C'est l'aduis de Salomon, qui entendoit tous les beaux secrets de choses diuines, naturelles, & humaines, & qui a representé ces trois vertus par trois figures, & non plus, qu'il fit mouler autour du grand vase de cuiure plain d'eau pure, auquel on lauoit tout ce qui seruoit aux sacrifices, ascauoir la figure de l'homme, du lion, & du beuf [I Kings, VII, 29]: pour faire cognoistre qu'il ne faloit pas seulement lauer les ordures exterieures du corps: ains aussi les soüilleures de l'ame, qui prennent leur source des trois uices opposites aux trois vertus, ascauoir la malice à la prudence, la lubricité à la temperance, la cholere furieuse à la magnanimité: & tout ainsi que ces trois vertus sont accompagnees de toutes les autres (pp. 77f).

Just as there are two forms of prudence so are there two "justices" which regulate the "prudences". There is firstly that internal psychic justice which harmonises the prudential moral virtues and again there is an external social justice which renders to each man his own and so assures the mutual peace of society. [42] This latter more practical form of justice

> ... n'est rien autre chose qu'vne espece de prudence ou practique de la science des loix, coustumes, & ordõnances ... pour ceste cause la science des loyx ou legitime est proprement appelee iurisprudence (p. 78).

But even practical justice goes beyond being merely an intellectual science and shares in religion and moral philosophy. It is explicitly linked with the Jewish virtue of *zedakah* or righteousness.

> ... la practique de iustice ne git pas seulemẽt à consulter, plaider, &iuger les proces & differẽs, ains aussi à la defense des plus foibles cõtre les plus puissans, en l'obeissance des particuliers enuers les magistrats, & au deuoir mutuel de chacun enuers son prochain, à departir aux poures necessiteux, laquelle vertu les Hebrieux

---

[41] The metaphors of the musical harmony of the virtues is to be found in a more general form in the *Oratio*. See above, Chapter II.

[42] Bodin actually identifies (pp. 87f) justice with *amitié* — the *amicitia* of the *Oratio*. See Chapter VI.

appellent *tsedaca*, c'est à dire iustice, d'autant que cela n'est point vne grace, mais vn debuoir que le plus riche doibt au poure (pp. 78f).

In this discussion of psychic and practical justice it might seem that Bodin is acknowledging a debt to Plato but the whole framework of the ethical thought here is fundamentally alien to Platonic philosophy for Bodin's psychic justice rests on a Judaised concept of free will and obedience to the revealed commands of a transcendent God. [44] How far Bodin has departed from Plato is shown graphically in his reinterpretation — and misrepresentation — of Plato's likening of the soul to a chariot pulled by unruly horses. Plato's original account in *Phaedrus* 246 and 253 depicted the driver of the chariot as prudence or judgement; Bodin, however, twists the simile to make will the charioteer and reason the reins while the chariot itself comes to symbolise prudence, magnanimity and temperance. This has the effect of adapting Plato's image to the demands of a Judaised concept of virtue resting on free will. Bodin carries out this critical substitution of will for judgement as the driver without the slightest indication to his readers of the radical change which has taken place (pp. 82-83).

But Bodin now goes on to expound another chariot metaphor which more easily expresses his Judaised conception of virtue. Mention of Plato's chariot and Solomon's vase with its three figures of the man, the lion and the ox

> ... me fait souuenir de la vision d'Ezechiel, ou le chariot celeste est tiré par quatre animaux, ascauoir l'homme, le lion, le beuf, & l'aigle... Salomon a signifié par les trois premiers, la prudence, la magnanimité, & la temperance: le quatriéme, qui est l'aigle, semble signifier la sapiéce qui éleue & rauit l'ame au plus haut qu'elle peut voler pour auoir la vision de Dieu: ... la sapience tirera auec foy la science: toutefois il y a peut estre quelque plus haut secret, que l'interprete de la vision a declare ne vouloir dire (Rabi Maimō libro 3. Nemor) (pp. 84f).

In the margin, almost as a signal of Bodin's Judaised mentality, is a reference to Maimonides, Book III with its marvellous interpretation of the divine chariot: the prophecy of Ezekiel indeed is the central topic of Maimonides' *Guide for the Perplexed*. With this in mind we may see how deeply immersed in Maimonidean thought were Bodin's ideas on virtue. Wisdom as a natural and at the same time religious concept is to be found in the closing chapters of Maimonides as we have earlier seen. So too is the understanding of virtue as essentially righteousness or *zedakah* and the recognition of free will as the basis of all non-illuminated "natural" virtue. At the same time Maimonides' theory of prophecy gave Bodin the framework for a doctrine of supernaturally illuminated virtue utterly different from the Christian idea of theological virtue. [45]

[44] The preference for Philo over Plato is plain enough in the *Methodus*, p. 123A. See below.

[45] For these Maimonidean ideas of virtue and prophecy see Chapters IV and VIII respectively. In ending his treatment of Judaised virtue Bodin discusses Aristotle's claim that truth is a moral virtue. For Bodin truth is rather a part of science (*Paradoxe*, pp. 85f). Nor is *amitié* to be classified as a moral virtue; it does not have a separate existence but must always be associated with justice (pp. 87f). Cf. Bodin's remarks on *amicitia* in the *Oratio*, Chapter I above and Chapter VI.

e) The Judaised Natural Virtue of Wisdom and the Christian Theological Virtues

In an earlier section (pp. 24-34) Bodin had distinguished between those virtues which form the subject of moral philosophy and the illuminated supernatural virtues of prophecy, love and joy which belong rather to the sphere of theology. Since the *Paradoxe* is not a theological treatise but deals with moral philosophy albeit in a religious context, Bodin does not return to the theme of prophecy; rather he concludes with a discussion of wisdom, the highest of the non-illuminated "natural" virtues. [46] But he does employ this last section (pp. 88-99) to show how the Hebraic virtue of wisdom subsumes and replaces the infused theological virtues of Christianity. For Bodin's wisdom embodies charity, faith and hope — virtues now robbed, however, of their Christian significance and made natural. [47]

This section, — which must be incomprehensible to any reader without an awareness of Bodin's Judaised structure of throught [48] — pursues three main arguments. Firstly Bodin demonstrates that the Christian theological virtues cannot be understood as virtues infused by grace. Secondly, these virtues of faith, hope and charity must be considered as forming together the Hebraic virtue of wisdom. Thirdly, wisdom itself is the peak of natural, non-infused virtue; but it is so difficult to attain that God almost has to draw or snatch (*ravir, tirer, trahere*) man near to Him if wisdom is to be gained. Yet, as Bodin carefully explains, God will grant man wisdom if man has the *will* to love God. Bodin's idea of God drawing man to Him in granting wisdom — the concept of *ravir* or *trahere* — is quite distinct from the idea of illumination which governs the award of prophecy or mystical love, for God will give his help to the man seeking wisdom who obeys and loves God. [49] Wisdom — and with it faith, hope and charity — depend then on free will and are naturally acquired virtues even if they require some degree of divine help.

Bodin begins by commenting that "the theologians call theological virtues those which are infused into us by God's grace and which have no other object

[46] There are some resonances in French thought of Bodin's notion that wisdom is a religious, if *naturally* acquired, virtue. (See Rice, *Renaissance Idea,* pp. 112ff. J. Victor, *Charles de Bovelles. An Intellectual Biography* (Travaux d'Humanisme et Renaissance 161, Geneva, 1978), pp. 33ff.) These resemblances, however, occur in the context of a Christian view of grace.

Incidentally Bodin is an exception to Rice's general statement (pp. 149ff) that wisdom evolved into a secular concept in sixteenth century France, becoming a code of ethical concepts indistinguishable from prudence. In fact, Bodin kept separate wisdom from prudence, nor was he a "secularist".

[47] Mesnard, 'Bodin critique', pp. 555f, notes Bodin's revolutionary rejection of Christian theological virtue.

[40] Thus Tentler, 'Meaning of Prudence', pp. 381-3, finds Bodin "confused" here, thinking that the philosopher first advocates a supernaturally infused theological virtue of charity and that Bodin then contradicts himself (three times over!) by explaining "charity" or wisdom as a natural virtue. Tentler has failed to distinguish between Bodin's own opinions and those of the theologians whom he is criticising in the *Paradoxe*! The distinction is quite clear in the text.

[49] See above for comparable passages in *Paradoxe,* pp. 37f.

or respect than God Himself" (p. 88). The theologians hold there to be three such virtues, faith, hope and charity, but Bodin drily remarks "that this (division) is not necessary if we accept the foundations laid above". [50]

Turning first to charity Bodin insists that as divine love, charity is a natural virtue.

> Parce que la charité ou amour diuin, qu'ils (*les théologiens*) font la principale vertu, est fondee sur les principes de nature, qui nous montre clairemēt qu'il faut aymer de toute sa puissance ce grand Dieu eternel, createur & conseruateur du monde, tresbõ & trespuissant (p. 88). [51]

Charity indeed is to be identified with wisdom Charity.

> ... n'est autre chose que la vraye sapience qui git en l'amour de Dieu tresardent, que les theologiens appellent charité, & Salomon l'appelle sapience & fruit de vie, comme nous auõs dit (pp. 88f).

Charity or wisdom is not therefore an infused virtue; if it were, then all the virtues would have to be regarded as infused.

> ... de dire que ceste vertu la est infuse diuinement, aussi sõt toutes les vertus & graces de Dieu, & generalement tout bien vient de Dieu (p. 89). [52]

Bodin now adduces a Judaising Philonic interpretation to explain that the highest virtues, like the best parts of sacrifices, pertain to God, the lower virtues to men. Charity, the supreme natural virtue, is directed like a burnt-offering solely to God, but all virtues must in some part be inspired by love of God.

> Tout ainsi q̃ de tous fruits les premices, & de tous sacrifices la graisse, & de toute oblation certaine portion estoit bruslee, & sacrifice à Dieu, & le surplus distribué aux sacrificateurs & ceux q̃ faisoient l'oblation: ainsi de toutes vertus les premices appartient à Dieu: le surplus aux hõmes: & tout ainsi qu'il y auoit vn sacrifice de louange qu'on appeloit *ola* [*Hebr.*] ou holocauste, qu'on brusloit entierement à l'honneur de Dieu ... ainsi entre les vertus la sapience qu'ils appellent charité, se doibt du tout rapporter à l'amour de Dieu ... ainsi est il de toutes autres

---

[50] The French version here (p. 88) is stronger than the Latin (*Paradoxon*, p. 89) which runs as follows: "Quot sunt huiusmodi virtutes? Tres illi quidem constituunt, scilicet, fidem, spem et charitatem, quas accutissimi theologi ab aliarum virtutum natura seiungi negant oportere."
In analysing this last section I have followed the French version which tightens the argument of the Latin edition while rearranging much of the material with several additions and omissions. The is, however, no basic inconsistency of thought between the two versions.

[51] The phrasing of the Latin strengthens the naturalistic emphasis: "Quamobrem (*in reply to the last answer quoted*)? Quia charitas illa sive amor divinus, quam omnium virtutum merito principem faciunt, firmissimis naturae principiis fundata sit, ac Deum optimum maximum ut summum bonum toto mentis impetu colendum ac prosequendum natura ipsa proponat..." (p. 89)

[52] Cf. *Paradoxon*, p. 90: "Quae igitur tua sententia est? Si theologicas virtutes definiunt quae divinitus infusae sunt, quaeque Deum ut immediatum obiectum habent, oportet virtutes omnes theologicas appellare, aut nullas eo genere censeri. Cur ita? Quoniam omne bonum divinitus influit, nec item virtus dici debet si primitiae alteri quam Deo tribuantur."

vertus, à scauoir de prudence, de temperance, magnanimité, voire de toutes actiôs
qui sont vicieuses ou imparfaites, si le premier sujet n'est fondé en l'amour de Dieu,
encor que la fin se rapporte au profit, ou bien d'autruy. mais la sapiêce ou amour
diuin a cela de special, qu'elle se rapporte du tout à Dieu (pp. 89f).

It is consciousness of the goodness and wisdom of God which draws man
to love of Him.

... seulement pour la seule bonté & sagesse de Dieu il est raui à l'aimer, & si cet
amour procedoit de la pure volôté & affection interieure de l'homme, la vertu en
seroit beaucoup plus grande & plus illustre que d'estre infuse diuinement, comme
il faut iuger en cas pareil de la foy (p. 90).

Bodin could not make it plainer that he believes that man is "ravi" to love
of God through man's free will and that this *ravissement* has nothing to do
with either the *infusion* of Christian theological virtue or Bodin's own prophetic
illumination. For Bodin, man's naturally willed love of God (i.e., wisdom) is
far superior in merit to any Christian conception which would make charity
a divinely infused and involuntary love of God.

Faith, the second of the theological virtues, also depends upon the will
and is the more to be valued as a willed virtue than if it were infused.

La vraye foy dépend d'vne pure & franche volonté, qui croit sans force
d'argumens, ny de raisons necessaires: & qui est en cela contraire à la science,
qui est fondee en demonstration forcee & necessaire: or si la foy est forcee, ce
n'est plus foy: & si elle est diuinement infuse, elle ne despend pas de la volonté
interieure de l'homme, ce qui est principalement requis en la foy, ains du commandement exterieur; il y a donc plus de merite quâd elle procede d'vne pure
volonté, que quand elle est infuse, & qu'elle vient d'autruy (pp. 90f). [53]

Hope is a form of willed faith and trust in God and must be combined
with charity if it has to have its proper effect.

Si nous prenons l'esperance pour la fiance que l'homme de bien a en Dieu
seul, c'est à dire qui ne fait ny mise ... il peut dire qu'il a vne vertu des plus belles
du monde, mais c'est tousiours ceste mesme sapience qui git en l'ardent amour de
Dieu, qui ne peut estre s'il n'est accompagné de ceste fiance, & ceux qui s'ap-
puyent & se fiêt és choses humaines, ils sont maudits, & declarez deserteurs
(Hieremie) (pp. 91f).

But the excellence of hope and wisdom brings Bodin to an apparent
confrontation between the claims of "grace" and free will.

... mais d'auoir ceste ferme fiance ou esperance, ou amour ardent enuers Dieu,
que nous auons dit estre le comble de sapience, il est bien difficile, & presque
impossible, si Dieu mesme ne nous rauit à luy (p. 92).

Is Bodin now admitting that hope and charity are after all infused virtues
dependent upon divine grace? Not at all; for Bodin is observing a crucial
distinction between *ravissement* and *infusion*. Charity or divine love is not
the same as the supernaturally infused or illuminated love of God which brings

[53] In the *Heptaplomeres* Bodin states that faith can only be seen as infused when
it accompanies the gift of prophecy. See Chapter VII.

with it the joy and vision of God. Rather is Bodin's charity the highest kind of naturally willed love of God. When man experiences this latter he is *ravi* or *saisi*. This *ravissement* is not "grace" but rather a response by God to the prayer of the good man. In that sense the *ravissement* is produced as a result of man's natural free will rather than being purely a manifestation of divine grace. As Bodin has argued in an earlier part of the *Paradoxe*, God never refuses His extraordinary help to the man who willingly turns to God for aid. [54] Throughout this discussion — and indeed throughout the whole *Paradoxe* — Bodin is careful to dissociate his idea of *illumination* from Christian grace for he never uses the term "grace" except when describing Christian ideas which are to be refuted. [55]

Bodin illustrates these ideas somewhat tersely in an important passage. First he asks whether the *ravissement* is in fact a matter of God's grace overriding the will of man.

> Mais c'est vne force quand Dieu rauit à foy quelqu'vn pour l'aimer, comme s'il ne deuoit pas l'aimer s'il ny estoit poussé, piqué, forcé, en quoy il me semble qu'il n'y a pas à lors grand merite, veu que nous y deuons courir à toute force (p. 92).

Bodin's reply to this illustrates the role of the human will in encouraging God to draw man to Him.

> Tout cela est beau à dire, mais oyez ce que dit l'amie de ce grand Roy, aprez auoir remarqué ses rares beautez, ses grandes richesses, ses perfections & puissances, Tirez moy, dit elle mõ amy, & nous courrons ensemble : elle est bien enflammee d'vn ardent amour, si est-ce neantmoins qu'elle desire & prie son amy de la tirer pour aller ensemble, & non pas deuant ny derriere (Io. c 19 nul ne vient à moy si mon pere ne le tire) (pp. 92f).

This reference to the Song of Songs VII, 10-11 (mistakenly cited as ch. III) is buttressed in the Latin text with a quotation from John, VI, 44 (again mistakenly cited as ch. XIX):

> Quid Christus? Nemo venit ad me nisi pater traxerit illum (p. 93).

The French version significantly weakens the Christian appeal by excluding the quotation from the *body of the text* and omitting Christ's name. Instead we have in the margin the simple reference to John and the words:

> Nul ne vient à moy si mon pere ne le tire (p. 93).

---

[54] *Paradoxe*, p. 37. Compare pp. 92 and 95. See notes 28 and 58.

[55] E.g. *Paradoxe*, p. 88: "Les théologiens appellent les vertus théologales, qui nous sont infuses par la grace de Dieu, et qui n'ont autre obiect ny respect que Dieu mesme." Bodin is especially careful to use a vocabulary of illumination — *éclaircir, effusion de la lumière divine, aide extraordinaire* — to describe the process of divine help, rather than such terms as *infusion* which he reserves for the description of Christion theological virtue. (The reference in note 53 above to the *Heptaplomeres'* use of "infusion" is to a passage where Bodin is criticising the Christian concept of infused theological virtue, and, to prove his point, says that the only time when faith may be said to be "infused" — in the language of Christian theologians — is when it accompanies prophecy. The tactical nature of the argument requires Bodin to use the term infusion in connection with prophecy although it is quite clear from passages in the *Heptaplomeres* and other works that he regarded prophecy as illuminated by the effusion of divine light, rather than infused). See Chapters VI and VII.

It must be emphasised that Bodin is here attributing salvation to God rather than to Christ who loses much of His redeeming office which would have been retained in such a verse as John, XIV, 6: "No man cometh unto the Father, but by me". The quotation of the earlier Johannine verse leaves the way open for the salvation of non-Christians, especially Jews. [56]

The point of citing John, VI in association with the Song of Solomon is not to suggest that none may come to God except through the saviour Christ, but rather to sustain with a Christian allusion the Hebraic belief that divine help will not be denied him who willingly seeks virtue and loves God.

Bodin has rejected the Christian theological virtues in favour of Hebraic wisdom or charity but some problems still remain. Is it against man's nature to be virtuous or is nature willingly so?

Commenting on this recurrent theme of the *Paradoxe* that nature and will must never be forced Bodin asks "who may doubt that men participating in a divine spirit may not mend themselves, bend and change (*to virtue*)" (p. 94). [57] Men may — "must" — voluntarily be virtuous and it is not against their nature to be so. They need only obey God's commandments which never go against nature. And here Bodin makes his final appeal to the Deuteronomic command to choose good.

> Mais pour lever toutes les excuses des hommes laschez de cœur, qui accusent iniurieusement la nature, affin de reieter leur faute en celuy qui est auteur de nature, il a dit haut et clair, Garde mes commandemens, et ilz te garder: tu as le bien et le mal, tu auras celuy qu'il te plaira; choise donc le bien et tu vivras; voila la conclusion du grand legislateur à la fin de tous ses mandemens (pp. 94f) (Deut. XXXI, 19, cited as XXVIII).

Nowhere is Bodin's vision of the Great God of Nature more essentially revealed than in this passage. The great legislator has created all nature of which human nature is a part. Human nature is imbued with morality in the form of moral choice: by this grant of free will God has made the universe of nature a moral universe for men. God and nature together direct man to virtue.

The closing pages of the *Paradoxe* resume the importance of religion for the achievement of virtue. The interlocutor, daunted by the difficulties of gaining wisdom, science and prudence, asks if there is a shorter way to wisdom. Bodin answers that there is; man may imitate Solomon in praying to God for wisdom and happiness and God may, heeding the prayer, bestow the gift. Once again as so often in the *Paradoxe* this may seem in Christian terms to be conceding after all that wisdom is a supernatural virtue granted by God's grace. But Bodin's meaning is that God gave Solomon wisdom only after the king had chosen willingly to pray to and fear God. (As ever God gives His help to man who willingly asks for it).

> (*Salomon*) conuie vn chacun de faire comme luy, asseurant par ses escripts que Dieu donne la sapience, & la prudence, mais il faut bien grauer en son esprit,

---

[56] As Mesnard, 'Bodin critique', pp. 558f, nicely points out.
[57] Compare, e.g., *Paradoxe*, p. 38.

que tous les saincts personages demeurēt d'accord, que le fondemēt & le comble de sapience git en la crainte de Dieu (p. 96). [58]

Fear of God, the foundation of wisdom, is in itself an act of free will and as such earns the gift of wisdom. Without such a willed choice God would not grant wisdom. Again Bodin's idea of grace and free will is very remote indeed from traditional Christian notions; as always, the Judaised idea of the Deuteronomic choice lies at the foundation of Bodin's moral thought.

In the end fear of God is inseparable from love of God and both are the basis of wisdom. By this Bodin does not mean the fear one has of enemies but rather that fear of offending a person whom one loves, as a mother fears to offend her small child and so constantly embraces it; it is the fear of "those whom one loves with the greatest affection". So much greater is the fear and love due towards God.

> Or il y a deux choses en Dieu qui manquent à toute creature, & qui doiuent engrauer en noz cœurs l'amour tresardent, & la crainte extreme de Dieu: c'est à scauoir vne bonté infinie, & vne puissance infinie: car il n'est pas moins bon qu'il est puissant: & n'est pas moins puissant qu'il est bon. mais d'autant que nous auons beaucoup plus de besoin de sa bonté que de sa puissance, & de sa douceur que de sa rigueur: pour ceste cause l'amour diuin doibt surpasser la crainte d'iceluy, & faut craindre l'offenser, non pas tant pour euiter la peine terrible de ses iugemēs, que pour l'obligation d'amour que nous luy deuõs, & des biens fais infinis que nous receuons sans cesse de ses mains (pp. 96f).

And here Bodin comes back to the political lesson to be learnt from his moral philosophy and religion, a political lesson incorporated into his writings on the League of 1589-91. It is a slackening of men's fear of God which has led to a general lack of fear and respect for authority and law and with it civil war. And this civil war is made much the more horrible by God's evident intention to use the war and its afflictions as a form of divine punishment and retribution which will bring men back to fear of His judgements. [59]

> Or l'opinion de l'Epicure, homme detestable, non seulement aneantit l'amour diuin qui est inseparable de sa crainte: ains aussi en arrachant du cœur des hommes la crainte de Dieu, il arrache aussi toutes les loix diuines & humaines, & rēuerse le fondement de toutes citez, empires, & societes, qui ne sont entretenues que par la crainte d'offenser Dieu: car si les princes & grāds seigneurs n'auoyent crainte que des magistrats, ausquels ils commandent, qui est-ce qui les empescheroit de mal faire? Et si les meschans sujets ne craignoyent q̃ les iuges & tesmoings, qui les retiendroit de faire mille mechancetez execrables à couuert? il faut dõc tenir pour tout resolu que la vraye sapience de Dieu git en son amour & en sa crainte: & d'autant que la plus part des hõmes est plus retenüe par la crainte que par l'amour, pour ceste cause la crainte de Dieu est beaucoup plus souuent recommandee, & trescõvenable à la Majesté diuine, & tresnecessaire au salut de tous empires, estats, & monarchies (pp. 97f).

---

[58] With marginal references to Proverbs, Psalms, Job and Ecclesiastes. For the belief that God never refuses His help to anyone who asks see *Paradoxe*, pp. 37, 92, 95. Cf. above, notes 28 and 54.

[59] Rose, 'Politique and the Prophet', pp. 787f, 808. The Latin version of the *Paradoxon* largely omits these remarks of immediate political significance. (According to Bellier's dedication of his 1575 translation of Philo, it was wisdom which revealed to men the truth that the religious wars were divine retribution for impiety and blasphemy.)

The *Paradoxe* echoes many opinions to be found in Philo and Maimonides. The most fundamental of these views is the Deuteronomic insistence that man's free will enables him to choose whether to obey God or not. [60] Such obedience is the essence of virtue and virtue becomes a quality attainable by the natural man. Christian grace is not essential to the achievement of such virtues as faith, hope, charity or repentance, which become in Jewish ethics natural religious virtues. When Bodin treated faith, hope and charity in the *Paradoxe* it was not the Christian meaning of these virtues he was discussing but rather their Judaised counterparts which were rooted in the dual love and fear of God, the two feelings which represented for Philo the poles of moral conscience. [61] Sometimes divine help was required, it is true, by men to attain fully these natural virtues, but such divine aid as Bodin called it was a far cry from Christian grace; for divine help in Bodin's mind was never denied to that man who of his own free will turned and prayed to God.

At the same time Philo, Maimonides and Bodin all regarded such natural religious virtues as charity and wisdom as preparation or disposition of man to receive the true happiness of a higher kind of virtue whose achievement lay beyond man's natural grasp. Only divine light could illuminate men with the actual ecstatic vision of God and the mystical love of the divine. [62] (Paradoxically it was in this thoroughly Judaised idea of prophetic illumination that Bodin came closest to the Christian idea of grace!).

Bodin's conceptions of virtue, free will and divine "grace" therefore form parts of a wholly Judaised structure of thought; to attempt to make sense of these ideas from a Christian perspective is a doomed undertaking. But Bodin's mental orientation, it should be remembered, is Judaising rather than Jewish. Bodin's treatment of one particular Gospel quotation illustrates this point vividly. In the *Paradoxe* Bodin quoted Matthew XI, 30, to show that religious virtue lay within man's power: "For my yoke is easy and my burden light". [63] By this quotation Bodin signalled that his private religious beliefs did not bind him to subscribe to the strict ritual requirements of Judaism and that he preferred to accept the Christian relaxation of the Law. Such an outlook made it easier for Bodin to conform to the Christian customs and habits — and politics — of sixteenth century France. But the end of this particular passage in the *Paradoxe* quotes tellingly the Jewish archetype from which the Christian guarantee derives: There is no difficulty in obeying God because "God has commanded nothing that is impossible to do — all his commands pertain to things that are easy, reasonable, equitable and natural". [64] Bodin's Judaising here consists in his conviction that both the Old and New Testaments depend on the fundamental Deuteronomic command to choose good; the implication is that most of the other specific religious requirements which shroud this commandment — whether the Christian requirement of belief in a redeeming

[60] Cf. Sandmel, *Philo*, p. 113.

[61] Cf. E. Bréhier, *Les Idées philosophiques et religieuses de Philon d'Alexandrie* (3rd ed. Paris, 1950), p. 310. See Chapter IV above.

[62] E.g. Sandmel, *Philo*, p. 101. Maimonides, *Guide*, II, xxxii (trs. p. 220).

[63] *Paradoxe*, p. 33. See above, note 22.

[64] *Paradoxe*, p. 37, citing Deuteronomy XXVIII nd XXIX. On Bodin's Judaising see also Mesnard, 'Bodin critique', pp. 558 ff, 562.

Christ or the Jewish ritual laws — are matters of indifference to true religion. If Bodin's ancestors had been Jewish he might well have observed the specific laws of Judaism. As it was he was educated in Christianity and so was willing to live and die in the Catholic Church. Once again the influence of Philo seems to be reassert itself in the whole character of Bodin's Judaising, an influence admitted in the *Heptaplomeres*:

> Philo the Hebrew said (*De Abrahamo, 5*) that the commandments depart not at all from nature and it is not a task of great effort to live your life according to the prescriptions of divine laws; for the tables of Moses contain nothing but the laws of nature and the life (*i.e. customs*) of our ancestors. [65]

[65] *Heptaplomeres*, ed. Noack, p. 190 (trs. p. 249). See Chapter VII for Latin text.

CHAPTER VI

THE EMERGENCE OF BODIN'S JUDAISED IDEA OF VIRTUE FROM THE "ORATIO" TO THE "THEATRUM" (1559-96)

When did the system of Judaised ethical ideas of the *Paradoxe* begin to take shape in Bodin's mind? If we cast a retrospective glance over Bodin's writings we will see that his thinking on virtue and man's power naturally to attain it underwent a considerable development between the *Oratio* of 1559 and his final conclusions on the subject reached thirty years later. Nevertheless from the start Bodin held a religious conception of virtue, recognising that ethics had to form part of a view of the world which expressed the relationship between God and nature. The development of this idea of virtue between the *Oratio* and his later works therefore consisted not in the movement from a secular to a religious ethics (his ethics had been religious from the beginning) but rather in the progressive Judaisation of his religious matrix. One may follow tentatively from one work to another that gradual Judaisation of Bodin's ideas of free will, grace, theological virtue and original sin which was to reach its climax in the *Paradoxe* and the *Heptaplomeres*. [1]

The appearances of virtue in various guises in the *Oratio*, the *Methodus* and the *République* have already been described in the first part of this book but it is now time to re-examine some of those earlier remarks in the light of what we know to be Bodin's later religious conception of virtue. In earlier chapters we were pursuing the role of virtue in the state and its relationship to learning and education; now we have to look for the religious essence of those ideas of virtue.

When Bodin wrote the *Oratio* he believed that "true wisdom is a conflation of firm virtue and the knowledge (*scientia*) of important things" and he avowed that it was this wisdom which brought man "close to the divinity of immortal God". [2] Throughout the *Oratio* Bodin seems to consider both virtue (represented pre-eminently by *amicitia*) and science as natural qualities although they were bred originally into human nature by God. For the young Bodin the main faculty involved in the furthering of both virtue and knowledge is reason and

---

[1] I shall in Chapter VIII attempt a more comprehensive account of the evolution of Bodin's religion.

[2] *Oratio,* ed. Mesnard, p. 14. See Chapters I and II for the Latin texts of most of the quotations given in English in this chapter.

indeed his whole philosophy in the *Oratio* is overwhelmingly rationalistic. *Scientia* may even "in revealing the causes of things educate us completely and give us faith (*fidem*) of a kind that enraged Epicureans could not dissipate". [3] Already Bodin has begun to reject the Christian idea of faith as given by grace even though his rationalistic idea of faith was in turn to be abandoned in the *Paradoxe* in favour of a concept of faith that was rooted in free will rather than intellect or rational argument. [4]

Reason itself is the great gift of God to man and Bodin describes it as a form of illumination without any hint of his later belief that illumination was prophetic. Light, it is clearly implied, is sent to all men in the form of reason, although some men, "like animals destitute of reason (*ratio*) are driven by instinct alone and... may refuse the light (*lux*) so divinely sent down to them". [5] Right itself is the light of the mind (*recta ratio, mentis lumen*). [6] Reason therefore is a natural faculty of man although it was originally placed or illumined in man by God.

Another respect in which Bodin's rationalistic attitude renders the *Oratio* somewhat remote from the Judaised thought of his mature works lies in its treatment of the will. There is very little attention paid to the rational will or free will (*voluntas*) in this early work. Indeed will seeems to be reduced to mere *appetitus* or the irrational will which must of course be curbed by reason. Thus, Cyrus is praised because he "learnt to govern himself and to subdue his appetite to reason which is the summation of all justice and natural law". There is no indication here (or in the opposite example of Circe who enslaved men to their appetites) of the crucial role to be played by free will in overcoming the appetite; the basis of moral philosophy is simply the rule of reason. [7]

The *Oratio*'s moral virtue of *amicitia* is itself seen as being born of reason rather than of free will; for *amicitia* is "connected with learning by the tightest of knots". [8] In the *Paradoxe*, however, Bodin eventually succeeded in Judaising amity by identifying it with justice — justice being the Judaised moral virtue *zedakah* which was born of free will. [9]

In three different respects, therefore, one may see how Bodin's later Judaising was to distance him from the ethical ideas so confidently and optimistically proclaimed in the *Oratio*. Adoption of a Judaised stance was to revolutionise his early rational theory of illumination, was to bring into prominence the central role of free will, and was to change *amicitia* from a more or less rational to a willed virtue. In a word, the Judaisation of Bodin's ethics meant transforming the entire basis of his ethics — and his religion — from rationalism to voluntarism.

Bodin's remarks on virtue in the *Oratio* are very fragmentary and elliptical but in the *Methodus* he is more direct. Here Bodin anticipates the *Paradoxe* in

---

[3] *Oratio*, p. 15.
[4] *Paradoxe* (1598), pp. 90f.
[5] *Oratio*, p. 14.
[6] *Ibidem*, p. 23.
[7] *Ibidem*, pp. 23f.
[8] *Ibidem*, p. 26.
[9] *Paradoxe*, p. 87.

dividing virtue into prudence, science and "religio".[10] Prudence distinguishes good from evil, science the true from the false, religion piety from impiety. But he then declares that these virtues joined together constitute wisdom (*vera sapientia*).[11] This is not wholly inconsistent with what Bodin later wrote about wisdom in the *Paradoxe* although he there defined wisdom as charity or the (natural) love of God. There is, however, a real discrepancy between one of these early remarks and his final thoughts. In the *Methodus* Bodin comments that "true wisdom is the highest and extreme good of man (*summum hominis extremumque bonum*)" and that it is "participation in this good which makes men happy in this life (*cujus boni qui sunt in hac vita participes beati appellantur*)".[12] Yet this earthly happiness secured by wisdom is surpassed by the highest happiness of the mystical ascent to the divine.

> By these steps (*the virtues and sciences*) man is carried on to things grasped only by the minde — that is, to the strength and power of immortal souls — until he is closely united (*conjungatur*) to God. In this consist the goal of human action, the final peace and the highest felicity.[13]

This visionary understanding of happiness and the supreme good of man anticipates the understanding of man's *extremum bonum* or *félicité extrême* in the *Paradoxe* as consisting in the illuminated love and vision of God.[14] But how is one to reconcile this mystical idea of happiness in the *Methodus* with the statement in the same work that true wisdom is the highest good which makes men happy in this life? The key is to be found in Bodin's phrase *in hac vita*; it is only in the present life that wisdom is the highest good of man. In the future or the spiritual life man's highest happiness is rather the mystical approach to God. In the *Methodus*, therefore, Bodin is advancing a bifurcated notion of supreme happiness, one branch of which is confined to the natural sphere, the other to the supernatural life of the soul. In the *Paradoxe*, however, Bodin moved beyond this unsatisfactory conceptual framework to insist that there was a single supreme happiness[15] which applied simultaneously to both lives of man and he took pains to explain that in speaking of a happy life "one should not understand by that merely the present life, but also the life of the future which will be still happier, as is indicated by the sacred tongue's use of the word *hayyim*, that is, lives."[16] In the *Methodus* Bodin posited two separate supreme forms of happiness, one for each life; in the *Paradoxe* he

---

[10] *Methodus*, p. 114B (trs., p. 15), quoted in Chapter II, note 1. The English version mistranslates *religio* as "faith", thereby imparting a Christian gloss to Bodin's virtues. Cf. my analysis of *Paradoxe*, pp. 65ff, given in the preceding chapter, section (d). Where page references to the *Paradoxe* are given in the present footnotes a fuller analysis as well as French quotations may usually be found in Chapter V.

[11] *Methodus*, p. 114B (p. 15).

[12] *Ibidem*.

[13] *Methodus*, p. 120A (p. 30). See Chapter II, note 3.

[14] For the terminology see *Paradoxon* (1596), p. 30. *Paradoxe* (1598), p. 28. In these texts Bodin certainly regarded wisdom as a good bringing a degree of happiness, but not as the highest or extreme good of man of which there was only one.

[15] *Paradoxe*, p. 18, asserts there can be only one *félicité extrême*.

[16] *Paradoxe*, p. 21. See Chapter VII, note 35, for further use of *hayyim* in the *Heptaplomeres*.

abandoned this for a single supreme happiness which was to be realised more often in the future life. Although, therefore, a mystical element had already entered Bodin's thinking by 1566 the alterations to his general structure of ideas it demanded were only half-executed in the *Methodus*. The full reconstruction of his theology and moral philosophy still lay ahead.

The same may be said of Bodin's new-found insistence on the will which emerges in the *Methodus*; he has the essence of the new idea but has not yet found a suitable framework in which to locate it.

> ... Will (*voluntas*) leads the way. For the will is the mistress of human actions whether it turns to reason or to the lower quality of the soul in seeking and avoiding things. [17]

Bodin has clearly recognised the domination of the will in the divided soul, but he has still not arrived at his mature theory of the unitary soul which will reveal and establish the full predominance of the will. Moreover, Bodin is still tied to a rationalistic position.

> Human actions produce errors daily unless guided by nature, that is, by right reason. [18]

Yet despite this initial confidence in human nature Bodin is pessimistic for "contact with earthly matter" and "the natural conflict of the passions in man" contaminate the human mind even if it be originally plucked from the divine mind. Hence,

> without divine aid (*ope divina*) the human mind may not attain any part of justice, nor may it achieve anything in accordance with nature. [19]

This gloomy statement seems to acknowledge a natural instinct to virtue while concluding that humanity is so flawed that it cannot fulfil this instinct by exercise of its will and reason without the aid of grace. But perhaps we should not jump to conclusions for it seems possible that Bodin was already influenced by Jewish ideas of free will and divine "aid", rather than by Christian "grace", and in the remark just quoted he may be using *opes divina* to convey the idea of divine aid as he does in his later writing. In the *Paradoxe* Bodin did not intend by *opes divina* the Christian idea of grace which comes to man without his having any say in the matter. Rather does Bodin seem to understand by the term God's quasi-natural response of aid to the good man who prays. Such aid Bodin terms in the *Paradoxe* the "ordinary aid of God which proceeds from natural causes". [20] In the *Paradoxe* the Judaised concept

---

[17] *Methodus*, p. 119B (p. 29). See Chapter II, note 14.

[18] *Methodus*, p. 115A (p. 17): "Atque omnino humanae actiones novis semper erroribus implicantur, nisi a natura duce, id est, a recta ratione."

[19] *Methodus*, p. 115AB (trs. p. 17): "ut sine opte divina nec se ipsam erigere, nec ullam justitiae partem adipisci, nec quicquam naturae congruenter agere possit."

[20] "Aide ordinaire" (*Paradoxe*, 1598, p. 35): "Ope divina ... opes ordinariae" (*Paradoxon*, 1596, p. 37). See Chapter V, note 26. Another aspect of Bodin's Judaised concept of grace may be seen in the non-volitional theory of prophecy to which he alludes in *Methodus*, p. 119B (p. 29). See Chapter VIII.

of grace designated by *opes divina* and *aide ordinaire* had in effect preserved the power of free will from that intrinsic weakness in the face of grace which afflicted it in Christian philosophy. Perhaps, then, Bodin as early as the *Methodus* was indicating by his terminology a basic departure from Christian grace, no matter how inchoate still may have been his Judaisation of the concept of divine aid.

Moreover, even if Bodin had not yet arrived at his later ideas of wisdom, the good and free will, the *Methodus* shows in one crucial respect at least that already in 1566 Bodin was moving towards a clearly Judaised ethics. For as an alternative to both Platonic and Aristotelian concepts of justice and prudence Bodin here elucidates a theory of Philo's which sets up four classes of "moral" virtue, namely prudence, temperance, magnanimity and integrity.

> Philo, avoiding ambiguity of words, preferred to call the highest good that justice which is nothing else than a certain righteousness and integrity in all plans, words and deeds. [21]

These four classes of prudential "moral" virtues are, it may be recalled, precisely those (if we read *justice* for *integrity*) which Bodin later expounded in the *Paradoxe* (pp. 76ff). As in the later philosophical work the *Methodus* sought to relate Philo's concept of justice to traditional Jewish views of charity by suggesting that Plato's theory that justice begins first in oneself is better put by the opinion of Philo that "each man initiates charity in himself". [22] This very notion recurs in the *Paradoxe* with the remark that "this virtue the Hebrews call *tsedaca* (i.e. *zedakah*, meaning also charity and righteousness) that is to say, justice" (p. 79). Philo was here the acknowledged source of Bodin's Judaised theory of virtue, expressed imperfectly in the *Methodus* but developing over the next two decades into the fully elaborated theory of the *Paradoxe*. [23]

The *République* [24] faithfully follows the distinction made in the *Methodus* between prudence, science and religion as different species of virtue. [25] Bodin is, however, now far more explicit on the supremacy of intellectual virtue and even asserts that man's "sovereign good depends on the intellectual virtues". [26] This phrasing suggests that Bodin had not yet fully thought out his Judaised religious conception of virtue for he seems to admit here the dependence of the sovereign good of man on intellectual virtue: in the *Paradoxe*, on the other hand,

---

[21] *Methodus*, p. 123AB (trs. p. 38), see Chapter II, notes 10ff, for quotations. The reference seems to be to Philo, *Post Caini*, #85. Cf. the *Paradoxe*, pp. 76ff, analysed in preceding chapter. The animals have prudential sense of *suum cuique* or equality as opposed to justice. Such a prudence can scarcely be either intellectual or moral.

[22] *Methodus*, p. 123AB. See Chapters II, and V, notes 43-44.

[23] One curious aspect of the transitional character of Bodin's thinking in the *Methodus* is the manner in which he *appears* to accept Aristotle's theory of virtue as the mean of two vices at p. 123A (trs. p. 38).

[24] Unfortunately my references are to the 1583 Paris edition and may indicate Bodin's thinking as it was in 1583 rather than in 1576 when the *République* first appeared.

[25] *République* (1583), p. 6, quoted in Chapter II, note 18.

[26] *Ibidem*, pp. 7f, quoted in Chapter II, note 20. As in the *Paradoxe* Bodin criticises Aristotle's notion of the "action of the intellect".

Bodin clearly understood the sovereign good of man to consist in the divinely illuminated enjoyment and vision of God (p. 24) and emphasised this to be a pure and free gift of God without any dependence on man's own virtuous achievement or intellect. [27] There is certainly an interest here in illumination but it is somewhat problematic since Bodin seems to regard the effusion of divine light as having a purifying function more or less equivalent to that of the moral virtues.

> Il est impossible, que l'ame puisse recueillir le doux fruict de contemplation, qu'elle ne soit esclarcie & purifiee par les vertus morales, ou par la lumiere diuine. [28]

It might seem at first that divine illumination has not yet fully taken the prophetic and mystic character it assumes in the *Paradoxe*; on the other hand, Bodin may well mean that illumination can by its very advent purify a man who has not already purified himself through moral virtue. [29] This seems to me to be the most likely meaning of Bodin's words.

By the time we come to the *Démonomanie* of 1580 Bodin's thought has clarified itself into the Judaised shape in which we have recognised it in the *Paradoxe*. Free will and the Deuteronomic choice now firmly emerge as the basis of virtue. [30] The choice of virtue may be indirect in the sense that a man might pray to God and be granted prudence and wisdom; in this case it may seem that the man receives prudence and wisdom through divine grace, but, as we have seen in the *Paradoxe* (pp. 33, 95, 98), the original choice to keep the commandments and pray to God is within man's natural powers. On the other hand, prayer to God will not obtain for man the gift of prophecy or illumination. Here then we have a strong intimation by Bodin of the separation made in the *Paradoxe* between wisdom and prudence as "natural" virtues and prophecy as a "supernatural" virtue.

> I'ay dict que c'est vn singulier don de Dieu, quand il enuoye son bõ esprit à celuy qu'il aime, pour estre entendu de luy, & guidé en toutes ses actions: Car il se peut faire que l'homme sera vertueux, & craignant Dieu, & le priera assiduelle-mẽt, & neantmoins Dieu, peut estre, ne luy donnera pas son esprit: mais bien luy donnera tant de sagesse & de prudence qu'il luy sera besoing. [31]

Bodin has already arrived at a Judaised concept of illumination which will replace Christian grace but he is still searching for an adequate terminology as may be seen from his loose use of the Christian term "grace" in the following

---

[27] Some other indications of Bodin's inconclusive thinking here are his loose references to moral and intellectual virtue (*République,* pp. 9f, quoted in Chapter II, note 24) and the imprecise remarks about the upper and lower souls (*République,* p. 6, quoted above Chapter II, note 18) which suggest he had not yet arrived at his final idea of the unitary soul.

[28] *République,* p. 8. See above, Chapter II, note 23.

[29] This interpretation is quote consistent with the prophetic thought of the *Démonomanie.* Illumination may also bring by its very introduction "faith". See *Heptaplomeres,* ed. Noack, p. 193 (trs. p. 252), and the next chapter.

[30] *Démonomanie,* (Paris, 1580), f. 8v.

[31] *Ibidem,* f. 9v.

passage where he summarises what is essentially the *Paradoxe*'s understanding of the relation between virtue and divine illumination.

> Et au contraire si l'homme s'adonne à bien, & qu'il éleue son ame à Dieu, à bien, à vertu, apres que son ame sera purifiée d'vne grace diuine, s'il s'exerce aux vertus morales, & puis aux vertus intellectuelles, il se pourra faire, qu'il ayt telle societé auec l'Ange de Dieu qu'il ne sera pas seulemẽt gardé par iceluy, ains il sentira sa presence, & cognoistra les choses, qu'il cõmande, & qu'il luy defend. Mais celà aduient à peu d'hommes, & d'vne grace, & bonté speciale de Dieu. [32]

This usage of grace was, as we have seen, to be expunged carefully from the descriptions of his own ideas which Bodin gave in the *Paradoxe* and replaced there by such terms as *effusion de la lumière divine*.

In both the *Consilium* and the *Sapientia* we see a continuation of the new ideas of the *Démonomanie* together with its obsolescent terminology. [33] One finds in the *Sapientia*, for instance, illuminative elements (no. 203) accompanied by the idea of the *sainte loy de grace* (no. 196). There is too a continuation of the *Démonomanie*'s fervent preoccupation with the idea of willing prayer as the road to conversion. At the same time the *Sapientia*'s broad Judaised structure of virtue looks forward to the *Paradoxe*: Faith and charity appear in a non-Christian form, constituting parts of a hierarchy of natural virtue including prudence, justice, science, faith and charity, and wisdom.

The virtues treated mainly in the *Paradoxe* are prudence and wisdom but Bodin's *Theatrum Universae Naturae* is devoted to demonstration of the third member of the triumvirate of virtue, *scientia*. As with the other virtues there is a religious dimension to Bodin's *scientia* for scientific knowledge of the natural universe leads man to God its creator. Yet, like prudence and wisdom, science is basically a natural virtue attainable by the exercise of man's natural understanding (*entendement* or *intellectus*). Understanding is a property of the soul and so most of the relevant discussion falls within the fourth book of the *Theatrum* where the soul is treated as a natural entity and part of the universe of nature. Here again the religious and the natural coincide.

As in the *Paradoxe* (pp. 59, 65) Bodin argues here that God Himself placed the seeds of virtue in men as part of their nature.

> So indeed in our souls have the seeds of all virtues and sciences been divinely sown as in the most flagrant gardens... (*If even animals have a certain natural reason then*) how much more truly will men draw out and express the seeds of sciences and virtues (*planted*) by the Father of nature? [34]

---

[32] *Ibidem*, f. 9. Cf. f. 25v: "L'infusion et grace prophétique." U. Lange, *Untersuchungen zu Bodins Démonomanie* (Frankfurt, 1970), p. 88, points out that the idea of grace and nature explained here is not the same as that which obtains in Christianity. For a reference to "grace" in the Jewish sense in the *Heptaplomeres* see Chapter VII, note 35.

[33] See Chapter III.

[34] *Universae naturae theatrum* (Lyons, 1596), pp. 475f: "Sic etiam in animis nostris, virtutum ac scientiarum omnium semina divinitus sparsa fuisse, ut quasi in hortis odoratissimis ... Quanto verius igitur homines ab ipso naturae parente scientiarum ac virtutum semina hauserunt et expresserunt?"

The French translation by F. de Fougerolles, *Théâtre de la nature universelle* (Lyons, 1597), p. 688, misleadingly adds some phrases not in the Latin original which seriously

This passage might seem to the uninitiated reader to be suggesting an Augustinian theory of grace and knowledge but in fact the remarks are all very much in keeping with the Judaised idea of grace and nature developed in the *Paradoxe*. The Judaised character of the argument is confirmed by Bodin's citation of Philo's *Legum Allegoriae* I in support of the quoted opinion even though he is careful to protect himself by camouflaging Philo among a group of slightly more conventional Greek philosophers. [35]

The *Paradoxe* and the *Theatrum* agree in placing science and all the virtues under the governance of the will. In the *Theatrum* Bodin outlines a unitary theory of the soul, seeing it as composed of various properties and qualities, all of which are commanded by the will; this psychology, as we have seen, is resumed succinctly in the *Paradoxe*. [36] It may be noted once more that the motive for Bodin's insistence on the primacy of the will and its accompanying psychology lies in his Judaised conviction that man's natural free will is sufficient to make the Deuteronomic choice and secure salvation. Considering that the *Paradoxe* and the *Theatrum* were composed at approximately the same time this complete congruence of opinion is not surprising.

The *Démonomanie*, the *Theatrum* and the *Paradoxe* were all published works and in a way the censor has eased for us the task of collating their points of view by forcing Bodin to resort in each of them to similar strategies of caution in speaking of grace, virtue and free will. In each of them Bodin goes only so far and no further and, so to speak, marks out the boundaries of his ideas. But when we come to compare the *Paradoxe* with the last of his works, the *Heptaplomeres*, difficult problems arise. The *Heptaplomeres*, in remaining in manuscript, permitted Bodin to transgress the boundaries placed on the expression of his earlier thought and to go so much further in his explicit critique of Christianity that his censure here is almost qualitatively different from that to be found in his other writings. This difficulty is compounded by the whole cast of the *Heptaplomeres* which was written in a far more complex form than his other dialogues, consisting as it does of a rich intellectual texture woven by the interplay of seven different religions. Let us now try to disentangle some of the main strands in this tapestry and discover whether they are also to be found in the less vividly coloured portrayal of virtue in the *Paradoxe*.

distort Bodin's thought. Fougerolles, for instance, has Bodin saying that the seeds of virtue and science emerge "moyennant la lumière qu'il (God) leur en a communiqué par son esprit"; this absurdly renders ordinary science and virtue dependent on divine illumination. (Fougerolles also added a marginal reference of his own to a psalm to prove this bogus point).

[35] E.g., Empedocles, Plato, the Academics (*Theatrum*, p. 476) Lange, *Untersuchungen*, p. 78, rightly remarks that Bodin is not proclaiming here an Augustinian theory of grace and knowledge.

[36] P. Mesnard, 'The Psychology and Pneumatology of Jean Bodin', *International Philosophical Quarterly*, II (1962), 244-264. Cf. *Paradoxe*, pp. 49f.

CHAPTER VII

JUDAISED VIRTUE AND PROPHECY. THE TRUE RELIGION OF THE "HEPTAPLOMERES"

The *Heptaplomeres* was written during the same years as the *Theatrum* and the *Paradoxe* and these three late works together evince a single mental universe, though one depicted from different angles. Much of the congruence of belief is left implicit in each of these books or indicated only by allusive phrasing. A major reason for this obliqueness is that the subject of each book varies and Bodin only explicates those points which seem directly germane to the subject in question. But there is also another, more prudential reason for this reticence. Bodin's religious vision was radically non-Christian and it brought him into conflict at so many points of contact with Christianity that to have made explicit the theological consequences of his views, for example, of the soul or of free will, would have placed him in danger of his life. Only in the unpublished *Heptaplomeres* did Bodin feel free to give a complete and forthright statement of his criticisms of Christianity, expounding the significance of ideas which he had treated all too elliptically in his published writings.

Yet, as we have seen, we cannot assume automatically that those statements in the *Heptaplomeres* which are critical of Christianity represent Bodin's authentic beliefs, for the work is written in the form of a colloquy involving seven speakers. The purpose of this chapter is to develop a critical method which will permit us to determine whether Bodin himself agreed with the *Heptaplomeres*' scepticism about the Christian doctrines of grace, sin and free will, a scepticism predominantly voiced by Salomon the Jew and Toralba the advocate of natural religion. The method consists in comparing the remarks in the *Heptaplomeres* with those expressed in Bodin's published writings, using the *Paradox* as the main control.

A basic principle of this method is the fact that Bodin could not — for fear of the stake — have put into print any forthright criticism of the crucial points of Christian doctrine: we should not therefore look for a denial of Christ in the published writings. Rather it is enough to show:

1. that there is some positive correlation between statements in the *Paradoxe* and the *Heptaplomeres* regarding virtue and free will;
2. that both works refute the Christian idea of theological virtue, whether or not they leave implicit the logical consequences of this refutation for the Christian ideas of grace and salvation;

3. that there is no contradiction in the *Paradoxe* of such Jewish statements of theology as appear in the *Heptaplomeres* (with the exception of Maimonidean rational faith, as will be seen in due course).

A final methodological factor should also be borne in mind, namely the fact that Bodin's choice of colloquium form enabled him to put some of his Judaised opinions into the mouth, not only of Salomon, but of Toralba and other speakers where there was some common ground between the religions they represented.

A full application of this critical method to the *Heptaplomeres* belongs in another place but an analysis of some of the key passages in the *Heptaplomeres* regarding virtue, controlled by reference to the *Paradoxe,* should be enough for the present to prove the sincerity of Bodin's Judaising in this inexhaustibly fascinating work.

The first of our passages to be examined occurs in the third book of the *Heptaplomeres* and links the problem of evil to the rejection of Aristotle's claim that virtue lies in the mean of two vices. The discussion of evil recalls the content of the opening section of the *Paradoxe* (pp. 6-15) and opens with Salomon giving a theological explanation of why evil does not exist in itself but is rather the privation of good as when God's protection or preserving power are withdrawn. Toralba then takes up the same line in a philosophical form. Effectively summarising the points made in the Aristotelian critique of the *Paradoxe* (pp. 45-64), Toralba castigates Aristotle for fallaciously believing that evil is the contrary of good and at the same time that evil is infinite; for, he says, only the First Cause is infinite and by definition that First Cause has no contrary. Besides, if evil were infinite "then it would have overwhelmed finite goodness and overturned the world" — in other words, evil would have defeated the good preserving power of God which holds the universe together and the natural forces of degeneration would have prevailed. [1] It is even more foolish of Aristotle, says Toralba, to think that virtue might be a mean between two vices; for then one vice would have two opposites — namely the mean virtue and the opposing vice — and in nature there is only one opposite. When the pagan Senamus objects that this means throwing away the golden mean and that moderation must be retained for the moral virtues if not for the intellectual, Toralba retorts that all the virtues must be intellectual in the Stoic sense since otherwise one would be praising moderaion in some virtues but not others. But the detailed argument on the mean and intellectual virtue stops here quite suddenly. The reason for this was that Bodin was reserving his Judaised explanation of virtue for the more appropriate setting of the *Paradoxe.* A similar consideration also restrained Bodin from discussing his Judaised ethics in the *Theatrum.* There Bodin's main concern had been with demonstrating the natural qualities of the soul; here in the *Heptaplomeres* the question

---

[1] *Heptaplomeres,* ed. Noack, pp. 86f (trs. p. 112f), speeches of Salomon and Toralba. *Ibidem,* p. 90 (trs. p. 117) cites Philo for the opinion that God cannot be the author of evil.

of virtue arises out of an investigation of angels and demons which raises the problems of whether demons may be said to be "evil". It should be stressed that the interlocutors in these pages are wholly in agreement with Bodin's view in the *Paradoxe* that the demons are God's good agents who inflict punishment on men for their disobedience of God's commands, a punishment which men tend to perceive as the presence of evil. [2]

.**.

Our next passage occurs in Book V where Toralba is seeking to prove his variety of natural religion to be the authentic *vera religio*. This is a critical section for when compared and controlled by the relevant remarks in his published writings on nature, virtue, prophecy and illumination, it will be seen that Bodin could agree only to a limited extent with the opinion he puts into the mouth of Toralba. Indeed, Salomon's modifications of Toralba's attitude recapitulate the beliefs of Bodin himself as expressed in the *Paradoxe* and other writings.

Salomon begins with an important speech explaining that human nature is strong enough to achieve virtue but is insufficient to attain that true mystical knowledge of God which requires illumination — a point of view which as we have seen is basic to the *Paradoxe*.

> There is a certain excellent power of nature planted in men's mind which excites them to piety, justice and all the virtues . But to attain divine knowledge unless God has inspired men is no more possible than for a picture in a dark place to seem distinct though painted by a skilled hand and in an elegant variety of colour .... Sometimes God allows men to be so blinded that, although they may have acquired a knowledge of all great things, they never enjoy the knowledge of God and true religion. [3]

Toralba immediately agrees: "Indeed, I agree that the power and force of nature are not so great that a man may attain the consummate wisdom of divine things without the aid and light of God". Such an admission of divine intervention should make one wary of routinely cataloguing Toralba as a deist in the mould of the natural religion of the Enlightenment. [4] His outlook seems rather more to be in the Platonic tradition if one is to judge not only from Toralba's statement but also the comment of Salomon who after damning

---

[2] *Ibidem*, p. 89 (trs. p. 115). Cf. *Paradoxe*, pp. 12ff.

[3] *Heptaplomeres*, p. 186 (trs. pp. 234f). "Praeclara quidem vis naturae est, hominum mentibus insita, quae illos ad pietâtem, justitiam, virtutes omnes exsuscitat: sed ut divinam sententiam assequaéur, nisi Deus ipsos afflaverit, non magis fieri poetst, quam inclusa tabula docta manu picta atque elegante colorum varietate distincta videri, sed oportebit perspicuo lumine illustrati.... Interdum Deus homines ita excoecari patitur, ut etiamsi rerum omnium magnarum scientiam adepti sint, nunquam Dei cognitione ac vera religione fruantur." The passage concludes by referring to Job's belief that wisdom "is granted by the gift and concession of immortal God alone"; "wisdom" here means the illuminated knowledge of the divine, as is shown by the context and also by Toralba's ensuing remark about the "consummate wisdom of divine affairs." For Bodin, *human* wisdom, although religious in character, did not require illumination See *Paradoxe*, pp. 88ff.

[4] *Heptaplomeres*, ed. Noack, p. 186 (trs. pp. 243f).

136

Aristotle for his impious ignorance of God, observes that "no one ought to think it strange if the divine light shone more abundantly for Plato than for all the other philosophers since he pursued God in all his writings with such reverence". [5]

Toralba and Salomon quickly agree that the inspired or illuminated knowledge and enjoyment of God represents man's happiness and highest good: "The highest good (*extremum bonum*) of man lies in the enjoyment of eternal God", says Salomon. This provokes an objection from Senamus that according to Aristotle the highest good (*sunnum bonum*) of man consisted in the action of virtue. Giving the floor to Toralba to explain the philosophical reasoning behind Salomon's religious statement, Bodin now offers a faithful summary of many of the ideas to be found in the second section of the *Paradoxe* (pp. 15-44). [6] The main charge is that Aristotle disastrously confused the end (*finis*) of man with his highest good (*summum bonum*): "The end of man is to have served the glory of God" while the highest good which man can enjoy is the enjoyment of God Himself, Who is the highest good of all things.

> Those are undoubtedly in error who say that the content or subject of moral philosophy is the *summum bonum*; for the highest good is God through Himself and cannot be thought as anything else. [7]

When Senamus asks what then is the subject of moral wisdom Toralba replies: "A man that is to be happy". The Latin here is exactly the same as that used in the first edition of the *Paradoxon* (p. 20) — *Homo beandus*, rendered in the French less cryptically as *l'homme disposé à recevoir la félicité humaine* (*Paradoxe*, p. 19). According to both the *Heptaplomeres* and the *Paradoxe*, moral wisdom which prepares man for the understanding of God is quite different from that divine knowledge or wisdom which signifies man's understanding and enjoyment of God and which is happiness itself.

On this fundamental point the *Paradoxe* is completely at one with the *Heptaplomeres*. The *summum bonum* — God Himself — is the subject of theology; the preparation of man to accede to this *summum bonum* is the subject of moral philosophy. The enjoyment of God the sovereign good of all things is indeed man's own highest good and is identified in both works with happiness itself which is the result of an effusion of divine light.

> The action of virtue is not the *extremum bonum* of man. That action is related to contemplation as motion is related to rest; contemplation is related to knowledge of the best thing, that is to knowledge of God, and knowledge is related to love and exceptional love to enjoyment. Indeed for what purpose do you love except that you enjoy the thing loved? Moreover, in this enjoyment the highest

---

[5] *Ibidem*, p. 187 (trs. pp. 244f). Salomon then points out that searching by the natural power of the mind is not enough to find God. "Moses, as well as Salomon, not once indicated that God is to be found by those who are driven by all the power (*impetu*) of the mind to search and revere Him."

[6] *Ibidem*, pp. 188-190 (trs. pp. 246-248).

[7] *Ibidem*, p. 189 (trs. p. 247): "Toralba: Ex quo sequitur illud etiam, eos scilicet aberrare, qui argumentum aut subjectum philosophiae moralis statuunt esse summum bonum aut subjectum philosophiae moralis statuunt esse summum bonum, quod per se ipsum Deus est, nec aliud cogitari potest."

measure of the soul consists in reflected action, that is, in the clearest effusion of the light and love of God towards us which we obtain passively and not through our action. [8]

So far Toralba has made most of the running and it might be tempting to assume that he and not Salomon is the main vehicle in the *Heptaplomeres* for those views which Bodin himself expresses in the *Paradoxe*. Yet Toralba is merely developing ideas of the highest good as the enjoyment of God and of happiness as an effusion of divine light — ideas which are first set forth by Salomon in these pages of the *Heptaplomeres*. More importantly still, Salomon takes over the exposition when Senamus raises a fatal objection to the idea of happiness as it is embodied in the context of Toralba's natural religion. Happiness in Toralba's religion could only exist for a man whose soul was no longer in his body; no living man might be happy.

> But because this happiness of divine enjoyment may touch no mortal as long as the mind (*mens*) is included in the debtor's prison of the mortal body, who will ever be happy? [9]

What Senamus is actually saying is that Toralba has proposed the idea of illumination in such vague terms that it is quite useless as a concept of happiness. Indeed Toralba never suggests a mechanism or medium for the transmission and reception of divine light; in a word, he has an inkling of illumination but no proper theory and is therefore wholly at a loss for any helpful description at all of the phenomenon. The proposal of a true theory of illumination is indeed left to Salomon who in his answer to Senamus' question sees prophetic revelation as the missing factor in Toralba's notion of illumination.

> Yet surely that happiness happened only to a few; for example to Moses alone when awake, to the other prophets when sleeping. Yet not to all did it happen. Isaiah said: "I see God on the sublime seat of majesty, and my eyes have seen God, the King of the armies." Likewise Ezechiel in a longer speech glories that he has attained this happiness. The stage of prophecy nearest to this happiness is when the divine light (*through*) an interceding angel joined to the human mind (*mens*) illuminates (*affulget*) during sleep. [10]

[8] *Ibidem*, p. 189 (trs. p. 248): "Toralba: Igitur actio virtutis non est extremum hominis bonum, quoniam ad contemplationem, ut motus ad quietem refertur, contemplatio ad optimae rei h. e. ad Dei cognitionem, cognitio ad ejus amorem, amor eximius ad fruitionem. Ad quod enim amas, nisi ut re amata fruaris? In hac autem fruitione summa voluptas animi versatur in actu reflexo h.e. in clarissima lucis et amoris Dei ergas nos effusione, quam patiendo adipiscimur, non agendo." (Cf. *Paradoxe*, pp. 18-44, passim, especially pp. 23 and 43). Salomon's remark on the same page of the *Heptaplomeres* that Aristotle erred in thinking the duty, end and happiness of man to be one and the same recapitulates *Paradoxe*, pp. 15ff.

[9] *Heptaplomeres*, ed. Noack, p. 189 (trs. p. 248): "Senamus: Sed cum haec beatitas divinae fruitionis mortalium nemini contingat tantisper, quam mortalis corporis ergastulo inclusa mens est, qui unquam beatus erit?"

[10] *Ibidem*: "Certe paucis admodum felicitas illa contigit, ut Mosi tantum vigilanti, caeteris prophetis dormientibus, nec tamen omnibus. Video, inquit Esaias, Deum in sublimi sede majestatis et viderunt oculi mei regem Deum exercituum. Item Ezechiel oratione longiore se hanc beatitudinem assecutum gloriatur. Huic felicitati proximus est prophetiae gradus, cum divina lux, intercedente angelo humanae menti copulato inter dormiendum affulget."

For Salomon happiness, which consists in the illuminated enjoyment of God, is to be identified with the highest degrees of prophecy.

Here is the lynchpin of Bodin's religion; for prophecy has a dual function — it *illuminates* the soul with love of God *and* it *reveals* the will of God to man. The two main poles of Bodin's *vera religio* — illumination and revelation — are reconciled in prophecy.

We have then Toralba admitting that the enjoyment of God comes only with illumination by divine light and at the same time we find Salomon proposing that this illumination is indeed prophecy which brings with it revelation; in other words Salomon denies Toralba's idea of natural, non-revealed religion. Can we say which of these two views is Bodin's own? Fortunately the question is an easy one and answered by Bodin himself in the published *Paradoxe*. In the *Paradoxe*, p. 31, Bodin outlines a Judaised argument from Philo and Maimonides which almost exactly parallels Salomon's views in the passages from the *Heptaplomeres* just cited.

> Since men have so little understanding of this sovereign good as long as they are attached to the body and much less the enjoyment of that good, whom may we call the most happy in this world after those whom you have called very happy? Those to whom God has sent the light of prophecy (*la lumière de prophétie*) and who have communication with the good angel, which others call the active intellect, by whose splendour good men are instructed by dreams and visions concerning all that is to be done and avoided and which informs princes and peoples of the will of God. ... (*Aristotle*) did not understand true human happiness. For the most divine personages never perceived this divine enjoyment except when sleeping (*margin*: excepté Moysé seul). This is why man's happiness is perfected when God acts in him through effusion of His light and the vision of His beauty which never happens to a man awake. [11]

Bodin's own Philonic belief in prophetic illumination, openly expressed in the *Paradoxe* and put into the words of Salomon in the *Heptaplomeres*, is that it is the prophets who receive the "effusion of God's light and the vision of His beauty"; illumination means for Bodin the light of prophecy — *la lumière de prophétie*. Toralba had admitted the reality of divine illumination but had, as an advocate of natural religion, denied the revelation of the prophets and *ipso facto* the whole phenomenon of prophecy. Bodin in the *Paradoxe,* like

---

[11] *Paradoxe*, p. 31: "Puis donc que les hommes ont si peu de cognoissance de ce bien souuerain tant qu'ils sont atachez au corps, & beaucoup moins de ioüissance d'iceluy, qui pouuons nous dire estre les plus heureux en ce môde apres ceux la que vous auez dit estre tresheureux? Ceux à qui Dieu à departi la lumière de prophetie, & qui ont la communication du bon Ange, que les autres appellent l'intellect actuel, de la splendeur duquel les gens de bien sont instruits par songes & visions de tout ce qu'il faut suiure & fuir, & auertir les Princes & les peuples de la volôté de Dieu ... void en cela qu'il [*Aristote*] n'a pas entendu la vraye felicité humaine: car les plus diuins persõnages qui furêt onques n'ont iamais perceu ceste ioüissance diuine sinon en dormant: c'est pourquoy. la felicité de l'hõme se parfait quand Dieu agit en luy par effusion de sa lumiere & vision de sa beauté, qui n'auiêt iamais à l'homme veillant." For Philonic and Maimonidean aspects of prophetic illumination see Chapters IV, note 65; V, note 21; this chapter, note 22; Chapter VIII. The reply here to an Aristotelian objection is very close to Salomon's response to the same objection raised by Senamus in *Heptaplomeres*, ed. Noack, p. 189 (trs. p. 248).

Salomon in the *Heptaplomeres*, asserted that illumination consisted precisely in prophecy. We must therefore take here Salomon's view rather than Toralba's as representing the convictions of Bodin himself.

For Bodin himself the natural religion of Toralba was inadequate since it required the addition of prophetic revelation before it might become *true religion* (as we shall see presently). The real purpose of Bodin's Judaising here, one might say, was to provide him with the critical revelatory factor which Toralba's otherwise congenial natural religion had lacked, namely prophecy. We shall see this clearly stated in the ensuing discussion of the place of nature and revelation in *vera religio*.

Upon advancing his idea of prophetic revelation as the highest happiness Salomon has immediately to defend it from appropriation by the Lutheran Fridericus who claims that the highest revelation is that of Christ Himself. ("I believe that the highest good finds its goal in the knowledge of God through Christ").[12] In brushing this claim aside Salomon takes the opportunity of putting Toralba's ideas into a more forceful Judaised form very close to their expression in the *Paradoxe*.

> About Christ is another matter. But the knowledge of God is the nearest step to that happiness which we seek. Indeed the Teacher of Wisdom spoke thus: "To have known God is consummate justice and the recognition of Your power is the root of immortality". Still that knowledge leads to worship, worship to love, love to enjoyment, which produces the highest pleasure of the soul, or rather is the very enjoyment of pleasure.[13]

The resemblance of this hierarchy of mystical experience to that propounded in the *Paradoxe* (pp. 32f) is striking. In the *Paradoxe,* of course, Bodin dared not rebuff Christ as intermediary so bluntly, but since he had not printed any reference to Christ as redeemer in that published work, and since in all other respects the *Paradoxe's* theory of the mystical love and knowledge of God agrees with that of Salomon in the *Heptaplomeres*, it may be taken that Salomon's words here faithfully represent Bodin's own feelings.

Toralba, however, does not give up easily and the rejection of Christian revelation now gives him a chance to insist that the revelation of Moses and the Hebrew prophets is equally superfluous to true religion which depends only on the law of nature.

> Therefore it is my opinion that those first parents of the golden age ... Abel, Enoch and Job, without the Law (*of Moses*) and Moses without Christ secured most purely that true enjoyment of divine pleasure by the law of nature.[14]

---

[12] *Ibidem*, p. 190 (trs. pp. 248ff).

[13] *Ibidem*, p. 190 (trs. p. 249): "De Christo quidem alias. Sed Dei cognitio proximus est ad illam, quam expetimus, felicitatem gradus. Sic enim sapientiae magister: Nosse Deum consummata justitia est, et tuae potestatis agnitio radix est immortalitatis. Illa tamen cognitio fertur ad cultum, cultus ad amorem, amor ad fruitionem, quae summam animi voluptatem parit, vel potius ipsa voluptatis est fruitio."

[14] *Ibidem*. "Haec igitur mea sententia est, primos illos aurei saeculi parentes, quos superius diximus, Abelem, inquam, Enochum, Jobum sine lege, Mosen sine Christo veram illam divinae voluptatis fruitionem purissime lege naturae adeptos fuisse. "

This elicits an important speech from Salomon which is avowedly inspired by Philo's observation (*De Abrahamo, 5*) that the Ten Commandments are in fact the revealed law of nature.

> I do not disagree with you (*replies Salomon*). For when we read that Abraham cherished the law of the most high, what does it mean other than that he followed the example of the law of nature? And indeed Philo the Hebrew said: "The commandments of the two tables depart not at all from nature and it is not a task of great effort to lead your life according to the prescriptions of divine laws, for the tables contain nothing but the law of nature and the life of our ancestors." [15]

Why then the need for the Decalogue, for revelation, for prophets? Bodin's answer is the same as that given years before in explaining his prophetic religion in the letter to Bautru of 1568-69: the prophets are sent by God to recall men from sin to virtue. [16]

> Because in Moses' time the law of nature had been so defiled by the crimes and shamefulness of men that it seemed to have been almost completely obliterated from their souls and made obsolete by its ancience, God the greatest and best, pitying the lot of men, wished to renew that same law of nature by His own word and comprehend it in the Decalogue which he inscribed on stone tables, especially those interdicts by which we are prohibited from violating nature. Therefore, when men grew deaf to the law of nature, the divine voice was required so that those who condemned nature might hear the father of nature proclaiming His words. [17]

Toralba's natural religion is thus transformed into a religion which is at the same time natural and revealed. The Great God of Nature — *the father of nature* — has endowed men with knowledge of the natural law and consolidated this law of nature with a prophetic revelation which serves to remind men of that same law. We have here yet again a mixture of categories which is unique to Bodin among major early modern thinkers, fusing as it does divine and naturalistic elements which are generally taken both in Christian *and* secular thought to be mutually opposed and irreconcilable; once more in

[15] *Ibidem.* "Non alia mihi mens est. Nam cum Abrahamum legem altissimi coluisse legimus, quid est aliud, quam naturae legis exemplar secutum esse: Et quidem Philo Hebraeus: Edicta, inquit, duarum tabularum nihil a natura discrepant, nec magno studio opus est, ut vitam exigas ad praescripta legum divinarum, quoniam nihil aliud, quam naturae legem et majorum nostrorum vita continent." For Philo's identification of the law of God with the law of nature see E.R. Goodenough, *By Light, Light* (New Haven, 1935), pp. 53f and below, Chapter VIII, section D. Philo is also invoked early in the *Heptaplomeres* for the view, fundamental for Bodin's theodicy, that God cannot create evil. See above, note 1, and also the analysis of the *Paradoxe* in Chapter V; and Chapter VIII, section C.

[16] For the letter to Bautru, see Chapter VIII.

[17] *Heptaplomeres*, ed. Noack, p. 190 (trs. p. 249): "Sed quoniam aetate Mosis naturae lex hominum sceleribus ac flagitiis ita inquinata erat, ut penitus ex animis obliterata videretur, et quasi sua vetustate antiquata, Deus optimus maximus, hominum vicem misertus, andem naturae legem sua voce renovare ac decalogo, quem tabulis lapideis inscripserat, complecti voluit, ac potissimum interdicta, quibus naturam violare prohibemur. Cum igitur homines ad naturae legem obsurduissent, divina vox necessaria fuit, ut qui naturam contemserant, naturae parentem sua verba resonantem exaudirent."

this Judaised universe is to be seen the impact of Jewish — specifically Philonic — concepts on Bodin's thought. [18]

Bodin's vision of a true religion which is simultaneously natural and revealed means that none of the participants in the *Heptaplomeres,* not even Salomon who comes closest to it, may properly be identified as the representative of *vera religio.* The true religion is not a formal or institutional one; it is invisible and has neither church nor congregation. For that reason there is no need for anyone to be converted to it from a sincere belief in his own religion. This perception is entrusted to the pagan Senamus whose own religion is of course deficient in revelation. After each of the speakers has asserted the truth of his own particular religion, Senamus suggests that each religion, while possessing part of the truth, is actually a just error.

> As this point Senamus (*the pagan*), who had hesitated for a while, but had wanted to speak said; I believe that all the religions of all people — the natural religion which Toralba loves, the religion of Jupiter and the gentile gods (which the Indians of the orient and the Tartars cherish), the religion of Moses, the religion of Christ, the religion of Mohammed — so long as they are pursued not with simulated pretense but with a pure mind, are not unpleasing to eternal God and are assuredly to be excused as righteous errors, even if that religion is the most pleasing of all which is the best. [19]

The last observation stimulates Toralba into making a last attempt to convince his friends that his own natural religion is indeed that best of religions and that "true religion is natural religion". Blithely invoking Salomon's earlier admission that the Decalogue is the law of nature Toralba rushes on to dismiss all the revealed religions as mere parables of nature. [20] But, as before, he comes to grief on the rock of illumination when Salomon answers him with a restatement of the need for prophecy.

> We have said above that all faith depends either clear arguments, or sound understanding, or divine oracles. Nor may faith be infused except by the oracle of prophecy divinely given to man and which is more certain than all science. [21]

Toralba cannot reply to this (and does not) because of his own commitment to a divine illumination of sorts; for illumination is possible only through

---

[18] For other contributions of Philo to Bodin's idea of God and religion see Chapter V; this chapter, notes 11, 15 and 22; Chapter VIII.

[19] *Heptaplomeres,* ed. Noack, p. 192 (trs. p. 250f): "Hic SENAMUS, qui aliquamdiu haeserat, cum loqui proposuisset: Omnes, inquit, omnium religiones, tum naturalis illa, quam amplectitur Toralba, tum Jovis gentiliumque Deorum, quos Orientales Indi ac Tartari colunt, tum Mosis, tum Christi, tum Muhammedis, quam suo quisque ritu non fucata simulatione, sed integra mente prosequitur, aeterno Deo non ingratos ac justos errores excusari confido, tametsi omnium gratissima est illa, quae optima."

[20] *Ibidem.* "If true religion is natural religion and this is made plain by clear reasons as not only Octavius but also Salomon himself confesses..." ("Si vera religio naturalis eaque perspicuis demonstrationibus explicatur, ut modo Octavius, sed etiam Salomo ipse confitetur.")

[21] *Ibidem,* p. 193 (trs. p. 253): "Superius dictum est, fidem omnem aut argumentis perspicuis aut sensibus integris aut divinis oraculis niti, fidem infusam nullam esse, nisi oraculo prophetae divinitus homini dato, quod omni scientia certius est." Referring to *Heptaplomeres,* ed. Noack, p. 133 (trs. p. 173), which follows Maimonides. But see below.

142

prophecy or some similar process which Toralba is unable to specify. To clinch the matter we may have recourse to the *Paradoxe* as a control to prove that Bodin himself in that published work regarded prophecy as the vehicle of illumination and must therefore be in broad agreement with Salomon's refutation of Toralba. [22] For Bodin, therefore, the Achilles' heel of Toralba's natural religion is indeed its very central feature — its rejection of revelation and prophecy!

It would be misleading to end the analysis of this particular section of the *Heptaplomeres* without mentioning one important respect in which Bodin diverges from Salomon's views, namely in the question of faith. According to Salomon faith may be evinced by man when he embraces clear arguments, is convinced by his senses or listens to the words of the prophets. Faith is "infused" (note Bodin's reversion to the Christian term purely for the purpose of criticising it) only when it accompanies the arrival of the prophetic light in man. The argument here is thoroughly Maimonidean as is shown by the earlier passage to which Bodin refers in his last quoted remark.

> Rabbi Moses Rambam (*Maimonides*) put the matter (*of the beliefs entailed by true religion*) more briefly and said that we must believe only three things, namely, proof, sense experience, and the oracles of the prophets; other things, he said, might be believed also but not by necessity. [23]

Now in the relevant controlling passage of the *Paradoxe* Bodin repudiates the Christian idea of faith as infused theological virtue, but he also denies the Maimonidean rationalism which would see faith as sometimes a matter of accepting cogent rational arguments. Faith depends on will, not on reason and cannot be forced or rational.

> True faith depends on a pure and free will which believes without force of argument or of necessary reasons. In this faith is contrary to science which is founded on cogent and necessary proof. If faith is forced it is no longer faith. [24]

This attitude has some resemblance to the tenor of certain remarks made by Toralba earlier in the *Heptaplomeres* which had insisted that faith depends on will not reason, and cannot be understood as an inspired virtue of a kind which would be completely independent of the will.

> Although several have tried to accomplish this (*rational proofs of true religion*) they did not succeed because faith is destroyed if it relies on proof and science.... The theologians call infused faith a theological virtue, granted as a divine gift and concession; if it is necessary and fixed so that it might not be lost, it is to be considered force rather than faith. But if it does rely on a free assent then it

---

[22] *Paradoxe*, pp. 31-33. See Chapter V, note 21. And above, note 11.

[23] *Ibidem*, p. 133 (trs. p. 173): "Rabbi Moses Rambam brevius rem contraxit ac tria tantum nostris credenda proponit, scilicet demonstrationem, sensum et oracula prophetarum; caetera, inquit, credi possunt, sed nulla necessitate."

[24] *Paradoxe*, pp. 90f: "C'est que la vraye foy dépend d'une pure et franche volonté, qui croit sans force d'argumens, ny de raisons nécessaires; et qui est en cela contraire à la science, qui est fondée en démonstration forcée et nécessaire. Or si la foy est forcée, ce n'est plus foy."

would be the height of impiety to try to uproot with human learning that doctrine which God in His great goodness has bestowed. [25]

It would be mistaken, however, to think that this agreement places Bodin in Toralba's camp. Toralba does not deny that faith is bestowed by God; he argues merely that the faith bestowed or infused by God must be received willingly, a position quite compatible even with Aquinas' view of theological virtue! The whole thrust of the *Paradoxe,* however, is that faith comes *entirely* from man's free will and does not depend on divine grace or infusion. In this emphasis upon free will Bodin remains close to Maimonides who retained, despite his rationalism, that fundamental belief in the freedom of the will — the Deuteronomic choice — which is intrinsic to all Jewish thought. Although Bodin might have differed from Maimonides concerning rational faith, he did not thereby disavow the core of Jewish ethics.

Again Toralba, in denying that faith has anything to do with prophecy or revelation (the "tables and the witnesses" as he calls them), [26] is effectively repudiating the whole theory of prophecy expounded by Bodin in the *Paradoxe* and his other writings. Here again Bodin's belief in prophetic revelation places him nearer to Maimonides who had made belief in the words of the prophets one of the criteria of faith.

We now come to the third passage in the *Heptaplomeres* where Bodin deployed his armoury of Judaised concepts to mesh together religion and ethics, prophetic illumination with moral virtue.

Where religion and morality are united in the mental universe of a thinker like Bodin any exposition of a non-Christian morality must sooner or later involve the rejection of the religious premises upon which Christian morality is based. [27] And it is in the last book of the *Heptaplomeres* that Bodin finally confronted and denounced the fundamental religious doctrines of Christianity. Here was the culmination of his Judaising for just as he used Jewish ideas to construct his own ideal of true religion, so he also used the parent religion to destroy the very foundations of Christianity, entrusting the final attack to the hands of Salomon. Toralba does assist but in the crucial section on virtue, grace, original sin and free will it is Salomon's speeches which pick

[25] *Heptaplomeres*, ed. Noack, pp. 129f (trs. p. 169): "Toralba: At nemo est, opinor, qui religionis cujusque demonstrationes tradiderit, etiamsi nonnulli efficere hoc sint conati, sed frustra, quia tantum abest ut fides cum demonstratione ac scientia stare possit, ut funditus evertatur.... Fidem autem infusam theologi appellant virtutem theologalem, quae Deum tantum sui argumentum ac objectum habet. Ea vero, fides divino munere ac concessu tributa, si tamen necessaria est et certa, ut amitti, summae, vis est, non fides. Si libera quadam assentione nititur, summae impietatis est, argumentis humanis doctrinam, quam Deus summa bonitate afflaverit, cuiquam eripere conari."

[26] *Ibidem*, p. 132 (trs. p. 172).

[27] On the question of religion and morality Bodin belongs to a stream of modern thinkers — including Hume, Heine and de Tocqueville — who have insisted on the need for a nexus between religion and ethics. (This remark, which may appear disconcerting to some readers, I hope to sustain in a future work.)

144

up themes and phrases left hanging for reasons of prudence in the *Paradoxe* and spell out to the full their anti-Christian consequences. [28]

In the *Paradoxe* Bodin had explained rather elusively his theory of "divine aid" (*opes divina* or *aide*) classifying it as either "ordinary" or "extraordinary". He had been careful in his published discussion to avoid the use of the work *gratia,* trusting perhaps that the Christian censor would simply assume that Bodin was in fact talking about Christian grace. Far from it; Bodin's theory of divine help and "grace" was deeply Judaised and designed to allow the maximum power to man's free will. [29] In the clandestine *Heptaplomeres* Bodin felt freer to state the natural consequence of his Judaised notion of divine help — that it annulled the cardinal Christian doctrine of original sin.

> All this discussion about the original Fall, which I think is no fall, has its beginning in the leaders of the Christian religion....
>
> And as Adam's repentance produced eternal salvation, so it was possible and always will be possible for anyone with divine help which never fails to restore men from depraved desires to right reason, from the senses to intelligible things, and never fails to obtain that salutary and everlasting life without any death and slaughter of beasts or men. [30]

Can we correlate this Jewish refutation of original sin with ideas expressed in the more discreet *Paradoxe*? Let us imagine Bodin's religion as a temple or sacred edifice and that in the *Paradoxe* he had sketched some of the architectural plan though only incompletely. For example, the building is to be supported by a range of columns; the supporting columns drawn in the *Paradoxe* might symbolise Bodin's non-Christian theory of grace or rather "divine aid"; [31] his strong emphasis on the role of free will in achieving virtue and salvation; [32] and the solid conviction that divine help would not be withheld from him who of his own free will turned to God. [33] But not all the columns are depicted in the *Paradoxe,* for the full blue-print of the temple is given only in the *Heptaplomeres* (even if in a somewhat cryptographic fashion). There one may find inserted in the plan the two missing pillars which were always required to support the edifice but which had been left out in the printed description. Certainly there were gaps in the design given by the *Paradoxe* but the columns to fill those gaps were logically entailed by the whole architecture of the temple, by the very structure of Bodin's Judaised theory of grace and free will. Indeed the columns which were sketched dictate the presence and the shape of the omitted pillars. These missing pillars — which we find drawn in detail by Salomon in the *Heptaplomeres* — were (1) the denial of original sin and (2) its corollary that free will is sufficient to secure salvation, that salvation which

---

[28] *Heptaplomeres,* ed. Noack, pp. 306ff (trs. pp. 404ff).

[29] *Paradoxe,* pp. 35ff. See above, Chapters V and VI (note 16).

[30] *Heptaplomeres,* ed. Noack, pp. 305, 307 (trs. pp. 404, 405f): "Tota haec disputatio de originis labe, quae nulla esse mihi videtur, a primoribus christianae religionis initium duxit.... Et quemadmodum Adamo resipiscentia peperit salutem aeternam, ita cuique licuit et semper licebit, ope divina, quae deesse nemini potest, a pravis cupiditatibus ad rectam rationem, a sensibus ad intelligibilia redire ac vitam illam salutarem ac sempiternam adipisci sine ulla bestiarum aut hominum caede ac mactatione."

[31] *Paradoxe,* pp. 35ff. See above.

[32] *Paradoxe,* passim, but especially in the last section on charity and wisdom.

[33] *Paradoxe,* p. 37 (cf. pp. 92, 95).

comes with the divine help produced by man's turning to God in repentance. So we have, as it were, a general or systematic reason for believing that the *Paradoxe* corroborates Salomon's caustic remarks on free will and original sin. But we can go further and identify some particular aspects of Salomon's critique which logically derive from Bodin's published statements in the *Paradoxe*.

Besides his theory of divine help Salomon offers two particular arguments against original sin which correspond nearly to statements in the *Paradoxe*. The first of these is the argument from illumination. That some men may experience illumination shows that man is not permanently stained with original sin.

> Why should God have offered Himself for contemplation and enjoyment to so many prophets if they were evil from their origin? The vision and enjoyment of the divine countenance happened to those clothed in flesh which they (*the Christians*) think most defiled.... [34]

The theory of divine illumination sketched in the *Paradoxe* entails the abandoning of original sin even though Bodin publicly suppressed that logical consequence out of discretion.

Salomon's second argument against original sin is the reality of free will: and here he comes into open conflict with St. Paul's opinion on original sin. When the Calvinist interlocutor helpfully reminds him of the Pauline doctrine, Salomon retorts with the Deuteronomic choice, that choice which procures salvation without Christ. God has promised life to those who choose good.

> Because grace, life and salvation were offered to those who obey the law, we read repeated a thousand times: "Do this and thou shalt live. This is your life, this is your salvation." Or do we consider these promises of God to be lies? Indeed, the most wise Solomon calls the divine law the tree of lives, by which he means present and future lives. [35]

It is absurd, says Salomon, to insist that Christ is necessary for salvation — "as if it were not in every man's power to execute the divine commands and as if the free will to follow the law had been removed from his posterity for the crime of Adam". [36]

---

[34] *Heptaplomeres,* ed. Noack, p. 308 (trs. pp. 407f): "Cur denique Deus tot ac tam multis prophetis, si ab ipsa origine scelerati essent, se contuendum ac fruendum praebuisset? Quae visio et fruitio divini vultus carne contectis, quam illi pollutissimam putant, obtigit."

[35] *Ibidem,* p. 311 (trs. p. 411): "Quod autem gratia, vita, salus legem amplectantibus proposita sit, millies repetitum legimus: Hoc fac et vives, haec est tua vita, haec tua salus est. An illa Dei promissa pro mendaciis habemus? Quid? Sapientissimus Salomo legem divinam appellat lignum vitarum, scilicet praesentis ac futurae vitae *hayyim* [in Hebrew script]." The choice is cited repeatedly in the work, e.g. pp. 312, 314 (trs. pp. 412, 415, etc.). For a similar reference to the Hebrew plural of "life" (*hayyim*) see *Paradoxe,* p. 21 (quoted in the text of Chapter V) and above, Chapter VI, note 16.
Note the use of "grace" here in a purely Jewish sense which has no connection with the New Testament concept. Cf. Chapter VI, note 32.

[36] *Heptaplomeres,* ed. Noack, p. 313 (trs. p. 413): "quasi non in hominis cujusquam potestate positum exsequi divina jussa et liberum exsequendae legis arbitrium, Adami scelere posteritati ereptum fuisset."

The Christian speakers continue to assert that Adam had lost his free will through original sin but this is sharply rebutted by Salomon:

> As innumerable errors follow from one error posited, so Christians think that the free will of doing good is snatched away by original sin — which does not exist — and that by this men are bound for eternal punishments. But laws are commanded in vain and the divine rewards would be empty promises if it were not within human power and will to obey the divine laws. [37]

This statement puts one immediately in mind of Bodin's remark in the *Paradoxe* stressing the paramountcy of free will and obedience to God's commandments:

> What must man do to arrive at a happy life? He must keep the commandments of God. Is it in man's power to do this? Why not — for it is not a commandment when one commands the impossible .... Those who say the contrary seek nothing other than the overthrow of all laws, human and divine ... For then the rewards of those who do good and the punishments of the wicked would be illusory. [38]

There can be no doubt after this corroborating statement in the *Paradoxe* that Bodin is fully in agreement with Salomon's opinions in the *Heptaplomeres* regarding free will and the absurdity of original sin and that Bodin believed as a result that a redeeming saviour was redundant. The power of free will and the Deuteronomic choice are repeatedly stated in the *Paradoxe,* nor is there the slightest indication in that published work that a Christ was needed to redeem men from original sin; men might choose life for themselves.

The Deuteronomic choice, — that is, the reality of free will — demands the repudiation of original sin. But where the *Heptaplomeres* was able to elaborate these consequences, the *Paradoxe* while accepting the choice diplomatically refrained from stating the latter part of the argument. Yet, as Bodin himself was assuredly aware, the premise of free will entails the rejection of original sin and with it Christianity itself.

When, therefore, one follows the maps of Bodin's religious thought (indistinct as they may sometimes be) in the *Paradoxe* and the *Heptaplomeres* one sees that the essential shapes and contours in these two works correspond almost exactly and actually represent a uniform religious vision. So much so that it might be said that the *Paradoxe* amounts to Bodin's own censored publication of the religious essence of the *Heptaplomeres.*

---

[37] *Ibidem,* p. 314 (trs. p. 414): "Ut uno errore posito innumerabiles consequuntur, ita ex originis peccato, quod nullum, est, Christiani liberam bene agendi voluntatem eripi, tum ex eo mortales suppliciis sempiternis obligari arbitrantur. At frustra leges jubent et inania forent divina promissa praemia, si leges divinas exsequi non sit humanae potestatis ac ne voluntatis quidem."

[38] *Paradoxe,* p. 3 (reiterated at p. 37): "quel est le deuoir de l'homme qui veut parvenir à ceste vie la si heureuse? C'est faire les commandemens de Dieu.

Est il en la puissance de l'homme de ce faire? Pourquoy non? autrement ce n'est rien commander quand on commande ce qui est impossible de faire ... ceux qui disent le contraire ne cherchent autre chose que l'éversion de toutes loix Divines & humaines.... Car non seulement les loyers des bienfaits, & la peine des forfaits seroyent illusoires."

Bodin's moral philosophy as it appears in both the *Paradoxe* and the *Heptaplomeres* drew heavily on Jewish ethical *and* religious thought. The whole basis of his ethics was free will and it is free will that made possible Bodin's belief in a theory of natural virtue sharply exclusive of the Christian theological virtues. At the same time Bodin substituted a Judaised idea of divine illumination for the Christian concept of grace and he reserved illumination to describe the phenomena of prophecy and mystical love of God; this allowed all the other virtues to be independent of "grace" and so naturally attainable by man. The highest happiness itself was removed from the domain of moral philosophy where it had resided in Aristotelian thought and placed instead — now identified as the vision of God — in the realm of prophecy and illumination. Yet moral virtue and wisdom, for all that they become natural rather than supernatural qualities, were thoroughly religious in character in that they depended ultimately on Bodin's Judaised religious doctrine of free will.

Even though Jewish ideas of moral virtue, wisdom and prophetic illumination dominate the *Paradoxe* and the *Heptaplomeres,* it would be a mistake to think that Bodin was recommending a return to Judaism. The thrust of Bodin's Judaising was not the conversion of the world — or even of himself — to Judaism. For Judaism remained a social religion more or less restricted to a given nation and set apart by its specific rituals and observances. If one considered it only from this civil aspect Judaism would have scarcely been superior to the Catholicism into which Bodin was born, which he adhered to during his life, and according to whose rites he was buried. Its civil character therefore, precluded Judaism as much as Catholicism from being that essentially pure *vera religio* sought after by Bodin.

Bodin valued Judaism rather because it was in its theology and revelation the purest of the revealed religions.

> But the purest and simplest religion of the Hebrews has no mingling of impurity, no heresies attached to it; it recognises nothing except the worship of one God. [39]

In its purest form Judaism was founded on pure monotheism and consisted of God's divine commandments to man as transmitted through the illuminated prophets. Prophecy, revelation, illumination, free will — these were the central Jewish ideas on which Bodin built his true religion. Such Jewish ideas helped Bodin to destroy the Christian doctrines of theological virtue and grace and simultaneously enabled him to transform natural religion — which singularly lacked revelation — into true religion. For Bodin the law of Moses expressed the law of nature and God had made Moses a prophet in order to reinforce the law of nature. Bodin's Judaising led him not to Judaism, but rather to a *vera religio* which united natural religion with prophetic revelation, a religion which was both natural and revealed, the true religion of the Great God of Nature.

---

[39] *Heptaplomeres,* ed. Noack, p. 197 (trs. p. 258): "Sed Hebraeorum purissima ac simplicissima religio nihil impure admistum habet, nullas haereses adjunctas, nullum praeterquam unius Dei cultum agnoscit."

PART C.

THE PROPHET

CHAPTER VIII

THE THREE CONVERSIONS OF THE PROPHET

Bodin's religious biography on the surface is a chapter of accidents and reversals, sudden conversions and enthusiasms: a young Carmelite monk in the 1540's who left the order, a professed Catholic in 1562, imprisoned as a suspected Huguenot in 1569, outwardly a *politique* Catholic from 1576-89, then a Leaguer Catholic from 1589-93, followed by a reversion to the *politiques*, and finally his death as a reputed crypto-Jew or at least *Achriste* in 1596, a matter which did not, however, prevent his receiving a Catholic burial. One might add too such embarrassments as a purported stay as a Calvinist pastor at Geneva in 1552, though on balance this seems to have been the coincidence of a namesake.[1] How is any sense to be made of this haphazard series of conversions? Can one penetrate beneath this enigma to the core of Bodin's religion — his *vera religio* — and perceive there a less capricious and more constant religious sensibility? Once we know what Bodin's inner faith amounted to, can we then use this knowledge to unravel the tangled skein of his frequent confessional shifts? I believe that all this is possible and that once it has been done Bodin's life will be seen to have been punctuated by one great conversion which occured in three distinct phases of increasing intensity: the first phase was accomplished by 1559 and saw Bodin's conversion away from Christianity

---

[1] E. Droz, 'Le carme Jean Bodin, hérétique', *Bibliothèque d'Humanisme et Renaissance*, X (1948), 77-94 seems to me to be right in identifying the Carmelite Jean Bodin tried for heresy at Paris on 7 August 1548 with our man. However, neither Droz nor H. Naef, 'La jeunesse de Jean Bodin, ou les conversions oubliées', *Bibliothèque d'Humanisme et Renaissance*, VIII (1946), 137-155 seem to have proven that Bodin was also the Calvinist pastor of that name at Geneva in 1552. J. Levron, 'Jean Bodin, sieur de Saint-Amand ou Jean Bodin, originaire de Saint-Amand?', *Bibliothèque d'Humanisme et Renaissance*, X (1948), 69-76 has cogently argued that (1) the pastor was described as "docteur en théologie" yet Bodin never used that title and in any case his two years of study as a Carmelite at Paris were scarcely enough to have obtained him the degree (2) the pastor's appellation "Jehan Bodin, natif de la ville Saint-Amand, diocèse de Bourges" rules out the possibility that it was our Bodin, who had been born in Angers. It is true that Bodin did call himself in later life "sieur de Saint-Amand" but he took this style only after 1576 when he settled at Laon in the Vermandois. There are at least two domains of the name Saint-Amand in the vicinity of Laon which would have been suitable sized for Bodin's lordship. The town of Saint-Amand in the diocese of Bourges (Cher(is too large a fief for a title of minor nobility. Finally, attempts to strengthen Bodin's links with the diocese of Bourges by citing his arrest at the priory of St-Denys-la-Châtre in that diocese in 1569 fall to the ground when one recognises that the priory in question is in fact St-Denys de la Charte in Paris (see below note 139). None of these objections has been answered by Naef and Droz.

to a sort of natural religion which nevertheless made allowance for theistic revelation; the second, occurring in the years 1559-66, was characterised by his distinctly Judaised recognition of the crucial importance of revelation and prophecy for *vera religio*; the third phase came with Bodin's own transformation into a prophet in 1567-69. These profound experiences, rather than his superficial alternations between Catholic and Protestant Christianity, are the real milestones of Bodin's religious career.

a) The Beginnings of "Vera Religio": Theistic Natural Religion and Confessional Indifference (1548-59)

There is now firm evidence to support de Thou's long distrusted allegation that Bodin had been a Carmelite in his youth. [2] In a notarial document of 1577 three Carmelites attest that they had known Bodin thirty-five years before when had studied with him at Paris for two years. They go on to say that Bodin had then returned to his home convent at Angers and afterwards they heard that he had left the order (presumably in good grace). This evidence would place Bodin's arrival at Paris around 1545 and his return to Angers around 1547. His departure from the order — which was secured apparently by his having taken vows while under age — would have occurred a year or two later, one would imagine.

Why did Bodin renounce the Carmelites? That Bodin was disillusioned by conventional Catholicism seems a likely explanation, especially if he is to be identified with a Carmelite 'Jehan Baudin' tried for heresy at Paris in 1548. [3] It would be unwise to place too much store by these early hazy

[2] J.-A. de Thou's claim (*Historiarum libri CXXXVIII ab anno 1546 ad annum 1607* (London, 1733), V, 641) that Bodin was a Carmelite has been confirmed by A. Ponthieux, 'Quelques documents inédits sur Jean Bodin', *Revue du XVIe siècle*, XV (1928), 56-99, pp. 57f. In the relevant document there is no reason given for Bodin's renunciation but de Thou asserts that the fact that he had taken his vows while under age facilitated his release from the order. During the sixteenth century the taking of vows at too young an age was recognised by the Carmelites as the source of many apostasies from the order. In 1530 the Prior-General Audet established minimum ages of 14 for the admission of candidates for the novitiate, 18 for the taking of vows, and 24 for the priesthood. See A. Staring, *Der Karmelitengeneral Nikolaus Audet und die Katholische Reform des XVI Jahrhunderts* (Rome, 1959), pp. 108, 211.
Guillaume Postel was also aware of Bodin's Carmelite past, alluding to him as "un moyne renié, qui fut carme angevin" and "instituti Eliani aliquando sectator". In my earlier 'Two Problems of Bodin's Religious Biography: The Letter to Jean Bautru des Matras and the Imprisonment of 1569', *Bibliothèque d'Humanisme et Renaissance*, XXXVIII (1976), 459-465, I took this to refer to Bodin's membership of a prophetic sect (such as the *libertins spirituels*) but I am now convinced it alludes only to his days as a Carmelite of which order the prophet Elijah was the patron. I hope to deal with this matter in a separate note.
[3] N. Weiss, *La Chambre ardente (1540-1550)* (Paris, 1889), p. 185. Idem, 'Huguenots emprisonnés à la Conciergerie du Palais à Paris en mars 1569', *Bulletin de la société de l'histoire de protestantisme français*, ser. v, XXI (1923), 86-97.
V. De Caprariis, *Propaganda e pensiero politico in Francia durante le guerre di religione* (Naples, 1959), pp. 325 and 329, tried to dissociate this Bodin from ours, but see Rose, 'Two Problems', p. 459.

incidents but they do encourage the suspicion that Bodin had embarked on the heretical road to his *vera religio* even as early as 1548.

Nevertheless in Bodin's youthful experience as a Carmelite may have lain the seeds of his eventual conversion and mature religious views. As we have seen in Chapter IV there are a number of intriguing parallels between Carmelite mystic spirituality and those doctrines of knowledge and love of God preached by Bodin in his *Sapientia* and *Paradoxe*. From the Carmelites' ascetic ideal of the attaining of prophetic perfection too Bodin may have conceived that devotion to prophecy which was to play such a dominant role in the later stages of his conversion to true religion . The other striking feature of Bodin's *vera religio*, "the purified heart", was also preeminent in Carmelite spirituality. Such concerns as these — mysticism, prophecy and purity and repentance — may well be the constants of Bodin's religious biography, instilled into him as a boy in the Carmelite monastery, but only finding their true fulfilment in his conversion from Christianity to a Judaised form of religion. [4]

There is no firm evidence for the religious direction taken by Bodin in the 1550's but there are some hints of things to come in the commentary on Oppian's hunting treatise *Cynegetica* which Bodin published in 1555. [5] Already there are traces of an incipient Judaising to be seen in his knowledge of Hebrew and more importantly in his preference for Moses' authority over that of Plato; most intriguingly there is an allusion to Philo's demonology. This Judaised demonology was to play a critical role in the prophetic theory of Bodin's later religious thought even if the significance of the citation was not apparent to Bodin when he was writing in 1555. [6] One might also conjecture an inclination to eclectic religion at this date to judge from the favourable reference to Pico della Mirandola's *900 Theses*. [7] It is in his discussion of the soul, however, that Bodin most clearly anticipates the *Oratio*. In his notes on Oppian's discussion of the intelligence of horses Bodin points out that although animals possess some aspects of reason or intelligence such as the

---

[4] See Chapter IV. For Carmelite spirituality see T. Brandsma, *Carmelite Mysticism. Historical Sketches* (Chicago, 1936). Joachim A. Smet, *The Carmelites. A History of the Brothers of Our Lady of Mount Carmel ca. 1200 AD until the Council of Trent* (privately printed, Illinois, 1975). The main document of Carmelite spirituality before St. John of the Cross and St. Teresa in the later sixteenth century is the *Institutio primorum monachorum,* printed in the *Speculum Carmelitanum* of P. Riboti (Paris, 1507). For English translation and comments see Fr.N. Werling, 'The Book of St. John, 44', *The Sword,* III (1939), 293-304; IV (1940), 20-24, 152-160, 309-320. (I am grateful to Father B. Pitman, O. Carm., for his advice and help in procuring copies of these items for me).

[5] *Oppiani de Venatione libri IIII Ioanne Bodino Andegavensi interprete* (Latin verse translation and commentary, Paris, Vascosanus, 1555; reissued Paris, Fouet, 1597). A Greek text issued anonymously by Bodin's publisher Vascosanus at Paris in 1549 may also have been the work of Bodin although he would have been rather young at the time. Turnèbe's Greek text (Paris, 1555), p. 207, accuses the editor of this edition (or perhaps Bodin on account of his commentary of 1555) of stealing his emendations. See *Oppien d'Apamée. La Chasse (Cynegetica)*, ed. P. Boudreaux (Paris, 1908), introduction. Also P. Mesnard, 'La Conjuration contre la renommée de Jean Bodin: Antoine Tessier (1684)', *Bulletin de l'Association Guillaume Budé*, XVIII (1959), 545-559, pp. 548f. Bodin's philological interest may have been steered to Oppian's natural history by Etienne Forcadel's *Aviarium jus civilis* (Lyons, 1550). See Chapter I.

[6] *Oppiani de Venatione,* Bodin's commentary, fol. 47, alludes to Philo. For details see below, section D.

[7] *Oppiani de Venatione,* fol. 84.

powers of phantasy, common sense and memory, nevertheless they do not share the true intellectual faculty of man, that is, the active intellect which illuminates the soul. Unlike animal intelligence which is "infused with the seed" human intelligence is "divinely implanted". According to Bodin Aristotle erred in not distinguishing between these two kinds of intelligence. So too did the Pythagoreans who in consequence accepted the transmigration of souls from humans to animals and so also did those Platonists who conceded immortality to the souls of animals. "I have always thought these opinions unworthy not only of Christians but also of philosophers", observes Bodin. [8]

This distinction between the animal and the human is resumed in the *Oratio* and the *Methodus* where Bodin admits too a sense of equity in animals although he reserves justice for men alone. [9] There is, of course, a strong religious motive for the line of argument that men's souls are intrinsically different from those of the animals. Once one believes that animals may have a properly intelligent soul it is a short step to pantheism or atheism. Such a belief destroys also the essential dignity of man which for Bodin is rooted in religion. Commenting on the Roman emperor Heliogabalus's practice of having his chariot drawn by four stags and four women Bodin remarks that this was done not out of zeal for the hunt but rather "in contempt of religion, of the gods, and of men". [10]

It seems an odd coincidence that Bodin's rival editor of Oppian should also have been responsible for the first extensive text of Philo (published at Paris in 1552). [11] Adrianus Turnebus (1512-65) taught at Toulouse before moving to Paris as Royal Professor of Greek in 1547. Although Bodin probably did not arrive in Toulouse until after Turnèbe's departure it seems that they moved in the same circles at Paris in later years, particularly in the group associated with Henri de Mesmes which included such friends of Bodin as Claude Fauchet. [12] Like that of Bodin Turnèbe's religious allegiance was somewhat perplexing to his contemporaries. Ronsard thought him a heretic though Turnèbe was as ready to denounce the Huguenots as he was the Jesuits. This religious ambiguity stemmed in part from his Platonic editing which covered the *Timaeus* as well as Philo. Indeed Turnèbe seems to have inclined towards novel Alexandrian ideas on religion and like Bodin espoused a Platonic belief in a universal order of nature. Yet Turnèbe is different from Bodin in that he seems to have remained a believing Christian; although there were no Catholic rites at his burial Turnebe died embracing "la doctrine des prophètes,

---

[8] *Ibidem,* fols. 53-54v.

[9] See Chapters I, note 35, and II, note 9.

[10] *Oppiani de Venatione,* fol. 68v.

[11] See below, section D.

[12] L. Clément, *De Adriani Turnebi regii professoris praefationibus et poematis* (Paris, 1899). G. Demerson, *Polémiques autour de la mort de Turnèbe* (Clermont-Ferrand, 1975). A. Cioranesco, *Bibliographie de la littérature française du seizième siècle* (Paris, 1959), pp. 669f. *Catalogus Translationum,* ed. P.O. Kristeller and F.E. Cranz (Washington DC, 1960-), I, 150; II, 14f. E. and M. Haag, *La France Protestante* (Paris, 1846-1859), IX, 433-436. J. Jehasse, *La Renaissance de la critique. L'essor de l'humanisme érudit de 1560 à 1614* (St-Etienne, 1976), pp. 55, 62, 142, 155. Janet Espiner-Scott, 'Note sur le cercle de Henri de Mesmes et sur son influence', *Mélanges offerts à M. Abel Lefranc* (Paris, 1936), pp. 354-361.

du Christ et des apôtres". Even this confession, however, might have influenced Bodin. The debt to Turnèbe remains problematic. [13]

In the *Oratio* ot 1559 there comes the first firm charting of Bodin's position and it suggests that he was now no longer a conventional Catholic, and perhaps no longer even a Christian in anything but name. The lengthy analysis in this work of religious aspects of education reveals a good deal of Bodin's thinking on religion and from it there emerge two main ideas; one is Bodin's indifference to confessional religion, the order is his belief in theistic natural religion. [14]

Bodin recognised here two forms of religion. In its first guise religion acted as a political and social bond between men:

> One thing in the state is to be sought above all from immortal God. It is that the will of the citizens in both spiritual and temporal matters (*divinae ac humanae res*) always be the same and in harmony (*consentiens*). This is the end of human society and of all public life. The laws of all nations, the religions and cults of all peoples, all the duties of judges and magistrates, indeed all institutions, rites and customs relate and are directed to one instance — that men may live in affection and trust (*Oratio*, ed. Mesnard, p. 25).

For this reason Bodin recommended that only one religion be followed in the state:

> Nor may one realise religious unanimity among all the citizens except that the people receive a common education from infancy, learn the same texts, acquire the same customs, honour the same God and finally be initiated into the same rites and imbued with the same learning (*Oratio*, p. 25).

Clearly any positive religion could function as a state-religion and Bodin expressed no particular preference for any one confession, Catholic or Protestant. [15]

[13] Haag, *La France,* p. 435. Clément, *Turnebi,* pp. 98-109. There is an echo of this confession in Bodin's letter to Bautru (see below, notes 131ff). There are also some parallels with the *Oratio*: Turnèbe's dedication of his Philo of 1554 anticipated Bodin's remarks of 1559 that all the arts and sciences were joined as by a chain (Clément, p. 31). The *Oratio's* optimistic confidence in the modern age may also have been affected by Turnèbe's works. Cf. Jehasse, *Renaissance,* p. 155.

[14] For further details and Latin texts of the quotations see Chapters I and VI. I follow the text as given in Jean Bodin, *Œuvres philosophiques* (Paris, 1951), ed. P. Mesnard, I.

[15] P. Mesnard, 'Jean Bodin à Toulouse', *Bibliothèque d'Humanisme et Renaissance,* XII (1950), 31-59, however, took the call for religious uniformity as evidence of Bodin's Catholicism in this period. Bodin was almost certainly a professing Catholic in public but my whole point — and I think Bodin's too — is that inner religious beliefs are not be same as external confessions. In any case, although I am sure that Bodin here is calling for Catholic uniformity at Toulouse, Mesnard misses the relativism of the argument which seems willing to accept any religion capable of uniting society. The only criterion seems to be pragmatic; the religion commanding the allegiance of the majority and of the powerful is to be the religion of the state. So too the denunciation of the multiplication of sects as the source of war (*Oratio*, p. 25) is not directed against the truth of the various sects, but rather against the fact that, lacking any common system of education, citizens have not been brought up in a single uniform religion. This does not strike me as the observation of a man who is entirely committed to the Catholic view of the Reformation.

But Bodin's neutrality with respect to positive religions sprang from more than just the belief that under differing circumstances one could function as well as another. It was rooted in his second concept of religion which he summed up thus in the *Oratio*:

> For God has placed in the souls of all of us the seeds of piety and religion, and these are so deeply rooted that they cannot be torn out without destroying also honour, trust, integrity and that justice without which not even God would reign. (*Oratio*, p. 25). [16]

This universally true religion incorporated all positive religions and was superior to them as the universal to the particular. Neither the Catholics nor the Huguenots could therefore lay claim to exclusive possession of *vera religio* and in discussing the nature of this true religion Bodin carefully avoided any mention of any church and even of Christianity. Instead what emerged was a religion with distinctly naturalistic tendencies and without the slightest mention of Christ. [17]

> Whence arose the impiety and false religion of the barbarians? Certainly out of ignorance. On the other hand, how was it that wise men recognised that the soul was an immortal principle, personal to them and flowing from the eternal mind? Whence did they extract the most certain knowledge of the one God? Assuredly out of the first principles and hidden causes of nature. They saw that these causes were all interrelated and led eventually as though by some necessity of nature, to a single one. Thus, even if nothing were published in our literature and books concerning God, the creator of the universe and of nature, if no voice from heaven had ever taught that souls live immortally, nevertheless that knowledge which reveals the causes of things would educate us completely and give us faith of a kind that enraged Epicureans could not dissipate. Is it not enough to contemplate that admirable might and nature of the most powerful God which is inscribed and comprehended in the causes of things? (*Oratio*, p. 15).

[16] In some passages Bodin's use of the term *vera religio* is confusing, e.g. *Oratio*, p. 25: "If it is the duty of pontiffs to ensure that the true religion (*religio vera*) is not polluted by the filth of any superstition or impiety, so it is the duty of the magistrates who hold the helm of state to prevent the distraction of its youth from one and the same religion to a multiplicity of religions, that is if we hope to have a state at all. But with private education some learn the pure religion (*pura religio*), some another religion, others none at all." (*Oratio*, p. 25.) See Chapter I for Latin texts of this and succeeding quotations. It might seem that Bodin here is merely saying that the duty of pontiffs is to enforce the religious orthodoxy of their particular church in the service of the state. But I think that Bodin has in mind the wider *vera religio* which makes the pontiffs responsible for the eradication of impiety towards universal *vera religio* as well as towards their own rites. e.g. witchcraft would be an example of such impiety against *vera religio*. In the *Methodus* Bodin took pains to clear up the possible confusion caused by his ellipsis and spelt out the fact that religion was more than just the uniformity of rites (*Methodus*, p. 121AB (33) or a department of state. See below. [References to the *Methodus* give respectively the page in the Latin text in Bodin, *Œuvres philosophiques*, I, and the page in the English translation by B. Reynolds, *Method for the Easy Comprehension of History* (New York, 1945).]

[17] In a Christian writer one would have expected some mention of Christ when Bodin remarks (p. 14) that when knowledge and virtue are combined man comes "close to the divinity of immortal God".

The Christian indifferentism of such groups as the Familists seems to be rooted in a quite different religious context. Cf. W. Kirsop, 'The Family of Love in France', *Journal of Religious History*, III (1964-65), 103-118. H. de La Fontaine-Verwey, 'The Family of Love', *Quaerendo*, VI (1976), 219-271.

In speaking of Bodin's religion as 'natural' one must be careful not to confuse it with some eighteenth century varieties of natural religion. Bodin's religion is natural in that it is rooted both in human nature as created by God (*Oratio*, p. 25, quoted above) and also in the structure of the natural universe.[18] But this naturalism does not rule out the possibility of revelation beyond the data of nature. In the passage just quoted, for example, Bodin cautiously allows for the role of divine revelation in his true religion ('even...if no voice from heaven had ever taught that souls should live immortally'). As we shall see the prophetic medium through which the divine will was revealed to men was to become a dominant concern in Bodin's religion a decade later.

The circumstances of Bodin's initial conversion to *vera religio* by 1559 are completely obscure but it may be worthwhile trying to interpret his preference for a universal natural religion over a too specific Christianity in the context of his drive towards a universalist philosophy in the 1550's and after. The *Oratio* of 1559 shows Bodin intent on a universal comparison of laws which would enable him to extract the essence of law, to penetrate the *vis et majestas legum,* the *norma aequitatis,* the *ultimum principium juris,* as he variously calls it in the *Oratio* (pp. 17f). Only then would jurisprudence, its inner nature revealed, be reduced to a true and certain science. All *vera scientia* depends on understanding the fixed and true essence which lies beneath the variety and mutability of laws and customs all over the world. In later years Bodin applied his method of universal comparison to discover the inner nature — the 'hidden causes' — of a whole range of subjects: in the *Methodus* he tried to analyse the hidden causes of historical change and the rise and fall of empires; in the *République* he seized upon sovereignty as the hidden cause of political power. The hidden cause of *vera religio* was to be pursued in the *Heptaplomeres,* but from the incidental remarks made in the *Oratio* it seems possible that as early as 1559 Bodin had applied his method to religion as well as to law and concluded that Christianity was not the hidden cause of *vera religio,* but only one of its various accidental manifestations.

What set Bodin on the trail of these inner truths, these hidden causes of law, religion and the universe? One crucial stimulus, it seems, was his reading of the works of Philo in the 1550's (see below, section D). But this is an external motive, as it were, and one would also like to have an inner psychological motive to make the picture more persuasive.[19] It is impossible to know for certain the motives of any conversion but there is a motif recurring throughout Bodin's writings which may suggest the key to his universal philosophy — the diversity of creation, a source of constant astonishment for Bodin. The bewildering variety of created forms, of rocks, vegetables, animals, men and societies, posed for Bodin as it did for Plato, Leonardo and Darwin, a miraculous riddle. For many sixteenth century minds it was also a dangerous riddle for it raised the issue of whether creation was simply an anarchy devoid of design and thus opened the high road to atheism. There were dangers too on an intellectual level for such a bounty of nature threatened the unity of creation.

---

[18] But note that Bodin does not say that God's *essence* may be learnt from nature. In his later writing Bodin was careful to distinguish between the attributes and the essence of God.

[19] See below Sections C and D.

Little wonder therefore that many of Bodin's contemporaries settled for a peremptory solution, pronouncing the diversity of creation to be simply the outcome of divine fiat and ordinance. Man might investigate and describe the myriad forms of creation, but he could not understand why it took such forms except to tax the diligence of the investigators and compel them to admiration of the creator's ingenuity. [20]

By way of contrast Bodin, far from being intimidated by nature's profusion, rejoiced in it:

> What is more admirable in the universe than excellence in the sciences? We wonder at the vastness of the earth, the depth of the sea, the immensity of the heavens, the splendour of the sun, the courses of the planets, the influences of the stars, the eclipse of the heavenly bodies; we marvel at lightning and thunder, storms and earthquakes, the forms of animals, the qualities of planets, the properties of metals, the variety of gems, the birth and death of all things; we are astounded by the virtue and power of immortal souls, the incredible divinity and nature of man. Yet none of these things is more admirable than that which is able to measure and comprehend these things. For this truly is the astounding miracle of the universe. And what pleasure can surpass the discovering of the hidden causes of these grand phenomena? What spectacle can be more beautiful than nature shedding profusely such a diversity of forms? (*Oratio*, p. 13). [21]

In his later writings Bodin went on to proclaim that in its magnificent diversity nature was not anarchic but resembled a choir of the universe wherein the diverse voices of all creation united in a harmonious worship of the creator. Not only did nature guide men to knowledge of God; it actually participated in His praise and through universal harmony was in communion with God. This religious vision of God and nature was later to be expressed in Bodin's fundamental formula of 'the Great God of Nature'. But how close was Bodin to this vision in 1559? It would be dangerous to assert too much about the religious beliefs outlined in a disconnected way in this early work but there is one significant clue that Bodin may already have had the structure of universal harmony worked out in his mind in a systematic form. In discussing the encyclopaedic unity of the arts and sciences Bodin introduces the metaphor of the choir:

> All the arts are connected and bound to one another by a certain kind of affinity and effect a wonderful harmony and agreement as with diverse kinds of voices. (*Oratio*, p. 17). [22]

[20] Pierre Charron, *De la sagesse* (1601), I, xxxix (quoted by E.F. Rice, jr., *The Renaissance Idea of Wisdom* (Cambridge, Mass., 1958), p. 185) took the diversity as a sign that nature and truth were beyond man's understanding.

[21] I am doubtful about the value of labelling Bodin a Platonist. If anything he was a Philonist. But in general such labels are too reductionistic and tend to rob their subject of the uniqueness or quiddity of his thought. See below, Section D. P. Mesnard, 'Le platonisme de Jean Bodin', in *Actes du Vᵉ congrès de l'Association Guillaume Budé* (Paris, 1954), pp. 352-361, surprisingly does not cite the *Oratio* to illustrate *his* case. For Leone Ebreo see Chapter IV and below, note 87.

[22] *Oratio*, p. 17: "cum omnes artes quadam inter seipsas affinitate connectuntur & colligantur, miramqve quasi ex diversis vocum generibus, harmoniam & concentum efficiunt." For contemporary Neoplatonic use of this choral metaphor see F. Yates, *The French Academies of the Sixteenth Century* (London, 1947), p. 106 and *passim*. For its origins in Philo and Plotinus see below Section D.

Even though the choral metaphor is not applied here to the universe itself Bodin's use of this universalistic image combined with his fascination at the diversity of creation suggests that the vision of the choir of creation was already in his mind.

The *Oratio,* therefore, suggests that by 1559 Bodin has espoused a religion that was essentially natural and universal and which allowed him to remain indifferent to the competing claims of the various positive religions. Yet for all that Bodin gained from this initial conversion from Christianity to natural religion the shift may have cost him dearly; for it may have diminished two major elements of his religious sensibility which had perhaps been with him since his youth. During his Carmelite years Bodin's spirituality had been directed towards purification and prophecy. But when his universalising tendency steered him to natural religion in his *Oratio* of 1559 it also persuaded him perhaps to suppress this earlier spirituality that had been rooted in the particularity of the Christian religion which he was trying to escape. The emergence of a Judaised mentality in subsequent years, however, was to permit Bodin to take possession again of the spiritual feelings of purification and prophecy by emancipating them from the unacceptable Christian doctrines in which those feelings had previously been situated. Until Bodin was able to fuse prophetic revelation with the naturalistic ideas of the *Oratio,* his conversion to *vera religio,* while it may have begun, was still a long way from fruition.

b) The Judaising of "Vera Religio": New Prophetic Themes (1559-66)

Our analysis of Bodin's initial conversion to *vera religio* should remove some of the difficulties which his formal profession of Catholicism as a Parisian *avocat* in 1562 has presented to recent biographers. Bodin's action on this occasion is quite consistent with the idea of true religion expressed in the *Oratio.* In matters of positive religion Bodin was willing to accept whichever confession was in command of the state. One might simulate adherence to a positive religion such as Catholicism without doing injury to *vera religio.* Indifferent as he was in matters of positive religion, Bodin would have had no qualms about taking the oath prescribed for the *avocats* on 10 June 1562. [23]

The *Methodus* makes explicit the distinction between political religion and true religion which had been a little obscure in the *Oratio:*

> We should not consider religion a part of civil science even if we see priests and pontiffs controlled by the power of the magistrates. This happens because the sacrifices and approved rites in the state must be zealously defended. But religion itself, that is, the turning of a purified soul towards God, can exist without

---

[23] R. Delachenal, *Histoire des avocats au Parlement de Paris 1300-1600* (Paris, 1885), pp. 29f, 405f. Two Jean Bodins subscribed to the oath, one of them our Bodin, the other his namesake Jean Bodin de Montguichet.

civil science, without association, in the solitude of one man; and he is thought, by the agreement of great men, to be happier the farther he is removed from civil society. (*Methodus*, 121AB; 33f).

State-religion is a matter of external rites and uniformity, true religion one of inner spirituality. [24]

From Bodin's distinction it follows that one may simulate adherence to the religion of the state without any prejudice to *vera religio*; all that is at stake here is external conformity to a positive religion of the kind exemplified by Bodin's own oath of 1562.

As long as Christianity was compatible with the fundamental monotheism of *vera religio* and as long as the oath-taker conformed to the rites of Catholicism, there was from Bodin's point of view no hypocrisy involved in such an oath. On the other hand, to deny what one believes to be the true religion — in a sense, to dissimulate — is denounced by Bodin as impiety:

> Indeed I would judge him impious who, believing whatever be his religion to be true, did not seek to protect it and overthrow opposing ones. (*Methodus*, 135A; 70). [25]

(There is an echo here of Philo's commendation of the Levites who "under the leadership of that high priest and prophet, Moses the friend of God, waged most bitter war for true religion and did not desist until they had destroyed all the false dogmas of their adversaries"). [26]

But had Bodin's idea of *vera religio* itself changed since 1559? Certainly the *Methodus* sees a clarifying of some of the ideas of natural religion which had been adumbrated in the Oratio. There is, for instance, a more systematic conception of the Great God of Nature than had appeared earlier. God is depicted as *naturae parens* — the father of nature — and all knowledge is related through a tripartite scheme of human, natural and divine history to man's gradual rediscovery of God:

> Of history, that is the true narration of things, there are three kinds: human, natural and divine. The first concerns man, the second nature, the third the Father of nature...
>
> Men should first notice the goodness of God and his pre-eminence in human affairs, then in manifest natural causes, then in the arrangement and splendour of the heavenly bodies; after that, in the admirable order, motion, immensity,

---

[24] For the Latin versions of these texts see Chapter II. Compare *Methodus*, p. 118A (25): 'Sed in eo genere historiarum (*divinity*), plus oratione frequenti et purgatae mentis in Deum conversione quam ullo studio proficiemus'; and *Methodus*, p. 154B (122): 'Primus (animorum ordo) quidem puras hominum mentes in Deum convertere'; and *Methodus*, p. 121AB (33): 'Religio vero ipsa, id est purgatae mentis in Deum recta conversio.'

[25] *Methodus*, p. 135: "ego vero impium judicarem nisi quancunque religionem veram judicaret, non eam quoque tueri & contrarias evertere conaretur." This is an exhortation to sincerity rather than religious war. But the underlying premise can, pushed to extremes, be turned to justification of religious war. This seems indeed to have happened so with Bodin in 1569. See below, Section E.

[26] Philo, *De Sacrific. Abel.*, 130. The Gelenius Latin translation renders true religion as *pro pietate*. Philo, *Lucubrationes omnes* (Lyons, 1555), p. 155.

harmony and shape of the entire universe, so that by these steps we may some-time return to that intimate relationship which we have with God, to the original source of our kind, and again be united closely to Him. (*Methodus,* 114B-115A; 15f). [27]

Here the natural basis of religion is explicitly rooted in the universal harmony and diversity of nature. At the same time the metaphor of the choir of nature emerges tied firmly to the concept of universal harmony:

> For if we refer all things to nature, which is chief of all things, it becomes plain that this world, which is superior to anything ever joined together by immortal God, consists of unequal parts and mutually discordant elements and contrary motions of the spheres, so that if the harmony through dis-similarity is taken away, the whole will be ruined .... As on the lyre and in song itself skilled ears cannot endure that sameness of harmony which is called unison; on the contrary a pleasing harmony is produced by dissimilar notes, deep and high, combined in accordance with certain rules.... (*Methodus,* 214B; 268).

The sharper focus of Bodin's natural theism renders all the more striking the signs of a reappraisal of the role of prophetic revelation in *vera religio* which appear in the *Methodus.* The belief in the immortality of the soul is now seen to spring from prophetic Scripture.

> What can be for the greater glory of God or of greater advantage that the fact that sacred history is the means of propagating piety (*religio*) towards God, reverence towards parents, charity to individuals and justice to all? Whence indeed do we draw words and oracles of the prophets and the eternal quality and power of souls if not from the sacred fount of history? (*Methodus,* 113A; 11).

This new perception of prophecy and revelation seems to reflect a fresh, more pronounced phase of Bodin's Judaising. The *Methodus* evinces a definite fondness for Jewish authorities, particularly Philo and Maimonides, which had not been evident in the *Oratio.* Favourable references to the Jewish nation

[27] The Latin texts of this and the two next excerpts are as follows: *Methodus,* pp. 114B-115A: "Historiae, id est verae narrationis, tria sunt genera: humanum, naturale, divinum. primum ad hominem pertinet, alterum ad naturam, tertium ad naturae paren-tem .... primum Dei bonitate ac praestantiam in rebus humanis, animadvertant : deinde in perspicuis naturae causis: tum in coelestium corporum descriptione & ornatu: postea in mundi totius admirabili ordine, motu, magnitudine, concentu, figura: ut iis gradibus ad eam, quae nobis est cum Deo, cognationem ac generis stirpem aliquando redeamus, rursusque cum eo penitus conjungamur."

Ibidem, p. 214B: "nam si ad naturam, quae rerum Princeps est, omnia revocemus, perspicuum fit mundum hunc, quo nihil pulchrius est ab immortali Deo coagmentatum, ex inaequalibus partibus, & maxime sibi repugnantibus elementis, orbiumque agitationibus contrariis ita sibi constare, ut sublata illa congruenti discordia interitus sit: non aliter optima Respublica, si naturam imitetur, id quod necesse est, ... & quemadmodum in fidibus & cantu ipso concentum aequalem, quem unisonum vocant, aures eruditae ferre non pos-sunt: contra vero dissimillimis inter se vocibus, tum gravibus tum acutis, moderatione quadam inter se confusis harmonia concors efficitur."

Ibidem, p. 113A: "quid ad veram utilitatem majus esse potest, quam quod ab historia sacra, religio adversus Deum, pietas in parentes, charitas in singulos, justitia in omnes propagatur?"

Cf *Methodus,* p. 114A (14): "If we neglect history, the cult of God, religion and prophecies are ruined with the passage of time." For further remarks on the religious and ethical ideas of the *Methodus* see above Chapter VI.

recur and Bodin gives himself over to an intense admiration for Moses as the supreme prophetic law-giver and philosopher: "Such is the authority with me of Moses alone that I place him far ahead of all the writings and opinions of all philosophers". [28]

If Bodin's final conversion of 1567-68 was one of prophetic transfiguration we may see in the *Methodus* of 1566 how he had laid out the Judaised psychological terrain on which the conversion was to take place. Prophecy is of course the most salient feature of this religious landscape but a number of other critical contours appear on the map of Bodin's religious sensibility sketched in the *Methodus* and these contours all seem to be the product of a new Judaised understanding.

Unlike the *Oratio* where reason had been seen as predominant one finds the will exalted as the "mistress of human activity" in the *Methodus*. [29] This new Judaised emphasis is reflected in Bodin's new sympathy for Philo's ethics and his adoption of the Jewish idea that righteous charity is true justice. [30] Will may in fact be said to have a central role in shaping the particular lines of Bodin's final conversion; it was through free-willed prayer that Bodin brought himself to the edge of human capability before surrendering the will at the moment he received the divine illumination of prophecy. (Such annihilation of the will is a common phenomenon in religious conversion). [31]

In Jewish thought the object of the will is to choose good and so purify the soul. This purification is rendered metaphorically by Philo as the "sacrifice" of a purified soul or mind. In the *Heptaplomeres* Bodin had actually cited Philo as a source for this metaphor of *mentes puras sacrificare*. [32] But already in the *Methodus* Bodin is citing not once, but three times the Philonic notion of the conversion of the purified soul:

> (In sacred studies)... frequent prayer and the turning of a purified soul towards God is better than study. [33]

---

[28] *Methodus*, p. 228B (303). Cf. *ibidem*, p. 253A (362): 'Illud etiam magis mirum videri possit, quod ab illis religiones, quae toto terrarum orbe usurpantur, velut a fonte fluxerunt'. See C.R. Baxter, 'Jean Bodin's Daemon and His Conversion to Judaism', in *Verhandlungen der internationalen Bodin Tagung*, ed. H. Denzer (Munich, 1973), pp. 1-21, at pp. 13f. For Bodin's frequent citations of Maimonides in the *Methodus* and elsewhere see (in the same volume) M. Isnardi-Parente, 'Le volontarisme de Jean Bodin: Maimonide ou Duns Scot?', pp. 39-51 (but see note 44 below). Also the references in Guttmann's article (cited below, note 77).

[29] *Methodus*, p. 119B (29). See Chapters II and VI for details.

[30] *Methodus*, p. 123AB (38). Again see Chapters II and VI.

[31] For the conversion of 1567-68 see the next section. Cf. William James, *Varieties of Religious Experience* (repr. London, 1977), p. 211. For the role of will in the conversions of Petrarch and others see W.J. Bouwsma, 'The Two Faces of Humanism: Stoicism and Augustinianism in Renaissance Thought', in *Itinerarium Italicum*, ed. H. Oberman (Leiden, 1975), pp. 5-60, especially pp. 37f.

[32] *Heptaplomeres*, ed. Noack (trs. p. 189). See Chapter VII for Latin text. For the critical impact of this idea on Bodin's final conversion see below, notes 48, 62, 73 and section D. The same metaphor of the purified soul appears in the letter to Bautru (see note 105).

[33] *Methodus*, p. 118A (25): "Plus oratione frequenti et purgatae mentis in Deum conversione, quam ullo studio proficiemus."

And a few pages later:

> Religion itself is the turning of a purified soul towards God (*purgatae mentis in Deum recta conversio*). [34]

Finally:

> The first order of souls turns the purified souls of men towards God (*puras hominum mentes in Deum convertere*). [35]

Yet there is a limit in Philo and Maimonides and in Bodin's *Methodus* to the power of free will. The power of the will stops short of prophecy.

> When God or divine fury inspires someone to prophesy, the action is not human but divine since it is not controlled by the will of man. [36]

Exactly so too is man's highest happiness, the mystical love of God, unattainable by the mere power of the will.

> Man is carried on to things grasped only by the mind, that is to the strength and power of immortal souls, until he is snatched up and deeply joined to God. In this consists the goal of human action, the final peace and the highest happiness. [37]

A basically Judaised religious structure is therefore present in the *Methodus*. It corresponds more or less exactly to the structure of ideas in his later *Paradoxe*: there, it will be recalled, Bodin insists that man may use his will to purify his soul through prayer and so naturally attain to virtue. Man is thus prepared to receive from God the highest happiness of ecstatic love of God, a happiness which is largely synonomous with the advent of the prophetic spirit.

By 1566, therefore, Bodin had discerned the Judaised way of true religion. First came free-willed prayer and purification of the soul; then, on a higher plane, that mystical love of God which comes with prophetic spirit. One might easily see, however, how this division between the two components of true religion could produce an acute state of religious and psychological tension in Bodin, and if we are to judge from his later recollections in the *Démonomanie* this is what indeed happened. Bodin had set up prophecy as the highest happiness of man, but he had made it an ideal beyond his own powers of achievement as he recognised in stating that it lay beyond the capability of free will. A profound recognition of this impotence may have provoked a religious and psychological crisis from which the only salvation was to fall back on his

---

[34] *Methodus*, p. 121AB (33): "Religio vero ipsa, id est purgatae mentis in Deum recta conversio." Ficino adopts a similar idea from Neoplatonic sources (and perhaps ultimately from Philo): "Prayer is nothing but an inner conversion of the soul towards God.» Quoted by P.O. Kristeller, *The Philosophy of Marsilio Ficino* (New York, 1943), p. 315. See below, note 45.

[35] *Methodus*, p. 154B (122): "Primus quidem puras hominum mentes in Deum convertere."

[36] *Methodus*, p. 119B (20): "Quem Deus aut furor divinus ad vaticinandum afflaverit, non humana, sed divina est actio, quia non ab hominis voluntate regitur." See Chapter VI.

[37] *Methodus*, p. 120A (30), quoted in Latin in Chapter II above.

admitted capacity for prayer and purification. The intensity of this prayer and the Philonic sacrifice of his purified soul would have cleared away all the obstacles in himself to the influx of divine light. One must stop short of saying that Bodin's introspection produced his transformation into a prophet; but one can say that, in Bodin's own terms, self-purification had prepared him to receive happiness.

c) The Third Phase of the Conversion: Bodin's Prophetic Transfiguration (1567-69)

In chapter two of the first book of *Démonomanie,* written in 1578-80, Bodin recounts in great circumstantial detail the religious conversion experienced by an unnamed friend at the age of 37. The vivid detail of this narrative has suggested to some readers that it is in fact an autobiographical account of Bodin's own religious crisis written up many years after the event. [38] There can be no doubt that the feelings attributed to the anonymous subject of the conversion are characteristic of Bodin's own mature religious sensibility as expressed in his later writings, particularly the *Paradoxe.* Such a coincidence of attitudes in itself would argue strongly for identifying the un-named convert of the *Démonomanie* with Bodin himself.

Furthermore, if there is a plain link between the conversion-narrative of the *Démonomanie* and Bodin's later religion, there is also a definite connection between the narrative and Bodin's earlier thought. The narrative of 1580 is set in the context of a description of a universe which pulsates with spirits. In the *Methodus* there had been hints of demonic activity in the natural universe

[38] See F. von Bezold, 'Jean Bodin als Okkultist und seine *Démonomanie*', *Historische Zeitschrift,* CV (1910), 1-64, references at pp. 26ff.

G. Roellenbleck, *Offenbarung, Natur und jüdische Überlieferung bei Jean Bodin* (Gütersloh, 1964), p. 120. I am greatly indebted to the accounts by C.R. Baxter (a) 'Jean Bodin's Daemon and his Conversion to Judaism', in *Verhandlungen der internationalen Bodin-Tagung,* ed. H. Denzer (Munich, 1973), pp. 1-21. (b) 'Jean Bodin's *De la Démonomanie des Sorciers.* The Logic of Persecution', in *The Damned Art,* ed. S. Anglo (London, 1977), pp. 76-105. My own account nevertheless differs somewhat from Mr. Baxter's in several major respects.

(A) There seem to me to be three separate stages to the conversion (before 1559, before 1566 and 1567-69) where Mr. Baxter sees only one, that of 1567-68. (B) The influence of Philo seems to be crucial but is touched on only incidentally by Mr. Baxter. (C) Mr. Baxter may underrate the voluntaristic and demonic content of the *Methodus,* largely there it seems to me as the result of the second stage of the conversion. (D) Mr. Baxter allows the importance of prophecy in the final stage of the conversion but I would argue vigorously that prophecy is absolutely central here and I hope I have been able to give a more precise explanation of its nature. (E) My redating of the letter to Bautru further supports the idea of a prophetic transfiguration in the period 1566-69. (F) Mr. Baxter's use of the term "Judaism" to describe Bodin's religion is somewhat misleading in that it suggests Bodin may have adhered to Jewish ritual. "Judaised religion" seems preferable.

From the vast but inconclusive literature on conversion one may cite particularly James, *Varieties of Religious Experience.* A.D. Nock, *Conversion* (Oxford, 1933). Margharita Laski, *Ecstasy. A Study of Some Secular and Religious Experiences* (London, 1961).

— the 'prince of fluid matter', 'the contagion of an evil spirit', 'the evil demon', 'the greater abundance of demons and witches', 'the agitating demon', 'the prince of darkness' — all these had made a perfunctory appearance. [39] They had, however, been left hanging in mid-air (so to speak) and not set in any systematic demonological context. Whether this was because Bodin had not conceived a demonology at this point, or because he thought such a history of spirits only marginally relevant to his present subject of human history, is open to debate but it seems to me that the latter is very much the case. [40]

We have seen from the references in the *Methodus* to prophecy, the will and purification that Bodin was by 1566 in possession of the structure of his mature *vera religio*. Moreover, according to the descriptions of the *Démono-manie* and the *Heptaplomeres* one of the essential features of *vera religio* is a spiritual universe which incorporates a demonology. It would be reasonable, therefore, to allow that behind the fragmentary demonic allusions of the *Methodus* there lies an awareness of their place in a general religious theory and to concede that Bodin had indeed framed a proper demonology by 1566. Bodin's *Démonomanie* represents in effect a systematic exposition of his already formed demonology rather than an abrupt shift in the whole direction of his thought.

An examination of the various elements of Bodin's religious vision presented in the conversion-narrative of the *Démonomanie* unveils intricate connections between, on the one hand, Bodin's spiritual universe with its angels and demons, and, on the other hand, the fundamentals of his *vera religio* — Deuteronomic free will, prayer and purification, and above all prophecy which is mediated through the angels. The demonology and the themes of *vera religio* are indeed functionally related and are not at all independent of one another.

The extent to which these religious ideas of Bodin's drew on a Judaised understanding is astonishing. In the *Methodus* Bodin's Judaised perceptions had appeared in merely allusive form, but coming to the *Démonomanie* one is struck at how soaked in Jewish ideas and deeply coloured by his reading of Philo and Maimonides is the conversion-narrative. Yet for all this contrast a comparison of the doctrines in the two works reveals how Bodin's third and final conversion proceeded along a road laid down during his second conversion. The Judaised structure was already there; all that was needed was the prophetic spirit itself.

The *Démonomanie* paints a vivid canvas of a universe teeming with angels and demons (good and bad spirits) operating in natural and human affairs

---

[39] *Methodus*, p. 115A (17); p. 116A (19); p. 119B (29); 153B (118); p. 233A (315); p. 234A (316). I cannot agree with Baxter, 'Bodin's Daemon', pp. 14, 16 (who does not cite these instances) that such slight demonic allusions as there are 'go against ... the main purpose of the *Methodus*'.

[40] Bodin does not lose sight of the ultimate interrelation of divine, natural and human history. It is only 'for the time being (*tantisper*) that (he) leaves divine history to the Theologians, natural history to the philosophers... (*for his object now is to*) concentrate long and intently upon human actions and the rules governing them' (*Methodus*, p. 115B (17)). See next footnote.

under the specific and constant direction of God; it is a vision which also dominates the *Theatrum* and *Heptaplomeres*. [41] In this dynamic universe man is intermediate between spirit and matter and so has an active role in the construction of universal harmony. [42] Such a connection between spirit and matter enhances Bodin's concept of the Great God of Nature.

> Car on void que ce grand Dieu de nature a lié toutes choses par moyens, qui s'accordent aux extremitez, & compose l'harmonie du monde intelligible, celeste, & elementaire par moyēns et liaisons indissolubles. Et tout ainsi que l'harmonie periroit, si les voix contraires n'estoyent liées par voix moyennes: ainsi est il du monde, & de ses parties. (*Démonomanie*, ff. 7rv). [43]

It might seem that Bodin's view of man as intermediate being is reminiscent of Renaissance Italian Neoplatonism but what he goes on to say is distinctively Hebraic and in a different category altogether from the religious philosophy of Ficino or Pico.

Although it is for God to decide whether to send man a good spirit or guardian angel to guide him, it is a man's free will which makes the decision to have commerce with evil spirits and turn to sorcery. The Deuteronomic choice between good and evil, life and death, is the core of Bodin's mature religious thought, and it is bound up with Bodin's demonology.

> Puis doncques que les Anges sont bons, & les Diables mauuais, aussi les hommes ont le franc arbitre pour estre bons, ou mauuais, comme Dieu dit en sa Loy (*Deut*. XXX, 15). I'ay, dit-il, mis deuant tes yeux le bien, & le mal, la vie & la mort, choisy donc le bien, & tu viuras. (*Démonomanie*, f. 8).

In the *Methodus* there had been a strong voluntaristic element, emphasising divine will but also admitting human will. 'Volition leads the way. For the will is mistress of human activity whether it follows reason or the lower faculty of the soul'. (*Methodus,* p. 119 B (29)). [44] While this statement may be reconciled with Christian thinking, free will in the *Démonomanie* takes on a fundamentally Judaised character expressed in the Deuteronomic choice. This choice, the turning of a purified heart towards God, has now become the essence of *vera religio*.

Those who of their own free will choose virtue and good and purify themselves through prayer thereby open themselves to divine illumination which may be mediated through the angels and spirits. Men who have so sanctified

[41] Again there is far more evidence of Providential intervention in human history in the *Methodus* than Baxter, 'Bodin's Daemon', p. 16, allows. See *Methodus,* p. 115A (16, 17): 'Dei bonitatem ac praestantiam in rebus humanis'; 'At humana historia quod *magna sui parte* fluit ab hominum voluntate'. The two statements are not contradictory. Free will does not infringe Providence.

[42] Bodin's conception of spirit is idiosyncratic: Angels and demons are corporeal, though not material. See Chapter V, and below, notes 93, 96.

[43] On harmony in the *Démonomanie* see U. Lange, *Untersuchungen zu Bodins Démonomanie* (Frankfurt, 1970), pp. 69-76. Bezold, 'Bodin Okkultist', p. 46.

[44] See M. Isnardi-Parente, 'Il volontarismo di Jean Bodin: Maimonide o Duns Scoto?', *Il pensiero politico,* IV, (1971), 21-45 (French version in *Verhandlungen,* ed. Denzer) for Bodin's later voluntarism. (Though the author seems to me to stress too much the Christian content of Bodin's theory — see Chapters IV and V).

themselves form therefore a crucial bridge between the two universes of spirit and matter.

> Or les saincts personnages, qui mesprisent la partie mortelle, & terrestre pour ioindre leur ame intellectuelle auec les Anges, font la liaison du monde intelligible auec le monde inferieur: Ce qui fut faict premierement lors que Adam fut creé en estat de grace, ayant neantmoins le franc' arbitre d'estre bon ou mauuais ... & non pas l'homme qui deuoit estre le lyen du monde intelligible & visible, laquelle liaison a continué entre les Anges, & les saincts personnages, par la priere, & moyen desquels le genre humain est conserué. (*Démonomanie*, ff. 7v-8).

It is within man's own natural powers and within the scope of his free will to pursue virtue and prayer and prepare himself for divine "grace".

> Si l'homme s'adonne à bien, & qu'il éleue son ame à Dieu, à bien, à vertu, apres que son ame sera purifiée d'vne grace diuine, s'il s'exerce aux vertus morales, & puis aux vertus intellectuelles, il se pourra faire, qu'il ayt telle societé auec l'Ange de Dieu qu'il ne fera pas seulemēt gardé par iceluy, ains il sentira sa presence, & cognoistra les choses, qu'il cõmande, & qu'il uy defend. Mais celà aduient à peu d'hommes, & d'vne grace, & bonté speciale de Dieu. Auerroës appelle celà l'adeption de l'intellect, & dict qu'en celà gist la felicité la plus grande, qui soit en ce monde: Ce que Socrate aperceut des premiers entre les Grecs. (*Démonomanie*, f. 9).

In the *Methodus* Bodin had insisted that true religion was 'nothing other than the turning of a purified soul towards God' but now in the *Démonomanie* the non-Christian character of this *vera religio* emerges quite arrestingly.[45] Although Bodin admits a first rupture between God and man brought about by the fall of Adam, he sees no need for a Christ to restore man to God. All that is necessary is sincere prayer and divine "grace"; man and God may come together through the angelic spirits and without Christ as intermediary. Such an outlook is remarkably close to Jewish ideas on God and man and Bodin himself cites a passage from Philo which moved him deeply.[46]

> Il[47] trouua en Philon Hebrieu au liure des sacrifices, que le plus grand & plus agreable sacrifice, que l'homme de bien, & entier peut faire à Dieu, c'est de soymesme, estant purifié par luy. Il suiuit ce conseil, offrant à Dieu son ame. Depuis il commença, comme il m'a dict, d'auoir des songes, & visions.[48]

[45] There is some resemblance here to the Neoplatonic notion of *conversio mentis ad Deum*, for which see this chapter, notes 34 and 35, and P.O. Kristeller, *The Philosophy of Marsilio Ficino* (New York, 1943), pp. 306ff. But that same idea, perceived in a Hebraic religious context, is frequently to be found in Philo, e.g. *Fuga*, 25: "Turn back to the Lord ... seek Him with all your heart and soul» (citing *Deuteronomy*, IV, 29). For other references including *Migr. Abrah.*, 195 and *Post. Cain.* 135, see P. Aubin, *Le Problème de la "Conversion"* (Paris, 1963), p. 227.

[46] I shall argue below that Philo played a crucial role in all three stages of Bodin's conversion.

[47] For the argument that "he" is Bodin see below.

[48] See below, note 62. The treatise in question is not *De Sacrificiis Abelis et Caini* but rather the sections "De Victimis" and "De Sacrificantibus" of *De Specialibus Legibus*, I, 162-345. Philo weakens the idea of temple-sacrifice in favour of the inner mystical sacrifice it symbolises. A general theme is that all sacrifices are equal given the purity of heart of the sacrificer: An important passage (257f) deals with the purification of the soul of the sacrificer. For the sacrifice of the purified soul see, e.g.: "The true altar of God is the thankful soul of the sage, composed of perfect virtues unsevered and undi-

Bodin's reading of Philo is apparent in the *Methodus* of 1566 which cites the philosopher as a source for Jewish history and discusses his opinions on the eternity of the universe. But there are also indications that by 1566 Philo's religious views had begun to affect Bodin. In chapter ten of the *Methodus* Bodin expounded a theory of Jewish history closely resembling Philo's interpretation of that history as a moral record of divine retribution for evil doing. Like Philo Bodin affirmed the unique role of the Jewish race as the recipients of divine revelation and the preservers of the purest positive religion. But most significantly of all, the *Methodus* repeats, not once but three times, Philo's own summation of true religion — that true religion is nothing other than the turning of a cleansed heart to God. [49]

In the *Démonomanie* Bodin developed these Philonic themes as well as others not immediately evident in the *Methodus*. One such new theme was Philo's notion that in the spiritual universe the angels and demons acted as the agents of God's justice. [50] Through this spiritual vision Philo had provided his solutions to the problems of divine transcendence and the existence of evil. God acted in the universe through the intermediation of angels and demons and used bad demons to provoke evil which nevertheless depended on human free will. Divine revelation to man also was mediated through the action of spirits which moved men to prophecy. The only exception to this procedure had been Moses who spoke with God face to face; Mosaic — and Jewish — revelation was therefore supreme. In Philo's Jewish synthesis prophecy therefore became the main vehicle of revelation; moreover, both prophecy and revelation were in turn inextricably bound up with the notion of a spiritual universe governed by providence. There can be no mistaking the echo of these Philonic connections between prophecy, revelation and spirits in such remarks in the *Démonomanie* as the following:

> O peuple heureux qui n'a point de sorcelerie ny de sortileges, mais auquel Dieu reuele les choses futures quãd il est besoin. Et combien que depuis la publication de la loy de Dieu, & apres tant de Propheties, visions, & iugemens de Dieu consignez es escriptures, & histoires sainctes, par lesquelles nous sommes bien enformez de la verité, & volonté de Dieu, & qu'il ne soit pas besoing de prophetes: neãtmoins il est bien certain, que Dieu ne laisse pas d'enuoyer aux hommes, songes, visions, & ses bons Anges, par lesquels il leur faict cognoistre sa volõté, pour se guider & instruire les autres. (*Démonomanie*, f. 27).

vided...." (281): "Sacrifice consists not in the victims but in the offerer's intention and zeal ... derived from virtue" (290). Cf. *Quod Deterius*, 21: ("Genuine worship is that of a soul bringing simple truth as its only sacrifice"); *De Somniis*, II, 74 ("... the best of sacrifices, even the whole soul, brimful of truths of all sincerity and purity..."); *De Vita Mosis*, II, 108 ("For the true oblation, what else can it be but the devotion of a soul which is dear to God. The thank-offering of such a soul receives immortality"); *De Sacrificiis Abelis*, 40 ("Offering the firstlings ... from the fat, showing that the gladness and richness of the soul, all that protects and gives joy, should be set apart for God").

[49] See notes 32ff.

[50] For such other Philonic themes as wisdom, virtue and grace see Chapters IV and V.

Two opposing schools of interpretation of Philo are represented by E.R. Goodenough, *An Introduction to Philo Judaeus* (2nd ed., Oxford, 1962) and H.A. Wolfson, *Philo* (Cambridge, Mass., 1947). Cf. L.H. Feldman, *Scholarship on Philo and Josephus 1937-62* (New York, 1963). For further notes on Philo see below Section D.

But even in the *Methodus* too there are hints that Bodin was already committed to Philo's vision of prophetic revelation in a spiritual universe. 'So Philo commended Moses with high praise, because alone among mortals he was at the same time the boldest general, the most prudent legislator and *the holiest prophet*',[51] says Bodin in the *Methodus,* agreeing with Philo's acclaim of Moses as the greatest of Jewish prophets.[52] Nor was Bodin's allusion to prophecy in the *Methodus* out of tune with Philo's definition of prophecy as a gift of divine grace beyond the power of human will. 'When God or divine frenzy inspires someone to prophecy, the action is not human but divine since it is not controlled by human will'.[53]

If we turn from these inconclusive allusions in the *Methodus* to the lavishly systematic analysis of prophecy in the *Démonomanie* we notice immediately the overwhelming role of prophecy in Bodin's religion — the crucial link between prophecy and revelation and its foundation in Bodin's spiritual universe of angels and demons is now fully articulated. In the *Démonomanie* prophecy is integrated into the spiritual universe as the highest form of angelic communication.

> Et entre ceux-là qui ont societé auec les bons esprits, il y a plusieurs degrez. Car aux vns Dieu donnoit vn Ange si excellent, que leurs Propheties, & predictions estoient tousieurs certaines & infaillibles, comme on dict de Moyse, Helye, Samuël, Helisée. Les autres n'ont pas tousiours esté infaillibles, soit que les esprits soient moins parfaicts les vns que le autre, oit que le suget n'es pas si propre ...aussi les passions de l'ame troublée, ou qui n'est pas coye & trãquille, ne peut si biẽ receuoir la clarté intellectuelle. l'ay dict que c'est vn singulier don de Dieu, quand il enuoye son bõ esprit à celuy qu'il aime, pour estre entendu de luy, & guidé en toutes ses actions ... Mais celuy à qui Dieu faict la grace speciale de cognoistre sensiblement la presence de son Ange, & communiquer intelligiblement auec luy, iJ se peut dire beaucoup plus heureux que les autres: & tresheureux s'il a le don de Prophetie, qui est le plus haut poinct d'honneur où l'homme peut estre esleué. (*Démonomanie,* ff. 9v-10).

Apart from the connection it makes between guardian angels and prophecy[54] this passage is notable for its arresting conception of prophecy as *clarté intellectuelle*. Such an emphasis on prophecy as an illuminated intellectual phenomenon, as an emanation from God through the angels to the human intellect, was clearly influenced by a reading of Maimonides and Bodin's theory of prophecy as elaborated in the *Démonomanie* incorporates many Maimonidean details. Yet the real source of this illuminative idea of prophecy seems to be really Philo as Bodin later acknowledged in the *Heptaplomeres* (below, note 114). In some ways of course Bodin's theory resembles also aspects of Neoplatonic angelology and anthropology, a kinship of which he was well aware.[55] But nevertheless

[51] *Methodus,* p. 152B (116) : 'Divinissimus propheta'.
[52] *Methodus,* p. 228B (303) etc.
[53] *Methodus,* p. 119B (29).
[54] Bodin seems to imply that the two are not identical. One may have a guardian angel yet not be endowed with the gift of prophecy. But while Bodin here associates prophecy with the higher and more excellent angels he later (*Dém.,* I, 4, f. 23, see below) makes the recognition of a guardian angel's presence the first grade of prophecy.
[55] For Neoplatonic ideas of angels and prophecy see J. Trithemius, *Oratio de vera conversione mentis ad Deum* (s.d., s.l., 1500?). Giovanni Pico della Mirandola, *Opera* (Basle, 1557), p. 25. (*Heptaplus,* III, 2). Marsilio Ficino, *Opera* (Paris, 1641), I, 2ff; 6f. Cf. Kristeller, *Philosophy of Ficino,* pp. 306ff. Cf. Bezold, 'Bodin Okkultist', pp. 48ff.

it would be a serious mistake to regard Bodin's conception of prophecy as being anything other than thoroughly Judaised in character, drawing as it does for the most part on the Old Testament, Philo and Maimonides. Indeed even the Neoplatonist most congenial to Bodin was Jewish, namely Leone Ebreo. [56]

Following Maimonides Bodin roots prophecy in divine will but sees it as transmitted through the natural means of the active intellect.

> Auquel passage les Hebrieux [*Numbers* XII] ont noté que la Prophetie est vne largesse enuoyee de Dieu, par le moyen et ministere de l'Ange ou intelligence actiue sur l'ame raisonnable premierement, & puis sur l'imagination: & n'exceptent que la Prophetie de Moyse, qu'ils tiennent auoir esté faicte à Moyse immediatement parlant à Dieu, sans moyen, & en veillant. Et par ainsi tous les propos de Dieu en toute la saincte escripture aux Prophetes, se font par le moyen des Anges, ou intelligences, ou en songes, & visions. (*Démonomanie,* ff. 21v-22). [57]

Bodin also agrees with Maimonides on the importance of self-purification through prayer as the necessary preparation for receiving the divine gift of prophecy.

> Or les moyens d'auoir les songes diuins, & d'approcher au degré de prophetie, est dépouiller premieremēt toute son arrogāce & vaine gloire, s'abstenir des voluptez deshõnestes, & d'auarice, puis apres s'adõner à viure vertueusemēt, & surtout à s'employer à contempler, & cognoistre les œuures de Dieu, & sa loy. (*Démonomanie,* ff. 22rv). [58]

Finally, Bodin's classification of the different kinds of prophetic experience into eleven grades imitates closely that offered by Maimonides. [59] But with one quite remarkable difference, for in discussing the first grade Bodin stretches the Jewish philosopher's definition in a curious way. Bodin at first follows Maimonides' definition of the first degree as the spirit of God coming upon someone and inspiring them to do good; Maimonidean examples are cited here. But then Bodin goes on to identify the spirit of God with the guardian angel sent by God, an identity not explicit in Maimonides:

> Le premier degré de Prophetie est la reuelation en songe de s'adonner à bien, & fuir le mal, ou pour euiter les mains des meschans, & alors cestuy-là sentira en son ame vn precepteur, qui le rendra sage, & aduisé (comme disent les Hebrieux) & de cestuy-cy l'escripture dict, que l'esprit de Dieu s'est reposé sur luy, ou bien que Dieu a esté auec luy. (*Démonomanie,* f. 23.) [60]

---

[56] Bodin's Judaised conception of prophecy appears clearly in *Heptaplomeres,* pp. 133-140 (trs. pp. 173-183). Cf. Bezold, 'Bodin Okkultist', pp. 49ff; and above, Chapters V and VII.

[57] Bodin gives a marginal reference to Maimonides, *Guides for the Perplexed,* bk. III (*sic,* for bk. II, ch. 36). Maimonides defines prophecy there as 'an emanation sent forth by the divine being through the medium of the active intellect, in the first instance to man's rational faculty, and then to his imaginative faculty'. (*Guide for the Perplexed,* trs. M. Friedländer (2nd ed., London 1904), p. 225). For Bodin's definition of angel, see *Démonomanie,* f. 30. (On the relationship between Bodin's prophetic theory and his ideas of God and nature see the Introduction above).

[58] Cf. the recommendations of Maimonides, *Guide,* II, ch. 36 (trs. p. 226).

[59] *Démonomanie,* I, 4f. 23rv. Cf. Maimonides, *Guide,* II, ch. 45 (trs. pp. 241ff).

[60] Cf. Maimonides, *Guides,* II, ch. 5 (trs. p. 241). See below.

This extension of Maimonides' definition is of the greatest significance for it was this same first grade of prophecy — characterised by the sensing of the presence of an angelic preceptor — that Bodin's unnamed friend had attained as a result of his conversion at the age of thirty-seven. Prophecy is therefore the key to understanding the nature of the particular conversion which Bodin described in the *Démonomanie* in order to illustrate the society of men and spirits.

*
**

In the narrative of the conversion three stages can easily be discerned. The first stage was one of disquiet and disturbance stemming from the prospective convert's anxiety to know exactly which of all religions was the true one. In pursuit of this knowledge the subject of the narrative had dedicated himself for a year to devout prayer accompanied by intense contemplation of God for two or three hours at a time and a profound reading of the Bible; God's guidance was invoked by the recital of Psalm 143 ("Hear my prayer, O Lord... teach me to do thy will..."). [61]   The second stage began with the convert's discovery in Philo's "treatise on sacrifices" that the greatest sacrifice a man could make was that of his own purified soul.   The subject followed this precept and offered his soul to God. [62]   This was the turning point of the conversion. There followed dreams and visions of instruction and while sleeping he heard the voice of God saying 'I will save your soul'. [63]   The third stage of

---

[61] *Démonomanie*, f. 10v: "Mais je puis asseurer d'avoir entendu d'un personnage, qui est encores en vie, qu'il avoit un esprit qui luy assistoit assiduellement et commença à le cognoistre, ayant environ trente sept ans, combien que le personnage me disoit, qu'il avoit opinion que toute sa vie l'esprit l'avoit accompagné par les songes précédens, et visions qu'il avoit eu de se garder des vices, et inconveniens ; et toutes fois il ne l'avoit iamais aperçue sensiblement, comme il feist depuis l'âge de trente sept ans: ce qui luy advint comme il dict, ayant un an auparavant continué de prier Dieu de tout son cueur soir et matin, à ce qu'il luy pleust envoyer son bon ange, pour le guider en toutes ses actions, et après devant la prire il employoit quelque temps à contempler les œuvres de Dieu, se tenant quelquesfois deux ou troi heures tout seul assis à méditer et contempler, et chercher son esprit, et à lire la Bible, *pour trouver laquelle de toutes les religions débatues de tous costez estoit la vray*, et disoit souvent ces vers:

> Enseigne moy comme il faut faire,
> Pour bien ta volonté parfaire,
> Car tu es mon vray Dieu entier,
> Fais que ton esprit débonnaire
> Me guide, et meine au droict sentier.

(*My italics*).   See Chapter III, note 15, for another reference to this psalm.

[62] *Ibidem*, fols. 10v-11: "Blasmant ceux-là, qui prient Dieu qu'il les entretiennent en leur opinion, et continuant ceste prière, et lisant les sainctes escriptures, il trouva en Philon Hébrieu au livre des sacrifices, que le plus grand et plus agréable sacrifice que l'homme de bien, et entier peut faire à Dieu, c'est de soymesme, estant purifié par luy. Il suivit ce conseil, offrant à Dieu son âme."   See above, notes 32, 48.

[63] *Ibidem*, f. 11: "Depuis il commença comme il m'a dict, d'avoir des songes et visions pleines d'instruction: et tantost pour corriger un vice, tantost un autre, tantost pour se garder d'un danger, tantost pour estre resolu d'une difficulté, puis d'un autre non seulement des choses divines, ains encores des choses humaines, et entre autres luy sembla avoir ouy la voix de Dieu en dormant, qui luy dist: Je sauveray ton âme: c'est moy qui t'ay apparu par cy devant.»

this conversion was the manifestation of a guardian spirit who would knock on the subject's door at 3 or 4 o'clock in the morning. At first alarmed that it might be a demon the subject prayed to God to send a good angel. Two days later the good spirit revealed itself while the subject was dining with one of the king's secretaries by knocking on a stool. Thereafter the subject felt courage and resolution in all matters and was strengthened by continual prayer to God and the reciting of psalms. On at least three occasions when he was in danger of his life the angel saved him by timely warnings. [64]

The narrative is explicit about the manner of communication between the convert and the spirit. The spirit could not be addressed direct but only indirectly through prayers to God. On the other hand the angel would often communicate with his protégé sensibly, whether by touching his ear or striking on the door with a hammer. Now, Bodin comments, the 'hearing of the striking of a hammer we read is the first mark of the prophets', and in a long passage he suggests that prophetic illumination is charasterised by the presence of a communicating guardian angel. [65] It therefore seems beyond doubt that the conversion amounted to the subject-s being transformed into a prophet of the first grade — a conclusion corroborated by Bodin's specific alteration (chapter 4) of Maimonides' definition of the first grade of prophecy to make it include the acquisition of a guardian angel. [66] The guardian angel and the advent of prophecy are, in consequence, indissolubly linked in Bodin's narrative of the conversion of his unnamed friend.

[64] *Ibidem,* fols. 11-12v.

[65] *Ibidem,* fols. 13rv: "l'ay bien voulu réciter ce que i'ay sceu d'un tel personnage, pour faire entendre que l'association des malings esprits ne doibt pas estre trouvée estrange, si les Anges et bons esprits ont telle société, et intelligence avec les hommes. Mais quant à ce qu'il dict, que le bon Ange luy touchoit l'oreille, cela est bien noté au livre de Iob chapitre XXXIII, et en Iesaye ay chapitre cinquantiesme, où il dict 'Dominus vellicavit mihi aurem diluculo'. Et Iob dict encores mieux, découvrant le secret aux hommes entendus, par le quel Dieu se faict peu à peu cognoistre sensiblement. Et quant à ce qu'il dict, qu'il oyoit fraper comme d'un marteau, nous lisons que c'estoit la première marque des Prophètes.... Or de dire que chacun a son bon Ange, cela n'est pas sans difficulté. Car combien que ceste opinion soit fort ancienne comme ces vers Grecs le monstrent ... C'est à dire, que chacun a un esprit conducteur de sa vie: toutesfois il semble du contraire. Car on void evidemment que Saul apres avoir esté beneit, et sacré de Samuel, et qu'il eut rencontré la bande des Prophètes au chemin, qui iouoyent des instrumens, l'esprit de Dieu le saisit, et se trouva (dit l'escripture) tout changé. C'est pourquoy Samuel luy dist, qu'il feist alors tout ce qui luy viendroit en la pensée. *Et quand il est dict que Dieu print de l'esprit de Moyse, pour en départir à LXXII personnes (que Dieu avoit choises entre six cens mil) et qu'ilz Prophètisoient, quand l'esprit de Dieu reposoit sur eux,* on peut recueillir que l'esprit de Dieu n'estoit pas encores avec eux ; *on recueillist aussi que l'esprit de Dieu est comme la lumière,* qui se communique sans diminution.... Toutesfois il se peut faire, comme i'ay dict, que la personne soit conduite et gardée par l'Ange de Dieu, sans l'apercevoir, ny avoir communication avec celuy qui le garde intelligiblement, ny sensiblement, soit que l'excellence des Anges est bien différente, comme i'ay dict de l'esprit de Moyse, de Samuel et d'Hélie, qui surpassoient de beaucoup tous les autres prophètes, soit que la personne n'est pas capable de l'intelligence spirituelle." (Italics added. For the "Seventy Prophets" see below, note 114.)

[66] See above note 60.

So far we have shown that in both structure and detail the experience of the unnamed convert is remarkably consonant with Bodin's religious sensibility as we have reconstructed it in this and earlier chapters from his other writings. This is particularly true of the core of the conversion — the prophetic transfiguration of the convert. There can be no doubting the centrality of prophecy in Bodin's religion for it served as the vehicle of both revelation and illumination, those two pillars of his religious thought. For prophecy both reveals God's will and crowns by divine illumination man's own efforts to perfect his natural virtue.

Yet granted that the conversion exemplifies all Bodin's religious concerns, is it really Bodin's own conversion that is being recounted? Certainly there is some anecdotal evidence that Bodin felt himself to be possessed of a guardian angel such as that which attached itself to the anonymous convert. François Pithou reported that

> Bodin était sorcier, comme m'a raconté Mr. le président Fauchet, qu'un jour qu'ils parloient d'aller ensemble, un escabeau se remua et Bodin dist: "C'est mon ange qui dit qu'il n'y fait bon pour moy." [67]

Since Fauchet was friendly with Bodin from at least 1568 and is even mentioned later in the *Démonomanie* his testimony (if accurately reported) may be taken as having some weight. [68]

There is too Bodin's bizarre behaviour to be considered; on occasion he would act as though he were an Old Testament prophet. One might cite his voluntarily protracted imprisonment of 1569-70 and the inflamed prophetic zeal of the famous letter to Bautru which may be dated to around 1569 (see section E). There are also the prophecies about the English throne which aroused the unwelcome attention of Walsingham in the 1580's and the predictions of the climactic religious wars in France after 1589. Finally some of his strange actions at Laon while it was under the control of the Catholics in 1589-94 can only be made sense of when understood as the actions of a convinced prophet. [69]

If we assume that the conversion in question is in fact Bodin's own and attempt to date it with reference to his biography, then additional circumstantial arguments may be discovered. [70] Bodin states that his friend underwent the conversion when about thirty-seven years old; it was then that the guardian angel began to manifest itself. [71] Bodin

---

[67] *Pithoeana*, appendix to J. Tessier, *Eloges des hommes savans* (Leiden, 1715), p. 6, quoted (with other references) by Bezold, 'Bodin Okkultist', pp. 26ff.

[68] *Démonomanie*, II, 6, f. 98 (and in *Republica* (1586), p. 612). He was known to Bodin by 1568 as *La Response de Jean Bodin à M. de Malestroit* (*1568*), ed. H. Hauser (Paris, 1932), p. 8, proves. See J. Espiner-Scott, *Claude Fauchet. Sa vie, son œuvre* (Paris, 1938).

A reference in the conversion-narrative (*Démonomanie*, I, 2, f. 11) to an unnamed *secrétaire du roy* was curiously deleted from the second edition published at Paris in 1581.

[69] See Chapter IX.

[70] This is not entirely a circular argument. I am merely trying to suggest a web of plausible arguments rather than attempting to *prove* conclusively the identity of the convert.

[71] *Démonomanie*, I, 2, f. 10v.

was born in 1529-30 and so the conversion, if it were his, would have occurred in 1566-67. And here we come to a fascinating parallel between the conversion-narrative and Bodin's account in a different part of the *Démonomanie* of an incident he experienced at Poitiers in the year 1567. While participating in the judicial proceedings known as the *Grands Jours* at Poitiers in that year Bodin had become acquainted with the case of some sorcerers who had brought ruin on a wealthy household for refusing them alms. [72] As Baxter has perceptively pointed out Bodin's account of the matter in book III rehearses several themes which had already figured in the narrative of the conversion in book I — Philo's idea of the sacrifice of a pure heart, the invocation of Psalm 91, the need for trust in God, for right-doing and for charity — these themes are common to both passages and it is tempting to see some kind of connection between the two narratives, one recounting the anonymous conversion, the other describing an acknowledged incident in Bodin's life. [73] Bodin in 1567, therefore, was apparently preoccupied with the same sort of feelings involved in his friend's conversion. It may be objected that Bodin in the later *Démonomanie*'s account was investing the Poitiers incident with a significance which he had not understood at the time, commenting, that is, on an incident of 1567 in the light of his beliefs in 1580. There is a great deal of point to this objection; nevertheless, the letter to Bautru is redolent with zeal suggesting a recent transfiguration while the imprisonment of 1569-70 indicates a period of fervent religiosity. This might be taken as indicating that Bodin's attitude to his convert in the *Démonomanie* of 1580 is not merely an expression of his current feelings but faithfully reflects a prophetic religious sensibility already present in Bodin's own character, writings and behaviour long before in the late 1560's.

Given the details of a pregnant personal experience in 1567 such as the Poitiers incident, it is at least plausible to date the conversion to around the time of that experience, if not to the actual encounter with the sorcerers. The *Démonomanie* itself, it should be remembered, was provoked by a chance encounter with witches in 1578 (sig. a iii verso) and it would not be surprising if a similarly fortuitous contact with sorcerers at Poitiers in 1567 precipitated Bodin's transfiguration as a prophet. The case of the sorcerers might well have prompted Bodin to reflect on the relationships between men and spirits and prepared him for the sudden realisation that he too was accompanied by a guardian spirit, albeit a good one unlike that of the sorcerers. [74] And it was the acquisition of a guardian angel which marked one's elevation to the first level of the prophetic calling.

---

[72] *Démonomanie*, III, 1, fols. 124v-125.

[73] See Baxter, 'Bodin's Daemon'. On Philo's sacrifice compare *Démonomanie*, I, 2, f. 11 with III, 1, f. 125. On Psalm 91 compare I, 2, f. 12v with III, 1, f. 125.

Philo's notion of the sacrifice of the soul seems to originate in prophetic literature and in Psalm 51, x and xvi-xvii: "Create in me a clean heart... For Thou desirest not sacrifice ... Thou delightest not in burnt offerings. The sacrifices of God are a broken spirit and a contrite heart."

[74] In *Démonomanie*, I, 2 (see notes 61, 63, 65 above) Bodin emphasises that the spirit had accompanied the man all his life and that a sudden recognition of its presence had been a critical stage in the conversion.

d) The Judaising Impact of Philo on Bodin's Conversions:
Purification and Prophecy

> He had studied in peace and prayed with
> fervour. He had distinctly felt that he was
> becoming purified.
>
> I.B. Singer, *The Manor.*

The conversion-narrative of the *Démonomanie* highlights the contribution
of Philo and Maimonides to two major aspects of Bodin's religion. To Philo
Bodin was deeply indebted for the theme that true religion was the sacrifice
of the purified soul and from Maimonides he drew extensively for the particulars
of his theory of prophecy. It is now time to look more generally at the impact
of Jewish theology on Bodin and to notice how Philo holds a special significance
for the evolution of Bodin's religious biography; for Philo seems to have affected
the successive steps or conversions by which Bodin advanced towards his
understanding of *vera religio*. The first of these steps was a vision of naturalistic theism, the second was Bodin's embracing of prophetic monotheism, and
the third was Bodin's own transfiguration as a prophet. Moreover, it seems
that Bodin's *vera religio* owes its structure to Philo's religion which rested
on the twin foundations of purification and prophecy.

There can be no doubt that Philo was well known to Bodin by 1559, indeed even by 1555. The 1550's were the decade in which Philo became widely
available in France. Budé's Greek text of *De opificio mundi* (Paris, 1526) and
his Latin translation of that and a few other works (Basle, 1527) had been
combined into a single volume (Basle, 1533) which was reprinted in 1550 and
1557. But it was in 1552 that Turnèbe published at Paris the first extensive
Greek text of Philo's works. [75] Two years later he brought out a Latin version
of Philo's *De vita Mosis* and in the same year (1554) there appeared at Basle
Gelenius' complete Latin translation which went into a second edition at Lyons
in 1555. [76] In his later works Bodin cites the Latin versions and it seems
plausible that he should first have seen them in the 1550's. [77] Bodin certainly

---

[75] *Philonis Judaei in libros Mosis de mundi opificio, historicos, de legibus. Ejusdem
libri singulares,* ed. Adrianus Turnebus (Paris, 1552). Bodin has been accused of pla-
giarising his translation of Oppian from Turnèbe but the charge seems unjustified to
me. See Mesnard, 'La conjuration'. R. Chauviré, *Jean Bodin, auteur de la République*
(Paris, 1914), pp. 26, 535. For Turnèbe see above, notes 5ff.

[76] Philo, *Lucubrationes omnes* (Basle, 1554), ed. S. Gelenius. See H.L. Goodhart
and E.R. Goodenough, 'A General Bibliography of Philo', in *The Politics of Philo
Judaeus* (New Haven, 1938). The first French translation was printed in 1575.

[77] For Bodin's knowledge of Philo see Roellenbleck, *Offenbarung,* pp. 87, 113. Lange,
Untersuchungen, pp. 93, 142ff. Lange claims (p. 143) that Bodin used the Lyons 1555
Latin version of Philo, while Baxter, 'Bodin's Daemon', p. 19, states that it was the 1554

knew one of the Greek texts by 1555 since he quoted Philo in Greek on the subject of demonology in his Oppian notes of that year.

The actual reference to Philo in the Oppian notes is important because it shows that Bodin had been struck by Philo's idea that there might be good demons as well as evil ones, an idea which might be taken to imply that it was through good demons that prophecy was mediated. [78]   There are other traces too of the Judaising influence of Philo in this early work, for instance in Bodin's acceptance of Moses as a superior authority to Aristotle. Bodin invokes Genesis for his contention that the four great rivers had their source in the garden of Eden and remarks that he prefers to go with Moses on this matter than with Aristotle: "The theologians who understand better interpret the source as Oceanus since the paradise of Moses, or Eden (*in Hebrew letters*) is nothing other than the whole earth according to the views of the Cabalists and the opinion of Jerome". [79]   Again, Moses is invoked as authority for the view that Noah and not Bacchus was the first cultivator of the vine, and also as evidence for the age of the earth. [80]   This lightly Judaising tendency emerges also in the faintly favourable remarks on Moses and the Jews at various points. [81]   Another aspect of an initial taste for Judaising may be the indications that Bodin knew some Hebrew by 1555; several Hebrew words are interspersed in the Oppian notes. [82]   Then too there are Bodin's anti-Greek views on the human and animal souls.   Bodin no doubt first imbibed from Christianity the opinion that man was made in the image of God and alone had an immortal soul, but it seems undeniable that a reading of Philo's works (which deal exhaustively with this aspect of the soul) would have strengthened Bodin's conviction. [83]

one.   There seems to me to be no way at present of knowing precisely which edition was in Bodin's hands.

The influence of Philo on the *Heptaplomeres* and *Démonomanie* is indicated in a rough way by the number of citations of the philosopher in those two works.   Cf. F. Bezold, 'Jean Bodin als Okkultist und seine *Démonomanie*', *Historische Zeitschrift*, CV (1910), 1-14, at pp. 50ff.   J. Guttmann, 'Jean Bodin in seinen Beziehungen des Judentums', *Monatsschrift für Geschichte und Wissenschaft des Judentums*, XLIX (1905), 315-348; 459-489, at pp. 330, 479f, says little about Philo and devotes more attention to the influence of Maimonides.   There is no doubt that Maimonides' rich and systematic doctrine deeply influenced Bodin, yet it was in a sens an elaboraton of Philo.   Moreover, as we have seen, it was reading Philo and not Maimonides that triggered Bodin's third conversion.

Philo also seems to have influenced Lipsius who equated the law of nature with the Decalogue.   See J.L. Saunders, *Justus Lipsius. The Philosophy of Renaissance Stoicism* (New York, 1955), pp. 60, 135, 200. Jehasse, *Renaissance*, p. 568.

[78] *Oppiani de venatione* (1555), fol. 47 : " Quanquam Psellus δαιμονας omnes maleficos esse putet, quod ex Proculo falsum esse satis intelligi potest, qui bonum cuique δαιμονα   praeesse scribit, et ex Philone Judaeo, in lib. de mundo... (*quotation in Greek*)." See section A above.

[79] *Oppiani de venatione*, fol. 72: "Aristoteles improbat ... magis tamen assentior Mosi ... Fontem interpretantur Theologi, qui melius senserunt, Oceanum: cum nihil sit aliud Mosis paradisus   (*Eden*), ex Cabalaeorum placitis, et Hieronymi sententia, quam universa tellus."

[80] *Ibidem*, fols. 78 (age of the earth), 107rv (Noah).

[81] *Ibidem*, fols. 48, 76v-77.

[82] *Ibidem*, fols. 72, 100, 107v.

[83] *Ibidem*, fols. 52-54.   See section A above.

In general Philo was a marvellous source for any Judaiser. This is scarcely surprising when we consider that some of Philo's works had been written expressly to attract gentile converts to Judaism. Expounding an allegorical interpretation of Scripture which drew exhaustively on Platonic metaphysical themes, Philo offered gentiles a religion which was at the same time cosmopolitan and yet founded on the particular but supreme Mosaic revelation of the Jews. [84] As historical justification for this fusion of Greek and Hebrew thought Philo asserted that the Greek philosophers had adopted the arcana of Moses, merely clothing these Jewish mysteries in a different garb.

In the *Oratio* there is little overt trace of the revealed Jewish components of this cosmopolitan religion. But the universal and naturalistic aspects of Philo's theism figure prominently. What Bodin has to say about human knowledge of God and the display of God's bounty is quite compatible with Philo's solution to the problem of how an eternal transcendent God manifests Himself immanently in the natural universe. Both Philo and Bodin see the beginning of knowledge of God in the contemplation of the universe by which the mind rises from the sensible world to the invisible order of God; God's existence, deduced from the design and rationality of nature, is attested by the universal consent of all peoples. [85] Again, like Bodin, Philo sees God's bounty as a manifestation of divine will which is responsible for the variety of the created universe. Bodin's vision of the harmonious unity among the diversity of created forms appears also in Philo who had also been fond of such musical metaphors as the choir of creation, the lyre of universal harmony and the choir of the soul. [86]

It may be tempting to label some of these views Platonic but Bodin adopted them in the Judaised form in which he encountered them in the writings of Jewish commentators such as Philo and, to a far lesser extent, Léon Hébreu. [87] Take for instance the doctrine of the immortality of the soul: "The immortal principle of the soul, personal to men and flowing to them from the eternal

---

[84] For bibliography on Philo see note 50.

[85] *Oratio*, pp. 15, 25. See above, notes 14ff; and Chapters I and VI. Philo takes a similar approach in the *Legum allegoriae* and elsewhere.
Note that God's essence or substance is not deducible from nature which as Bodin points out in the *Theatrum* is a "mere shadow" of God. Cf. Philo's remark that "God is everywhere in His powers, nowhere in His essence".

[86] For the choir and the lyre see Philo, *Cherubim*, 110ff; *Vita Mosis*, 115, 210; *De migratione Abrahami*, 104. Plotinus, who appears to have been influenced by Philo, uses similar images in the *Enneads*, III, 2/2; IV, 4/2, 4/12, 4/32; VI, 9/8. In general see E. Bréhier, *Les idées philosophiques et religieuses de Philon d'Alexandrie* (3rd ed., Paris, 1950), pp. 140ff, 147. See Chapter I above for further references to the *Oratio*.

[87] See note 21 above. The work of Leone Ebreo (born 1460) whose *Dialoghi dell' Amore* (1501-02) were published in French in 1551 (see the recent facsimile edition by T.A. Perry, *De l'Amour* (Chapel Hill, N. Carolina, 1974) was certainly well-known to Bodin but it seems to me that Philo and the non-Platonic Maimonides were far greater influences on his thought. Mesnard, 'Platonisme de Bodin', admitted some Hebrew influence, including that of Leone, but did not appreciate the impact of Philo. It is significant that Bodin does not adopt those strange views of God and creation which were peculiar to Leone. Many of Leone's statements about God and the unity and diversity of creation are also common to Philo and it was these, rather than the more idiosyncratic ones of Leone, that Bodin took up. (Despite the publishers' claims in later editions of the *Dialoghi* it now seems doubtful whether Leone was ever actually converted to Christianity as alleged). See Chapter IV.

mind" as Bodin puts it in the *Oratio*. [88]   One might easily ascribe this notion to the influence of Plato but we should remember that in the Oppian notes of 1555 Bodin had already denied the Platonic doctrine of the transmigration of souls.   The *Oratio's* reference can only plausibly be taken as a Christian or Jewish allusion to the immortality of the soul.   In view of Bodin's demonstrated reading of Philo from 1555 on and his apparent agreement with major aspects of Philo's theology the Jewish philosopher is likely to have been a source of his doctrine of the soul although here one would still be willing to admit the preponderant weight of Christian tradition on Bodin.

While stressing the universal and philosophical aspects of Philo's religion the *Oratio* still contains intimations of the more theistic ideas of prophecy and revelation.   In a pregnant passage already cited Bodin enigmatically combined natural and revealed religion in affirming that men would have acquired faith in God "even if nothing were published in our books concerning God the creator of the universe and nature, and if no voice from heaven had ever taught that souls live immortally..." [89]   There is too in the *Oratio,* one might add, a suggestion of divine will intervening in human affairs as when Bodin in speaking of the sudden unforeseen revival of the project to found an academy at Toulouse remarks that it occurred "with a certain high sign of divine will (*divinae voluntatis*)". [90]

**

Despite the strong evidence that Bodin had read Philo by 1555 it must be be admitted that these indications of the impact of Philo on precise aspects of Bodin's thought in the *Oratio* are all very tentative.   When we come, however, to look at parallels between Philo and various elements of Bodin's later religion of prophetic monotheism we are on somewhat surer ground.

Philo and Bodin agree on the most fundamental matter of religious thought; the problem of divine transcendence and immanence.   Moreover, both use the machinery of a spiritual universe populated by angelic intelligences to reconcile these two aspects of the divine.   Philo had combined the Stoic view that divine power pervades the world as an immanent force with Plato's belief in a supracosmic — though not transcendent — deity.   Such a combination was not original [91] but Philo added the Hebraic dimension of prophecy to these vaguely immanent conceptions of God.   He thereby transformed what were really pantheistic notions into a theistic religion where a truly transcendent deity first created the universe *ex nihilo* [92] and subsequently constantly governed and

[88] *Oratio*, p. 15.
[89] *Ibidem*, p. 15.
[90] *Ibidem*, p. 7.
[91] Cf. the *De Mundo* of Pseudo-Aristotle which was during the Renaissance often published in the same volume as Philo's *De opificio mundi*.
[92] See D. O'Connor and F. Oakley, eds., *Creation. The Impact of an Idea* (New York, 1969), for the intrinsic difference between Jewish and Greek theories of creation. Only in Jewish thought was there any conception of creation being achieved *ex nihilo* by a transcendent God rather than by an immanent deity who merely ordered *pre-existing* matter.

178

preserved it through the intermediation of the *logos* and the angelic spirits. In Philo we find apparently for the first time in religious thought the reconciliation of transcendence and immanence. [93]

As early as the Oppian notes Bodin was aware of Philo's reference to good and bad demons and in his later writings he frequently resorts to Philo's usage in referring to God's active immanent spirits as powers or *dynameis*. [94] While there is no use of Philo's term *logos* to signify the chief of these immanent spirits (perhaps because of its Christian connotation) nor of its rabbinical equivalent *shekinah* (*presence*), Bodin's attested knowledge of Jewish sources make it certain that he knew the function of these concepts in representing the immanent aspect of the transcendent Jewish God. [95] One also finds in the *Theatrum* a notable debt to Philo's doctrine of *pneuma* which had distinguished between three different kinds of spirit: the purely incorporeal spirit of transcendent God Himself, the immanent corporeal spirits of the *logos* and angels, and the spirit of the human soul. [96] Upon this pneumatology rested Philo's — and Bodin's — ideas of prophecy.

Bodin's Judaised theory which understands prophecy as a combination of divine will and natural agency follows Philo (and more so Maimonides who had painted in the details of what had been left as only a rough sketch by the Alexandrian philosopher). [97] Prophecy reflects immanence in that it is mediated through angelic intelligences and demons which are natural spirits. But prophecy also implants in the natural universe the divine law of a transcendent God. God's will and law are revealed through the immanent spirits to those prophets who are to communicate these *fiats* to humanity. By this means God's will and law are made immanent although God Himself does not become so; a transcendent theism is thereby preserved from the danger of pantheism.

This conception of a divine law that is immanent is embodied in Bodin's identification of the law of God with the law of nature. The Decalogue as communicated by God to Moses, the greatest of prophets, is indeed nothing other than the prophetically revealed law of nature: Revelation and nature are no paradox! That Philo was the source of this insight into the identity of divine and natural law is clear from the *Heptaplomeres*.

[93] See Wolfson, *Philo,* for an estimate of Philo's critical position in Western thought. On his angelology see A. Laurentin, 'Le Pneuma dans la doctrine de Philon', *Ephemerides Theologicae Lovanienses,* XXVII (1951), 390-437, at pp. 398ff (also printed as *Analecta Lovaniensia Biblica et Orientalia,* ser. II, fasc. 25, 1952). Bréhier, *Idées,* pp. 126ff.

Philo is cited on the nature of the angels in *Heptoplomeres,* pp. 30 and 44 (trs. 41 and 59).

[94] Especially in the *Démonomanie, Theatrum* and *Heptaplomeres.* For Philo's terminology of powers see Bréhier, *Idées,* pp. 136ff.

[95] For Bodin's knowledge of Jewish traditions see Guttmann, 'Bodin in seinen Beziehungen des Judentums'. Cf. J. Abelson, *The Immanence of God in Rabbinical Literature* (London, 1912).

[96] *Universae Naturae Theatrum* (Lyons, 1596), pp. 500-536. See P. Mesnard, 'The Psychology and Pneumatology of Jean Bodin', *International Philosophical Quarterly,* II (1962), 244-264. Laurentin, 'Le Pneuma'. G. Verbeke, *L'évolution de la doctrine du pneuma du Stoïcisme à Saint Augustin* (Paris-Louvain, 1945), pp. 236-260.

[97] See note 109 below.

Philo the Hebrew said (*De Abrahamo*, 5): "The commandments depart not at all from nature and it is not a task of great effort to lead your life according to the prescriptions of divine laws for the Tables of Moses contain nothing but the law of nature and the life of our ancestors." [98]

In the *Démonomanie* Bodin offers an expression of this relationship between divine and natural law which throws a very interesting light on his conception of the Great God of Nature. It is a mistake, observes Bodin, to ascribe the magical effects of stones, plants and metals — or stars and angels — to their own intrinsic powers. Rather it is God's power which is operating through these natural phenomena. Bodin approves of Seneca's remark that it is absurd to say "Nature does this, nature does that" for this means merely that

> *Tu natura Deo nomen mutas*, c'est à dire, tu changes nature en Dieu. Cõbiẽ seroit il plus beau de dire Dieu fait cecy, Dieu faict celà. En toute l'escripture saincte, ce mot de Nature, ne se trouue iamais, ains tousiours il est dict, Dieu a faict faire cecy, Dieu a faict faire celà, vsant du verbe transitif Hebrieu *hifil* c'est à dire, faict faire, que les Grecs & Latins ont troduict par vn verbe actif, lequel abus a esté cause de plusieurs erreurs, de ceux qui ont attribué choses indignes à la maiesté de Dieu ... C'est la coustume de l'escriture saincte, d'attribuer à Dieu les œuvres de ses creatures, soit bien ou mal ... Ce n'est pas que les Hebrieux ayent ignoré la difference des œuures de Dieu & de nature: car Salomon l'a souuent remarqué, quand il dict aux allegories. L'enfant est sage, qui obeïst aux mandemens du pere, & n'oublie pas la loy de la mere: Il entend les commandemens de Dieu, & la loy de nature. [99]

Sometimes the will of God comes into conflict with the laws of nature and it is then that miracles occur. This idea of the miraculous presented no paradox to Philo. For Philo's voluntaristic theory acknowledged the role of God's will in establishing habitual or conventional laws of nature and at same time allowed God's will to suspend these laws as He wished. [100] This Philonic dual framework of what might be called God's absolute and conventional power was adopted by Bodin as early as the *Methodus*. [101]

> Natural history presents a necessary and stable sequence of causes unless checked by divine power or for a brief moment abandoned by that power to the prince of fluid matter and the father of all evils. From God's abandonment are derived spectacles of distorted nature and huge monsters; from God's intervention arise extraordinary miracles. [102]

---

[98] *Heptaplomeres*, p. 190 (p. 249). For Latin text see Chapter VII, note 15. Cf. E. R. Goodenough, *By Light, Light. The Mystic Gospel of Hellenistic Judaism* (New Haven 1935; reprint, Amsterdam, 1969), pp. 53f.

[99] *Démonomanie*, I, 5, fols. 36v-37. *Hifil* is given in Hebrew letters.

[100] See R.M. Grant, *Miracle and Natural Law* (Amsterdam, 1952). H.A. Wolfson, 'Philo on Free Will and the Historical Influence of His View', *Harvard Theological Review*, XXXV (1942), 131-169.

[101] For this framework see Chapter V. The distinction was also maintained by the Scotists and Ockhamists.

[102] *Methodus*, p. 115A(17): "Naturales enim necessariam habent et stabilem causarum consecutionem, nisi divina potestate prohibeantur, vel paulo momento ab ea deserantur, et quasi fluentis materiae principi omniumque malorum parenti permittantur. Ex altero quidem ostenta depravatae naturae et immania monstra; ex altero egregia Dei miracula."

Such notions of divine and natural law and of the role played by prophecy in revealing God's laws, lead to a Philonic theory of ethics which was known to Bodin from at least 1566 and cited approvingly in the *Heptaplomeres* as we have seen.[103] The Ten Commandments are the revealed law of nature and, far from being repugnant to nature, they are easy to follow through the choice of man's free will. For both Philo and Bodin the Deuteronomic command to choose life is fundamental, a command often described by Philo as the doctrine of the two ways of good and evil. In Philo and Bodin free will is absolutely vital for without free will there can be no meaning or purpose to human existence. Moreover, free will is central to their theodicies. Since God cannot be the author of evil, then evil must originate as the result of free will choosing to do wrong and attracting retribution inflicted by the spirits. In the *Heptaplomeres* Bodin openly cites Philo as a source for this theodicy and — most revealingly — quotes a passage which in the original ties the idea that God cannot be the author of evil to the theme of the sacrifice of the purified soul![104]

The Philonic theme of the sacrifice of the purified soul and the associated principle that true religion is the turning of the purified soul towards God stand out prominently in several of Bodin's works. Not once but three times Bodin had affirmed in the *Methodus* that true religion was the turning of the purified soul towards God and the same formula reappears tellingly in the letter to Bautru of 1568-69.[105] The theme of sacrifice of the purified soul dominated the conversion-narrative of the *Démonomanie* and, as we have seen, the definition of true religion was at last credited explicity to Philo in the *Heptaplomeres*. Such a persistent recurrence is incontrovertible evidence of the manner in which the Philonic idea of the purified soul prevailed in Bodin's thinking during the crucial years 1566-69 and beyond.

The purified soul is indeed one of the foundations of the religious thought of both Philo and Bodin. For them free-willed purification of the soul is really the preparation of the soul to receive prophetic illumination. Both Philo and Bodin envisage a *vera religio* constructed on the two levels of purification and prophecy. One level consists of what one might call the purifying of the soul by the cultivation of ethics and moral philosophy, that is the achievement of moral virtue as preparation to receive the happiness of illumination. The other, higher level is that on which divine prophetic illumination takes place. In consequence both thinkers, while regarding virtue as a naturally attainable excellence, understood ethics as a composite part of religion.[106]

*
**

[103] See Chapters II and VI for remarks in the *Methodus* on Philo's ethics of free-willed righteousness or integrity.

[104] *Heptaplomeres*, p. 90 (117), quoting Philo, *De Fuga*, 80. See also Philo, *De Opificio mundi*, 75, 152. (Cf. Goodenough, *Light*, p. 53).

A Judaised theory of free will does not contradict the belief that the whole universe was an act of God's grace. Cf. Philo, *Legum allegoriae*, III, 78.

In general see above Chapters V, note 12, and VII.

[105] See notes 32ff, 62, 73 above, and section E below.

[106] See Philo's *Quis Heres*, cited by Bodin in *Heptaplomeres*, p. 97 (125). Also Goodenough, *Light*, p. 238. See below.

If free will is essential to the theodicy of Philo and Bodin so too is prophetic illumination. It is precisely because men's free will enables them to stray willingly from their natural goodness that involuntary prophetic revelation is necessary. The Jews were punished, comments Bodin in the *Heptaplomeres*, because

> They had fallen away from the true worship of God and we have witness of this from the words and writings of the prophets [107] ... When men grew deaf to the law of nature, the divine voice was required so that those who contemned nature might hear the father of nature proclaiming His words. [108]

Bodin's theory of prophecy is in broad agreement with that of Philo even though he is indebted for many of the details to Maimonides whose *Guide for the Perplexed* had actually been cast in the form of an exposition of prophetic revelation. Prophets are seen by Philo as men inspired by a revealing God to recall men back to virtue. [109] For Philo prophecy is the unique channel of revelation, mediated by such natural means as the angels and *logos* (or in Maimonidean terms, the active intellect). [110] Illumination too plays a role for Philo understood the *logos* as a light-stream transmitting prophecy as a divine gift bestowed on selected purified men. [111] But Philo's theory of prophecy is ecstatic as well as illuminative for the divine spirit of prophecy not only illuminates but also inspires the soul of the prophet with the ecstatic vision and mystical love of God. [112]

As we have seen in Chapter V Bodin follows these Philonic ideas of ecstatic illumination very faithfully, even to the extent of using ambiguous and apparently contradictory terms so as to befuddle what is really a consistent argument. [113] In one of the most interesting passages in the *Heptaplomeres* Bodin reveals fully his awareness of Philo's dual idea of prophecy as ecstasy and illumination, and acknowledges Philo's main work on the theme.

> Philo the Hebrew said clearly: "When the divine light arises the human light sets. When the divine light sets, the human light rises." (*Quis heres, 263; cf. 249, 258ff*). The prophets experienced this, that their soul seemed to depart with the arrival of the divine spirit .... Thus, it is made clear that the light of the passive intellect flows from the active intellect, but the light of the active intellect flows

[107] *Heptaplomeres,* p. 199 (260). Cf. *Methodus,* ch. 10. See above Chapter VII, notes 16ff.

[108] *Heptaplomeres,* p. 190 (249). Latin text in Chapter VII, note 17. Cf. Laurentin, 'Pneuma', pp. 416f. The idea of prophecy here subsumes Philo's Jewish philosophy which sees history as the unfolding of divine justice.

[109] For Philo's idea of prophecy see Wolfson, *Philo,* II, 395-426. Bréhier, *Idées,* pp. 179-205. Laurentin, 'Pneuma', pp. 416ff.

[110] On Jewish views of prophecy as exemplifying immanence see Abelson, *Immanence,* Chapter 18 etc.

[111] Goodenough, *Light,* pp. 53f, 192ff, 217f, 382.

[112] *Ibidem,* pp. 247, 382. Bréhier, *Idées,* pp. 179ff.

[113] See Chapter V, notes 18, 22. Bodin's summary of his views on prophecy in *Démonomanie,* I, Chapters 1-4 (see especially f. 27) effectively rehearses Philo's ideas. Cf. Bezold, 'Bodin Okkultist', pp. 50ff.

from a higher and more divine light. Let no one think that the active intellect is God or that it is to be worshipped as God. [114]

* * *

Bodin's citations of Philo at crucial junctures demonstrate how deeply Philonic religion affected the development of Bodin's own *vera religio*. We may also see the impact of Philo if we try to summarise the Philonic themes to be found in Bodin's religious writings: Free will and obedience of the Deuteronomic command; purification of the soul; purification as the prelude to prophecy; revelation through prophecy; prophecy as divine illumination which instils a mystical love and knowledge of God; the mediation of prophecy by angels; a theodicy which depends on a moral universe populated by good and evil spirits doing the bidding of God; a God Who is transcendent and yet immanent and Whose revelation is in accordance with the law of nature — all these parallels can be drawn between the two authors. But it is their shared conviction that men must both love and fear this God wholeheartedly that makes the prophetic monotheism of Philo and Bodin a vividly emotional belief rather than a purely intellectual mysticism. [115]

Philo emerges as perhaps the key to Bodin's religious biography, appearing at each stage of the conversion. (1) A first reading of Philo during the 1550's may have contributed to Bodin's original conception of the Great God of Nature. (2) Further reading of Philo then probably forced Bodin's evolving sense of *vera religio* into a coherent and formulation. This may have happened by 1566 for in the *Methodus* there are unmistakable suggestions of a *vera religio* based upon the two foundations of Philo's religion, purification and prophecy. [116] (3) And, finally, from Bodin's own words in the *Démonomanie*

---

[114] *Heptaplomeres*, p. 97 (125). "Quod apertius Philo Ebraeus: Exoriente, inquit, divino lumine humanum occidit, occidente divina luce humanum exoritur, quod vatibus contingit, ut immigrante spiritu divino mens eorum emigrare videatur .... Ita planum fit, lumen intellectus patibilis ab intellectu agente, agentis vero lumen a luce superiore et diviniore manare, ne quis intellectum actuosum putet Deum esse aut pro Deo colat." Compare *ibidem*, p. 189 (248); *Paradoxe*, p. 31; *Démonomanie*, fols. 9v-10 (above, note 54). Cf. Chapter VII, notes 10-11. (Salomon's explanation meets with the immediate approval of the Calvinist Curtius in *Hept.* p. 97 (125)).
The passage cited raises some difficulties; for example, Bodin's distinction here between the three kinds of light is a little perplexing. It is probably entailed by the celestial analogy; in effect, there is only one true prophetic light which emanates originally from God although it is mediated by the active intellect and the angels.
Bodin brings out the illuminative aspect which is often implicit in Philo. See for instance Bodin's treatment of the Seventy Elders of Numbers, XI, 16 (*Démonomanie*, fols. 10, 13v): "The divine spirit (*of prophecy*) is like light which communicates itself without diminution" (quoted above, note 65). Philo (*Gigant.* 24) had apparently regarded the Seventy Elders as an instance of the light-stream or *logos* mediating the prophetic spirit but had not said so explicitly. See Goodenough, *Light*, pp. 217f, 232.
Bodin's discussion of ecstasy in *Theatrum*, pp. 500ff, should be treated with caution. It pertains really to the question of whether the soul can leave the body. As Bodin points out, the matter of divine prophetic ecstasy belongs to a "different doctrine" (p. 504). Even here, however, Bodin significantly quotes the Abrahamic ecstasy described in Philo's *Legum allegoriae*, II, 59, in the body of his text (p. 506).

[115] See Chapters V, note 61, and IX. Cf. Bréhier, *Idées*, p. 310.

[116] Cf. Goodenough, *Light*, p. 238.

we may argue that a renewed, intense reading of Philo's book "on sacrifices" during his spiritual crisis of 1566-68 triggered Bodin's prophetic transfiguration. For Bodin himself purification was to culminate in prophecy.

e) The Letter to Bautru and the Imprisonment of 1569

Much of the preceding argument about the events of 1567-68 has depended on the later testimony of Bodin's *Démonomanie* written in 1578-79, but there is one document which is probably nearly contemporary with the conversion and which may be used to throw light on Bodin's spiritual transformation. This is the famous letter to Jean Bautru des Matras.[117] Although it has generally been dated to 1561-63 I believe there is a far greater probability of its belonging to the years 1568-69.[118] My reasons for saying so are:

1. The usual attribution to 1561-63 seems unlikely since during that period Bodin swore his oath of Catholicism at Paris (in June 1562). The scathingly anti-Catholic sentiments of the letter make it most improbable that its author would have been willing even to simulate public adherence to the Catholic religion.[119]

2. The references to the contemporary "civil wars which have set ablaze all France" and their putative religious origin clearly suggest that the letter was written during the religious wars of the 1560's. If we discount the first war of religion lasting from 1561 to March 1563 as a likely period for the reason given above, then the second or third religious wars become the much more likely objects of Bodin's reference. These wars lasted from September 1567 to August 1570, the period to which we have dated (on the evidence of the *Démonomanie* and other writings) Bodin's final conversion to true religion. The intensity of Bodin's still recent conversion would account for the strange religious zeal of the letter. Most importantly, the letter evinces several prophetic preoccupations which as we have already seen came into prominence only after the conversion of 1567-68.

3. One such preoccupation is the upholding of the purity of monotheism, a concern evident in Bodin's sarcastic abuse of Catholic rites and doctrine.

---

[117] The letter was originally printed in Paul Colomiès, *Gallia Orientalis* (The Hague, 1665), pp. 76-80. I have used the text reprinted in Chauviré, *Jean Bodin*, pp. 521-524.

[118] This section expands the arguments to be found in my earlier article, 'Two Problems of Bodin's Religious Biography'.

[119] For the letter's attack on Catholic rites see below, point 3. In his important early article 'La pensée religieuse de Bodin', *Revue du seizième siècle*, XVI (1929), 77-121, P. Mesnard fully recognised the anti-Catholic tenor of the letter. But in his later writings Mesnard tended — possibly reflecting his own religious feelings — to make Bodin a good Catholic from 1562 on. This seems to be the reason why Mesnard persistently used a strained argument to date the letter to the period 1561-63, specifically to the time before Bodin took the Catholic oath of June 1562. As we shall see (below, point 5) Bodin refused a similar oath of Catholicism in November 1568. This would make the latter year a much more likely approximate dating for the document. Mesnard was aware of the refusal of 1568 but never seems to have tried to explain it.

"There was no (*worship of*) statues for 800 years (after Christ), no idolatry of bread (*artolatreia*) for 600 years, no apotheosis of mortals for 400 years..." [120] Is this nothing but a conventional Huguenot attack on Catholic tradition? There is one very good reason for suspecting that something more is involved: the recipient of the letter Jean Bautru des Matras came from a strongly Huguenot family and had apparently refused — unlike Bodin — to take the oath of Catholicism in 1562. [121] Yet Bodin clearly states his disagreement with Bautru's religious opinions in the letter. [122] How then may Bodin be regarded as a straightforward Huguenot or his letter be taken as nothing more than a run-of-the-mill Huguenot attack on Roman superstition? The mood of the letter is rather more in tune with Bodin's denunciations of idolatry in his writings after 1567, suggesting that the fervour of the letter sprang more from devotion to his newly discovered true religion of prophecy and monotheism than from ordinary Huguenot prejudices. [123]

4. Bodin's commitment to prophecy, which we have dated earlier in this chapter to the conversion of 1567-68, appears in various disturbing forms in the letter. The first of these is a somewhat surprising justification of religious war. Like the *politiques* Bodin was willing to tolerate differences of religious opinion between friends but he parts company with them in maintaining that a threat to true religion should be resisted if necessary by war. [124] The letter to Bautru starts by refuting the common notion that religion causes wars and follows Augustine in acquitting the Christians of the charge of fomenting dissension at Rome. In this context religion is seen as only an accidental cause of war. [125] But later in the letter Bodin explains how resistance to the impiety of idolaters is the true cause of religious war:

[120] Chauviré, *Jean Bodin*, p. 524.
[121] Mesnard, 'La pensée religieuse de Bodin', p. 79, alleged that Bautru was a Catholic, but in a later work (*Œuvres de Jean Bodin* (Paris, 1951), I, p. xvi) Mesnard reversed himself and stated that Bautru was a Huguenot without noting, however, the difficulties which this revision presented to his interpretation of the letter. Mesnard did, nonetheless, argue on this basis that the letter was writen before June 1562 when Bodin was won back to the Catholic fold. How then would Mesnard explain the imprisonment of Bodin in 1569 for refusing to take an oath of Catholicism? Mesnard cites no sources for the claims that both Jean and his father Maurice Bautru des Matras refused the Catholic oath of 1562. But E. Haag, *La France Protestante* (2nd ed., Paris, 1877), I, 1036, is positive that Maurice refused the judges' oath at Angers in 1562 while Jean does not appear in the list of Paris *Avocats* who took the oath in June of that year.
[122] Chauviré, *Jean Bodin*, p. 521: "cum dissentiamus inter nos in rerum divinarum opinione".
[123] Where prophecy entered the picture even Catholics might develop doubts about the sacraments similar to Bodin's. Guillaume Postel, for example, proposed before 1547 the abolition of the sacraments as a result of enhanced awareness of the role of prophecy in Catholic Christianity.
See F. Secret, 'L'émithologie de Guillaume Postel', in *Umanesimo e esoterismo*, ed. E. Castelli (V Congresso Internazionale di Studi Umanistici — Archivio di Filosofia, Padua, 1960), pp. 381-437.
[124] Bodin never adopted the Catholic nor the Huguenot view that saw religious war as a justified defence or crusade in favour of a specific confessional religion. His notion of religious war depended on a prophetic vision of war and peace. The letter to Bautru is the most extreme case of Bodin's defence of religious war but he later accepted war as divine punishment and purgation. See Chapter IX.
[125] Chauviré, *Jean Bodin*, p. 522: "Est ergo religio bellorum principium κατασυμβεβ-ηκως."

Constantine, elected emperor by the legions of the Gauls, Germans and Britons, trusting in Christ's name, undertook on behalf of the Christian religion as a private person a holy war against his prince and the Roman state. Thus he dispossessed of empire those tyrants who had abused the handsome title of princes to do cruelty. Before him Moses and Judas Maccabeus had not hesitated to do the same, levelling and making deserted temples and flourishing cities so that no vestige of such great impiety might be left. Who may doubt that this very thing was attempted with God's permission on account of the murder and persecution of those good men who had tried to abolish the most shameful *eidolomaneia*? I believe this, my dear Bautru, to be the cause of holy war. *(Sacrum bellum).* [126]

Does this favourable reference to Constantine mean that Bodin was a Christian? To answer this requires a very close examination of the letter. The first point to note is that early in the letter Bodin defines true religion by the same Philonic formula as in the *Démonomanie*: "True religion is nothing other than the turning of a purified spirit to the true God". [127] Nevertheless this true religion has often attracted the opposition of the impious and in this sense has been a source of war and conflict. "Indeed, there can be no greater mark of true religion than that human forces conspire to attack it strongly; hence the vulgar opinion that sees religion as the source of war". [128] One such persecuted group of believers in *vera religio* had been the early innocent Christians, but it is clear from what follows that the Christians are only a particular instance of a general history of the persecution of the true religion of the prophets. Bodin's theory of religious war is thus based on a prophetic concept of religion:

We agree that man, although created a distinguished character and adorned with the brightest virtues by God, has turned aside from the right path. Because of this eternal ruin has invaded the soul of mortals in such a way that they may neither be stirred to virtue by any rewards nor deterred from vices by the harshness of punishments. We should therefore live in perpetual night and fog had not God at fixed times excited the highest virtue in certain men so that they might guide other mortals who wander from the true way of virtue. Such during two thousand years were those ten men gathered in the Bible at the beginning of the book of Chronicles [*from Adam to Noah*] and the prophets of both ages. I pass over Pythagoras, Thales, Solon, Anaxagoras, Socrates, Plato, Xenophon, Hermodorus, Lycurgus, Numa, the Scipios, the Catos — what men, flourishing in suck virtue, integrity, and wisdom! None of these escaped the calumnies of the impious; many were punished by exile, several cut down in front of the altars, others condemned to punishment as though they were seditious citizens; never-

[126] *Ibidem*, p. 523: "Constantinus Augustus, Gallorum, Germanorum, Britannorum legionibus Christiani nominis fiducia erectus, sacrum bellum ipse privatus, adversus suum principem, adversus S.P.Q.R. pro Christiana religione suscepit, ac tyrannos, speciosa principum appellatione abutentes ad crudelitatem, de imperio deturbavit. Idem antea Moses ac Judas Macchabaeus facere non dubitarant, templaque et urbes florentissimas solo aequaverant, ut ne vestigium quidem tantae impietatis ullum extaret; quis dubitet quin hoc ipsum tentatum sit, Deo permittente, propter caedes ac sectiones bonorum, qui turpissimam ειδωλομανειαν abolere conantur?
Hanc igitur, mi Botrue, sacri belli causam esse opinor."

[127] *Ibidem*, p. 522: "... veram religionem aliud nihil esse quam purgatae mentis in Deum verum conversionem" — Bodin's characteristically Philonic definition. See section D above.

[128] Chauviré, *Jean Bodin*, p. 522: "illud etiam addo, verae religionis argumentum nullum majus esse, quam cum in ea fortiter oppugnanda vires humanae conjurant; tum illa jactantur in vulgus, ab religione bellorum initia proficisci."

theless all were united with the highest virtue and piety and little was lacking, as Augustine says, that the Platonists be made Christians. When Plato preached everywhere the worship of the one God and the nature and power of immortal souls, he said that he was to be believed just until a more excellent one than he should bring something more sacred. [129]

Clearly prophecy *is* revealed religion here as it is in the *Démonomanie,* a religion which embraces Moses, Plato and Christ. But although he seems to be following Augustine's well known argument that Plato was a forerunner of Christ, Bodin never actually admits the divinity of Christ. As in all his other writing (with the sole exception of the forthright but secret *Heptaplomeres*) Bodin is extremely cautious in his phrasing about Christ. Granted that Christ is the bearer of "a more sacred" doctrine than Plato, yet he is never described as the redeemer, but merely as the greatest prophet. Christ, like Plato, bears a prophetic message summoning men to the worship of the one God; but Christ is never referred to as the incarnation of God.

> It was Christ who, sent down from heaven to earth, as though seizing with (*Prometheus'*) rod the sacred fires of eternal Pallas, breathed on those select men of pure life, so as to purify a world polluted by the infamy of vices and crimes and lead men bound by abominable superstition to the true worship of omnipotent God. He and his followers were, however, punished with the cruellest and most shameful of punishments, because they had grasped at the state and violated religion. But of such power was his discipline that it withstood the treachery of evil men and the extraordinary cruelty of tyrants who attacked it for three hundred years. [130]

Christ is acclaimed as the most excellent guide ot he true religion of the one great God, the foremost of those prophets sent down by God to guide men to

---

[129] *Ibidem,* pp. 522f: "Illud autem constat inter nos, hominem eximia quadam conditione creatum ac praeclaris virtutibus a Deo subornatum de vie deflexisse, ex quo labes aeterna mortalium animum sic invasit, ut nec praemiis ullis ad virtutem incitari, nec suppliciorum acerbitate a vitiis deterreri possint. Itaque in perpetua nocte et caligine versaremur, nisi Deus O.M. statis temporibus summam virtutem in quibusdam excitaret, ut ab iis reliqui mortales a recto cursu virtutis aberrantes dirigerentur. Tales extiterunt duobus circiter annorum millibus decem illi quos Historia S. complectitur initio των παραλειπομενων, et utriusque aetatis Prophetae. Omitto Pythagoram, Heraclitum, Thalem, Solonem, Aristidem, Anaxagoram, Socratem, Platonem, Xenophontem, Hermodorum, Lycurgum, Numam, Scipiones, Catones, quos viros! qua virtute, integritate, sapientia florentes!
Nulli ex his omnibus impiorum calumnias evaserunt; multi exilio mulctati, nonnulli ante aras caesi, alii alio supplicio damnati sunt quasi seditiosi cives: tametsi omnes summa virtute ac pietate conjuncti, ac parum abest, ait Augustinus, quin Platonici fiant christiani. Cum autem Plato unius Dei cultum animorumque immortalium vim ac potestatem ubique praedicaret, tantisper sibi credendum esse dicebat, dum se praestantior sacratius aliquid afferret."

[130] *Ibidem,* p. 523: "is erat Christus qui, caelo delapsus in terras, quasi ferula Palladis aeternae sacros ignes arripiens selectos vitae purioris homines afflavit, ut flagitiorum et scelerum immanitate pollutum orbem perpurgaret, ac mortales execranda superstitione obligatos ad verum praepotentis Dei cultum perduceret; ipse tamen cum suis crudelissimo ac turpissimo genere supplicii affectus est, quod violatis religionibus regnum affectare diceretur. Sed tam magna vis extitit ejus disciplinae, ut contra omnes hominum improborum insidias, contraque mirabiles Tyrannorum crudelitates, quos annos amplius trecentos illam oppugnarunt." For the argument that the letter to Bautru is not that of a believing Christian see Mesnard, "La pensée religieuse de Bodin". In his later writings Mesnard seems to have ignored the perceptions of this important article.

virtue, repentance and recognition of divine majesty. It was only in this curious and restricted acceptance of Christ that Bodin was a Christian; in none of his writings did Bodin ever confess the divinity of Christ, admit the resurrection, or hail Him as the saviour or redeemer.

Was Bodin then a Socinian? There is certainly much of the religion of Lelio Sozini and the Socinians in the letter to Bautru. The Socinians held that salvation is to be found in God Himself to Whom supreme worship and reverence of both heart and mind are due; Christ is worshipped not as a primary saviour but as a representative of God's authority. Christ suffered not for the atonement of men's sins (which are forgiven by God alone) but rather as an example of how men may return to God. For the Socinians Christ is a prophet and teacher. Accompanying this Christology one finds many of the Judaised themes already encountered in Bodin: belief in the supremacy of the Decalogue, emphasis on free will and the rejection of original sin. [131] It was perhaps these Socinian beliefs which Bodin had in mind when he alluded in the letter to Bautru to "my religion, or rather that of Christ". [132]

Yet for all this Christian Socinianism there is one point to be noted: Bodin *never* refers to the Socinian principle that belief in Christ (even if he were not the Redeemer) is required if a man is to be "justified". Although the elect are not justified by the death of Christ they are justified by faith in Christ as God's representative.

Nowhere in Bodin's writings does one find any admission that justification is achieved through faith in Christ; indeed in the *Heptaplomeres* the entire notion that any man can be justified in the sight of God is abruptly dismissed. [133] Bodin, it seems, went along with the Socinians as far as recognising Christ as a great prophet; whether he went any further is open to doubt.

On the whole it might be wise to interpret the Bautru references to Christ, not as Socinian, but rather as aspects of that prophetic *vera religio* to which Bodin's Judaising led him and which is so evident in nearly all his other writings. The letter's emphatic insistence on prophets and prophecy is strikingly reminiscent of the *Démonomanie* and at least one detail of vocabulary — the repeated word for evil demon, *kakodaimon* — ties in with the theory of prophecy elaborated in the later work (*Kakodaimon* is one of Philo's favorite terms). [134]

---

[131] E.M. Wilbur, *A History of Unitarianism* (Boston, 1945), I, 85ff, 408ff. Many of these Socinian ideas were not made explicit until Fausto Sozzini published his *De Jesu Christo servatore* in 1594 and the promulgation of the Racovian Catechism in 1605. (There are also some less striking parallels between the Bautru letter and the Arian heresy although here again Arianism held to a belief in a Christ who was of a special nature and more than a mere prophet).

[132] Chauviré, *Jean Bodin*, p. 522: "... meam vel potius Christi religionem".

[133] *Heptaplomeres*, p. 322 (424). (See Chapter IV, note 89). The *Heptaplomeres* (e.g. pp. 190, 199 (trs. 249, 260)) absorbs the prophetic elements of the Bautru letter while giving a sharp critique of the Socinian notion of a justifying faith in Christ.

[134] *Ibidem*, p. 522: "κακοδαιμονα", and p. 524: "omnes homines, exceptis (sic enim vox divina testatur) millibus septem, teterrima κακοναιμονων λατρεια και δουλεια, vixisse permiserit". Compare *Démonomanie*, I, i, fol. 6v: "κακαδαιμον"; and I, iii, fol. 14: "κακαδαιμονας". Philo introduces the word *kakodaimon* in *Cherubim*, 39, using it constantly in his other writings to denote unhappiness and misery. See G. Mayer, *Index Philoneus* (Berlin, 1974), p. 154. The term was taken up later in Plotinus' *Enneads*. Curiously enough it was also used by Servetus. See *Registres de la Compagnie des Pasteurs à Genève*, ed. R.M. Kingdon *et al.* (Geneva, 1962-), II, 43.

The whole structure and sense as well as the massing of references and allusions leave little room for doubt that the *vera religio* expounded in the letter of Bautru is founded above all on prophecy; notice the ten Adamite prophets, the prophets of both ages, the seven thousand prophets on whom God remarks to Elijah, the gentile prophets of the Greeks, the setting of Christ within a purely prophetic context.[135]

Were it not for the acceptance of Christ within the line of prophets Bodin's view of prophecy would be wholly in accord with Jewish tradition. This tradition understood prophecy to have two main objectives. One was to recall men from vice to repentance and to virtue and Jewish Messianic tradition saw the Messiah as a great prophet come to recall men to repentance.[136] Bodin wholeheartedly accepted the connection of prophecy with repentance but he departed from Jewish tradition in being willing to admit Christ as a prophet and perhaps even as Messiah, though this would scarcely have been the divine Messiah of the Christians. Yet curiously enough Bodin's early Carmelite training may have contributed to his distinctly un-Christian idea of Christ. The Carmelites had placed great store on the prophets as leaders of men to contrition and tended to assimilate their divine Christ into the prophetic tradition represented by their patron Elijah. When Bodin subsequently lost his faith in the divinity of Christ his experience as a Carmelite may have left a strong enough impression on him to enable him to retain his belief in an authentically prophetic Christ; this idiosyncratic concept of a non-divine but prophetic Christ would have inexorably cut off Bodin from all the major religious traditions leaving him alone with a *vera religio* that was neither Christian nor Jewish but uniquely personal.

The second major purpose of prophecy in Jewish thought was the preservation of a pure monotheism, the summoning of men back to the worship of the true God. Bodin's denunciations of Catholic *eidolomaneia* are coloured by this prophetic purpose and he follows Jewish tradition also in seeing Moses and the Maccabees as warrior-prophets sent to purify religion by war. Bodin indeed conceives the purification of monotheism as the true — and good — cause of religious war. But again he places himself outside the Jewish tradition when he accepts Christ as one of those prophets who had come to restore men "to the true worship of almighty God", a restoration requiring the waging of a holy war of the spirit rather than the toleration of an impious peace.[137]

Bodin's fusion of religious war, true religion and prophecy in the letter to Bautru vividly illustrates how prophecy had come to be the central — and the revolutionary — element of his religion. Bodin now saw the prophet as the revealer of true religion, prepared to carry out his mission to the point of death. In this way prophecy had become the foundation of both true religion and religious war. There had been premonitions of these beliefs in the *Methodus* but their intensity of expression in the letter reflects a recent and profound

---

[135] For the Adamites (I Chronicles, I, 1) and the prophets of the two ages see the text in Chauviré, *Bodin*, p. 522, quoted above in note 88. For the 7,000 prophets left in Israel (I Kings, XIX, 18) see Chauviré, p. 524 (quoted above, note 91).

[136] Abelson, *Immanence*, p. 317. G. Scholem, *The Messianic Idea in Judaism* (New York, 1972), For Philo's idea of the prophet recalling men to virtue see Laurentin, 'Le pneuma', pp. 416ff.

[137] See the passages from the letter in Chauviré, pp. 522-24, already quoted.

spiritual experience such as had occurred with the transfiguration of 1567-68. In later years Bodin's writings continued to embody these feelings but they took on a more subdued form in keeping with the passage of time from their initial revelation. The letter to Bautru seems to be the actual point of division between Bodin's early and later writings, the point where the author's awareness of prophecy is to be seen in its sharpest, freshest and most dramatic form. [138] It would be psychologically plausible, therefore, to place the letter as near as possible in time to the conversion and, for the reason given above as point 2, 1568-69 would be the likeliest date.

5. One critical biographical fact which supports a later dating of the letter to 1568-69 is Bodin's mysterious arrest and imprisonment from March 1569 to August 1570 after failing to take a second oath of Catholicism in November 1568. [139] Like many of his fellow-prisoners Bodin could easily have secured an early release from prison by simulating adherence to the Catholic church but he chose to linger on in gaol for a year and a half until rescued by a general amnesty. Why? As we have seen Bodin's revulsion against Catholic rites in the letter to Bautru arose out of the fear that those rites smacked of idolatry and endangered the sanctity of monotheism. This fear alone may have prevented him from taking the Catholic oath of 1568 as readily as he had sworn it in 1562 and in this decision he may have been counselled by his recently acquired guardian angel. Most importantly the letter to Baudru regards persecution as the common mark of prophets and to Bodin, emerging from his conversion of 1567-68 convinced that he was a prophet of the first degree, [140] a period of imprisonment may have seemed almost welcome as authentication of his new prophetic status. In sum, the conversion of 1567-68, the imprisonment of 1569-70 and the letter to Bautru — redated to 1568-69 — together constitute what may be regarded as the central crisis of Bodin's life, a crisis which took place in the years 1567-70.

[138] Among those to miss the letter's central theme of prophecy has been De Caprariis, *Propaganda*, p. 327, who argues that Bodin believed in divine revelation coming direct to man without intermediaries.

[139] Bodin's name does not appear in the list of those who took the oath of 12 November 1568 (Archives Nationales, Paris, *X. 1A 1625*. fols. 1v and ff).
He was arrested on 6 March 1569 and released on 23 August 1570 according to documents in Weiss, 'Huguenots emprisonnés à la Conciergerie'. The arrested man is described as "Jehan Baudin soy disant avocat en la court de Parlement, natif d'Angers, et demeurant au prieuré Sainct-Denys de la Châtre". Weiss identifies this priory as that of Saint-Denis de Jouhet, département Cher, arrondissement La Châtre. La Châtre is only 40 kms west-south-west of Saint-Amand in the diocese of Bourges, a fact which might seem to strengthen Bodin's connection with the Saint-Amand of Bourges rather than of Laon-Vermandois and so identify him with the Calvinist pastor Jean Bodin of "Saint-Amand in the diocese of Bourges" who turns up at Geneva in 1552 (as Naef and Droz, — footnote 1 above — have argued). Levron, however, objected — to my mind rightly — that Bodin's connection was with Saint-Amand in Laon-Vermandois. The present case again seems to be a mere curious coincidence. The priory in question is far more likely to have been in Paris and may be identified as that of Saint-Denis de la Charte, an ancient Benedictine priory on the left bank. This makes better sense than having to believe that Bodin was arrested in the Cher and brought all the way to Paris. (See *Gallia Christiana*, (reprinted, Gregg, 1970), VII, (Paris, 1744), col. 550). What Bodin was doing in a Catholic priory I have no idea. It was definitely our Bodin and not his namesake Jean Bodin de Montguichet who was imprisoned in in March 1569. Montguichet was appointed to a court post in May 1569 while our Bodin was still a prisoner.

[140] Cf. *Démonomanie*, I, iv, fol. 23.

f) Conclusion

Bodin's case may serve to throw light on one of the central problems of conversion, namely the relationship between the personality and ideas of a convert *before* and *after* the conversion. In which respects does a convert change and in which respects does he remain the same? What are the constants and the variables? What is accidental and what is substantial in his thought and personality? We are, in other words, enquiring about the nature of an individual's psychic energy.

There are two kinds of variables in Bodin's conversions. The former, superficial kind concern his confessional vacillations between Catholicism in 1562, heresy in 1569, and Catholicism again in 1589. Bodin's wavering actually sprang from a deep and enduring conviction that his real allegiance was to *true religion*; Bodin was constant in his indifference to positive confessional religion. The second species of variables is more significant. These variables consist in the shifts from a natural theism in the *Oratio* to the prophetically revealed religion of the later writings, from a Carmelite to a Judaised spirituality. Certainly there were shifts in these respects but here again we can discern an underlying constancy beneath the flow of belief. The Great God of Nature, the theistic God who reconciled transcendence with the world of nature pervades all of Bodin's writings and one might be more justified in thinking of the religious visions of the *Oratio* and the *Methodus* as successive refinements of Bodin's understanding of his basic concept rather than as abrupt shifts. A revelational element was definitely present in the *Oratio* even if it were largely glossed over. Given Bodin's theistic idea of God, this element could only grow more insistent with the passage of time and with reflection. As to Bodin's spiritual progress, connecting lines can be drawn between his early Carmelite and later Judaised spirituality; both phases shared a preoccupation with purification, prayer and prophecy. By 1566, it seems, Bodin had attained an understanding of the two-fold structure of true religion as a combination of purification and prophecy. It is unthinkable that someone of Bodin's intensity of religious feeling should have been content to remain with one half of the religious experience, that of purification. The same psychic energy which inspired him to devise this Judaised form of true religion with its two tiers of purification and prophecy continued to drive him to the height of religious experience — the achievement of prophetic transfiguration.

Bodin was never a Jew [141] but rather a profound Judaiser who had a deep spiritual kinship with the Jews which was rooted in a shared prophetic monotheism. Bodin would certainly have considered himself one of the "children of

---

[141] Though there seems to be a general tendency to refer to Bodin's "Judaism". E.g., Baxter, 'Bodin's Daemon'. Roellenbleck, *Offenbarung*. D.P. Walker, *Spiritual and Demonic Magic from Ficino to Campanella* (London, 1958), p. 171.

Israel" by which he meant "all those who trust in God".[142]   From 1566 at least Bodin trusted in a God Who revealed Himself through prophecy and Whose prophet he became in 1567-68.   Prophecy was vital to Bodin's Judaised monotheism because it rescued him, as it did Philo and Maimonides, from the perils of natural and philosophical religion.[143]   Moreover, prophecy fulfilled a unifying function in *vera religio* since Bodin's Judaised theory of prophecy bound together two of the foundations of that religion — illumination and revelation.[144] Yet prophecy was of more than religious significance to Bodin. It came to dominate his political thought and actions as we shall see in the ensuing account of his dealing with the Catholic League at Laon.   It was by these actions that Bodin would prove himself a true prophet of God.   "As to the true marks by which to recognise those (*true prophets*) who have such (*divine*) grace, one must consider carefully and examine all their actions, and above all one must know which God they worship".[145]

[142] *Démonomanie*, I, 5, f. 30v. An analogous idea of Philo's is described in Wolfson, *Philo*, II, 401.

[143] On prophecy, nature and revelation see e.g., Maimonides, *Guide*; Philo, *Quis Heres*.

[144] See Chapters V-VII.

[145] *Démonomanie*, I, 4, f. 27. These true prophets worship transcendent God and not the immanent angelic or demonic spirits who transmit His laws and will.

CHAPTER IX

THE POLITIQUE AND THE PROPHET (1589-94)

> For it befits the servants and lieutenants of God that like
> generals in war they should inflict vengeance on deserters
> who leave the ranks of justice. But it befits the Great King
> that the general safety of the universe should be ascribed to
> Him, that he should be the guardian of peace and supply richly
> and abundantly the good things of peace ... For indeed God is
> the Prince of Peace while His subalterns are the leaders in
> war.
>
> Philo, *De Decalogo*, 178.

By the time Bodin published the *République* in 1576 the original incandescence of the prophetic conversion had waned and he was sufficiently composed to describe what was essentially a religious vision of politics without allowing the religion to become rancorous or obtrusive. Most likely the zeal of the new convert had subsided some years before 1576. In 1570 Bodin had been released from prison still apparently unrepentant; in 1571 however, he took up a court post and the following year permitted himself to be saved from what would perhaps have been a fittingly prophetic death in the St. Bartholomew Massacre. Nevertheless the imprint of the conversion is clearly visible in the *République's* moderated remarks on universal religion, virtue and prophecy; for all its loss of initial fire Bodin's *vera religio* is still a real presence in his great academic political treatise.

It comes through in the Judaised conception of law upon which the *République* is built: for Bodin, following Philo's formula, the divine law is the law of nature. But even more telling is the emergence of prophecy as a crucial facet of Bodin's perception of kingship. In a curious passage in the *République* Bodin compares the prophetic communication between God and His elect prophets to the relationship between a king and his subjects. In both cases the governing emotions are love and fear. Nowhere perhaps are the religious foundations of Bodin's political thought more disturbingly exposed than here.

> Now the love of his subjects for a sovereign is far more necessary for the
> preservation of a state than is fear of him. For love cannot exist without fear
> of offending him who is loved, but fear can exist without love and very often does.
> It seems that this great God who is sovereign of the universe has shown human
> princes who are His true images how they are to communicate with their subjects

193

("if they are to be loved and feared"). For God communicates with men only by means of dreams and visions and then but to a very small number of the elect and most perfect ("of the highest sanctity and righteousness (*integritatis*)"). When God's voice promulgated the Decalogue displaying His fire in the sky and with His thunder and thunderbolts shaking the mountains with such a terrifying blast of trumpets that the people fell prostrate beseeching Him to speak to them no more lest they die, then, it is said, they were hearing His voice so that they might ever more be fearful of offending Him. ("But (*henceforth*) they were to be commanded through Moses"). Nevertheless to encourage men to love Him ardently God loaded them with His great favours, largesse and infinite bounty. [1]

Among the ideas enunciated in this pregnant passage we may now recognise many of the themes which have appeared in foregoing chapters. The Great God of Nature finds His weak counterparts in earthly monarchs and His revealed will of the Decalogue its parallel in the positive laws of kings. Love and fear ultimately register man's relations with God and are reflected in the subject's attitude in his sovereign. The sovereign in turn communicates with his people as God does with His prophets. Here in the sober philosophical *République* are the clear signs of a prophetic vision of politics which was to be fulfilled in Bodin's own eccentric political conduct when the last of the Religious Wars broke out in 1589.

Among the many apparent paradoxes of Jean Bodin's personality one of the most striking was the sudden transformation of the defender of royal sovereignty and religious toleration into the apologist of the rebelling Catholic League at Laon in 1589. Throughout the middle period of the Wars of Religion (1572-84) Bodin had been attached to the parties opposing the Guise and the Catholic League; he had been active first in the royalist party of Henri III and subsequently he rose to prominence in the retinue of the king's brother, the *politique* duke of Alençon. After the duke's death in 1584 Bodin seems to have been attached loosely to Henri of Navarre, supporting (so it seems) his claim to the French throne and earning through his services to Navarre the promise of a reward in 1587. Yet despite this royalist and *politique* history Bodin in March 1589 to all appearances threw overboard his old loyalties and went over to public support of the League. In so doing he appears at first sight to have repudiated political, religious and jurisprudential convictions of long standing. The League demanded that the king of France

---

[1] *République* (Paris, 1583), IV, 6, pp. 616ff: "Or l'amour des subiects envers le souverain, est bien plus nécessaire à la conservation d'un estat, que la crainte. Et d'autant plus nécessaire, que l'amour ne peut estre sans crainte d'offenser celuy qu'on aime. Mais la crainte peut bien estre, et le plus souvent, sans amour. Et semble que ce grand Dieu Prince du monde, a monstré aux princes humains, qui sont ses vrayes images, comme il se faut communiquer aux subiects ("*et amari possint, et metui*"). Car il ne se communique aux hommes que par visions et songes, et seulement à bien petit nombre des esleus, et plus parfaicts ("*ac integratis*"). Et quand il publia de sa voix le décalogue, faisant voir son feu iusques au ciel, et de ses foudres et tonnerres trembler les montagnes, avec un son si effroyable de trompettes, que le peuple pria se rapissant sur sa face, que Dieu ne parlast plus à eux, autrement qu'ils mourroyent tous; encores est-il dit, qu'ils n'ouyrent que sa voix, à fin qu'ils eussent à iamais crainte de l'offenser. ("*Sed per Mosem, quae vellet, iuberentur*"). Et néantmoins pour inciter les hommes à l'aimer ardamment, il les comble assiduellement de ses grandes faveurs, largesses et bontés infinies." I have added some variants from Bodin's own Latin translation of 1586 (*Republica*, p. 455). These are given inside quotation marks set within parentheses.

be Catholic whereas Bodin had never regarded a religious test as a fundamental law of the French crown; the League demanded sectarian religious war of the kind which the *République* had proscribed; the League abhorred the principle of religious toleration advocated in the *République*; the League overruled the juristic right to the throne of Henri of Navarre which Bodin, it is often said mistakenly, had justified as late as 1586. [2] What motives could conceivably have driven Bodin to commit this act of apostasy (if such it really be)? The answer is of the greatest significance for an understanding of Bodin's mind not only in his later years but from his youth onwards. For Bodin's change from *politique* to *ligueur* is but one of the several conversions which punctuate his life and the details of this particular alteration may illuminate his personality and thought in general.

For all its importance the problem of Bodin's adherence to the Catholic League in 1589-90 has received often unsatisfactory solutions which have tended to treat the question simplistically instead of giving it the complex analysis it deserves. [3] To begin with the simple question of why Bodin supported the League comprises not one but a series of questions each of which requires a separate answer. What were Bodin's true feelings about the League? Why did he join? How far was he committed? Which policies of the League did he support and which did he reject? How did he square his *politique* views with his acceptance of the League? Did his attitudes change in the course of the conflict? How did the deaths of Henri III and the cardinal de Bourbon variously affect his views? And what of the impact of six years of wasting civil war?

In answering these questions it is not enough to provide each of them with a simple and restricted explanation. It is instead necessary to imitate Bodin's own intricate and rambling treatment. Bodin's writings concerning the League, like all his works, are a rich woven texture incorporating what may seem to a modern mind to be highly discordant themes. Legal and constitutional, prophetic and numerological, political and prudential, religious and moral — all these modes of thought combine to form a fantasy of an argument rather than a rationally put case. To do justice to the complexity of Bodin's political ideas and conduct during his last years at Laon requires indeed an approach as variegated as his own.

Yet amid all this complexity we should also seek for an inner consistency to Bodin's political behaviour in the two decades between the first edition of the *République* and his death in 1596. Bodin's political "progress" from being a *politique* in the period 1576-89 to being a prophet in 1589-94 has perplexed both his contemporaries and his biographers who have discovered no other consistency in these two phases of career beyond the fact that in both there was involved a certain element of political prudence. The real

---

[2] I believe that Bodin's alleged "change of sides" occurred in any case in 1586, not 1589 as is usually said. See P.L. Rose, 'Bodin and the Bourbon Succession to the French Throne 1583-1594', *Sixteenth Century Journal*, IX (1978), 75-98.

[3] The best account to date is J. Moreau-Reibel, 'Bodin et la Ligue d'après des lettres inédites', *Humanisme et Renaissance*, II (1935), 422-440. Less satisfactory are S. Baldwin, 'Jean Bodin and the League', *Catholic Historical Review*, XXIII (1937), 160-184. R. Chauviré, *Jean Bodin, auteur de la République* (Paris, 1914), pp. 76ff. K.D. McRae, ed., *Jean Bodin: The Six Bookes of a Commonweale* (Cambridge, Mass., 1962), p. Aii.

constant, however, is to be found in the role of *vera religio*. Bodin's universal *vera religio* in the first period promoted an indifference to specific confessional religion which disposed him towards a *politique* standpoint. This confessional indifference did not suddenly vanish in 1589 with the advent of the Catholic League; Bodin always remained faithful to his idea of *vera religio*. Bodin was always indeed a *politique* just as he stayed a prophet after 1567-68; in this sense, there was really no abandoning of his position as a *politique* for a new interest in prophecy. But in 1589 Bodin did enter a new and more active phase of his prophetic vocation. The sinfulness of France and the scandalous conduct of the Ahab-like king Henri III provoked Bodin's prophetic instinct and convinced him that divine retribution must be at hand. That retribution was to be inflicted by the scourge of religious war. In the face of God's wrath Bodin assumed the role of God's servant interpreting His will to men.

*
**

Our knowledge of Bodin's relations with the League derives in the main from two chief sources. One is the *Mémoires* of Antoine Richart, a contemporary burgess of Laon during Bodin's stay there in the 1580s and 1590s. [4] These are invaluable for the information given on Bodin's actual conduct during the period of the civil war although his actions are seen in a somewhat unsympathetic light. Bodin's political behaviour at Laon was, however, coloured by the fact that he held public office in the city from 1587.

The general revolt of the League against Henri III in the early months of 1589 placed Bodin, then *procureur du roy* at Laon, in an extremely difficult position. As a public official he was obliged to execute the orders of the *procureur général* of Paris requiring local *procureurs* to administer an oath of allegiance to the Catholic League. Bodin tried to save himself by a rambling speech at the oath taking on 21 March 1589 where he insisted that he was acting in his capacity of *procureur* of the royal estate, rather than of the king himself. [5] At a further public meeting on 4 April 1589 he welcomed three commissioners who had been sent by the League to try a group of royalists but was howled down when he hypothesized about an eventual restoration of Henri III. [6] Bodin continued to be regarded with suspicion by the Leaguers of Laon and on 20 January 1590 his house was subjected to a search and several of his books burnt on his doorstep. [7] After this warning Bodin desisted from public acts except to protect an unjustly condemned youth in 1593; on this occasion Bodin acted as an Old Testament prophet fulminating against

---

[4] A. Richart, *Mémoires sur la Ligue dans le Laonnois* (Laon, 1869).

[5] *Ibid.*, p. 66. Bodin had already postponed the taking of the oath. There had in 1587 been objections raised at Paris that a reputed Huguenot sympathiser such as Bodin should be permitted to hold royal office at Laon. Bodin was subsequently examined and cleared. See *Lettres de Catherine de Médicis*, ed. H. de la Ferrière (Paris, 1880-1943), IX, 453. Chauviré, *Bodin*, p. 77, thought wrongly that Bodin was examined because of a doubtful book. (See below, note 41).

[6] Richart, *Mémoires*, p. 83.

[7] *Ibid.*, p. 228ff. (mispaginated).

the injustice of the acting governor of the city.[8] As the successes of the now converted Henry IV drove the League to desperation Bodin fled Laon in April 1594 to join the new king. Richart's unfavourably sardonic comments on this manoeuvring by Bodin have largely been followed by subsequent writers.

The other source is Bodin's own correspondence of the period 1589-94 as represented by a group of six letters, five of which were discovered in manuscript and published some time ago by Moreau-Reibel.[9]. One of these edited letters had appeared in print anonymously in 1589 as the *Lettre d'un lieutenant-général de province*. The sixth letter the notorious *Lettre de M. Bodin,* was published in 1590 but was not reprinted with the others. Taken as a group and in sequence these letters permit us to see the problem of the League through Bodin's eyes and to place a more sympathetic interpretation upon his public acts endorsing its opposition to Henri III and his Bourbon successor. The present account will try not only to analyse some of the main themes and motifs — above all the theme of religious war — embedded in this correspondence but also to discern how Bodin's convictions and sensibility changed in the course of these turbulent few years.[10]

The first letter of the manuscript correspondence is undated but was probably written in late March 1589; it was published anonymously in the same year under the title *Lettre d'un Lieutenant-Général de Province à un des premiers magistrats de France,* M. Iouin, Paris, 1589.[11] It is a cautious but unembarrassed account of Bodin's administering of the oath of Sainte-Union at Laon on 21 March 1589 and probably contains the substance of the speech he made on that occasion.[12] Bodin clearly felt he was writing to an official of like mind who had finally joined the League in protest at the king's tyrannical conduct. Bodin's own legal friend of thirty years at Paris, Barnabé

---

[8] *Ibid.,* p. 415.

[9] Printed by Moreau-Reibel, 'Bodin'. Also cited by Baldwin, 'Bodin'. Although grouped together in the manuscript (Bibliothèque Nationale, Paris, Ms. Français 4897) it is most unlikely that all these letters were addressed to the same person. For discussion of the various recipients see below.

[10] I hope to add something to the earlier analyses by Moreau-Reibel and Baldwin who did not attempt to trace the evolution of Bodin's feelings about the succession and war during these years.

[11] Issued by the same publisher as *Advis d'un lieutenant-général...,* 1589. See R.O. Lindsay and J. Neu, *French Political Pamphlets 1547-1648. A Catalog of Major Collections in American Libraries* (Madison, Wisc., 1969), No. 1551. D. Pallier, *Recherches sur l'imprimerie à Paris pendant la Ligue (1585-1594)* (Geneva, 1976), No. 411. The *Lettre* of 1589 is reprinted with variants by Moreau-Reibel, 'Bodin', pp. 425-30. Dated April by a later hand in the manuscript but probably written before 26 March to judge from the references to the receipt of orders for the oath. 'Dimanche dernier dix neufiesme de Mars' (p. 1). Its inclusion in this manuscript series of letters is external evidence of the letter's authenticity. Taken together three remarks in the letter may serve as internal evidence. 'J'ay veu un Ambassadeur Polaque qui estoit Huguenot (p. 5) ... en ceste ville (*of the Carolingians*) (p. 8) ... que j'ay estimé et publié par escript aussi bien climatérique aux monarchies (p. 8)....'

[12] Chauviré, *Bodin,* p. 82 (following J.-A. de Thou) accepts the *Lettre de M. Bodin* (1590) as a reflexion of Bodin's speech of 1589, thus losing sight of any evolution of feeling between the two dates. There are in fact key differences between the letters of 1589 and 1590.

Brisson, springs to mind as a likely recipient.[13]   Like Bodin, Brisson had formerly been a *politique* supporter of Henri III but following the king's degeneration in 1588 had deserted to the League, replacing the royalist Achille de Harlay as president of the Parlement de Paris after the latter's removal from office by the Leaguers.[14]

The letter opens with a restrained call for resistance to Henri III. Unlike those Leaguers who openly called for tyrannicide, Bodin was reluctant to rebel against a king who by reason of his office was sacred and he felt compelled to justify his action to himself and his correspondent.[15]   The king's behaviour, says Bodin, is causing his people to perish and has provoked not an isolated rebellion but a general revolution.   There is no choice but to join the League which is now chastising Henri; let the security of the people be the law (pp. 1-3). *Salus populi suprema lex esto* — this is the political foundation of Bodin's support of the League in 1589.[16]

Yet it is clear from Bodin's public actions in these same months that he understood that the people were in almost as much need of protection from the League as from the tyrant.   At the very oath taking ceremony of the 21 March he demanded justice and protection for twenty-five royalist prisoners who had almost been lynched by rioters, and his insistence that the guilty be punished brought forth threats to hang him.[17]   Two weeks later on 4 April Bodin infuriated a public assembly by conjecturing what would happen if the king were by some chance restored to authority.[18]   It is tempting to interpret these two episodes as evidence of Bodin's lack of sincerity in supporting the League but they make better sense when seen as the actions of a man genuinely disgusted by Henri III's crimes, committed to the League as the instrument of punishment and yet concerned to protect the monarchy and moderate the

[13] Brisson is suggested by Moreau-Reibel, 'Bodin', p. 430. Cf. the concluding phrases at p. 9 of the *Lettre*: '... il y a tantost trente ans pour amy et collègue et maintenant que la dignité vous est donnée illustre et grande', referring to Brisson's presidency of the Leaguer Parlement de Paris. Brisson had in 1574, it seems, attended the Académie du Palais. See above, Chapter IV, note 10. (He was the uncle of the mathematician François Viète).

[14] There is some doubt about Brisson's sincerity. He had covered himself with a secret deposition that he was acting under duress. See P. Gambier, *Au temps des guerres de religion. Le président Barnabé Brisson, Ligueur (1531-1591)* (Paris, 1957).

[15] Bodin always had serious reservations about the legality of rebellion though once successful it might be accepted as a fait accompli. (See below, notes 49, 58, 76, 83 for other comments on this difficult topic.) The important point is that Bodin did not justify the rebellion but rather saw in its success a sign of divine will and displeasure with Henri III. (This is not to say that Bodin felt that the rebels could lay claim to being divinely inspired. See below, notes 82 and 83).

For tyrannicide in contemporary thought see R. Mousnier, *The Assassination of Henry IV* (trs. London, 1973), pp. 98ff., 214. K. Cameron, 'Henri III, the Anti-Christian King', *Journal of European Studies*, IV (1974), 152-63. M. Yardeni, *La conscience nationale en France pendant les guerres de religion (1559-1598)* (Paris-Louvain, 1971), ch. VII.

[16] In a crisis of state 'ceste maxime générale ... ne souffre point d'exception. Salus populi suprema lex esto', *République* (Paris, 1583), IV, 3, p. 576. See also *Sapientiae Moralis Epitome* (Paris, 1588), maxim 121. Cf. Chapter III, note 19.

[17] Richart, *Mémoires*, p. 66. Chauviré, *Bodin*, pp. 87ff.

[18] Richart, *Mémoires*, p. 83.

excesses of the Leaguers.[19]   Bodin's conduct is not without parallel among his own acquaintances.   The prominent lawyer and philosopher Guillaume Du Vair, had earlier belonged with Bodin to the duke of Alençon's circle and he and Bodin had many mutual friends at Paris including Christophe de Thou and Barnabé Brisson.   In early 1589 Du Vair shared to the full Bodin's revulsion at the king's crime and gave his support to the League.   At the same time Du Vair recognized the need for moderation of the League's extremism: "We must not undo ourselves to no purpose...We may retard and slacken cunningly the course of violence...Peace and concord is re-established by the modest and impartial carriage of a good citizen".[20]

Bodin's anger at Henri III betrays a strong tendency to reduce politics to religious and biblical terms which may clearly be seen in his discussion of the impregnability of Paris.   The city of Paris cannot be ruined by human power for it is under God's protection; its sustaining strengths are fear of God, charity and justice.   Charity in particular is of great moment for the sight of it extinguishes divine wrath.   Paris' weaknesses too are moral rather than political; they are incontinence and the traffic in silver (pp. 4ff).   Fortunately, however, the happy day of the Barricades, though detested by some, had cleansed Paris, routing the thieves of the court and the vermin of courtiers who despoil all cities (pp. 5ff).   This attack on Parisian vice continues moral and religious feelings which may be traced back to Bodin's Carmelite spirituality.   Aversion to cities was prominently featured in the *Institutio primorum monachorum* which in its exposition of the Fifty-fifth Psalm had added usury to the list of urban sins: "I have seen violence and strife in the city... wickedness, deceit, guile (Psalm LV, 9-10).[21]   Feelings of this sort had indeed already appeared in two of Bodin's printed works.   "Souvent la damnable cité est sauvée par charité", he had written in the *Sapientia* of 1588.   This moral tone is not surprising in a moral treatise but for all its technical analysis of economics the *Response à M. Malestroit* of 1568 had also ended up by affirming that economics rested on religious and moral presuppositions.   Conspicuous consumption and waste were seen as being carried on "en despit de Dieu" and in the revision of 1578 Bodin spelt out that divine retribution was at hand ("aussi Dieu s'en vengea").

But it is upon Henri III's head in particular that Bodin invokes divine punishment in the *Lettre* of 1589.   The religious theme of divine vengeance

[19] Chauviré, *Bodin*, pp. 78-9, 88 believes Bodin yielded only momentarily to the League out of prudence and fear.   This does not take into account the bitterness of Bodin's attack on the king.   Nevertheless from the beginning Bodin must have had severe misgivings about the demagoguery of some of the more extreme Leaguers in the city.   Following the attempted lynching of the royalists in March, Innocent la Biche proscribed a list of suspected royalists and more than 200 suspects were obliged to take flight in May.   See E. Fleury, *Cinquante ans de l'histoire du chapitre de Notre-Dame de Laon ... 1541 ... 1594* (Laon-Paris, 1875), pp. 319ff.

[20] Guillaume Du Vair, *Traité de la constance* (Lyons, 1595 edn), pp. 335, 338.   Cf. R. Radouant, *Guillaume Du Vair. L'homme et l'orateur jusqu'à la fin des troubles de la Ligue (1556-1596)* (Paris, 1907), p. 403.

[21] G. Wessels, 'Pars ascetica Regulae Iohannis 44', *Analecta Ordinis Carmelitarum*, III (1914-16), 346-367, at p. 352.   (See above Chapter IV, note 49).
Bodin had been saved at the *journée des barricades* (May 1588) by his friend the advocate Dauger or D'Ogier.   See also the letter of 1590 discussed below.   For the "traffic in silver" cf. *Lettre de M. Bodin* (1590), p. 18.

is now added to the earlier political principle of *Salus populi* as a justification of the League's revolt.

> Mais quant au Roy, ie tiens que sa ruine est proche et inevitable car Dieu qui donne la crainte sur les Rois, l'a du tout retirée de son peuple ... L'autre point est qu'il a osté à luy et à son conseil le iugement ... en matière d'estat.... Ces deux poincts sont remarquez en Iob et Samuel, pour argumens très certains de la fureur de Dieu, envers les Princes. Quand à l'infraction de la foy publique, ie n'ay iamais leu que Dieu en ayt oublié la vengeance, et d'un double parricide, et mesme en la personne d'un homme sacré et ministre de Dieu. Combien que ie voy une cause plus haute et universelle, c'est que Dieu a resolu et continuera comme il a commencé de chastier les Rois et grands seigneurs pour donner les exemples terribles aux successeurs, de marcher droit, vo' avez vu ... Et croy que Iob parloit de ce règne quant il dit, *qui facit regnare hipocritam propter peccata populi* (pp. 6-7).

Such fervent denunciation is more than an example of the common sixteenth-century practice of citing scripture of justify political action; it unmistakeably expresses an intensely prophetic vision of divine vengeance on tyrants. [23]

To this moralizing Hebraic prophecy Bodin adds the corroboration of another kind of prophecy, this time natural rather than religious. Henry III is the sixty-third king of France since Pharamond and the number sixty-three, 'que i'ay estimé et publié par escript', is climacteric for monarchies. [24] Nevertheless for Bodin this is an inferior sort of prophecy which is binding (as he earlier wrote in the *République*) only on those 'qui laschent la bride aux appétits desréiglés, et cupidités bestiales'. By 1589 Henri III clearly came within this category. [25] Even in this case, however, there is no necessity that the prophecy be fulfilled 'veu que leurs sceptres sont tous en la main de Dieu pour les donner et oster quant et à qui luy plaist...Ie m'en rapporteray tousiours au iugement de Dieu' (p. 8).

Bodin's objections to Henri of Navarre in this letter are also religious rather than political:

> On nous menace du Roy de Navarre, à tort et sans cause, car il ne la fera pas longue et ne touchera iamais la couronne pour des raisons que vous sçavez mieux que moy: encores a il faict une faute grande, en laquelle il persévère, c'est

---

[22] *Sapientiae Moralis Epitome* (Paris, 1588), maxim 166. (See above, Chapter III, note 20). *La Response de Jean Bodin à M. de Malestroit 1568. La vie chère au XVIe siècle*, ed. H. Hauser (Paris, 1932), pp. 20f. (For an appeal to Moses as an economics expert see pp. 33f. where the theme of virtue is introduced into the economic discussion).

[23] Bodin's vision of divine retribution becomes increasingly collective and universal in contrast to the inflamed pamphlet literature of 1589 which concentrated on the individual vilification of Henri III, 'that Judas ,that Nero'. Henri's crimes reawakened a prophetic spirit long present in Bodin's mind that had earlier appeared, slightly muted, in the *République's* praise of the prophets who had brought low the house of Ahab. See C.R. Baxter, 'Problems of the Religious Wars', in *French literature and its background*, ed. J. Cruickshank (Oxford, 1968), I, 166-85.

[24] Bodin, *République* (1583), IV, 3, p. 567. Cf. *Lettre* (1590), p. 17. Chauviré, *Bodin*, pp. 85ff. Bodin probably availed himself of natural prophecy in his prediction of the Babington Conspiracy which earned him the attentions of Walsingham in 1586. See below, note 77.

[25] *République*, IV, 3, p. 572, speaking of astrology as an example of naturalistic prophecy.

qu'il n'a pas la crainte de Dieu, et se ioue des biens de l'Eglise, qui est un feu en sa maison qui le consumera.... (pp. 7-8).

This is not the visceral hatred of Navarre felt by many Catholic Leaguers but rather a considered indignation at the impieties of the Protestant leader.

From the letter of March 1589 it is clear that Bodin's support of the League depended on a combination of political and religious factors. [26] Politically Bodin saw the League as representative of a general revolution aimed at overthrowing the tyranny of Henri III. By invoking the maxim *Salus populi suprema lex esto* Bodin admitted that the French were in need of protection from a tyrant and at the same time justified to himself his commission of the city of Laon to the League. On the religious level Bodin believed that Henri's dementia signified a withdrawal of divine favour and sanction of the king. Yet while Bodin might share the League's abhorrence of Henri III there were two fundamental differences in outlook. First, although the success of the rebellion was a sign to Bodin that God was punishing Henri III, nevertheless his political justification of the revolt — which he based on the universality of the uprising against Henri III, not on a legal doctrine of resistance — was far from complete. In fact, as he admitted in the *Lettre* of 1590 [27] Bodin was never really convinced of the legality of resistance even to the most inhuman and irreligious tyrant. In the second place, the League held the revolt to be a crusade against Henri the heretic and the ally of heretics, but Bodin condemned the king not as a heretic but as an impious tyrant deserted by God. Here at the very start could be found a discrepancy between Bodin's and the League's conception of religious war. In supporting the League Bodin never abandoned his earlier stance against sectarian religious war aiming at the extinction of the Protestants in France. The fact that Bodin and the League initially coincided in condemning the tyrannical Henri III largely papered over such basic disagreements. But the differences were real and needed only time and a change of circumstances for them to be uncovered and for the limitations of Bodin's loyalty to the League to become clearly noticeable. Those very same political and religious beliefs which had permitted Bodin to join the League in good conscience in 1589 also circumscribed his new allegiance.

The assassination of Henri III on 1-2 August 1589 marked the fulfilment of Bodin's initial purpose in supporting the League and his next letter of 15 August rejoices in the tyrannicide as an act inspired by God. 'Dieu soit

---

[26] The religious dimension of Bodin's politics is often missed. See for example J.H. Franklin, *Jean Bodin and the Rise of Absolutist Theory* (Cambridge, 1973), p. 98, note, where in considering in exclusively political terms Bodin's justifications of revolution he misses the religious foundation of these views. At this point should be mentioned an awkward piece of evidence. According to documents published by A. Ponthieux, 'Quelques documents inédits sur Jean Bodin', *Revue du Seizième Siècle*, XV (1928), pp. 56-99, at pp. 61ff., it seems that from November 1587 until April 1589 Bodin was receiving payments 'pour estre du conseil du Roy de Navarre'. I have no way of accounting for this except to say that the pension seems to have been owed for past legal services rendered. I doubt if Bodin were a secret agent of Navarre in the period 1589-90. Certainly as long as the cardinal de Bourbon was alive Bodin was a genuine member of the League. For a man of Bodin's intricate conscience advice and legal representation of Navarre might not have been incompatible with criticism of his patron.

[27] See below, note 49.

loué qui nous a tous délivrez de la puissance d'un tyran fin et dangereux...
Nous pouvons bien louer Dieu et le remercier et admirer ses jugemens.' [28]
But the death of Henri III did not satisfy Bodin and in this and subsequent
letters he enlarged his prophetic denunciation of tyrants into a national jeremiad.
Convinced that God was intervening in the affairs of France Bodin now came
to welcome war as the instrument of divine vengeance on corrupt and evil
men. [29] It was to be, he prophesied, a seven year war and so far only two
of those years had elapsed.

> Mais je n'ose m'en resjouyr, ayant leu en la Bible que celui se resjouyt du
> malheur d'autruy, n'eschappe jamais le chastiment. C'est pourquoi Job protestait
> devant Dieu qu'il ne s'estoit jamais resjouy de la calamité de ses ennemiz. Et à
> dire vrai, nous avons encore de la guerre pour cinq ans, et verrons mourir la plus
> grande part des Princes et de la Noblesse, et les villes forcées des uns ou des
> autres, ou chastiées par leurs habitans mesmes. Car Dieu est descendu du Ciel
> pour faire Justice en terre, et enfin nous donner un Roi à son plaisir, et tel le sera
> qui ne l'espère pas, et ceux qui pensent y parvenir, n'y toucheront pas. [30]

While the League scarcely moved from its conception of religious war as a
crusade against heresy, Bodin now perceived war to be religious in the Hebraic
sense that it was inflicting divine retribution on all parties. [31]

God's intervention, Bodin believed, would bestow on France a king of his
own choosing and so rendered futile any human attempt to determine the
succession to the French throne by law or by arms. But Bodin did have
definite opinions on the laws governing succession even if he had little confidence in their validity in the face of divine wrath. The letter of August 1589
interprets the Salic law of succession in terms of degree of consanguinity
rather than primogeniture. [32] 'Or la loi salique', Bodin asserts, 'défère la

[28] Printed by Moreau-Reibel, 'Bodin', pp. 431-3. Although the editor (p. 429, n. 5)
appears to regard this as addressed to the same recipients as the succeeding letters it
seems much closer in spirit to that of March 1589 and is clearly addressed to a fellow
sympathizer with the League, perhaps Brisson again. ('J'ay ey peur que vostre ville
(Paris) ne fut contrainte par faute de vivres de capituler à dures conditions (to
Henri III)...'). For Jacques Clément as deliverer see Mousnier, Assassination, p. 214.

[29] For other participants in this mood see Baxter, 'Problems'.

[30] Moreau-Reibel, 'Bodin', p. 432. A letter to the Chevalier de la Mauvissière
(printed by Chauviré, Bodin, pp. 529ff.), dated 30 September 1585, remarks: 'Pas ung de
toutz ceux que les hommes ont élu, choisi et nommé ne touchera ny sceptre ny couronne
de France'. But this may be simply a repudiation of elective monarchy, rather than
a religious expression.

[31] For the League's conception of religious war see, e.g. the anonymous Le martel
en teste des catholiques françois (Paris, 1590): 'Où il s'agit de la religion contre les
hérétiques, il n'y a père, mère, frère, sœur, parens ny amis, qui doivent nous retenir'
(quoted by R. Schnur, Die französischen Juristen im konfessionellen Bürgerkrieg des 16.
Jahrhunderts (Berlin, 1962), pp. 14ff.).

[32] In so doing Bodin departed from a view earlier expressed in the République, VI,
5, p. 994. For a detailed explanation of this change of mind (evident in the Latin
De Republica of 1586) see my 'Bodin and the Bourbon Succession'. Cf. R. Giesey, The
Juristic Basis of Dynastic Right to the French Throne (Transactions of the American
Philosophical Society, N.S., LI, V) (Philadelphia, 1961), p. 31. F.J. Baumgartner, 'The
Case for Charles X', Sixteenth Century Journal, IV (1973), 87-98, at p. 96. Id. Radical
Reactionaries. The Political Thought of the French Catholic League (Geneva, 1976),
p. 166. Neither author has investigated the complexity of Bodin's thought on this topic.

couronne au plus proche et la représentation en succession collatérale n'a jamais lieu par les coustumes de France, ny de droit commun, que jusques aux enfans des frères'. [33]   By 'plus proche' Bodin means the claimant closest to the original joint ancestor (or genearch) of both the deceased king and the collateral house now succeeding.   By Bodin's count Navarre was fourteen degrees removed from Louis IX — the original genearch — but the cardinal Charles de Bourbon (Navarre's uncle) had a better claim in that he was only thirteen degrees removed.   Bodin sets aside the purely primogenitural argument by rejecting the legal fiction of representation.   (According to representation Navarre is deemed to represent his late father, Antoine de Bourbon, who had been the cardinal's elder brother and so had the right by primogeniture.) [34]

Navarre's claim was thereby overridden by the prior right of his uncle the cardinal de Bourbon, the uncrowned Charles X.   But Bodin realized, as did the cardinal himself, that the very argument which put Charles X on the throne also placed Navarre indisputably next in line of succession. [35]   Only by repudiating the crown could the cardinal have averted the rightful succession of his nephew and it was now too late for this.

> Mais je m'esmerveille pourquoi le conseil de l'union, et ceux qui possèdent le Cardinal de Bourbon, ne lui ont persuadé qu'il repudiât la Couronne. Car en ce faisant, il faisait place au duc de Montpensier et à son fils ... (le) Roi de Navarre ... ne peut toucher la couronne si premièrement le Cardinal de Bourbon ne l'appréhende qui sera pour trois jours peut estre qu'il a à vivre et asseurer la couronne au Roi de Navarre. [36]

[33] Moreau-Reibel, 'Bodin', p. 433.

[34] Curiously enough representation was also rejected by such protagonists as François Hotman on the Protestant side (Giesey, *Juristic Basis,* p. 35) and the foremost advocate of the League, Louis d'Orléans.   The latter's *Second avertissement des catholiques anglois aux françois catholiques* (Lyons, 1590) argued that Roman law lacked validity in France and consequently the device of representation which was based on the private Roman law of intestate inheritance (*Institutes,* III, 2, 5) was inadmissible.

[35] Cf. Baumgartner, 'Case for Charles X', who does not, however, examine Bodin's views very closely.
The cardinal himself is said to have recognized the rights of his nephew and to have protested that he agreed to the League's acclamation in order to protect the rights of the Bourbons.   Gambier, *Brisson,* p. 78, quotes Charles' remark that 'le roi de Navarre, mon neveu, cependant fera fortune, ce que je fais n'est que pour la conservation du droit de mon neveu'. See Nicholas de Villeroy, *Mémoires d'état 1574-1594,* in *Nouvelle collection des mémoires sur l'histoire de France depuis le XIIIᵉ siècle* (Paris, 1836-54), XI, 141.   In November 1589 Charles had sent a messenger to his nephew to recognize Navarre as king of France and exhort him to convert.   See E. Saulnier, *Le rôle politique du cardinal de Bourbon (Charles X) 1523-1590* (Paris, 1912), pp. 226ff. Some Leaguers such as Matteo Zampini (*De la succession du droict et prérogative du premier prince du sang de France* (Paris, 1588) might adopt degree of consanguinity as the principle of succession but at the same time exclude Navarre from the throne without saying who should in fact succeed the cardinal. Cf. Baumgartner, *Radical Reactionaries,* pp. 62ff.

[36] Moreau-Reibel, 'Bodin', p. 432. The possible right of duc François de Montpensier is based on the fact that he stands in the same degree of consanguinity as the cardinal.   The cardinal had first right over the crown being the elder (and not because he was descended from the senior house of Bourbon).   If the crown had not entered the house of Bourbon-Vendôme via the cardinal then it would have been contested anew between François and Navarre and the former, being senior by one degree, would have prevailed.   For this somewhat peculiar argument — but one that is consistent with Bodin's views on the laws of succession — see my 'Bodin and the Bourbon Succession'.

Navarre's eventual succession to the throne was *assured* by law. Nor was there any religious obstacle; Bodin makes no stipulation here that Catholicity is one of the fundamental laws governing the succession. In these respects Bodin was sharply at odds with the League. On the other hand his support of the primacy of the cardinal's claim was wholly unacceptable to Navarre who had been designated as heir — provided he convert — by Henri III on his death-bed. Bodin's answer to this nomination would have been (as it was in 1590) that the crown is not inheritable as private property by the disposition of the testator and that it is assigned according to the fundamental laws of succession. [37] Moreover, Bodin's reservations about Navarre's moral fitness to hold the crown continued for another two years as we shall see and allowed him to remain with the League for the time being. In 1589, therefore, Bodin might still be termed a sincere, if rather unsound, member of the Catholic League.

As to whether the legitimate claims of either the cardinal or Navarre would ever be respected in fact, Bodin was deeply sceptical. All his theorizing about the laws of succession was no more than an empty exercise in the face of God's entry into the arena. Human justice must give way to divine justice operating through war. Military might was in itself uncertain in the midst of this general chastisement in which Bodin himself shared.

> Et combien que nous soyons en haute montagne qui ne se peut miner, sapper ny battre, si est-ce que je prévoy que nous tomberons ez mains de noz ennemis, et qu'il faudra quitter ma maison, pour retourner à Paris achever mes jours. Car je ne vaux pas mieux que les autres qui sont chastiez. [39]

The idiosyncrasy of Bodin's character and ideas not surprisingly rendered him suspect in the eyes of the League at Laon. Richart remarks somewhat simplistically that 'il estoit bien cogneu en la ville pour ung politicque et dangereux catholique'. [40] In the excitable closing months of 1589 a Jesuit extremist, Antoine le Toulousain, conducted a personal vendetta against Bodin culminating in the latter's arrest on 20 January 1590. Although Bodin was freed soon after with a warning, the search of his house disclosed some dubious materials (including a genealogy of Henri IV, fortunately not in Bodin's hand) and his books, which threatened 'to draw the wrath of God within the town', were publicly burnt. [41] Some of his personal correspondence may also have

---

(The case of François' father the late duke Louis II comes up for discussion in the *Lettre* of 1590, pp. 13ff.)

The argument here, it should be noted, is purely hypothetical since once Charles de Bourbon had accepted the crown it could not be repudiated. Cf. the *Lettre* (1590), p. 15: 'Un droit souverain impérial ... qui se peut bien répudier, mais estant une fois accepter il ne se peut donner, quitter, céder ny transporter.' The crown is not a private inheritance at the disposal of the testator. See below, note 50.

[37] See previous note.

[38] Moreau-Reibel, 'Bodin', p. 433.

[39] *Ibid.*, p. 433.

[40] Richart, *Mémoires*, p. 68.

[41] *Ibid.*, pp. 228ff. Chauviré, *Bodin*, pp. 80ff. Bodin had previously been arrested in 1587 but that seems to have been the result of a purge of suspect Huguenot officials in royal service rather than because of his interests in magic or sorcery as Chauviré (p. 77) believed. See McRae, *Bodin ... Six Bookes*, introduction, p. Aii. (See above, note 5).

been seized and this might explain how the notorious *Lettre de M. Bodin* dated 20 January 1590 came to be published by the League printer Chaudière at Paris and elsewhere that same year. [42] To a sophisticated reader the *Lettre* seemed (like the preceding letter) to support the claims of the cardinal de Bourbon and Navarre at the same time and this contrivance, when published, might have served to discredit Bodin universally with the League, the *politiques* and the party of Henri IV. [43] To the uncritical reader, however, the *Lettre* might be useful propaganda since it showed a well known royalist and *politique* coming out in apparent support of the League's candidate. In this respect it certainly was a success to judge from the five editions it went through in the one year 1590. [44]

Evidently addressed to a *politique* and so to a different recipient than the two letters of 1589 the *Lettre de M. Bodin* is an extended apology for Bodin's support of the League. [45] It starts in an injured tone.

[42] Lindsay and Neu, *French Political Pamphlets*, No. 1674. Pallier, *Recherches sur l'imprimerie*, No. 654. Published by Chaudière, Paris; Pillehotte, Lyons; Moreau, Troyes; Colomiez, Toulouse; Velpius, Brussels. (All in 1590). Manuscript versions, none autograph, are in Bibliothèque Nationale, Paris, Ms. Français 4897, fols. 36-7v; Français 20153, fols. 459-464; suppl. Français 4255 (not seen); Dupuy 744, fols. 104-9.

H. Hauser, *Sources de l'histoire de France. XVIᵉ siècle* (4 vols., Paris, 1906-15), IV, 139f., doubted the authenticity of the bulk of the letter. While we have no way of knowing precisely how the League might have tampered with particular passages the text as a whole is in keeping with the mood, tone and opinions of Bodin's authentic correspondence.

I have not yet been able to undertake a full collation of the variants in the manuscript and printed versions because of difficulties in obtaining a microfilm of the text described as "Bibliothèque Nationale Paris, Ms. suppl. Français 4255 (ex-15222)", printed by E. de Barthélemy, *Etude sur Jean Bodin. Sa vie et ses travaux* (repr. Paris, 1876, *from the Annales de la Société Académique de Saint-Quentin*, ser. 3, t. XIII), pp. 47-52. This appears to conflate the various letters of 1589 and 1590 adding many new phrases and omitting several passages. Among the most important variants are: (1) The placing of the cardinal and Navarre respectively in the twenty-first and twenty-second degree of consanguinity (to Henri III?) as opposed to the thirteen and fourteen degrees in which they stand to Louis IX in the *Lettre*. (2) A variation of the passage on the Montpensier claim to the throne in which the duc (François) de Montpensier is now correctly stated to be younger than and in the same degree as the cardinal. On this claim see Appendix I to my 'Bodin and the Bourbon Succession'. (3) The introduction of a passage, very similar to one in the letter of August 1589 (see above, note 36), on the need for Navarre first to acknowledge the cardinal if he intends to establish his own subsequent right to the throne.

[43] K.D. McRae, 'The Political Thought of Jean Bodin's (unpublished Ph.D. thesis, Harvard, 1954), pp. 124ff., suggests that his enemies arranged the publication. Chauviré, *Bodin*, p. 82, thinks Bodin had to publish the *Lettre* to clear himself with the League. But it is clear from his private correspondence that it was published without his consent: 'Toutefois je me plains que l'on a publié des lettres à Paris sous mon nom sans que je sçay qu'elles portent...', letter of 1590-1, in Moreau-Reibel, 'Bodin', p. 434.

[44] Its admission of the right of Navarre to succeed the cardinal would scarcely have seemed good publicity for the League after the cardinal's death in May 1590.

[45] Not to Brisson, *pace* McRae, 'Political Thought of Bodin', p. 124, who seems to be following a note on the manuscript copy Ms. Dupuy 744, fol. 108v. Cf. Chauviré, *Bodin*, p. 83.

Note the reference at p. 5 to the unpublished book which Bodin hoped to show his correspondent. This was most likely the *Theatrum Naturae*. Cf. the mention of another unpublished book in a letter of 1595 to Roland Bignon, printed by Chauviré, *Bodin*, p. 534. (It is unlikely that Bignon was the recipient of the *Lettre* of 1590; he was a supporter of the League at that time).

Monsieur,

> Depuis trois iours, un de mes amis vous ayant visité, m'a rescript que vous
> estiez demeuré fort estonné de ce que i'estois Liguevr: & pour response ie vous
> diray que ie suis très aisé sçauoir que vous portiez bien. Et quant à la Ligue, ie
> ne vous sçaurois dire autre chose, sinon qu'estant dans une ville il est très-néces-
> saire, ou estre le plus fort, ou du party plus fort, ou ruyné du tout (p. 3).

Some have taken this brusque remark to be sufficient explanation for Bodin's
attachment to the League but the justifications that follow are far more
important. The first of these is *salus populi*, the principle which Bodin had
emphasized in the *Lettre d'un Lt-Général* of March 1589. He now explains the
particular circumstances governing his invocation of this principle. He had
maintained the cause of Henri III 'as much as the office I hold and honour
have permitted me'. He had delayed the taking of the oath at considerable
personal risk and it was only when 'the regiment of captain Bourg had been
on the verge of entering the city to kill, pillage and sack those called royalists'
that Bodin had abandoned the king finally.

> ie vous confesse ie passay carrière, me souvenant de la maxime tant vulgaire,
> qui dit que. Le salut du peuple est pour loy souveraine: ioinct qu'une nécessité
> forcée n'est iamais sujette à la recherche des Loix humaines. Et néanmoins nous
> sommes presque les derniers de deux cents bonnes villes, & sept Parlements qu'il
> y a en France, qui avons entre ouuertement au party qu'on appelle La saincte
> Union des Catholiques (pp. 3-4).

Although Bodin's scruples had inhibited him from rebelling against the king
for so long, once it was forced on him Bodin became wholly and religiously
convinced of the rightfulness of the League's revolution. He realized now
that God was intervening in the crisis, had withdrawn His grace from Henri III
and was now inflicting general retribution on the French.

> Mais après auoir le tout bien & meurement consideré, je trouve que c'est icy
> un vray iugement de Dieu; qui n'est point seulement pour mon particulier; qui puis
> auoir meffait comme estant homme: mais général pour toute la France, qui a com-
> mencé aux plus grands Princes, & continuera tant & savant qu'il n'y aura ville,
> place ny chasteau, bourgade ny village: qui ne soit chastié des uns ou des autres;
> & quant & quand remply de séditions, massacres, querelles & inimitiez intestines:
> & dupuis les plus grands iusques aux plus petits chacun fera chastié en sa per-
> sonne, ou en ses biens, & moy, peut estre, des premiers: car ie ne vaux pas mieux
> que les autres. Et préuoy que cette ville (encor que elle ne se puisse battre que
> mal-aisément à force de canon, & qu'elle soit hors de la sappe, mine & escallades)
> néantmoins elle est pour estre prise, & tumber entre les mains de nos ennemis:
> & de ma part, ie souffriray patiemment la perte de mon Estat, & de mes biens,
> voire de ma vie; pourveu que je puisse seruir au public (pp. 4-5).

The chastisement of war will last seven years and only then will God grant
France a king of His own choosing, not men's.

> Que ie préuoy que cette guerre ne finira de cinq ans, & que la plupart de la
> noblesse y tumbera: & que les forces du Royaume seront tellement affaiblies &
> diminuées; que chacun s'en esbahira: & en fin Dieu, qui tousiours a aymé ce
> Royaume & ne l'habandonnera point, nous donnera un Roy à son plaisir, tout
> autre que les hommes ne pensent. Ce que ie dissemble peut estre un songe, &
> toutes fois ie préuoy que ce sera, peut estre, un oracle & prophétie, d'autant que

206

mon opinion est fondée en grand iugement & raison: laquelle donne loy a toutes choses. Et pour confirmer mon opinion, l'ay'apperceu par la connoissance des histoires tant sacrées que prophanes, que les grands & notables changemens des Empires, Royaumes & Monarchies, se font en cinq ou six ans, le septiesme estant le nombre sacré, mystic & diuin, auquel le repos & la tranquilité se donne: à fin que l'homme n'entre en désespoir, & qu'il ne perde courage, & qu'il trouve relasché en ses misères. L'année passée que commencèrent les Barricades fut la première, cette-cy est la seconde, qui a estè plus rude que la précédente: & toutesfois ce n'a este que jeu au prix des autres qui suyvront, lesquelles seront horribles, estranges, & merveilleuses (pp. 5-6).

Peace before the lapse of five more years is impossible because the protagonists are so inutterably opposed both in religion and politics, but in any case, God is now taking a hand.

> Vous me direz; la Paix se fera: les Princes s'accorderont: cela ne se peut espèrer; car les prétendans, les Chefs & les partisans sont appointez contraires, tant en l'Estat qu'en la Religion; qu'en leurs mœurs, façon & inclinaisons: & ne se peuvent aucunement accorder, à parler naturellement, car Dieu est par dessus, & en fera comme il luy plaira (p. 6). [46]

The central portion of the *Lettre* of 1590 clarifies Bodin's thinking on two major aspects of the French succession. Namely, the principle governing collateral succession to the crown and the need for the king to be Catholic. The earlier letter of 15 August 1589 had sketched Bodin's view on the fundamental law of succession but now he elaborates the case (pp. 10-15). [47] Bodin here clearly and firmly interprets the Salic law in terms of degree of consanguinity to the ancestral king and this argument brings the cardinal to the throne.

> Puis la Loy du Royaume défère la Couronne à la plus proche maison venant en directe ligne de la race des Roys. Et ceste coustume est conforme à la loy de Dieu: et a esté suivie et approuvée par la loy des douze tables. Or est il que Monseigneur le Cardinal de Bourbon, à compter depuis le Roy Sainct Loys, se trouve descendu par son fils Robert de France Conte de Clermont, du quel est venue la branche de Bourbon, à prendre de père à fils, au treiziesme degré: et le Roy de Navarre au quatorziesme, et partant plus esloigné d'un degré. Et d'autant que chacun y vient de son Chef, et que la Couronne n'a iamais déférée à la maison de Bourbon, sinon maintenant: Et que le feu Roy de Navarre estant mort du vivant du Roy Charles, n'y eut iamais aucun droict pour le transmettre à son fils: sans aucune difficulté par la loy du Royaume (comme i'ay dict) la Couronne appartient à Monseigneur le Cardinal de Bourbon, et n'en peut estre frustré que par l'usurpation et violence, contraire à la loy, et reprouvée de Dieu et des hommes.... (pp. 9-10).

Navarre must claim in his own right (*de son chef*) and he may not claim to represent his dead father Antoine de Bourbon. In any case representation has little or no place in the fundamental law of succession to the crown and to pretend so, 'cela est induire une nouvelle Iurisprudence' (p. 10). Neither

[46] Note the similarity of these phrases to the concluding paragraph of the letter of 15 August 1589.

[47] For details see my 'Bodin and the Bourbon Succession'.

is it permissible in cases of direct succession as Charlemagne's exclusion of his grandson Bernard of Italy (child of his deceased elder son) in favour of his younger son Louis the Pious shows (pp. 11-12). As far as collateral succession is concerned representation has an extremely limited validity and applies even in Roman law only to cases where the relationship of the claimant to the deceased is below the tenth degree. [48] Therefore, 'faut par nécessité que chacun y vienne de son chef sans se pouvoir aucunement ayder de représentation' (pp. 12-13).

This argument might make the cardinal the legitimate king of France but it would also, as Bodin had taken for granted in his letter of the previous August, place Navarre next in line for the throne. Now Bodin almost openly admits Navarre's right to succeed when he admits that all the latter has to do is first recognize his aged uncle's prior right and then himself rejoin the Catholic church. [49]

> Par ainsi le Roy de Navarre, quelque bon conseil et subtil qu'il puisse avoir, est à mon iugement mal fondé, et trèsmal conseillé, qu'il ne reconnoist Monseigneur le Cardinal de Bourbon pour Roy. Car advenant qu'il luy eust faict repudier son droict par force, pour ces raisons que nous avons dict cy dessus, il n'y auroit rien, et cela retourneroit à d'autre. [50] Au contraire s'i lle faisoit couronner Roy et se gouvernast sagement, montrant avoir affection au bien et déffense de cette Couronne: et faisant publique profession de la Religion Catholique, de bonne foy et sans fraude, pourroit attirer à foy la bien veillance des Princes, provinces, et villes Catholiques: et s'estant reconcilié à l'Englise, et faict absoudre des censures Ecclésiastiques par nostre S. Père, et faisant acte de bon et vray

[48] *Lettre de M. Bodin,* p. 13: 'Car comme princes descendus de la maison de France, toute leur parenté qui de l'estoc paternel passoit le dixiesme degré....' (Referring to the Roman law of intestate inheritance, *Institutes of Justinian,* III, 2, 5; III, 5, 5). Giesey, *Juristic Basis*, pp. 24ff., points out that in collateral lines representation was limited to three degrees of consanguinity. This certainly seems to be the case with French law as Bodin saw it. In both the letter of August 1589 and the *Lettre* of 1590 Bodin limits representation to the sole case of a nephew succeeding an uncle. The relationship here, counting from the nephew through his father to the grandfather and thence to the uncle, is in the third degree.

It should be noted that Bodin counts his degrees of consanguinity from the ancestral king or genearch to the claimant ('à prendre de père à fils', p. 10). Thus between Louis IX and Navarre Bodin reckons fourteen degrees. On the other hand Roman civil law counts the degrees between the immediately deceased king and the claimant. If applied to the present case this wouuld place more than twenty degrees between Henri III and Navarre.

[49] So convincing was Bodin's advocacy of the fundamental law of succession that Chauviré (*Bodin,* p. 86) regarded this letter as evidence that Bodin was an unrepentant *politique* and took it merely as an oblique encouragement of Navarre's claim to the throne ('une apologie hypocrite de la Ligue'). In truth Bodin was still a faithful, though circumscribed, adherent of the League. Indeed after the death of Henri III the League's cause became better founded in his mind by virtue of the fact that it was no longer a revolt against the king but rather a movement fighting in support of the new legitimate king Charles X. See the *Lettre* o. 1590, p. 16: 'Vous voyez donc maintenant, Monsieur, que la cause de l'union est mieux fondée que vous ne pensiez, encores qu'on vueille dire que de commencement elle estoit malfondée à cause de la rebellion pretendue contre son Roy....' See below, notes 58, 72 and 83.

[50] A repudiated inheritance might have gone not to Navarre but to the house of Bourbon-Montpensier. However, Bodin was speaking hypothetically about the *late* duke Louis II de Montpensier as the heir of the cardinal (pp. 13ff). (See above, note 36).

Catholique, *asseureroit* par ce moyen l'Estat de sa maison après le décèds de son Oncle âgé de soixante et sept ans, lequel auiourd'huy il détient iniustement en captivité (p. 15).

Although Bodin and the League agreed on the need to have a Catholic king it seems hardly likely that their reasoning was the same. At the Estates of Blois in 1576 the League had proclaimed Catholicity as the fundamental law of the French crown. Catholicity was indeed elevated to become the *principal* law governing succession, and later Leaguer writers such as Louis d'Orléans asserted that even the Salic Law yielded to the law of Deuteronomy which barred the godless and heretical from royal office.[51] In 1588 the current Estates of Blois insisted that Catholicity be made a formal 'loi fondamental et irrévocable' and the League's Edict of Union in the same year enshrined the principle 'pour loy inviolable et fondamentale de cestuy nostre royaume'.[52]

Did Bodin subscribe to this notion? Certainly not before 1589. At the first Estates of Blois in 1576 he had actually led the opposition to the League.[53] Moreover, subsequent editions of the *République* stipulate only three *lois royales ou impériales*, i.e. the Salic Law of succession, the indivisibility of sovereignty and the inalienability of royal demesne.[54] Nor does there appear to have been any basic change after 1589. The letters of 1589-90 are careful to avoid speaking of Catholicity as fundamental crown law and make Navarre's conversion more a matter of prudence and custom than of law.

> Quant à la Iustice et bonté de la cause (*de la Ligue*): qui doute que les Catholiques ne soient en possession depuis tantost seize cents ans? N'est-ce pas assez pour prescrire, quand l'on voudroit débattre leurs tiltres de nullité? Ne sont ils pas bien fondez en l'interdict commun? Et qui sont les Iuges non suspects, qui ne donnent arrest à leur proffict, et qui ne dient (*sic*) que pendant la vuidange du procez ils ne doivent estre troublez? Ie dis mesme par la confession du Roy de Navarre, qui se submet (par apparence) au iugement de l'Eglise, et consent de passer par l'advis d'un Concile libre (p. 9).[55]

This prudential argument for Catholicity was widespread among *politiques* and royalists. Henri III on his deathbed had recognized Navarre as his

---

[51] *Introduction des gens des troys estats* (Blois, 1577). The basis of this view was the promise in the coronation oath to protect the Church. Cf. Baumgartner, *Radical Reactionaries*, pp. 56ff., 67 ff.

[52] F. Isambert, *Recueil général des anciennes lois françaises depuis l'an 420 jusqu'à la révolution de 1789* (20 vols., Paris, 1821-33), XIV, 618, 630.

[53] Jean Bodin, *Recueil de tout ce qui s'est negotié en la compagnie du Tiers Estate de France... Blois... 1576* (Sine loco, 1577).

[54] *République*, I, 8. Cf. A. Lemaire, *Les lois fondamentales de la monarchie française d'après les théoriciens de l'ancien régime* (Paris, 1907), pp. 114ff.

[55] I am unable to agree with Baumgartner, *Radical Reactionaries*, pp. 165ff., when he claims that 'it is clear that Bodin was persuaded to join the League largely on the basis of the fundamental law of Catholicity. He accepted the necessity of the League to defend Catholicism'. There is no evidence that Bodin regarded Catholicity as a fundamental law whereas he certainly agreed with the League's support of Charles X on the ground that this was in keeping with the fundamental law of succession. The legitimacy of Charles X seems to have been the critical factor in Bodin's committing himself to the League *in good conscience*.

successor *provided* he convert. Navarre himself later acknowledged the force of the case for conversion in July 1593, so opening the way for his coronation the following year and eventual religious peace. *Politiques* in Bodin's own circle subscribed to the need for conversion. Du Vair in late 1592 urged the League to accept Navarre if he convert; [56] Bodin's close friend, the Angevin advocate Pierre Ayrault (1520-1604), urged unconditional recognition of Henri IV but at the same time hoped the king would convert 'for the sake of honour and utility'. [57] Although Bodin's arguments about succession and religion put him on the side of the League in 1590 his views were not really so out of tune with *politique* feeling as might seem. For Bodin's position assured the succession of Navarre, preserved legitimacy and, without admitting Catholicity as a new fundamental law, argued that the king must convert if he were to put an end to the wars of religion. Well might he reassure his *politique* correspondent: 'Vous voyez donc maintenant, Monsieur, que la cause de l'Union est mieux fondée que vous ne pensiez'. [58]

Bodin might think that Navarre had the right to succeed but would he in fact ever do so? As in the earlier letter of August 1589 Bodin is sceptical that human notions of legitimacy have any validity in this divinely inflicted war. Bodin saw as clear evidence of God's intervention the assassination of Henri III.

> la mort duquel non précogitée par iugement humain, ains venant de la main de Dieu, qui use de son bras droict contre les Roys et Princes, quand ils se mesconnoissent; faict plus qu'entière preuve du mérite de ses actions: et monstre que sa vie passée a esté peu agréable à la Majeste divine. Car la Loy de Dieu dict en paroles expresses ; *Tu ne tueras point, et quiconque prendra le glaive, perira par le glaive.* Cela est verifié en luy (p. 16) ... l'adiusteray ce qu'on m'a faict souvenir que i'avois dict en plaine table l'année passée, que le Roy n'eschaperoit pas l'année (p. 17).

Natural prophecy too had forewarned Bodin of Henri's fall:

> l'auois aussi escript en ma République que non seulement aux Monarchies & Royaumes l'année 63. estoit climatérique: mais aussi pour le regard de la personne des Princes. Et que ie feu Roy estoit à conter depuis Pharamond iusques à luy el soixante & troisiesme en ordre. Le Roy qui estoit Prince curieux, & qui vouloit tout sçauoir, comme iadis le Roy Loys onziesme, (des humeurs duquel il tenoit beaucoup) auoit leu mon livre, à ce que m'a dict un grand Seigneur de ce Royaume portant tiltre de Mareschal de France: adioustant qu'il auoit bien remarqué ce passage, mais qu'il se mocquoit de tout cela, & qu'il espèroit finir ses iours en repos, ne se souciant de successeur nonplus que l'Empereur Neron, qui désiroit après sa mort que le Ciel & la terre veinssen a se mesler pesle-mesle: ce qu'il a bien monstré en seize ans qu'il a esté Roy.... (pp. 17-18). [59]

---

[56] *Exhortation à la paix adressée à ceux de la Ligue*, in Guillaume Du Vair, *Actions et traictez oratoires*, ed. R. Radouant (Paris, 1911), pp. 63ff. Cf. Radouant, *Guillaume Du Vair*, pp. 282ff.

[57] Pierre Ayrault, *Supplication et advis au roy de se faire catholique* (Angers, 1591). (Bibl. Nat., Ms. Dupuy 317). Cf. Radouant, *Du Vair*, pp. 292ff. A. Cioranesco, *Bibliographie de la littérature française du seizième siècle* (Paris, 1959), p. 98. A letter of 1595 from Bodin to Ayrault is printed by Chauviré, *Bodin*, pp. 532ff.

[58] *Lettre* of 1590, p. 16. See above note 49 for quotation.

[59] Cf. *Lettre d'un Lt. Général*, p. 8. Chauviré, *Bodin*, pp. 85ff.

Henri III had bequeathed only misery to France. Like Caligula he had pillaged the treasury and squandered his resources running up a debt of 20 *millions d'or* to the city of Paris alone. From this legacy 'nous ne pouvons espérer que pauvreté et famine' (p. 18). It is a misery compounded by the disputed succession. The legitimate king Charles is held prisoner by his nephew Navarre while Mayenne proclaims himself lieutenant-general of the Royal State and Crown of France. 'Il n'y a que Dieu qui sçache sur le chef de quel Prince doibt tumber la Couronne pour y demeurer. Ie ne voy pas par iugement humain que l'un ny l'autre l'emporte s'il ne se faict autre chose' (pp. 18-19).

The cardinal de Bourbon died in May 1590 so rendering Navarre the legitimate claimant according to Bodin's logic yet the remaining three manuscript letters of the correspondence seem to avoid the topic of the succession altogether and no mention is made of Henri IV. [60] Why? The answer may be found in the intensified prophetic mood which characterizes these later letters and results in Bodin's treating the succession entirely as a matter of divine will. Arguments as to legitimacy now seem wholly marginal and irrelevant to the real crux of the matter — divine intervention. At the same time these letters mark a new phase in Bodin's relations with the League. His earlier justifications for supporting the League have successively disappeared; Henri III had died, then the cardinal de Bourbon. What is left now is no longer a justification of the League but rather a justification of war itself. War is God's chastisement of Leaguer and royalist evildoers alike; as the outpouring of divine vengeance this war cannot be settled by human alliances, no matter how strong. 'La victoire dépend de Dieu, qui sans doubte, monstrera un tour de sa main puisqu'il y va de la Religion et chastiera ceux qui de la part ou d'autre couvent (*sic*) leurs ambitions et voleries du voile de Religion.' [61]

In an undated letter to a Leaguer written after January 1590 Bodin gives free rein to his prophetic vision almost exulting in war as divine justice:

> Si est-ce et je prie Dieu tous les jours qu'il lui plaise ruiner tous ses ennemis parce qu'il n'y a que lui seul qui les puisse bien connoistre. En quoi faisant les siens vivront en paix quelques jours après qu'il aura chastié les uns par els autres, comme il dit. *Ulciscar inimicos meos per inimicos meos.* Car jamais il n'a fait plus belle Justice qu'il fait à présent: qui fait que les villes superbes qui estoient fondues à toutes sortes de voluptez, se réduisent au petit pied. Et ceux que jamais n'ont voulu jeusnez volontairement, maintenant, ils y jeusnent par force, et ceux qui n'ont jamais fait aumosne, le demandent. Bref, tous les juges de France ne sçauroyent juger tant de coupables de mort que la guerre en fera mourir en quattre ou cinq ans comme je voy par chacun jour. [62]

There is a sense in this letter of the weakness of human peace. 'Vray est que j'estime bien qu'il se fera une paix fourrée qui ne sera pas de longue durée,

[60] I am aware that this silence may be accidental. Unlike the two printed letters none of these manuscript letters is intended to give an extensive account of Bodin's thinking.

[61] Moreau-Reibel, 'Bodin', p. 434.

[62] Printed by Moreau-Reibel, 'Bodin,, pp. 433ff. and datable to after February 1590 by the reference to letters of Bodin's (presumably the *Lettre de M. Bodin*) recently published without authorization at Paris.

non plus et encore moins que les dix traictez faits depuis trente ans', says Bodin. [63]   Only God's peace is secure and that will come only after God's justice has been done through seven years of God's war. [64]   Justice, war and peace are thus bound up with one another in Bodin's mind.

The harshness is considerably softened in the next letter of 7 November 1591.   War and the *calamité si générale* have assuaged Bodin's prophetic anger; the cry of vengeance has now turned to lament and hope for a peace which will not come soon:

> Mais il me semble que ce n'est pas une guerre, ains une rage civile, de vouloir assiéger villes en hyver, hyverner ez compaignes, camper sans pavillons, estant tout le plat pays pillé, brûlé, saccagé, pour affamer aisément une armée ou la voir périr de froidures, pluyes et famines.   Telles gens qui prennent tant de peine à se ruiner en nous ruinants ne seront pas fort pleurez ... la guerre continue encor deux ans, comme je ne voy pas que nous puissions jouir d'une paix asseurée, le reste de la noblesse françoise sera bien petit.

As a citizen of Laon Bodin was still a Leaguer [65] but it now seemed to him only a matter of time before God put an end to such factions as the League by bestowing a king of peace upon France.

> La France sera en danger d'estre en proye aux estrangers.   Car le françois est mal propre à faire et entretenir ligues, et incompatible avec les Aristocraties et Democraties.   C'est pourquoi je tiens pour tout asseuré que Dieu nous donnera un Roi paisible de son estat dedans deux ans.   Je prévoy bien qu'on parlera de la paix sur la fin de cette année et commencement de l'autre, mais l'exécution ne se pourra faire si tost.   Toutefois, je prie Dieu que je soy trouve menteur. [66]

It is clear from this letter that Bodin had serious reservations about the League's conduct on the ground that it seemed likely to provoke a foreign invasion of a weakened France. [67]   The brutal execution of Bodin's old friend Brisson by the Sixteen of Paris eight days after this letter was written must have shaken Bodin and alarmed him about the democratic excesses arising out of the League.   More than ever the restoration of royal power and with it peace seemed imperative.   The last letter of the correspondence, dated 12 January 1593, no longer dwells on retribution but rather on the expectancy of peace through a king sent by God:

> Il y a tantost cinq ans, ou quoi que soit, c'est la 5e annee de noz guerres civiles laquelle j'ay predite et préveu nous devoir apporter notable changement par la paix comme je m'assure qu'il aviendra devant la fin d'icelle, qu'il *faudra ployer ou rompre*.   Et en ceste asseurance, je prieray Dieu qu'il dispose des armées et des

---

[63] Moreau-Reibel, 'Bodin', p. 434.

[64] Bodin stands by his earlier predictions of a seven-year war.   'Nous en avons eschappé un an, qui n'est que jeu.   Car les quatre ans qui restent à mon avis serait (sic) bien plus fascheux à passer', in Moreau-Reibel, 'Bodin, p. 434.

[65] For the *Lex Solonis* see below.

[66] Moreau-Reibel, 'Bodin', p. 435f.

[67] For the foreign threat see Yardeni, *Conscience nationale en France.*

212

victoires, des sceptres et couronnes, qu'il luy plaise nous donner sa paix très heureuse... [68]

Six months later Henri IV rejoined the Catholic church and February 1594 saw his coronation. In March 1594 Paris was taken by the king; the following month Bodin finally fled Laon. Closely besieged by the king the extreme Leaguers of Laon surrendered only in August 1594. By 1596, the seventh year of God's war, the religious wars were at an end.

The League letters of Bodin register the evolution of his political and religious thinking on war. In 1589 Bodin had welcomed the League's prosecution of what he saw as a just war against the tyrant Henri III. By 1590 Bodin was rather understanding war as a divine revenge unleashed on the impieties of the French. But by 1593 the tone of the correspondence was being softened by increasing expectations of peace. The purgative efficiency of the war had run its course. This changing perception of war was paralleled by shifts in the mood of the letters after 1591 from vengeance to lament, from retribution to fear and desolation, from the prophetic acclaim of war to pity and exhaustion.

Bodin's support of the League came in for a good deal of criticism among some *politiques* at the time and his subsequent critics have for the most part been scarcely less severe. The historian de Thou remarked that 'considering he was once a Protestant and never far from that doctrine Bodin acted with unworthy levity in publicly persuading the people of Laon to take the oath to the League'; [69] Guy Patin saw the matter more harshly, remarking that Bodin 'became a Leaguer for fear of losing his office'. [70] For the nineteenth-century biographer Baudrillart Bodin's adherence to the League was 'contrary to all his principles' and the whole matter was 'a regrettable episode' in which 'the *fonctionnaire* aligned himself for a moment with the party of Mayenne; the philosopher and, except for this short eclipse, the public man, were always on the side of rationality and toleration'. [71] The subsequent biography by Chauviré took a more sympathetic view of the affair but still concluded that Bodin was acting all along against his conscience: Bodin remained a royalist and *politique* whose relations with the League were governed by fear and prudence and whose 'conscience yielded momentarily, and with regret, to circumstances'. [72]

[68] Moreau-Reibel, 'Bodin', p. 436. Cf. C. Vivanti, *Lotta politica e pace religiosa in Francia fra cinque e seicento* (Turin, 1963) on hopes for a king of peace. In discussing Bodin Vivanti (pp. 64ff.) concentrates on the *Heptaplomeres* and does not consider the problem of Bodin's membership of the League.

[69] Jacques-Auguste de Thou, *Historiarum sui temporis libri CXX (1543-1607)* (7 vols., London, 1733), IV, 641 f., 698.

[70] Quoted by Chauviré, *Bodin*, p. 88.

[71] H. Baudrillart, *Jean Bodin et son temps* (Paris, 1853), pp. 131-5.

[72] Chauviré, *Bodin*, pp. 78ff., 85-8. Thus the *Lettre* of 1590 becomes 'une apologie hypocrite de la Ligue' published by Bodin to save himself. See above, note 49. Chauviré considerably softens the strictures of Richart. Most modern writers seem to accept the argument from fear, e.g. J.W. Allen, *A History of Political Thought in the Sixteenth Century* (repr. London, 1957), p. 397. Franklin, *Bodin and Absolutist Theory*, p. 97 n. See below.

Though sounding plausible and containing some truth these arguments from fear and expediency are too simple to explain the complexity of Bodin's feelings about the League and completely miss the sincerity of his allegiance — even if that sincerity were temporary and that allegiance always limited. [73] The private correspondence of 1589-94 makes it clear beyond the shadow of a doubt that Bodin was a convinced supporter of the League; the question therefore, one should be asking, is not whether Bodin was sincere in supporting the League but rather how he persuaded himself to join it in good conscience, how his reasons changed with political developments, and whether or not his new allegiance signified a reversal of previously held principles.

The two letters of 1589 show that Bodin's conclusion that God had forsaken Henri III originally permitted him to join the League in good conscience. After the initial commitment had been made Bodin always found a good reason for remaining with the League. Henri III might be removed from the scene in the summer of 1589 but then Bodin found himself agreeing with the League's support of the legitimate king Charles X. After the cardinal's death in May 1590 a fatalistic acceptance of seven years of civil war inflicted as divine vengeance on France meant that there was little point in supporting Navarre, especially considering that the new king was far from being without sin himself and could never be accepted by the nation as long as he remained a Huguenot. There was, therefore, always a religious, if not a specifically Catholic, dimension to Bodin's perception of the League and, indeed, his opinions revolved around his constantly prophetic sensibility. In 1589 this sensibility took the form of an Elijah-like indignation at the new Ahab and Nero, Henri III; thereafter it changed into a different prophetic mode, keyed to a vision of universal punishment by war.

What was the citizen of Laon to do amidst these divine vicissitudes? Should Bodin have fled the city in 1589 as the moralistic Richart (who himself stayed on comfortably and unobtrusively) judged? [74] In the first year of the

[73] Recent attempts by Baldwin ('Bodin and the League', *loc. cit.*), Giesey (*Juristic basis*, pp. 30ff.) and Baumgartner (*Radical Reactionaries*, pp. 65ff.) to argue that Bodin's Catholicism made him a sincere supporter of the League seem to be as simplistic as efforts to argue from expediency. The only account which seems to sense the complexity of the issue is that of Moreau-Reibel ('Bodin et la Ligue') although he does not closely analyse the correspondence.

[74] Richart, *Mémoires*, p. 230 (the second p. 230 in the mispagination), remarks: '... il luy eust mieux par son honneur sortir la ville au commencement de ces guerres comme feirent beaucoup d'aultres de sa qualité sans nager entre deux eaues comme il penssoit faire où il a perdu tout l'honneur et la réputation qu'il s'estoit acquis de long-temps....'
Richart was convinced that Bodin had gone against his conscience (p. 68): 'De Bodin il demeura seul sans fréquentation de personne, combien qu'en sa harangue il se fust efforcé de monstrer son affection à la Ligue en foullant aux piedz devant tous vraiz françois les droictz et auctoritez des estatz de France, mais en vain, car il estoit bien congneu en la ville pour ung politicque et dangereux catholicque, dont c'est une chose très vraie que les hommes saiges n'ont pas tousjours une discrétion ou jugement par-faict. De quoy il est nécessaire que souvent se demonstrèrent des signes de la faiblesse de l'entendement humain tel qu'il feit à ceste église cathédralle où il uza des parolles assez mal sonnantes que je ne veulx réciter. Ceste acte lui donna une grande tâche entre les gens d'honneur, il luy sembla ses parolles estre propres pour se rendre (contre sa conscience) plus agréable aux ligueurs à s'estendre ainsy par trop en sa harangue

war Bodin felt that his duty as an officer of the crown obliged him to remain in the hope of rescuing the prestige of the monarchy by dissociating it from the criminal king. But why did Bodin not take flight after 1590 when the city was in revolt against the new legitimate king Henri IV? A curious remark in the *Lettre* of 1590 has been seized upon by some commentators intent on seeing Bodin's conduct as dictated entirely by fear and self-preservation:

> Et quant à la Ligue, ie ne vous sçaurois dire autre chose, sinon qu'estant dans une ville il est très nécessaire, ou estre le plus fort, ou du party du plus fort, ou ruyné du tout. [75]

In fact the superficial frankness of this statement conceals a deeply held moral belief in the necessity of taking sides in a civil war. In the *République* Bodin had attached the greatest importance to the ancient *Lex Solonis* which compelled all citizens to take sides during civil war and disorder rather than flee or remain neutral. This law, says Bodin, may seem unjust but it is absolutely necessary and must be obeyed even if both sides are in the wrong. Neutral men are able, like the priests of Mars, to stir up contention between factions and the purpose of the law is to prevent such men fishing in troubled waters. In any event, the unaligned citizen, like Theramenes in the Peloponnesian War, has no support and is likely to be turned on by both sides. [76] This seems to be the principle of political conduct underlying Bodin's superficially blatant statement of 1590, a statement that is actually elliptical and cryptic.

Such a state of mind was shared by Bodin's own friends and acquaintances caught in other cities dominated by the League. Brisson and Du Vair stayed on in rebel lious Paris and the latter also invoked the law of Solon which prevented the citizen withdrawing from the midst of civil disorder. [77] Du

au mespris de son Roy, et comme depuis il feit encores à une response qu'il signa en ung exploit d'un huissier ainsy qu'il sera dict cy apres, mais pour tout cela Bodin non fut davantage emploié aux affaires publicques, les ligueurs se servans de lui seullement comme d'un baston à ruer aux noix. Voila doncq Bodin demeure seul à faire comme on dict des chasteaux en Espagne.'

[75] *Lettre* (1590), p. 3. Allen, *History*, p. 397, comments that 'there is little need to search for other reasons for his unheroic and very excusable conduct'.

[76] *République*, IV, 7. The Latin version greatly elaborates the remarks at pp. 655f. of the French edition of 1583. For an English translation of the Latin text of 1586 see Bodin, *Six Bookes of a Commonweale*, pp. 536-40: 'By this means the conscience of an honest man is forced to take either the one or other part, when perhaps he thinks both naught, and that they are both in the wrong.... In brief, the law of God (*Deuteronomy*) forbids him that knows the truth to follow the common opinion of them which are out of the way, whereunto Solon's law seems to repugn in forcing a man to take either the one part or the other, although that they both be naught.' Bodin seems to let the anti-nomy stand. But he does assert that religious conscience is not a sufficient reason for rebellion (*Six Bookes*, pp. 539f., quoted below at note 87). It should be emphasized that Bodin's advocacy of the *Lex Solonis* did not mean that he encouraged civil war and factions (*Six Bookes*, p. 519). But once war had broken out then sides must be taken. His views in this respect parallel those on rebellion and revolution; once a rebellion became a successful revolution it should be accepted as a fait accompli. See above, note 15.

[77] Du Vair, *Constance*, bk. III. Cf. Radouant, *Guillaume Du Vair*, pp. 196ff, 266f. Michel de Castelnau-Mauvissière (1520-92) also advocated a policy of conciliation without neutrality. Mauvissière and Bodin were friendly during these last years at Laon and some of their correspondence is printed in Chauviré, *Bodin*, pp. 529ff. Curiously enough Giordano Bruno had been an intimate associate of Mauvissière at the London embassy

Vair and Bodin both knew that if they openly took the royalist side they would simply be destroyed to no purpose. They could not remain neutral like Theramenes, nor did the law of Solon allow them to take flight. Only by staying on could they hope to 'slacken the violence cunningly'. [78] Yet when the time was ripe both men took decisive action. Du Vair spoke out at great risk against the League's involvement with Spain. [79] Bodin for his part left Laon to join the now converted and legitimate king Henri IV who was advancing on the city; changed political circumstances meant that Bodin was no longer fleeing civil war within Laon, but was rather declaring himself for the king's side in the civil war in France. This option had not been open to Bodin in 1589 given the general revolution against the impious — and in any case remote — Henri III. Nor was Bodin's flight an easy decision; it involved real risk to his house, books and property which he left behind at the Leaguers' mercy. Such a strong royalist and anti-Leaguer as Ayrault did not allow the events of 1589-94 to damage his close friendship with Bodin and one should be wary of rushing to moral judgements on Bodin's conduct in these years and ascribing it to self-interest or cowardice. Certainly the complex and unique attitudes of Bodin, Brisson and Du Vair and other such 'moderates' suggest the danger of using fixed labels like *politique, ligueur* or *royaliste* to denote the states of mind current in the confused and volatile situation of 1589-94.

This attempted justification of Bodin might seem to be special pleading of the kind precisely to confirm Bodin's slipperiness and lack of principle in joining the League. One may not deny, for instance, that events in Laon affected his behaviour; had he lived in a royalist town there is little doubt that Bodin would have been an open supporter of Henri IV from at least May 1590 when the cardinal died if not before. But whatever political expediency triggered his support of the League there can be no doubt that Bodin was also acting at the same time in accord with deep personal convictions. Bodin did believe sincerely in some of the League's programme though for reasons other than those advanced by his fellow members; his adherence to the League was always circumscribed by political and religious principles quite his own.

while the latter was ambassador to England (1575-85) and dedicated *Cena delle Ceneri* and *De l'Infinito Universo* to his host. It is, however, doubtful whether Bruno and Bodin ever met. Cf. G. Hubault, *Michel de Castelnau, ambassadeur en Angleterre (1575-85)* (St. Cloud, 1856, repr. 1970), pp. 139ff. F.A. Yates, *John Florio. The Life of an Italian in Shakespeare's England* (Cambridge, 1934), pp. 61-76, 90ff. Idem, *Giordano Bruno and the Hermetic Tradition* (London, 1964), pp. 203f, 229, 235, 245, 254, 292. It was through intercepted correspondence between Mauvissière and Mary, Queen of Scots, that Walsingham learned of the Babington Plot in 1586. Bodin was suspected of involvement because he had prophesied the death of the English queen and his arrest was demanded by Walsingham. No doubt the secretary had become apprised of Bodin's predictions through correspondence between Bodin and Mauvissière. See McRae, 'Political Thought', pp. 116f who cites *Calendar of State Papers, Venetian 1581-91* (Public Record Office), No. 407; *Calendar of State Papers, Foreign 1586-88,* (P.R.O.), p. 94.

[78] See above, note 20. Contrast the case of Pierre Charron who also initially embraced the League and then moved to the side of Henri IV. In later years Charron regretted his conduct. He considered that he had joined the League under the impulse of his passions which a good Stoic would have suppressed. Bodin, however, was led not by passion, but by principle and religious sensibility into supporting the League. See E.F. Rice, jr., *The Renaissance Idea of Wisdom* (Cambridge, Mass., 1958), p. 201. A. Levi, *French Moralists. The Theory of the Passions 1585-1649* (Oxford, 1964), p. 97.

[79] *Suasion pour la loi salique,* in Du Vair, *Actions et traictez,* ed. Radouant.

Yet most commentators have preferred to accept Baudrillart's allegation that Bodin's conduct in 1589-94 was contrary to all his principles. Thus, Chauviré has declared that Bodin failed to obey his religious and political convictions; instead he found himself sanctioning rebellion, repudiating Navarre as the legitimate successor to the throne and abandoning religious toleration to support a policy which insisted on the Catholicity of the French king and nation and demanded religious war to achieve the extermination of the Huguenots! [80]   The truth, however, is that Bodin never reversed any of his basic principles. [81]   To take first the problem of Bodin's support of the rebellion against Henri III in March 1589. In the *République* (II, 5) Bodin had forbidden the slaying of a rightful king, no matter how tyrannical he was, and had also forbidden rebellion unless it were inspired, like Jehu's uprising against Ahab, by the express commandment of God. [82]   Bodin's purpose was to forestall any subject or faction arbitrarily claiming the right to rebel against their lawful king. These words, however, had been written in 1576 long before anyone could have remotely foreseen Henri III's deranged murders of the Guises in December 1588. The events of the first few months of 1589 did not result in the reversal of Bodin's views on tyrannicide and resistance, but rather persuaded him that God had turned against the king. As Bodin carefully explains in the opening pages of the letter of March 1589 he decided to join the League only after becoming convinced of the near universality of the rebellion against Henri III. Bodin indeed never approved entirely of the initial rebellion — in the *Lettre* of 1590 he confessed that it might have been *mal fondée* because of its resistance to a king — but the extent of the revolt was enough to suggest to him that it had developed into a successful revolution and that as such it had come to express God's verdict on the criminal king. [83]

After the question of Bodin's stand on resistance comes the problem of his views on the legitimate succession to the throne. While it *may* be true that in 1583 Bodin implicitly preferred the right of Navarre to that of his uncle the cardinal Charles de Bourbon, nevertheless the Latin *Republica* of 1586 clearly supported the cardinal and this at a time when there was no unwarranted

[80] Chauviré, *Bodin*, p. 88.

[81] Even if he did abandon his ties with Navarre — a connexion which scarcely amounted to a matter of principle — he did so with the principle of the *Lex Solonis* in mind.

[82] *République* (1583 edn), II, 5, pp. 305f.: 'Théologiens tiennent qu'il n'est iamais licite, non pas seulement de tuer, ains de se rebeller contre son prince souverain, si ce n'est qu'il y eust mandement spécial de Dieu, et indubitable: comme nous avons de Iehu, lequel fut eslu de Dieu, et sacré Roy par le Prophète avec mandement exprès de faire mourir la race d'Achab ... Mais il ne faut pas parangonner ce mandement spécial de Dieu aux coniurations et rébellions des subjects mutins contre le Prince souverain.'

[83] Bodin was always cautious about his opinion of the post hoc legitimacy of a successful revolt. See Lemaire, *Lois fondamentales*, pp. 113f.

For his caution even in March 1589 see above note 15; and for the admission in the *Lettre* of 1590 that the initial revolt had perhaps been 'malfondée' see above, notes 49 and 58. Franklin, *Bodin and Absolutist Theory*, p. 97 n, thinks Bodin's resistance to the king in 1589 curious though he was 'not guilty of violating his principles'; Bodin 'did not justify the act of rebellion. He merely treated it as a fait accompli which Henry had brought upon himself'. I hope I may have elucidated Mr. Franklin's perceptive remarks here. (Incidentally Bodin supported the claim of Charles — not Antoine — de Bourbon and he did *not* recognize Mayenne as next in line in 1590).

pressure on Bodin to do so. This switch — if it were indeed one — arose out of Bodin's continuing reflexion on the juristic principle of representation, not out of fear or prudence or expediency. Moreover, it did not entail any fundamental change of the law of succession. Salic Law was preserved as the inviolable principle of succession to the crown and Bodin's disallowance of representation was merely a clarification of that law. [84] Bodin never rejected the crown law of succession any more than he abandoned the belief that France was an *estat royal*; the democratic policies of some Leaguers always filled him with repugnance. [85]

Nor did the religious policy of the League find any favour with Bodin. He never reversed or altered his conception of fundamental law to make Catholicity a law of the Crown. [86] All that he asked was that Navarre convert, a recommendation made by many other royalist and *politique* writers including Du Vair, Ayrault, not to mention Henri III himself, and a suggestion eventually adopted by Navarre. Again there is not the slightest hint in the correspondence that Bodin had reversed his belief in religious toleration; certainly there is a preference for a Catholic king but no call for the extirpation of heresy.

Finally, did Bodin ever lose his '*politique*' conviction that religious war was a great evil? [87] In the *République* he had proscribed religious war between sects as politically destructive and had gone so far as to advocate banning all religious disputation and debate as dangerous; the Latin edition of 1586

[84] See above, notes 32ff. Also my 'Bodin and the Bourbon Succession'. I am not entirely convinced that Bodin intended to support Navarre's claim in 1583.

Franklin, *Bodin and Absolutist Theory*, p. 97, notes, but does not explain, the switch from the nephew to the uncle's side. Giesey, *Juristic Basis*, pp. 30f., does not consider any juristic reason for the change and seems to attribute it solely to the 'changed religious atmosphere'. McRae, 'Political Thought of Bodin', p. 130, and in his introduction to *Six Bookes of a Commonweale*, p. A.11, asserts that 'Bodin's new views on the succession cannot be accepted as sincere', though he admits that Bodin's argument would establish Navarre as the cardinal's successor. The *Republique*'s maintenance of the prior right of the nephew is taken as Bodin's 'genuine' view. This is too simple.

[85] Moreau-Reibel, 'Bodin et la Ligue', pp. 437f., rightly points out that Bodin did not support the democratic and religious programme of the League.

[86] *Pace* Giesey, Baumgartner and Baldwin (above, note 73). For the *République* on fundamental law, see above note 54.

[87] In two early writings Bodin had apparently favoured war in the interests of *vera religio*. The first is in the *Methodus* of 1566 ('Ego vero impius judicarem nisi quancumque religionem veram judicaret, non eam quoque tueri et contrarias evertere conaretur', in *Œuvres philosophiques de Jean Bodin*, ed. P. Mesnard (Paris, 1951), I, 135A). However, V. De Caprariis, *Propaganda e pensiero politico in Francia durante le guerre di religione* (Naples, 1959), I, 329, has suggested that this is more an avowal of sincerity than advocacy of religious war. The second source is the famous letter to Bautru which I would date to 1568-9. (See Chapter VIII). These remarks should be contrasted with Bodin's position in the Latin version of the *République* issued in 1586, quoted here after the Knolles translation (*Six Bookes*, pp. 539f.): 'Yet when we may not publicly use the true religion, which still consists in the worshipping of one almighty and everlasting God, lest by contemning of the religion which is publicly received we should seem to allure or stir the subjects unto impiety or sedition, it is better to come unto the public service, so that the mind still rest in the honour and reverence of one almighty and ever living God.' Cf. *Republica* (Paris, 1586), pp. 485f: "Quando vero religione, quae in unius sempiterni Dei vero cultu versatur publice uti non licet, ac ne publicae religionis contemptu ad impietatem cives, aut ad seditionem incitare videamur, publicis sacrificiis adesse praestat, dum tamen in unius sempiterni Dei cultu mens acquiescat."

had significantly extended the section on religious war by arguing that religious war and oppression led to that greatest of evils, atheism, which placed both the soul and the state in peril. [88] When the League launched its war against Henri III and Navarre Bodin recognized it as a political conflict and he was able to justify it as a war directed against the tyranny of Henry III and then, after August 1589, as a war for the legitimate succession to the throne. But he also welcomed it as a religious war, not in the *Republique's* sense of war between sects, nor in the League's sense as a crusade against heresy. The correspondence like the *Paradoxe* [89] graphically reveals Bodin's prophetic conviction that the war was expression of divine justice and retribution, a visitation of punishment on the impiety of both sides: 'God has descended from heaven to do justice on earth.' [90] Bodin's welcoming of religious war in 1589 did not signify any withdrawal of his earlier condemnations of religious war; he was simply recognizing God's hand.

This chapter has sketched one side of Bodin's prophetic personality in his last years, depicting him as Elijah or Jeremiah *redivivus*, the fiery invoker of war as divine vengeance. But there was an irenic and pacific side to him which was closer to the visions of universal peace and reconciliation to be found in Isaiah and Micah. In the very same years that Bodin wrote his incensed letters on the League he was also composing the visionary *Colloquium Heptaplomeres* where he rejected formal confessional beliefs in favour of an inner spirituality which, adopted universally, would enable men to live in peace and harmony. [91] This simultaneous belief in the League and in religious toleration — in war and peace — was not so much a paradox as a twofold reflexion of the prophetic character of Jean Bodin. [92]

[88] *République*, IV, 7, pp. 652ff. in the French edition of 1583; extended in the *Six Bookes of the Commonweale*, pp. 539ff., which follows for the most part the Latin text of 1586 (pp. 485f).

[89] The Latin *Paradoxon* (pp. 3ff, 12-14) understood war as divine retribution inflicted by demons. It also (p. 12) saw war as the privation of God's bounty.

[90] See above, note 30. There may be a parallel between this and Francis Bacon's comment (*Considerations touching a warre with Spain*, 1624, in *Certaine miscellany works* (London, 1629), p. 3) that 'warres are suits of appeale to the tribunal of God's justice, where there are no superiours on Earth to determine the cause'. In the *Lettre* of 1590 Bodin had devoted several pages (pp. 6-9) to proving that since the sides were so evenly and powerfully matched only God could determine the issue.

[91] External war may have intensified Bodin's search for inner religious peace as it did with other such spirituals as Abraham Ortelius. Cf. Frances Yates, The *Valois Tapestries* (London, 1959), p. 106.

[92] Bodin was fond of quoting Jeremiah. See the letter of 1590-1 in Moreau-Reibel, 'Bodin et la Ligue', p. 435. ('Ulciscar inimicos meos per inimicos meos', earlier cited in the 1583 edition of the *République*, IV, 7, p. 657: 'Ie me vengeray (parlant en la bouche de Hieremie) de mes ennemis, par mes ennemis'). He would have certainly known the distinction between prophets of war and of peace in Jeremiah, XXVIII, 8-9: 'The prophets that have been before me ... of old prophesied ... of war, and of evil ,and of pestilence. The prophet which prophesieth of peace ... the Lord hath truly sent him....'

BIBLIOGRAPHY

Abel, G., *Stoizismus und frühe Neuzeit. Zur Entstehungsgeschichte modernen Denkens im Felde von Ethik und Politik,* Berlin, 1978.

Abelson, J., *The Immanence of God in Rabbinical Literature,* London, 1912.

Allen, J.W., *A History of Political Thought in the Sixteenth Century,* repr. London, 1957.

Altmann, A., "Ibn Hayya on Man's Ultimate Felicity", in *Harry Austryn Wolfson Jubilee Volume,* Jerusalem, 1965, I, 47-87.   »

Aristotle, *Works,* trs. J.A. Smith, W.D. Ross, *et al.,* Oxford, 1908-52.

Aubigné, Agrippa d', *Œuvres,* ed. Pléiade, Paris, 1969.

Aubin, P., *Le Problème de la "Conversion",* Paris, 1963.

Ayrault, P., *Supplication et advis au roy de se faire catholique,* Angers, 1591 (Bibliothèque Nationale, Paris, MS Dupuy 317).

Bacon, Francis, *Certaine miscellany works,* London, 1629.

Bady, R., *L'Homme et son Institution de Montaigne à Bérulle (1580-1625),* Paris, 1964.

Bainton, R.H., *Hunted Heretic. The Life and Death of Michael Servetus (1511-53),* Boston, 1953.

Baldwin, S., "Jean Bodin and the League", *Catholic Historical Review,* XXIII, 1937, 160-184.

Barber, G., "Haec a Joanne Bodino lecta", *Bibliothèque d'Humanisme et Renaissance,* XXV, 1963, 362-365.

Barker, E., *The Political Thought of Plato and Aristotle,* rev. ed., New York, 1959.

Baron, S.W., *A Social and Religious History of the Jews,* 2nd ed., New York, 1952.

Barthélemy, E. de, *Etude sur Jean Bodin. Sa vie et ses travaux,* repr. Paris, 1876.

Berg, R., "Un demi-Juif: Jean Bodin", *La Revue Juive de Lorraine,* XIII (1937), 29-35.

Bezold, F. von, "Jean Bodin als Okkultist und seine *Démonomanie*", *Historische Zeitschrift,* CV, 1910, 1-64.

Blau, J.L., *The Christian Interpretation of the Cabala in the Renaissance,* New York, 1944.

"E. Bodin" (i.e., Jean Bodin), *Sapientiae moralis epitome,* Paris, 1588.

Bodin, Jean: See *List of Abbreviations* for full titles of major works.

Bodin, Jean, *Colloquium Heptaplomeres,* ed. L. Noack, Schwerin, 1857, reprint, Stuttgart, 1966.

— *Colloquium of the Seven About Secrets of the Sublime,* trs. M.L.D. Kuntz, Princeton, 1975.

— *Consilium de principe recte instituendo,* ed. J. Bornitius, Erfurt, 1603.

— *Démonomanie des sorciers,* Paris, 1580.

— *Method for the Easy Comprehension of History,* trs. B. Reynolds, New York, 1945.

— *Œuvres philosophiques de Jean Bodin*, ed. P. Mesnard, Paris, 1951, I (*Oratio, Methodus, Distributio*).

— *Oppiani de Venatione libri IIII Ioanne Bodino Andegavensi interprete*, Paris, Vascosanus, 1555; reissued Paris, Fouet, 1597.

— *Le Paradoxe de Jean Bodin Angevin qu'il n'y a pas une seule vertu en médiocrité, ny au milieu de deux vices. Traduit (par Bodin) de Latin en François et augmenté en plusieurs lieux* (Denys du Val), Paris, 1598.

— *Paradoxes de M.J. Bodin doctes et excellents discours de la vertu...* traduit du Latin en François par Claude de Magdaillan (T. Du Bray), Paris, 1604.

— *Paradoxon quod nec virtus ulla in mediocritate nec summum hominis bonum in virtutis actione consistere possit* (Dionysius Duvallius), Paris, 1596.

— *Recueil de tout ce qui s'est negotié en la compagnie du Tiers Estat de France... en la ville de Blois, en novembre 1576*, s.l., 1577.

— *De Republica* (trs. Bodin), Paris, 1586.

— *République*, Paris, 1583.

— *La Response de Jean Bodin à M. de Malestroit 1568. La vie chère au XVIe siècle*, ed. H. Hauser, Paris, 1932.

— *Selected Writings of Jean Bodin on Philosophy, Religion and Politics*, ed. P.L. Rose, North Queensland, 1980.

— *Le Théâtre de la nature universelle*, Lyons, 1597. (Trs. F. de Fougerolles).

— *Universae naturae theatrum*, Lyons, 1596.

Boisset, J. de and Stegmann, A., (eds.), *Aspects du libertinisme au seizième siècle*, Paris, 1974.

Bouwsma, W.J., *Concordia Mundi. The Career and Thought of Guillaume Postel (1510-81)*, Cambridge, Mass., 1957.

— "The Two Faces of Humanism: Stoicism and Augustinianism in Renaissance Thought", in *Itinerarium Italicum for P.O. Kristeller*, ed. H. Oberman, Leiden, 1975, pp. 5-60.

Brandsma, T., *Carmelite Mysticism. Historical Sketches*, Chicago, 1936.

Bredvold, L.I., "Milton and Bodin's *Heptaplomeres*", *Studies in Philology*, XXI, 1924, 399-402.

Bréhier, E., *Les Idées philosophiques et religieuses de Philon d'Alexandrie*, 3rd ed., Paris, 1950.

Brown, J.L., *The Methodus ad Facilem Historiarum Cognitione of Jean Bodin. A Critical Study*, Washington, D.C., 1939.

Busson, H., *Le Rationalisme dans la littérature française de la Renaissance*, 2nd ed, Paris, 1957.

Cabos, A., *Guy du Faur de Pibrac. Un magistrat poète au XVIe siècle (1529-84)*, Paris, 1922.

Calvin, J., *Opera omnia* (Corpus Reformatorum, 40), Brunswick, 1863-97.

Cameron, K., "Henri III, the Anti-Christian King", *Journal of European Studies*, IV, 1974, 152-163.

Chauviré, R., *Jean Bodin, auteur de la République*, Paris, 1914.

Cioranesco, A., *Bibliographie de la littérature française du seizième siècle*, Paris, 1959.

Clément, L., *De Adriani Turnebi regii professoris praefationibus et poematis*, Paris, 1899.

Cohen, K., *The Throne and the Chariot. Studies in Milton's Hebraism*, The Hague, 1975.

Colomiès, P., *Gallia Orientalis*, The Hague, 1665.

Copleston, F., *Aquinas*, London, 1955.

Dagens, J., *Bérulle et les origines de la restauration catholique (1575-1611)*, Bruges, 1952.

Damiens, S., *Amour et intellect chez Léon l'Hébreu*, Paris, 1971.

De Caprariis, V., *Propaganda e pensiero politico in Francia durante le guerre di religione, I, 1559-1572*, Napes, 1959.

Delachenal, R., *Histoire des avocats au Parlement de Paris 1300-1600*, Paris, 1885.

Demerson, G., "Un Mythe des libertins spirituels: le prophète Elie", in *Aspects du libertinisme au XVIe siècle*, ed. J. de Boisset and A. Stegmann, Paris, 1974, pp. 105-120.

— *Polémiques autour de la mort de Turnèbe*, Clermont-Ferrand, 1975.

Denzer, H., (ed.), *Jean Bodin. Verhandlungen der internationalen Bodin Tagung in München*, Munich, 1973.

Dictionnaire de spiritualité ascétique et mystique, ed. M. Viller *et al.*, Paris, 1932.

Droz, E., "Le carme Jean Bodin, hérétique", *Bibliothèque d'Humanisme et Renaissance*, X, 1948, 77-94.

Du Perron, J., *Diverses œuvres*, Paris, 1622.

Du Vair, G., *Actions et traictez oratoires*, ed. R. Radouant, Paris, 1911.

— *De la Constance*, 2nd ed., Lyons, 1595.

— *De la Sainte Philosophie: Philosophie morale des Stoïques*, ed. G. Michaut, Paris, 1945.

— *The Moral Philosophie of the Stoicks*, trs. R. Kirk, New Brunswick, 1951.

Duby, M., *Jean Bodin et Toulouse*, thèse en droit, Toulouse, 1944 .

Dunn, J., *The Political Thought of John Locke. An Historical Account of the Argument of the Two Treatises of Government*, Cambridge, 1969.

Elisée de la Nativité, P., "Les Carmes imitateurs d'Elie (1370-1668)", in *Elie le prophète* (Etudes Carmélitaines, 35), Bruges, 1956, II, 82-110.

Encyclopaedia Judaica, London-Jerusalem, 1971.

Epstein, I, (trs.), *The Babylonian Talmud*, 34 vols., London, 1935-48.

— *Judaism. A Historical Presentation*, Harmondsworth, 1959.

Erasmus, D., *The Education of a Christian Prince*, trs. L.K. Born, New York, 1936.

Espiner-Scott, J., "Note sur le cercle de Henri de Mesmes et sur son influence", *Mélanges offerts à M. Abel Lefranc*, Paris, 1936, pp. 354-361.

Espiner-Scott, J., *Claude Fauchet. Sa vie, son œuvre*, Paris, 1938.

Febvre, L., "L'universalisme de Jean Bodin", *Revue de Synthèse*, LIV, 1934, 165-168.

Feldman, L., *Scholarship on Philo and Josephus (1937-1962)* (Studies in Judaica, I), New York, 1963.

Festugière, A.J., *La Philosophie de l'amour de Marsile Ficin et son influence sur la littérature française au XVIe siècle* (Etudes de Philosophie Médiévale, 31), Paris, 1941.

Ficino, Marsilio, *Opera*, Paris, 1641.

Fleury, E., *Cinquante ans de l'histoire du chapître de Notre-Dame de Laon... 1541... 1594*, Laon-Paris, 1875.

Forcadel, E., *Aviarium jus civilis*, Lyons, 1550.

— *Œuvres poétiques*, ed. F. Joukovsky, Geneva, 1977.

Fox, M., "Maimonides and Aquinas on Natural Law", in *Studies on Maimonides and St. Thomas Aquinas*, ed. J. Dienstag, New York, 1975, pp. 75-106.

Franklin, J.H., *Jean Bodin and the Rise of Absolutist Theory*, Cambridge, 1973.

— *Jean Bodin and the Sixteenth Century Revolution in the Methodology of Law and History*, New York, 1963.

Fremy, E., *L'Académie des derniers Valois 1570-85*, Paris, 1887.

Friedman, J., *Michael Servetus . A Case Study in Total Heresy*, Geneva, 1978.

— "Michael Servetus. The Case for a Jewish Christianity", *Sixteenth Century Journal*, IV, 1973, 87-110.

— "The Reformation and Jewish Anti-Christian Polemics", *Bibliothèque d'Humanisme et Renaissance*, XLI, 1979, 83-97.

Gadave, R., *Les documents sur l'histoire de l'Université de Toulouse et spécialement de sa faculté de droit civil et canonique (1229-1789)*, Toulouse, 1910.

Gallia Christiana, Paris, 1744 (reprint, Gregg, 1970).

Gambier, P., *Au temps des guerres de religion. Le président Barnabé Brisson, Ligueur (1531-1591)*, Paris, 1957.

Garosci, A., *Jean Bodin. Politica e diritto nel rinascimento francese*, Milan, 1934.

Giblet, J., "L'Homme image de Dieu dans les commentaires littéraux de Philon d'Alexandrie", *Studia Hellenistica*, V, 1948, 93-118.

Giesey, R., *The Juristic Basis of Dynastic Right to the French Throne (Transactions of the American Philosophical Society, N.S. LI, 5)*, Philadelphia, 1961.

Gilson, E., *The Christian Philosophy of St. Augustine*, London, 1961.

— *The Christian Philosophy of St. Thomas*, London, 1957.

— *Jean Duns Scot. Introduction à ses positions fondamentales*, Paris, 1952.

Goodenough, E.R., *An Introduction to Philo Judaeus*, 2nd ed., Oxford, 1962.

— *By Light, Light. The Mystic Gospel of Hellenistic Judaism*, New Haven, 1935 (reprint, Amsterdam, 1969).

— *The Politics of Philo Judaeus*, New Haven, 1938.

Goodhart, H.L. and E.R. Goodenough, "A General Bibliography of Philo", in E.R. Goodenough, *The Politics of Philo Judaeus*, New Haven, 1938.

Grant, R.M., *Miracle and Natural Law*, Amsterdam, 1952.

Guhrauer, G.E., *Das Heptaplomeres des Jean Bodin*, Berlin, 1841, reprint, Geneva, 1971.

Guttmann, J., "Jean Bodin in seinen Beziehungen des Judentums", *Monatsschrift für Geschichte und Wissenschaft des Judentums*, XLIX, 1905, 315-348; 459-489.

Guy, H., "Les *Quatrains* de Pibrac", *Annales du Midi*, XV, 1903, 449-468; XVI, 1904, 65-80; 208-222.

Haag, E. and M., *La France Protestante*, Paris, 1846-1859.

Hauser, H., *Sources de l'histoire de France. XVI siècle*, Paris, 1906-15.

Horowitz, M.C., "Natural Law as the Foundation for an Autonomous Ethic: Pierre Charron's *De la Sagesse*", *Studies in the Renaissance*, XXI, 1974, 204-227.

Hubault, G., *Michel de Castelnau, ambassadeur en Angleterre (1575-85)*, St. Cloud, 1865 (repr. 1970).

Imbart de la Tour, P., *Les origines de la Réforme*, Paris ,1915-35.

Introduction des gens des troys estats, Blois, 1577.

Isambert, F., *Recueil général des anciennes lois françaises depuis l'an 420 jusqu'à la révolution de 1789*, Paris, 1821-33.

Isnardi-Parente, M., "A proposito di un'interpretazione cinquecentesca del rapporto teoria-prassi in Aristotele e Platone", *Parola del Passato*, LXXXVII, 1962, 436-447.

— "Le volontarisme de Jean Bodin: Maimonide ou Duns Scot?" in *Verhandlungen der internationalen Bodin Tagung in München*, ed. H. Denzer, Munich, 1973, pp. 39-51.

— "Il volontarismo di Jean Bodin: Maimonide ou Duns Scoto", *Il pensiero politico*, IV, 1971, 21-45.

Jaeger, W., *Paideia. The Ideas of Greek Culture*, Oxford, 1939-45.

James, W., *Varieties of Religious Experience*, repr. London, 1977.

[Exposition] "Jean Bodin et Toulouse", *Annales de la Faculté de Droit de Toulouse VIII*, 1960, 151-203.

Jehasse, J., *La Renaissance de la critique. L'essor de l'humanisme érudit de 1560 à 1614*, St. Etienne, 1976.

Jundt, A., *Histoire du Panthéisme populaire au moyen âge et au seizième siècle*, Paris, 1875.

Kingdon, R.M., J.-F. Bergier and A. Dufour, (eds.), *Registres de la Compagnie des Pasteurs de Genève au temps de Calvin*, Geneva, 1962.

Kirsop, W., "The Family of Love in France", *Journal of Religious History*, III, 1964-65, 103-118.

Kogel, R., *Pierre Charron*, Geneva, 1972.

Krailsheimer, A.J., *Rabelais and the Franciscans*, Oxford, 1963.

Kristeller, P.O., "A Thomist Critique of Marsilio Ficino's Theory of Will and Intellect", *Harry Austryn Wolfson Jubilee Volume*, Jerusalem, 1965, II, 463-494.

Kristeller, P.O. and F.E. Cranz (eds.), *Catalogus Translationum*, Washington, D.C., 1960-.

La Boétie, Etienne de, *Discours de la servitude volontaire*, ed. P. Bonneton, Bordeaux, 1892.

La Ferrière, H. de, (ed.), *Lettres de Catherine de Médicis*, Paris, 1880-1943.

La Noue, F. de, *Discours politiques et militaires*, ed. F.E. Sutcliffe, Geneva, 1967.

Lange, U., *Untersuchungen zu Bodins Démonomanie*, Frankfurt, 1970.

Lasker, D.J., *Jewish Philosophical Polemics Against Christianity in the Middle Ages*, New York, 1977.

Laski, M., *Ecstasy. A Study of Some Secular and Religious Experiences*, London, 1961.

Laporte, J., "Philo in the Tradition of Biblical Wisdom Literature", in *Aspects of Wisdom in Judaism and Early Christianity*, ed. R. Wilken, Notre Dame, Indiana, 1975, pp. 103-141.

Laurentin, A., *Le Pneuma dans la doctrine de Philon*, (Analecta Lovaniensia Biblica et Orientalia, ser. II, fasc. 25), Louvain-Bruges, 1952. (Also in *Ephemerides Theologicae Lovanienses*, XXVII, 1951, 390-437).

Leff, G., *Medieval Thought*, London, 1959.

Lefranc, A., "La Détention de Guillaume Postel au prieuré de Saint-Martin-des-Champs (1562-81)", *Annuaire-Bulletin de la Société de l'Histoire de France*, XXVIII, 1891, 211-230.

Lemaire, A., *Les lois fondamentales de la monarchie française d'après théoriciens de l'ancien régime*, Paris, 1907.

Léon l'Hébreu, *Dialogues de l'Amour. The French Translation attributed to Pontus de Tyard and published in Lyon 1551*, ed. T.A. Perry (Studies in Comparative Literature, 59), Chapel Hill, N. Carolina, 1974.

Leone Ebreo, *Dialoghi d'Amore*, Rome, 1535.

— *The Philosophy of Love*, trs. F. Fredeberg and J.H. Barnes, London, 1937.

Levi, A.H.T., "Ethics and the Encyclopedia in the Sixteenth Centurty", in *French Renaissance Studies 1540-70*, ed. P. Sharratt, Edinburgh, 1976, pp. 170-184.

— *French Moralists. The Theory of the Passions 1585-1649*, Oxford, 1964.

— *Pagan Virtue and the Humanism of the Northern Renaissance*, Society for Renaissance Studies, Occasional Paper 2, London, 1974.

Levron, J., *Jean Bodin et sa famille . Textes et commentaires*, Angers, 1950.

— "Jean Bodin, sieur de Saint-Amand ou Jean Bodin, originaire de Saint-Amand?", *Bibliothèque d'Humanisme et Renaissance*, X, 1948, 69-76.

Lindsay, R.O. and J. Neu, *French Political Pamphlets 1547-1648. A Catalog of Major Collections in American Libraries*, Madison, Wisc., 1969.

McRae, K.D., (ed.), *Jean Bodin: The Six Bookes of a Commonweale*, Cambridge Mass., 1962.

—. "The Political Thought of Jean Bodin (unpublished Ph.D. thesis, Harvard University, 1954).

— "Ramist Tendencies in the Thought of Jean Bodin", *Journal of the History of Ideas*, XVI, 1955, 306-323.

— "A Postscript on Bodin's Connections with Ramism", *Journal of the History of Ideas*, XXIV, 1963, 569-571.

Maimonides, Moses, *Guide for the Perplexed*, trs. M. Friedländer, 2nd ed., London, 1904.

— *The Guide of the Perplexed*, trs. S. Pines, Chicago, 1963.

(Anon,). *Le martel en teste des catholiques françois*, Paris, 1590.

Mastellone, S., "Gallicani e libertini", *Il Pensiero Politico,* VI, 1973, 249-253.

Melczer, W., "Platonisme et Aristotélisme dans la pensée de Léon l'Hébreu", in *Platon et Aristote à la Renaissance* (De Pétrarque à Descartes, 32), Paris, 1976, pp. 293-306.

Mesnard, P., "La conjuration contre la renommée de Jean Bodin: Antoine Tessier (1684)", *Bulletin de l'Association Guillaume Budé*, XVIII, 1959, 535-559.

— "Etat présent des études Bodiniennes", *Filosofia*, XI, 1960, 687-696.

— "L'importance de la cité dans l'éducation nationale au temps de la Renaissance française", in *Pierre Mesnard: Images de l'homme et de l'œuvre*, Paris, 1970, pp. 238-243.

— "Jean Bodin à la recherche des secrets de la nature" in *Umanesimo e esoterismo*, ed. E. Castelli (Archivio di Filosofia, 5), Padua, 1960, pp. 221-34.

— "Jean Bodin à Toulouse", *Bibliothèque d'Humanisme et Renaissance*, XII, 1950, 31-59.

— "Jean Bodin devant le problème de l'éducation", *Revue des Travaux de l'Académie des Sciences Morales et Politiques*, 1959, 217-228.

— "Jean Bodin et la critique de la morale d'Aristote", *Revue Thomiste*, LVII, 1949, 542-562.

— "Jean Bodin et le problème de l'éternité du monde", *Bulletin de l'Association Guillaume Budé*, ser. III. v. I, 1951, 117-131.

— "Le nationalisme de Jean Bodin", *La Table Ronde*, CXLVII, 1960, 66-72.

— "La pensée religieuse de Bodin", *Revue du Seizième Siècle*, XVI, 1929, 77-121.

— "Le Platonisme de Jean Bodin", *Actes du Ve Congrès de l'Association Guillaume Budé*, Paris, 1954, pp. 352-361.

— "The Psychology and Pneumatology of Jean Bodin", *International Philosophical Quarterly*, II, 1962, 244-264.

— "Un rival heureux de Cujas et de Bodin: Etienne Forcadel", *Zeitschrift der Savigny-Stiftung für Rechtesgeschichte*, LXVII, 1950, 440-458.

Moreau-Reibel, J., "Bodin et la Ligue d'après des lettres inédites", *Humanisme et Renaissance*, II, 1935, 422-440.

Mousnier, R., *The Assassination of Henry IV*, London, 1973.

Naef, H., "La jeunesse de Jean Bodin, ou les conversions oubliées", *Bibliothèque d'Humanisme et Renaissance*, VIII, 1946, 137-155.

Newman, L.I., *Jewish Influence on Christian Reform Movements*, New York, 1925.

Nock, A.D., *Conversion*, Oxford, 1933.

O'Connor, D. and Oakley, F. (eds.), *Creation. The Impact of an Idea*, New York, 1969.

Oestreich, G., *Geschichte und Gestalt des frühmodernen Staates*, Berlin, 1969.

Oppien d'Apamée. La Chasse (Cynegetica), ed. P. Bourdeaux, Paris, 1908.

Orléans, L. d', *Second avertissement des catholiques anglois aux françois catholiques*, Lyon, 1590.

Pallier, D., *Recherches sur l'imprimerie à Paris pendant la Ligue (1585-1594)*, Geneva, 1976.

Pandochaeus, E. (i.e. Postel, G.), *Panthenosia*, Basle, 1547.

Paparelli, G., *Feritas, humanitas, divinitas. L'essenza umanistica del Rinascimento*, Naples, 1973.

Philo, *Lucubrationes omnes*, ed. S. Gelenius, Basle, 1554, and Lyons, 1555.

— *Philonis Judaei in libros Mosis de mundi opificio, historicos, de legibus. Ejusdem libri singulares*, ed. A. Turnebus, Paris, 1552.

— *Les Œuvres de Philon Juif*, ed. trs. P. Bellier, Paris, 1575.

— *Philo in Ten Volumes With an English Translation*, ed. F.H. Colson, *et al.*, Cambridge, Mass., 1929-62.

Plato, *Collected Dialogues*, ed. E. Hamilton and M. Cairns, Princeton, 1961.

Plotinus, *Opera omnia*, trs. M. Ficino, ed. F. Creutzer, Oxford, 1835.

Pibrac, G. du Faur de, *Discours de l'ire et comme la faut modérer*, in E. Fremy, *L'Académie des derniers Valois 1570-85*, Paris, 1887.

Pico della Mirandola, G., *Opera*, Basle, 1557.

Pintard, R., *Le libertinage érudit dans la première moitié du XVIIe siècle*, Paris, 1943.

Ponthieux, A., "Quelques documents inédits sur Jean Bodin", *Revue du Seizième Siècle*, XV, 1928, 56-99.

Postel, G., *Restitutio rerum omnium conditarum per manum Eliae profetae*, Paris, 1552.

— *Le Thrésor des prophéties de l'univers*, ed. F. Secret (Archives Internationales d'Histoire des Idées, 27), The Hague, 1969.

Radouant, R., *Guillaume Du Vair, L'homme et l'orateur jusqu'à la fin des troubles de la Ligue (1556-1596)*, Paris, 1907.

Reulos, M., "Une institution romaine vue par un auteur du XVIe siècle: La censure dans Jean Bodin", *Etudes offertes à Jean Macqueron*, Aix-en-Provence, 1970, pp. 585-590.

Riboti, P., *Speculum Carmelitanum*, Paris, 1507.

Rice, E.F., Jr., *The Renaissance Idea of Wisdom*, Cambridge, Mass., 1958.

Richart, A., *Mémoires sur la Ligue dans le Laonnois*, Laon, 1869.

Roellenbleck, G., *Offenbarung, Natur und jüdische Überlieferung bei Jean Bodin*, Gütersloh, 1964.

Ronsard, P., *Œuvres complètes*, ed. G. Cohen, Pléiade ed., Paris, 1958.

Rose, P.L., "Bodin and the Bourbon Succession to the French Throne 1583-1594", *Sixteenth Century Journal*, IX, 1978, 75-98.

— "The *Politique* and the Prophet: Bodin and the Catholic League 1589-94", *The Historical Journal*, XXI, 1978, 783-808.

— (ed.), *Selected Writings of Jean Bodin on Philosophy, Religion and Politics*, North Queensland, 1980.

— "Two Problems of Bodin's Religious Biography: The Letter to Jean Bautru des Matras and the Imprisonment of 1569", *Bibliothèque d'Humanisme et Renaissance*, XXXVIII, 1976, 459-465.

— "A Venetian Patron and Mathematician of the Sixteenth Century: Francesco Barozzi (1537-1604)", *Studi Veneziani*, N.S. I, 1977, 119-178.

Rosin, D., *Die Ethik des Maimonides*, Breslau, 1876.

Roth, L., *The Guide for the Perplexed: Moses Maimonides*, London, 1948.

Roubichou-Stretz, A., *La Vision de l'histoire dans l'œuvre de la Pléiade*, Paris, 1973.

Rule of St. Albert, trs. B. Edwards, Aylesford, 1973.

Sabrié, J.-B., *De l'Humanisme au rationalisme. Pierre Charron 1541-1603*, Paris, 1913.

Sandmel, S., *Philo of Alexandria. An Introduction*, New York, 1979.

Saulnier, E., *Le rôle politique du cardinal de Bourbon (Charles X) 1523-1590*, Paris, 1912.

Saunders, J.L., *Justus Lipsius. The Philosophy of Renaissance Stoicism*, New York, 1955.

Schmidt, C.G.A., *Les libertins spirituels. Traités mystiques écrits dans les années 1547 à 1549*, Basle, 1876.

Schnur, R., *Die französischen Juristen im konfessionellen Bürgerkrieg des 16. Jahrhunderts*, Berlin, 1962.

Scholem, G., *On the Kabbalah and its Symbolism*, New York, 1969.

— *The Messianic Idea in Judaism*, New York, 1972.

Sealy, R.J., "The Palace Academy of Henri III", *Bibliothèque d'Humanisme et Renaissance*, XL, 1978, 61-84.

Secret, F., *Bibliographie des manuscrits de Guillaume Postel*, Geneva, 1970.

— "Un cheval de Troie dans l'église du Christ: La Kabbale chrétienne" in *Aspects du libertinisme au seizième siècle*, ed. J. de Boisset and A. Stegmann, Paris, 1974, pp. 153-166.

— "L'Emithologie de Guillaume Postel" in *Umanesimo e esoterismo*, ed. E. Castelli (V Congresso Internazionale di Studi Umanistici — Archivio di Filosofia, 5), Padua, 1960, pp. 381-437.

— *Guillaume Postel (1510-81) et son interprétation du Candélabre de Moyse*, Nieuwkoop, 1966.

— "Notes sur les Hébraïsants Chrétiens", *Revue des Etudes Juives*, CXXIII, 1964, 141-168.

— "La première académie française de musique selon les témoignages de Genebrard et de Jean Bodin", *Bibliothèque d'Humanisme et Renaissance*, XL, 1978, 119-120.

— "De quelques courants prophétiques et religieux sous le règne de Henri III", *Revue de l'Histoire des Religions*, CLXXII, 1967, 1-32.

Sharratt, P., ed., *French Renaissance Studies 1540-70*, Edinburgh, 1976.

Skinner, Q., *Foundations of Modern Political Thought*, Cambridge, 1978.

Smet, J.A., *The Carmelites. A History of the Brothers of Our Lady of Mount Carmel, ca. 1200 A.D. until the Councnl of Trent*, privately printed, Illinois, 1975.

Sozzini, F., *De Jesu Christo servatore*, Basle, 1594.

Speculum Carmelitanum sive historia Eliani ordinis fratrum Beatissimae Virginis Mariae de Monte Carmelo, ed. Fr. Daniel a Virgine Maria, Antwerp, 1680.

Speculum Ordinis Carmelitanum, Venice, 1507.

Staring, A., *Der Karmelitengeneral Nikolaus Audet und die katholische Reform des XVI. Jahrhunderts*, Rome, 1959.

Stegmann, A., "Un thème majeur du second humanisme français (1540-70): l'orateur et le citoyen. De l'humanisme à la réalité vécue", in *French Renaissance Studies 1540-70*, ed. P. Sharratt, Edinburgh, 1976, pp. 213-233.

Tessier, J., *Eloges des hommes savans*, Leiden, 1715.

Tenenti, A., "Libertinisme et hérésie", *Annales ESC*, XVIII, 1963, 1-19.

Tentler, T.N., "The Meaning of Prudence in Bodin", *Traditio*, XV, 1959, 365-384.

Thou, J.-A. de, *Historiarum sui temporis libri CXX (1543-1607)*, London, 1733.

Trithemius, J., *Oratio de vera conversione mentis ad Deum* (s.d., s.l., 1500?).

Urfé, H. d', *Epîtres morales*, Lyons, 1598.

Vanderlinden, E., "Les Divers modes de connaissance de Dieu selon Philon d'Alexandrie", *Melanges de science religieuse*, IV, 1947, 285-304.

Verbeke, G., *L'Evolution de la doctrine du pneuma du Stoïcisme à S. Augustin*, Paris-Louvain, 1945.

Verwey, H. de la Fontaine-, "The Family of Love", *Quaerendo*, VI, 1976, 219-271.

Victor, J., *Charles de Bovelles. An Intellectual Biography*, Geneva, 1978.

Villeroy, N. de, *Mémoires d'état 1574-1594*, in *Nouvelle collection des mémoires sur l'histoire de France depuis le XIIIᵉ siècle*, Paris, 1836-54.

Vivanti, C., *Lotta politica e pace religiosa in Francia fra cinque e seicento*, Turin, 1963.

Walker, D.P., *Spiritual and Demonic Magic from Ficino to Campanella*, London, 1958.

Weiss, N., *La Chambre ardente (1540-1550)*, Paris, 1889.

— "Huguenots emprisonnés à la Conciergerie du Palais à Paris en mars 1569", *Bulletin de la Société de l'Histoire du Protestantisme français*, ser. v, XXI, 1923, 86-97.

Werling, Fr.N., "The Book of St. John 44", *The Sword*, III, 1939, 293-304; IV, 1940, 20-24; 152-160; 309-320.

Wessels, G., "Pars ascetica Regulae Iohannis 44", *Analecta Ordinis Carmelitarum*, III, 1914-16, 346-367.

Wilbur, E.M., *A History of Unitarianism*, Boston, 1945.

Williams, G.H., *The Radical Reformation*, Philadelphia, 1967.

Wirth, J., "'Libertins' et 'Epicuriens'. Aspects de l'irreligion au XVIᵉ siècle", *Bibliothèque d'Humanisme et Renaissance*, XXXIX, 1977, 601-627.

Wolfson, H.A., *Philo*, Cambridge, Mass., 1947.

— "Philo on Free Will and the Historical Influence of His View", *Harvard Theological Review*, XXXV, 1942, 131-169.

Yardeni, M., *La conscience nationale en France pendant les guerres de religion* (*1559-1598*), Paris-Louvain, 1971.

Yates, F., *The Art of Memory*, London, 1966.

— *Astraea*, London, 1975.

— *The French Academies of the Sixteenth Century*, London, 1947.

— *Giordano Bruno and the Hermetic Tradition*, London, 1964.

— *John Florio. The Life of an Italian in Shakespeare's England*, Cambridge, 1934.

— *The Occult Philosophy in Elizabethan England*, London, 1979 (not seen).

— *The Valois Tapestries*, 2nd ed., London, 1975.

Zampini, M., *De la succession du droict et prérogative du premier prince du sang de France*, Paris, 1588.

Zanta, L., *La Renaissance du Stoïcisme au XVIe siècle*, Paris, 1914.

Zimmerman, B. (ed.), *Acta Capitulorum Generalium Ordinis Fratrum B.V. Mariae de Monte Carmelo*, Rome, 1912.

— "Les Carmes humanistes", *Etudes Carmélitaines*, XX, 1935, 19-93.

INDEX

233

Wolfson, H.A., 85n, 87n, 168n, 179n, 180n, 182n, 192.

Women, 23, 33, 33n, 34, 39-40, 40n, 51n. 60.

Yardeni, M., 40n, 198n, 212n.

Yates, Frances, 53n, 73n, 75n, 158n, 216n, 219n.

Zampini, Matteo, 203n.
Zanta, L., 75n.
Zimmerman, B., 79n, 80n, 82n.
Zohar, 85n, 91n.

ACHEVÉ D'IMPRIMER
AUX « PRESSES DE SAVOIE », AMBILLY-ANNEMASSE (H.-S.),
EN NOVEMBRE 1980